Virginia

GREGG SHORTHAND FOR COLLEGES DIAMOND JUBILEE SERIES

volume one

LOUIS A. LESLIE
COAUTHOR DIAMOND JUBILEE SERIES
OF GREGG SHORTHAND

CHARLES E. ZOUBEK
COAUTHOR DIAMOND JUBILEE SERIES
OF GREGG SHORTHAND

RUSSELL J. HOSLER
PROFESSOR OF EDUCATION
UNIVERSITY OF WISCONSIN

SHORTHAND WRITTEN BY
CHARLES RADER

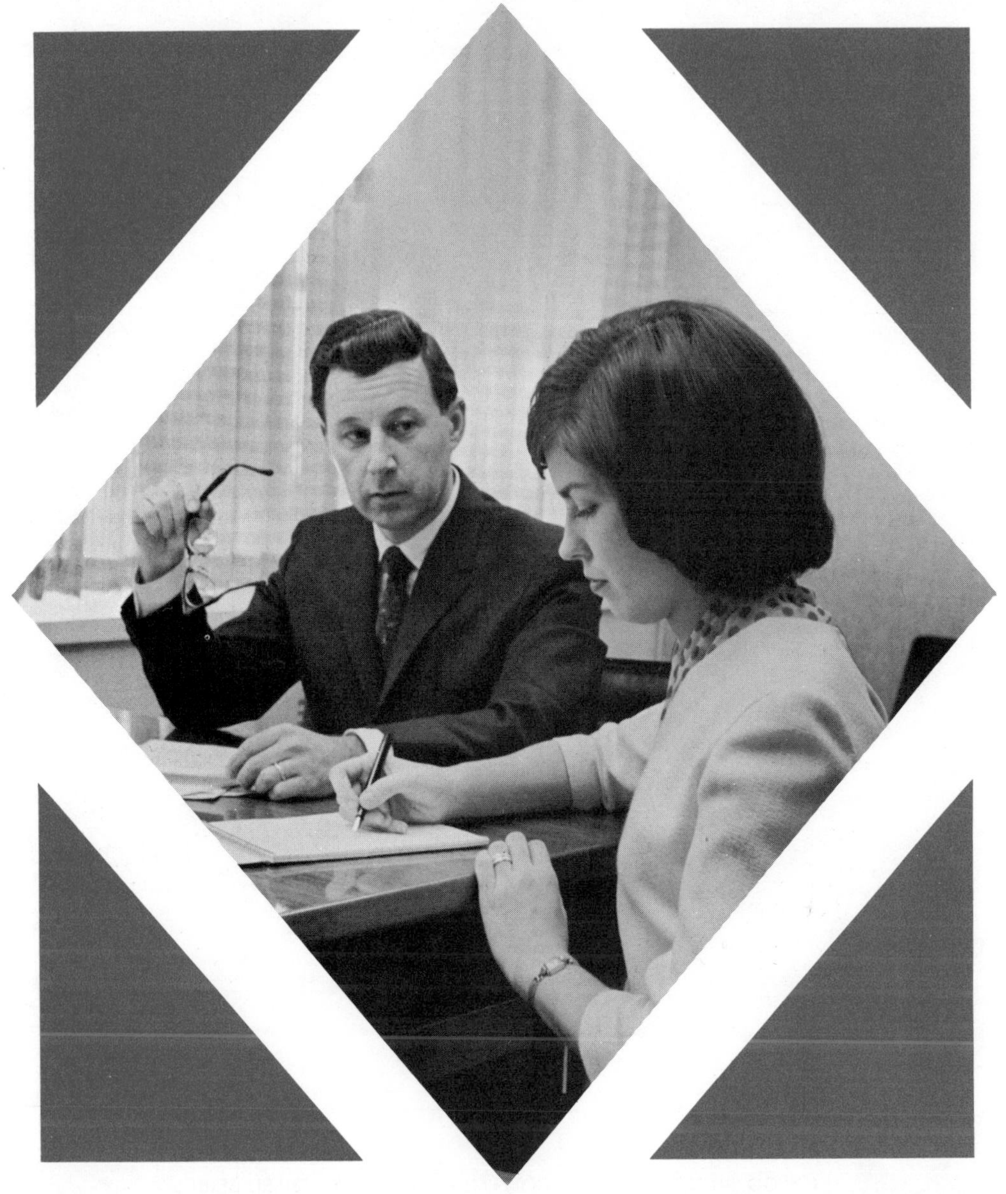

FOR COLLEGES VOLUME ONE

DIAMOND JUBILEE SERIES

GREGG DIVISION McGRAW-HILL BOOK COMPANY

NEW YORK CHICAGO DALLAS SAN FRANCISCO TORONTO LONDON SYDNEY

Photographs: Joe Ruskin

Design: BARBARA DU PREE KNOWLES

GREGG SHORTHAND FOR COLLEGES, DIAMOND JUBILEE SERIES
VOLUME ONE

Library of Congress Catalog Card Number 64-8974.

11 12 13 14 15 16 RRD-65 0 9 8 7 6 5 4 3 ISBN 07-037317-5

GREGG SHORTHAND, THE SYSTEM OF MILLIONS

Gregg Shorthand is the world's most widely used system of shorthand. In fact, to many people the terms "shorthand" and "Gregg" are synonymous. Gregg Shorthand is written by millions of people throughout the world, not only in English but in many foreign languages as well. It is used by stenographers and secretaries as a vocational tool to enable them to obtain and hold interesting and rewarding positions in business. It is used as a personal tool by business and professional men and women to relieve them of the burden of writing cumbersome longhand when they make notes, compose important memoranda, and draft speeches and reports.

GREGG SHORTHAND, DIAMOND JUBILEE SERIES

The Diamond Jubilee Edition of Gregg Shorthand, the first revision of Gregg Shorthand since 1949, further refines the system so that the student can achieve greater shorthand skill in less time than was previously possible. The changes in the system represent refinements of the 1949 edition based on the research of the authors, on the suggestions of experienced shorthand teachers on the post-high school level, and on a study of the application of the shorthand principles by stenographers and secretaries on the job.

Gregg Shorthand, Diamond Jubilee Series, has three important objectives:

1▸ To eliminate the hesitation caused when a writer had to make choices in the reading and writing of shorthand outlines.

2▸ To eliminate abbreviating devices that are no longer used with sufficient frequency in business dictation to justify the effort to learn them.

3▸ To eliminate abbreviating devices which, though they could be used with sufficient frequency in business dictation, are seldom or never used by the stenographer and secretary on the job.

GREGG SHORTHAND FOR COLLEGES, DIAMOND JUBILEE SERIES

To meet the needs of private schools, colleges, junior colleges, and other post-high school institutions, the Diamond Jubilee Series revision has been made available in a college edition — *Gregg Shorthand for Colleges, DJS* — in two volumes, of which this is Volume One. *Gregg Shorthand for Colleges* provides shorthand instructional materials that are different from those used in high schools, materials that are more challenging and more mature in interest level and in vocabulary content.

ORGANIZATION OF GREGG SHORTHAND FOR COLLEGES, DJS, VOLUME ONE

Gregg Shorthand for Colleges, DJS, Volume One, is organized into 3 parts, 10 chapters, and 70 lessons.

PART 1: Principles — Chapters 1-8. Each chapter contains six lessons — the first five lessons are devoted to the presentation of principles, and the sixth lesson is a recall. The last of the new principles are presented in Lesson 47.

PART 2: Reinforcement — Chapter 9. Chapter 9 contains eight lessons, each of which reviews intensively the principles in one of the chapters in Part 1.

PART 3: Shorthand and Transcription Skill Building — Chapter 10. This chapter consists of fourteen lessons, each of which is designed to strengthen the student's grasp of a major principle of Gregg Shorthand. In addition, each lesson continues to develop the student's vocabulary and to improve his ability to spell, to punctuate, and to apply rules of grammar correctly.

TRANSCRIPTION EMPHASIS

At the urgent request of college shorthand teachers, *Gregg Shorthand for Colleges, DJS,* places even more emphasis on the nonshorthand factors of transcription than previous college editions. *Gregg Shorthand for Colleges, DJS,* contains:

Spelling and Punctuation Practice • A very popular transcription feature introduced in the 1949 edition of Gregg Shorthand was in the form of marginal reminders, which taught the student spelling and punctuation concurrently with shorthand. *Gregg Shorthand for Colleges, DJS,* retains this helpful learning device with two slight, but useful, modifications:

1 ▸ The punctuation marks are encircled in color in the shorthand plates of the Reading and Writing Practice; in addition, the reason for their use is given *above* the circle rather than in the margin.

Thus the student is saved the eye movements that were previously necessary when the reason was given in the left margin of the shorthand.

2▸ The correct word division is now provided for the words singled out from the Reading and Writing Practice for spelling attention. In addition, the shorthand outlines for those words are printed in color.

Business Vocabulary Builder • Beginning with Chapter 3, each lesson contains a Business Vocabulary Builder, which consists of several words or expressions and their definitions. The Business Vocabulary Builder helps to overcome a major transcription hurdle – a limited vocabulary.

Similar-Words Drill • These drills teach the student the differences in meaning between similar words that stenographers often confuse; for example, *their-there; accept-except.*

Spelling Families • An effective device for improving spelling is to study words in related groups or spelling families. In this volume the student studies five of these families.

Common Word Roots • By studying the more common Latin and Greek word roots, the student increases his command of words. In this volume the student studies five such roots.

Grammar Checkup • In a number of lessons, drills are provided on rules of grammar that stenographers often apply incorrectly.

Transcription Quiz • Beginning with Lesson 57, each lesson contains a transcription quiz consisting of a letter in which the student must supply the internal punctuation. This provides him with a test on how well he has mastered the punctuation rules presented in earlier lessons.

OTHER FEATURES

Chapter Openings • Each chapter is introduced by a beautifully illustrated spread that not only paints for the student a vivid picture of the life and duties of a secretary but also inspires and encourages him in his efforts to acquire the necessary skills.

Student Helps • To be sure that the student gets the greatest benefit from each phase of his shorthand study, he is given step-by-step suggestions on how to handle it when it is first introduced.

Reading Scoreboards • At various points in the text, the student is given an opportunity to determine his reading speed by means of a scoreboard. The scoreboard enables him to calculate the number of words a minute he is reading. By comparing his reading speed from scoreboard to scoreboard, he sees some indication of his shorthand reading growth.

Check Lists • To keep the student constantly reminded of the importance of good practice procedures, an occasional check list is provided. These check lists deal with writing shorthand, reading shorthand, homework, proportion, etc.

Charts and Lists • The last lesson of each chapter in Part 1 contains a recall chart that reviews all the principles of the chapter as well as the principles of previous chapters.

In the Appendix is a cumulative list of word beginnings and endings and phrasing principles given in the order of presentation in the text.

On the back inside cover is a chart of the brief forms in the order of their presentation in the text, as well as a list of commonly used phrases.

GREGG SHORTHAND FOR COLLEGES, DJS, VOLUME TWO

Gregg Shorthand for Colleges, DJS, Volume Two, is carefully written to follow Volume One in sequence. It has as its objectives:

1▸ To review and strengthen the student's knowledge of the shorthand system.

2▸ To develop his power to construct new outlines from dictation.

3▸ To extend his knowledge and skill in the basic elements of transcription.

4▸ To lay a solid foundation for the further development of dictation and transcription skill.

This Diamond Edition of *Gregg Shorthand for Colleges* is published with pride and with the confidence that it will help teachers of Gregg Shorthand to do an even more effective job of training rapid and accurate shorthand writers and transcribers.

LOUIS A. LESLIE
CHARLES E. ZOUBEK
RUSSELL J. HOSLER

contents

SHORTHAND PRACTICE PROCEDURES

The rate at which your shorthand skill develops will depend largely on two factors—the amount of *time* you devote to your practice and the *efficiency* with which you practice. The person who practices efficiently will derive far more benefit from an hour's practice than another who may spend several hours on his practice but follows no plan.

You will be sure to derive the maximum benefit from your investment in practice time if you follow these effective practice procedures.

READING WORD LISTS

Each principle of Gregg Shorthand that you will study is accompanied by a list of illustrations in shorthand and in type. Practice each list in this way:

1▸ With the type key to the shorthand exposed, pronounce and spell aloud—if possible—each word and shorthand outline in the list, thus: *say, s-a; see, s-e.* Reading aloud will help to impress the shorthand outlines on your mind. Read all the shorthand words in the list in this way—with the type exposed—until you feel you can read the shorthand outlines *without* referring to the key.

2▸ With a card or piece of paper, cover up the type key to the first column of the list. Then read aloud from the shorthand, thus: *s-a, say; s-e, see.*

3▸ If the spelling of a shorthand outline does not immediately give you the meaning, move your card or piece of paper aside and refer to the type key. Do not spend more than a few seconds trying to decipher an outline.

4▸ Follow this procedure with the remaining columns of words in the list.

5▸ After you have read all the words in the list from the shorthand, reread the entire list once or twice again.

NOTE: In reading brief forms and phrases, it is not necessary to spell the shorthand outlines.

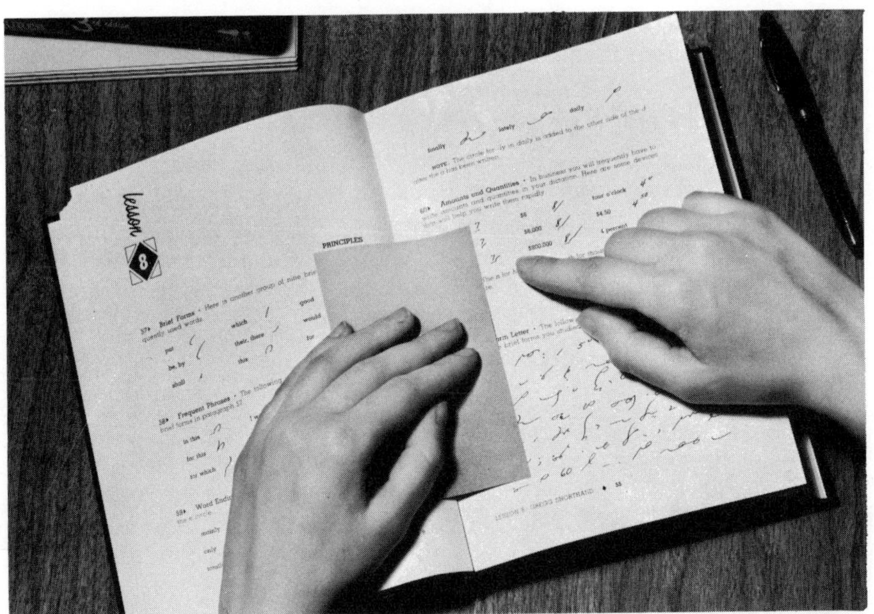

The student places a card or slip of paper over the key and spells and reads the shorthand words aloud.

READING LETTERS AND ARTICLES

Each lesson contains a Reading and Writing Practice consisting of either letters or articles written in shorthand. Reading these shorthand letters and articles will help to impress the shorthand principles on your mind and enable you to develop a large shorthand vocabulary rapidly.

Two procedures are suggested. Procedure 1 is to be used by those students who have been supplied with a *Student's Transcript of Gregg Shorthand for Colleges, Diamond Jubilee Series, Volume One.* Procedure 2 is to be used by those who will work without a *Student's Transcript.*

PROCEDURE 1: With Student's Transcript

1▸ Place your *Student's Transcript* to the right of your textbook and open it to the transcript of the Reading and Writing Practice you are about to read.

2▸ Place your left index finger under the shorthand outline that you are about to read and your right index finger under the corresponding word in the *Student's Transcript.*

3▸ Read the shorthand outlines aloud until you come to an outline that you cannot read. Spell the outline. If the spelling does not immediately give you the meaning, anchor your left index finger on the outline and look in the transcript, where your right index finger is resting near the point at which you are reading.

4▸ Determine the meaning of the outline you cannot read and place your right index finger on it.

5▸ Return to the shorthand from which you are reading—your left index finger has kept your place for you—and continue reading.

6▸ If time permits, reread the material aloud a second time, once again spelling any outline you cannot read and referring to the transcript when the spelling does not immediately give you the meaning.

By following this procedure, you will not lose any time finding your place in the shorthand and in the transcript when you cannot read an outline.

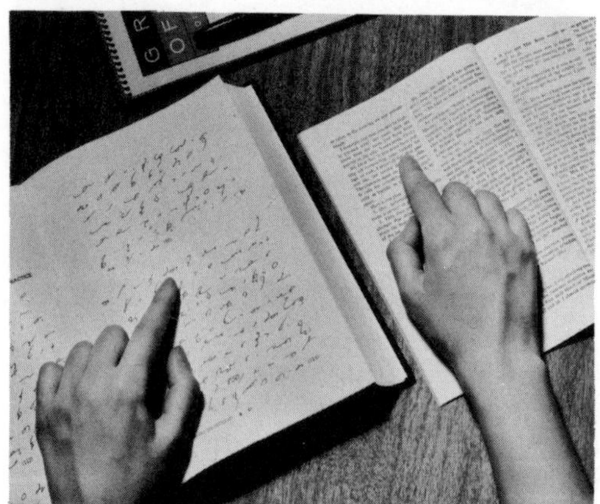

The student reads from the shorthand and refers to the STUDENT'S TRANSCRIPT whenever he cannot read an outline after spelling the shorthand characters in it.

PROCEDURE 2: Without Student's Transcript

1▸ Before you start your work on a Reading and Writing Practice, have a blank card or a sheet of paper and a pencil handy.

2▸ Read the shorthand outlines aloud.

3▸ When you come to an outline that you cannot read, spell it. If the spelling does not immediately give you the meaning of the outline, write the outline on your card or sheet of paper (or encircle it in your book if the book is your personal property) and continue reading. Do not spend more than a few seconds trying to decipher the outline.

4▸ After you have gone through all the material in this way, repeat the procedure if time permits. On the second reading you may be able to read some of the outlines that escaped you the first time. When that happens, cross those outlines off your sheet or card.

5▸ Finally—and very important—at the earliest opportunity ask your teacher or a classmate the meaning of the outlines you could not read.

Do not be disappointed if your shorthand reading rate in the early stages is low. That is only natural because you are in a sense learning a new language. If you read each day's lesson faithfully, you will find your reading rate increasing almost from day to day.

The student reads from the shorthand and writes on a card any outline that he cannot read after spelling the shorthand characters in it.

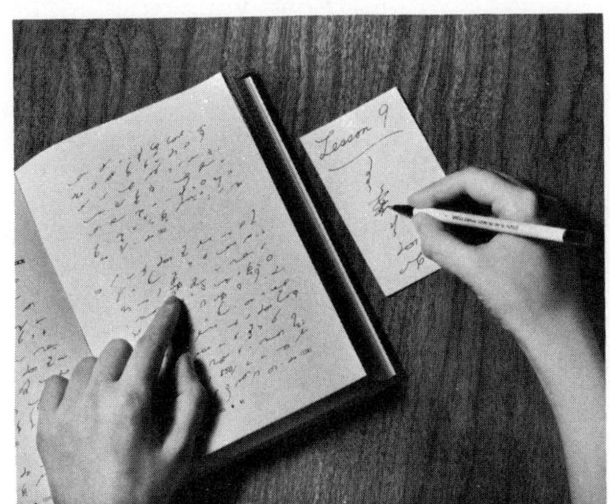

WRITING THE READING AND WRITING PRACTICE

After you have read the Reading and Writing Practice of a lesson, you should make a shorthand copy of it. Before you do any writing, however, you should give some thought to the tools of your trade—your notebook and your writing instrument.

Your Notebook • The best notebook for shorthand writing is one that measures 6 x 9 inches and has a vertical rule down the middle of each sheet. If the notebook has a spiral binding, so much the better, as the spiral binding enables you to keep the pages flat at all times. The paper, of course, should take ink well.

Your Pen • If it is at all possible, use a fountain pen or a good ball-point pen for your shorthand writing. Why use a pen for shorthand writing? It requires less effort to write with a pen; consequently, you can write for long periods of time without fatigue. On the other hand, the point of a pencil soon becomes blunt; and the blunter it gets, the more effort you have to expend as you write with it. Pen-written notes remain readable almost indefinitely; pencil notes soon become blurred and hard to read. Pen-written notes are also easier to read under artificial light.

Having selected your writing tools, you should follow these steps in working with each Reading and Writing Practice:

1▸ Read the material you are going to copy, following the suggestions given under the heading, "Reading Letters and Articles," on page 11. Always read the Reading and Writing Practice before you copy it.

2▸ Read a convenient group of words from the printed shorthand and then write that group. If possible, say each outline aloud as you write it. Keep your place in the shorthand with your left index finger if you are right-handed; with your right index finger if you are left-handed.

* * *

Quite naturally, your early writing efforts may not be very rapid; nor will your shorthand outlines look as pretty as those in your book. With regular practice, however, you will soon become so proud of your shorthand notes that you won't want to write any more longhand!

When copying, the student reads a convenient group of words aloud and then writes the group in his notebook.

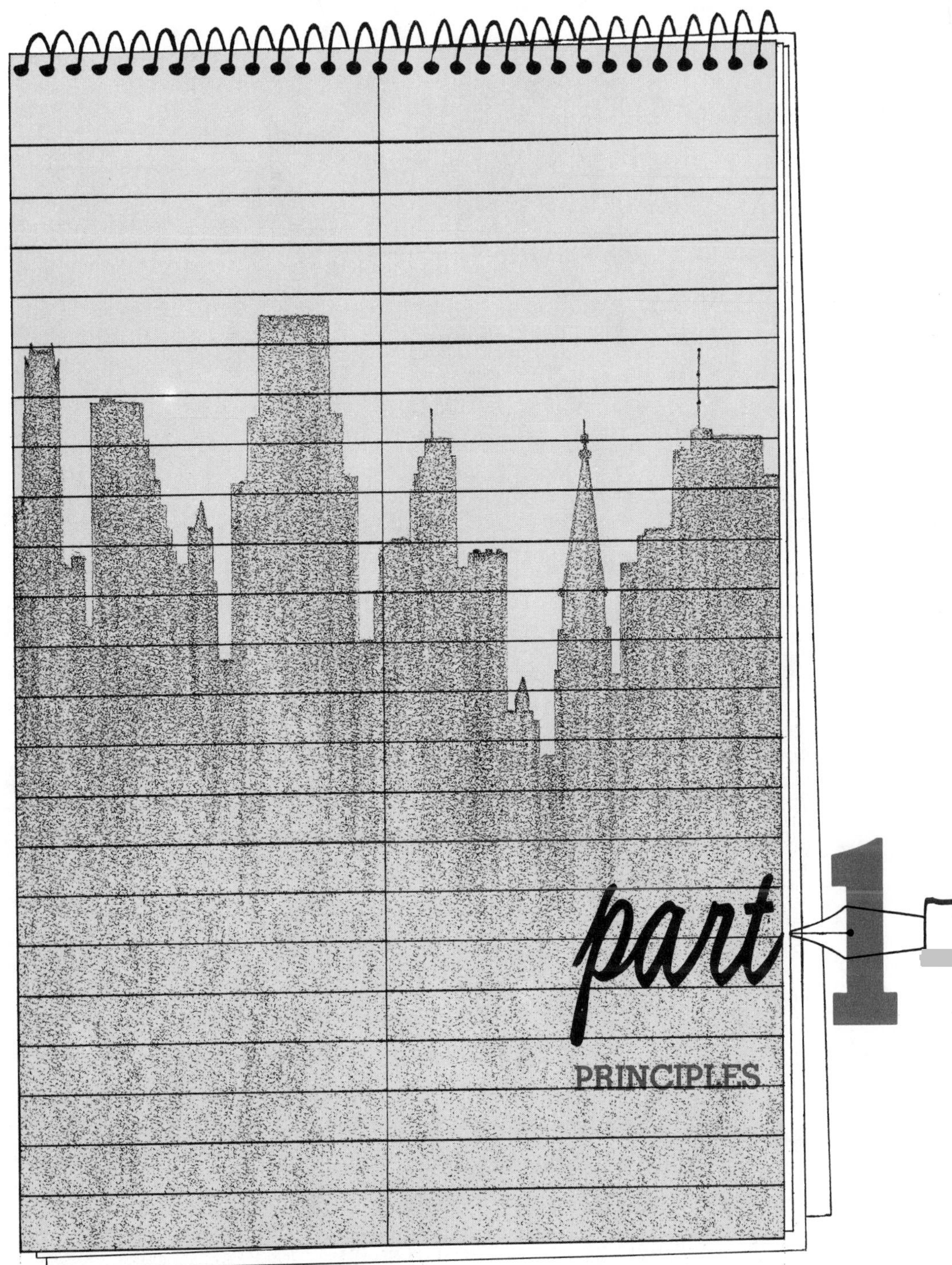

part 1

PRINCIPLES

"Help Wanted — Shorthand Required" You will find this advertisement — or one that says the same thing in different words — in almost any daily newspaper. One large city newspaper carries over 1,000 such ads in a single Sunday issue! And there are thousands upon thousands of openings for shorthand writers that aren't even advertised in the newspaper.

Shorthand is a sought-after skill, and its value increases every year. Just as there will always be a need to write, there will always be a need to write rapidly. Longhand is too laborious, especially for the busy executive. It is true that the spoken word can be recorded in numerous ways, including electronic methods, which have been available for many years; nevertheless, in spite of technical advances, the demand for shorthand writers is far ahead of the supply.

Shorthand is convenient. You can write it anywhere as long as you have a piece of paper and a pen or pencil. You don't have to plug anything into an electrical outlet or to haul a machine with you. If the dictator changes his mind while he is dictating, the shorthand writer can make corrections in her notes easily and quickly without mechanical adjustments.

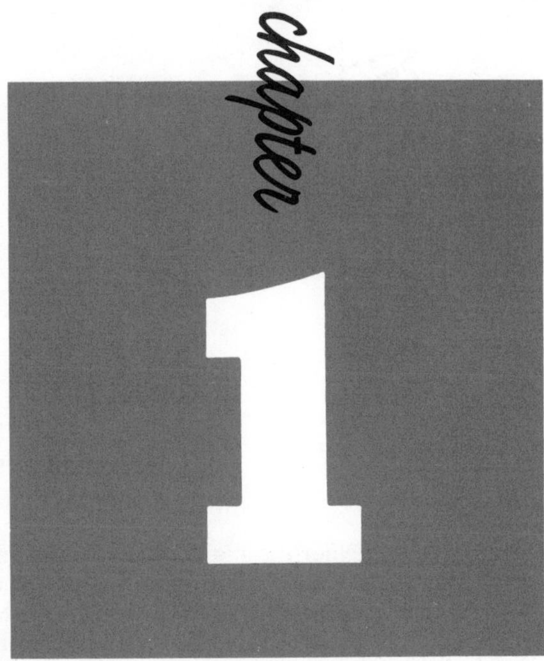

SHORTHAND IS AN ENDURING SKILL

You can use shorthand to take dictation in a secretarial job, to make notes of lectures and discussions in college classes, to help you organize papers and reports, to make notes while doing research, to help you organize a talk, to take notes at meetings that you have the responsibility of recording, and in dozens of other ways. Shorthand has almost unlimited uses. Some executives know shorthand; consequently, they write their letters in Gregg Shorthand and give them to their secretaries to transcribe. You can see how this saves an enormous amount of time for both the executives and the secretaries.

Once you have learned shorthand and learned it well, it doesn't leave you—especially if you use it at every opportunity. Those who claim to have learned shorthand and forgotten it completely probably never really learned it. Thousands of mature women who left the job years ago to marry reenter the secretarial field every year. Most of them require only a brief "refresher" course to rebuild their shorthand skill. The alphabet of Gregg Shorthand has not changed, and the skill comes back very rapidly.

So remember this: Once you have become proficient in Gregg Shorthand, you have acquired an enduring skill that will last a lifetime. By keeping that skill sharp, you have employment insurance and, for the foreseeable future at least, a ready market for your talents.

GREGG SHORTHAND IS EASY TO LEARN

If there is the slightest doubt in your mind whether you can learn to write Gregg Shorthand rapidly and accurately, dismiss it now! If you can write longhand, you can learn to write Gregg Shorthand – it is as simple as that! In writing Gregg Shorthand, you will use the same strokes and the same writing movements that you employ in writing longhand.

Learning to write Gregg Shorthand is actually easier than learning to write longhand. If you find this statement a little difficult to believe, the following illustration should convince you of its truth.

In longhand, *f* may be expressed in many different ways, all of which you had to learn. Here are six of them:

In addition, in many words the sound of *f* is expressed by combinations of other letters of the alphabet; for example, *ph*, as in *phase*; *gh*, as in *rough*.

In Gregg Shorthand there is only *one* way to express the sound of *f*, as you will learn later in this lesson.

With Gregg Shorthand, you can reach almost any speed goal that you set for yourself – provided that you practice faithfully and intelligently.

PRINCIPLES

GROUP A

1▸ **S-Z** · The first shorthand stroke you will learn is *s*, perhaps the most frequently used letter in the English language. The shorthand *s* is a tiny downward curve that resembles the longhand comma. Because *s* in English often has the sound of *z*, as in *saves*, the same downward curve is used to express *z*.

S-Z 

2▸ **A** • The second shorthand stroke you will learn is the shorthand *a*, which is simply the longhand *a* with the final connecting stroke omitted.

A 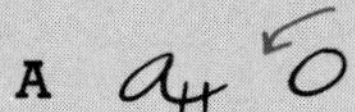

3▸ **Omission of Silent Letters** • In the English language, many words contain letters that are not pronounced. In shorthand, these silent letters are omitted; only the sounds that are pronounced in a word are written. For example, in the word *say*, the *y* would not be written because it is not pronounced. For the word *face* we would write *f-a-s;* the *e* would be omitted because it is silent, and the *c* would be represented by the shorthand *s* because it has the sound of *s*.

In the following words, what letters would not be written in shorthand because they are not pronounced?

eat	**day**	**dough**	**hole**
save	**main**	**date**	**right**

4▸ **S-A Words** • With the strokes *s* and *a*, you can now form shorthand outlines for the following words:

NOTE: The *c* in *ace* is represented by the shorthand *s* because it has the *s* sound.

5▸ **F, V** • The shorthand stroke for *f* is a downward curve the same shape as the shorthand *s*, but it is somewhat larger—about half the height of the space between the lines of your shorthand notebook.

The shorthand stroke for *v* is a very large downward curve the same shape as *s* and *f* — almost the full height of the space between the lines of your shorthand notebook.

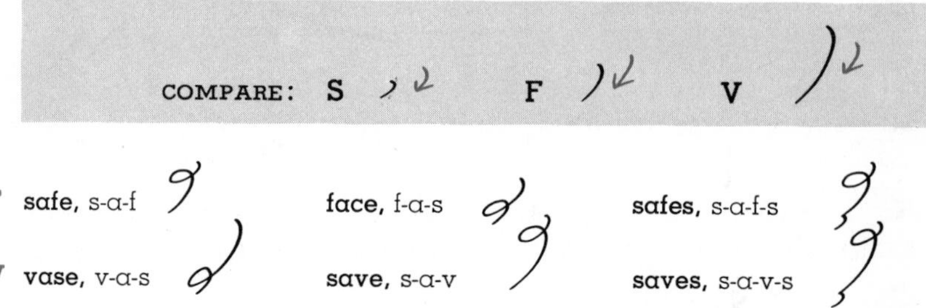

COMPARE: S F V

F	**safe,** s-a-f	**face,** f-a-s	**safes,** s-a-f-s
V	**vase,** v-a-s	**save,** s-a-v	**saves,** s-a-v-s

6▸ **E** · The shorthand stroke for e is a tiny circle. It is simply the longhand e with the two connecting strokes omitted.

E

see, s-e	**fee,** f-e	**ease,** e-s
sees, s-e-s	**fees,** f-e-s	**easy,** e-s-e

SUGGESTION: At this point, turn to page 10 and read the procedures outlined there for practicing word lists. By following those procedures, you will derive the greatest benefit from your practice.

GROUP B

7▸ **N, M** · The shorthand stroke for *n* is a very short forward straight line.

The shorthand stroke for *m* is a longer forward straight line.

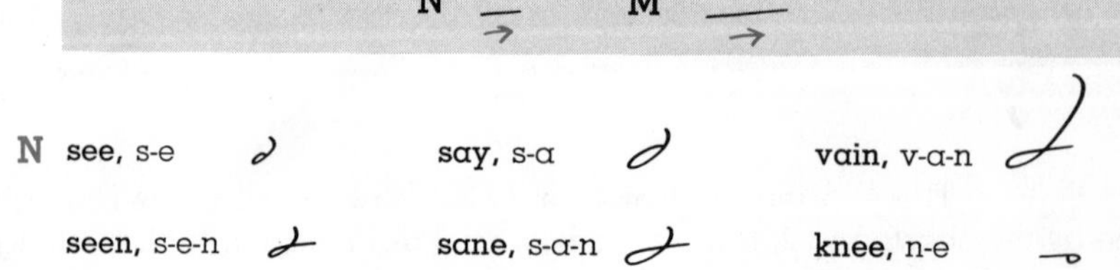

N M

N	**see,** s-e	**say,** s-a	**vain,** v-a-n
	seen, s-e-n	**sane,** s-a-n	**knee,** n-e

NOTE: The *k* in *knee* is not written because it is not pronounced.

M	me, m-e	main, m-a-n	seem, s-e-m
	mean, m-e-n	name, n-a-m	same, s-a-m
	may, m-a	aim, a-m	fame, f-a-m

8▸ **T, D** · The shorthand stroke for *t* is a short upward straight line. The shorthand stroke for *d* is a longer upward straight line.

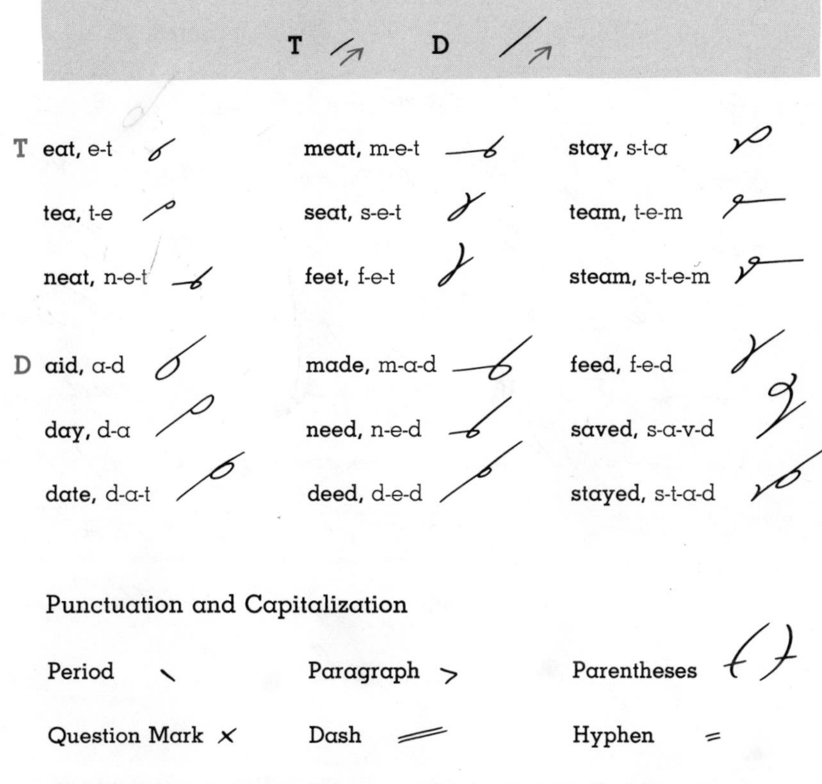

9▸ **Punctuation and Capitalization**

Period	Paragraph	Parentheses
Question Mark	Dash	Hyphen

The regular longhand forms are used for all other punctuation marks.

Capitalization is indicated by two upward dashes underneath the word to be capitalized.

Fay Dave Mae

READING PRACTICE

With the strokes you have learned in this lesson, you can, with the help of an occasional longhand word, read complete sentences.

Read the following sentences, spelling each shorthand word aloud as you read it, thus: *F-a, Fay; m-e-t, meet; m-e, me.* If you cannot read the word after you have spelled it, refer to the key.

1 Fay will meet me on East Main.
2 The dean stayed all day.
3 Dave made me save.
4 Amy gave me a vase.
5 Dean can eat meat.
6 Fay made Dave stay for tea.
7 I stayed for tea the same day.
8 Dave's knee hurts.
9 The Navy team stayed until May 15.
10 Dave is mean and vain.
11 Amy saved me money.
12 Fay's home faced east.
13 Can Fay see me on May 18?
14 Dave made a date with me.
15 Dave gave me the deed.

PRINCIPLES

10▸ Alphabet Recall • Here are the shorthand strokes you studied in Lesson 1. How rapidly can you identify them?

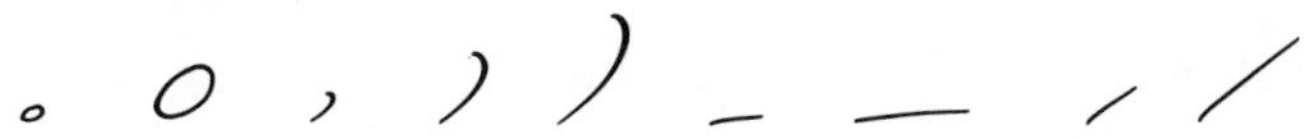

11▸ O, R, L • In this paragraph you will study three new, very frequently used letters of the alphabet—o, *r*, *l*.

The shorthand stroke for o is a small deep hook.

The shorthand stroke for *r* is a short forward curve.

The shorthand stroke for *l* is a long forward curve, about three times as long as the stroke for *r*.

Notice how these shorthand strokes are derived from their longhand forms.

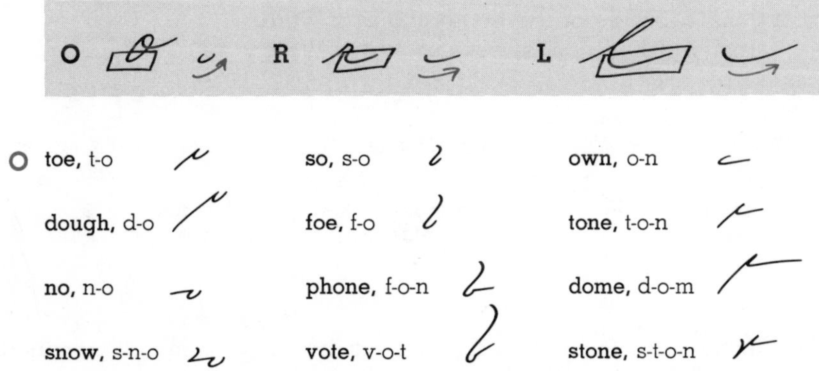

NOTE: In the words in the third column, the o is placed on its side. By placing o on its side before *n* and *m* in these and similar words rather than writing it upright, we obtain smoother, faster joinings.

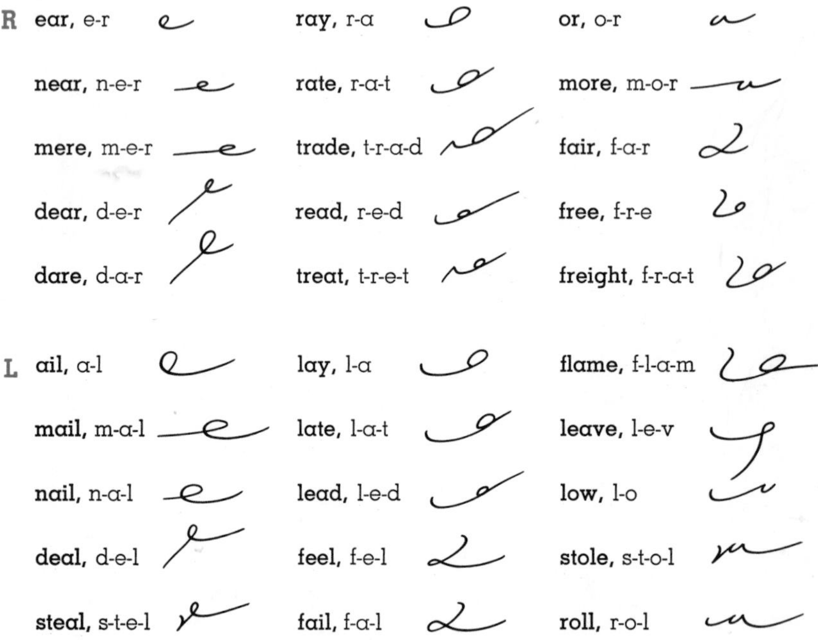

NOTE: *Fr,* as in *free,* and *fl,* as in *flame,* are written with one sweep of the pen, with no stop between the *f* and the *r* or *l.*

12▸ H, -ing • The letter *h* is a dot placed above the vowel. With few exceptions, *h* occurs at the beginning of a word.

Ing, which almost always occurs at the end of a word, is also expressed by a dot.

H	**he,** h-e	**home,** h-o-m	**whole,** h-o-l
Ing	**heating,** h-e-t-ing	**hearing,** h-e-r-ing	**heeding,** h-e-d-ing

13▸ Long I • The shorthand stroke for the very common long sound of *i,* as in *high,* is a large broken circle.

I

high, h-i		**light,** l-i-t		**life,** l-i-f	
my, m-i		**mile,** m-i-l		**sign,** s-i-n	
night, n-i-t		**tire,** t-i-r		**side,** s-i-d	
right, write, r-i-t		**file,** f-i-l		**fine,** f-i-n	

14▸ Omission of Minor Vowels • Many words in the English language contain vowels that are sounded only slightly or are slurred. Such vowels may be omitted if they do not contribute to speed or legibility.

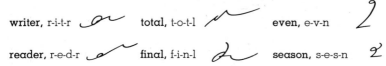

writer, r-i-t-r		**total,** t-o-t-l		**even,** e-v-n	
reader, r-e-d-r		**final,** f-i-n-l		**season,** s-e-s-n	

READING PRACTICE

With the aid of a few words in longhand, you can now read the following sentences. Remember to spell each shorthand word aloud as you read it and to refer to the key when you cannot read a word.

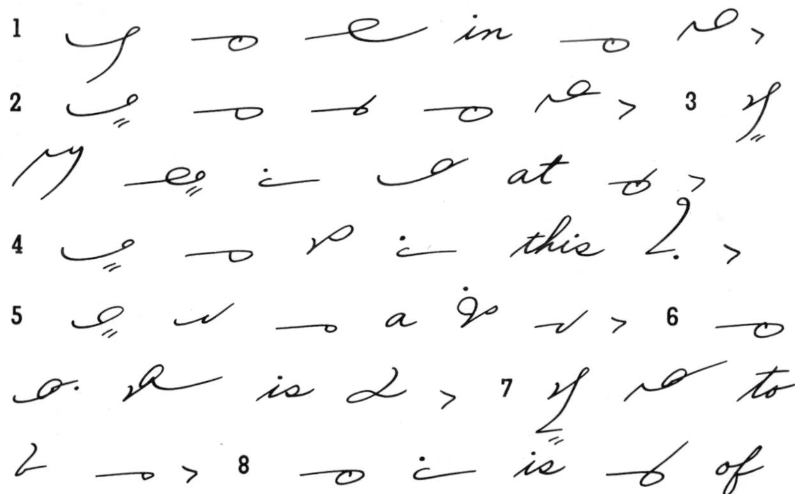

1 Leave my mail in my tray.
2 Lee may meet my train.
3 Steve drove Mary home late at night.
4 Lee may stay home this evening.
5 Ray wrote me a hasty note.
6 My writing style is fair.
7 Stephen tried to phone me.
8 My home is made of stone.
9 Mary dyed her hair.
10 I own a retail store in Erie.
11 Ray may buy a snow tire.
12 Lee made a high score.
13 I need more light.
14 Is it raining or snowing?
15 Ray came late; Lee came even later.
16 He made a hasty retreat.
17 Ray Taylor is flying to Rome.
18 My reading rate is low.
19 Lee made me a loan.
20 Mary can drive me home later.

PRINCIPLES

15▸ Alphabet Recall • Here are the strokes you studied in Lessons 1 and 2. How rapidly can you identify them?

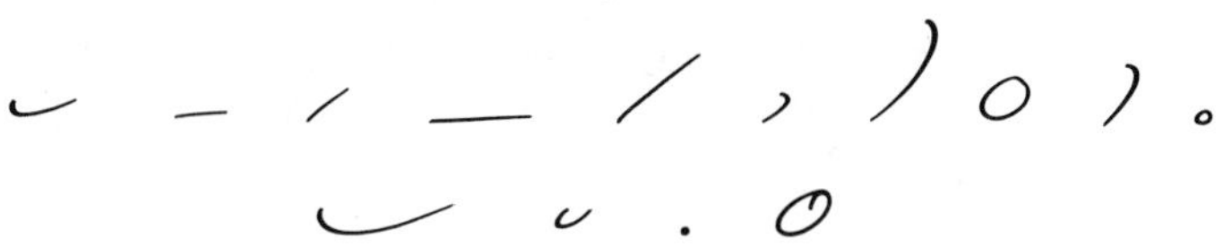

16▸ Brief Forms • There are many words in the English language that are used over and over again. As an aid to rapid shorthand writing, special abbreviations, called "brief forms," are provided for many of these common words. For example, we write *m-r* for *Mister; v*, for *have.*

This process of abbreviation is common practice in longhand, too. You are, of course, familiar with such abbreviations as *Ave.* for *Avenue; memo* for *memorandum; Sat.* for *Saturday*, etc.

Because the brief forms occur so frequently, make a special effort to learn them well.

am		**Mr.**		**are, our, hour**	
I		**will, well**		**in, not**	
have		**a, an**		**it, at**	

NOTE: A number of the brief forms have two or more meanings. When you are transcribing material you have taken from dictation, context will help you select the correct meaning of a brief form.

17▸ Phrasing • The use of brief forms for common words enables us to save writing time. Another device for saving writing time is called "phrasing," or the writing of two or more shorthand outlines together. Here are a number of phrases built with the brief forms you just studied.

I will	**I will not**	**he will not**
I have	**I have not**	**he will**
I am	**in our**	**are not**

18▸ Left S-Z • In Lesson 1, you learned one stroke for *s* and *z* — the small downward curve that resembles a comma. Another stroke for *s* is also used in order to provide an easy joining in any combination of strokes — a backward comma. For convenience, it is called the "left *s*."

At this stage it is not necessary for you to know which form of *s* to use in any given word; this will become clear to you as your study of shorthand progresses.

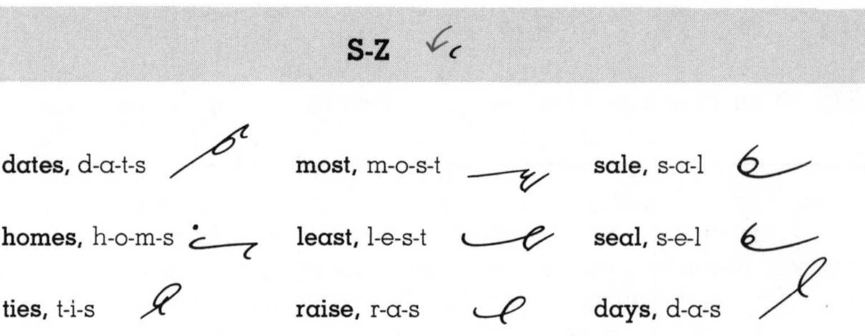

S-Z
dates, d-a-t-s
most, m-o-s-t
sale, s-a-l
homes, h-o-m-s
least, l-e-s-t
seal, s-e-l
ties, t-i-s
raise, r-a-s
days, d-a-s

19▸ P, B • The shorthand stroke for *p* is a downward curve the same shape as the left *s*, except that it is larger — approximately half the height of the space between the lines in your shorthand notebook.

The shorthand character for *b* is also a downward curve the same shape as left *s* and *p*, except that it is *much* larger — approximately the full height of the space between the lines in your shorthand notebook. Note the difference in the sizes of the left *s*, *p*, and *b*.

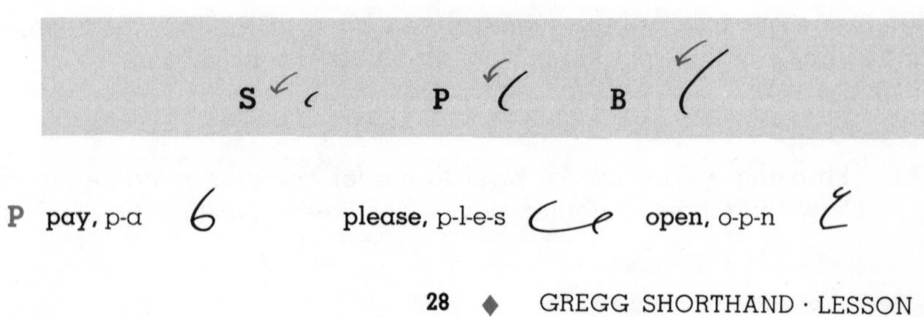

pays, p-a-s	**plain,** p-l-a-n	**hope,** h-o-p
space, s-p-a-s	**place,** p-l-a-s	**paid,** p-a-d
spare, s-p-a-r	**price,** p-r-i-s	**prepare,** p-r-e-p-a-r
B **bay,** b-a	**brief,** b-r-e-f	**neighbor,** n-a-b-r
obey, o-b-a	**bright,** b-r-i-t	**labor,** l-a-b-r
base, b-a-s	**blame,** b-l-a-m	**able,** a-b-l
boat, b-o-t	**buy,** b-i	**label,** l-a-b-l

NOTE: The combinations *pr, pl, br, bl* are written with one sweep of the pen without a pause between the *p* or *b* and the *r* or *l.*

READING PRACTICE

You have now reached the point where you can read sentences written entirely in shorthand.

SUGGESTION: Before you start your work on this Reading Practice, take a few moments to read the practice procedures for reading shorthand on page 11. By following those procedures, you will be able to read these sentences quickly and at the same time derive the most benefit from your reading.

GROUP A

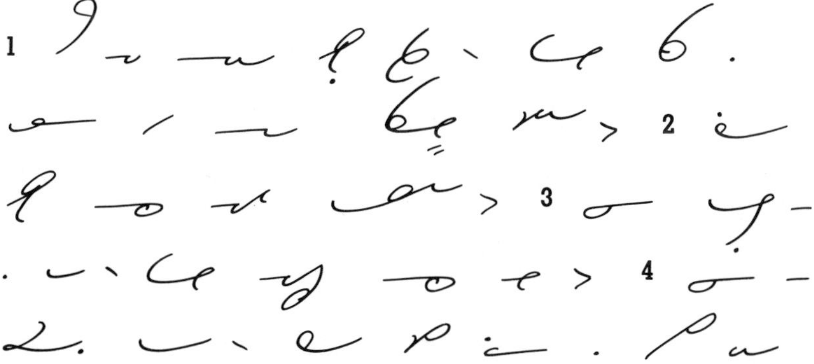

5

(53)

GROUP B

6

7

8

9

10

(49)

GROUP C

11

12

13

14

15

(44)

PRINCIPLES

20▸ Alphabet Recall • In Lessons 1 through 3 you studied 17 shorthand strokes—more than half the strokes in Gregg Shorthand. How rapidly can you identify them?

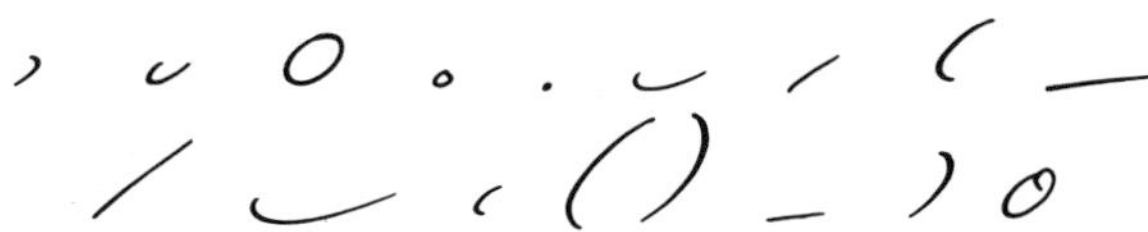

21▸ Sh, Ch, J • The shorthand stroke for *sh* (called "ish") is a very short downward straight stroke.

The shorthand stroke for *ch* (called "chay") is a longer straight stroke approximately half the height of the space between the lines in your shorthand notebook.

The shorthand stroke for the sound of *j*, as in *James* and *age*, is a long downward straight stroke almost the full height of the space between the lines in your shorthand notebook. Note carefully the difference in the sizes of these strokes.

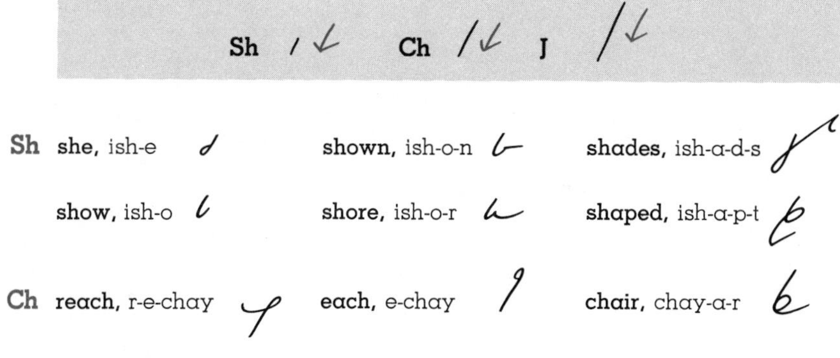

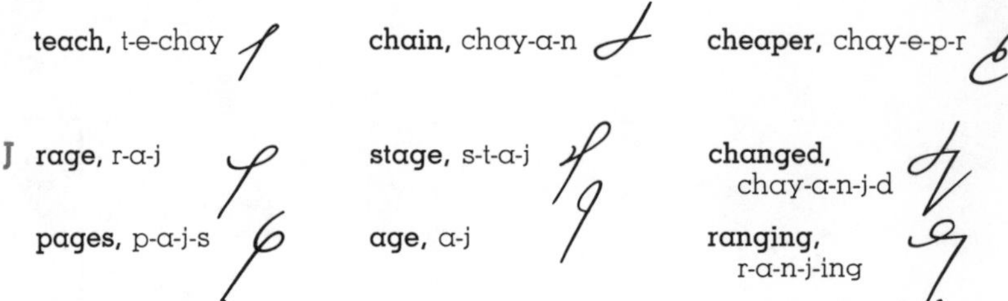

22▸ OO, K, G • The shorthand stroke for the sound of oo, as in *too*, is a tiny upward hook.

The shorthand stroke for *k* is a short forward curve.

The shorthand stroke for the hard sound of *g*, as in *gave*, is a much longer forward curve—almost three times as long as *k*. It is called "gay."

OO **K** **G**

OO

too, to, two, t-oo	**true,** t-r-oo	**rule,** r-oo-l
do, d-oo	**drew,** d-r-oo	**pool,** p-oo-l
who, h-oo	**proof,** p-r-oo-f	**move,** m-oo-v
shoe, ish-oo	**room,** r-oo-m	**noon,** n-oo-n

NOTE: The oo hook is placed on its side in *move* and *noon*. By placing the oo hook on its side rather than writing it upright in these and similar words, we obtain smoother, faster joinings.

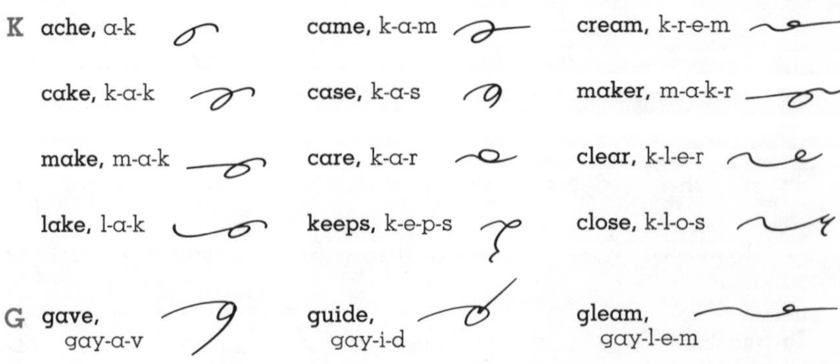

K
ache, a-k
came, k-a-m
cream, k-r-e-m
cake, k-a-k
case, k-a-s
maker, m-a-k-r
make, m-a-k
care, k-a-r
clear, k-l-e-r
lake, l-a-k
keeps, k-e-p-s
close, k-l-o-s
G
gave, gay-a-v
guide, gay-i-d
gleam, gay-l-e-m

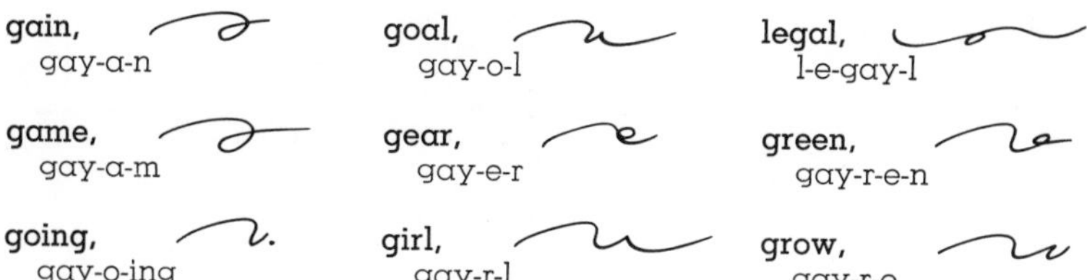

NOTE: *Kr* and *gl* are written with one smooth, wavelike motion; *kl* and *gr* are written with a hump between the *k* and the *l* and the *g* and the *r*.

READING PRACTICE

You can now read the following shorthand sentences. In these sentences you will find many illustrations of the shorthand strokes, brief forms, and phrases you learned in Lessons 1 through 4.

You may find it profitable to take a few moments to reread the practice suggestions on page 11 before you begin your work on this Reading Practice.

GROUP A ▸

GROUP B

6

7

8

9

10

(82)

GROUP C

11

12

13

14

15

(47)

GROUP D

16

17

18

19

20

(50)

GROUP E

21 22

23

24 25

26 27

(30)

PRINCIPLES

23▸ Alphabet Recall • Here are the 23 alphabet strokes you studied in Lessons 1 through 4. Can you read them in 30 seconds or less?

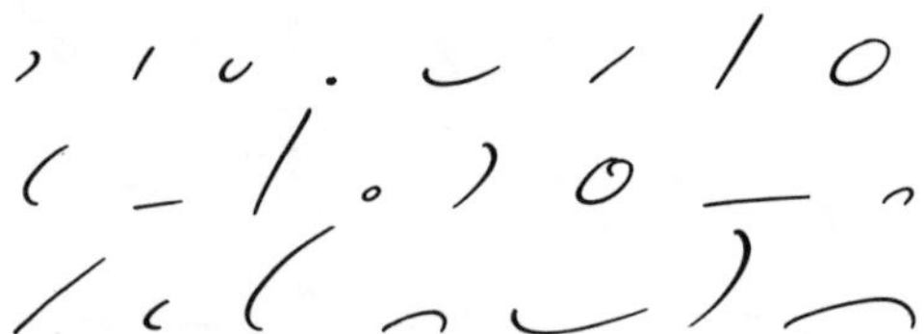

24▸ A, Ä • The large circle that represents the sound of ā also represents the vowel sounds heard in *act* and *arm.*

A	**act,** a-k-t	**had,** h-a-d	**last,** l-a-s-t
	facts, f-a-k-t-s	**man,** m-a-n	**past,** p-a-s-t
	as, a-s	**matter,** m-a-t-r	**fast,** f-a-s-t
Ä	**arm,** a-r-m	**mark,** m-a-r-k	**calm,** k-a-m
	far, f-a-r	**dark,** d-a-r-k	**start,** s-t-a-r-t
	charges, chay-a-r-j-s	**park,** p-a-r-k	**large,** l-a-r-j

25▸ E, I, Obscure Vowel • The tiny circle that represents the sound of ē also represents the vowel sounds heard in *rest* and *if,* as well as the obscure vowel sound heard in *her, urge.*

E	**rest,** r-e-s-t	**let,** l-e-t	**checked,** chay-e-k-t

test, t-e-s-t	**letter,** l-e-t-r	**telling,** t-e-l-ing
best, b-e-s-t	**sells,** s-e-l-s	**any,** e-n-e

I **if,** e-f	**bills,** b-e-l-s	**bid,** b-e-d
him, h-e-m	**still,** s-t-e-l	**middle,** m-e-d-l
did, d-e-d	**shipped,** ish-e-p-t	**remit,** r-e-m-e-t

Obscure Vowel

her, h-e-r	**hurry,** h-e-r-e	**first,** f-e-r-s-t
urge, e-r-j	**hurt,** h-e-r-t	**church,** chay-e-r-chay
earn, e-r-n	**firm,** f-e-r-m	**learn,** l-e-r-n

26▸ Th • Two tiny curves, written upward, are provided for the sounds of *th*. These curves are called "ith."

At this point you need not try to decide which *th* stroke to use in any given word; this will become clear to you as your study of shorthand progresses.

Over Th **Under Th**

Over Th

then, ith-e-n	**teeth,** t-e-ith	**smooth,** s-m-oo-ith
thick, ith-e-k	**faith,** f-a-ith	**booth,** b-oo-ith
these, ith-e-s	**bath,** b-a-ith	**theme,** ith-e-m

Under Th

three, ith-r-e	**though,** ith-o	**health,** h-e-l-ith

threw, ith-r-oo	**thorough,** ith-e-r-o	**clothing,** k-l-o-ith-ing
throw, ith-r-o	**both,** b-o-ith	**clothes,** k-l-o-ith-s

27▸ Brief Forms • Here is another group of nine brief forms for very common business words. Learn them well.

the	**can**	**with**
that	**is, his**	**but**
you, your	**of**	**Mrs.**

READING PRACTICE

At this stage you can already read complete business letters written entirely in shorthand. Be sure to follow the suggestions for reading shorthand on page 11 as you work on this Reading Practice.

28▸ Brief-Form Letter • The following letter contains one or more illustrations of the brief forms you studied in this lesson.

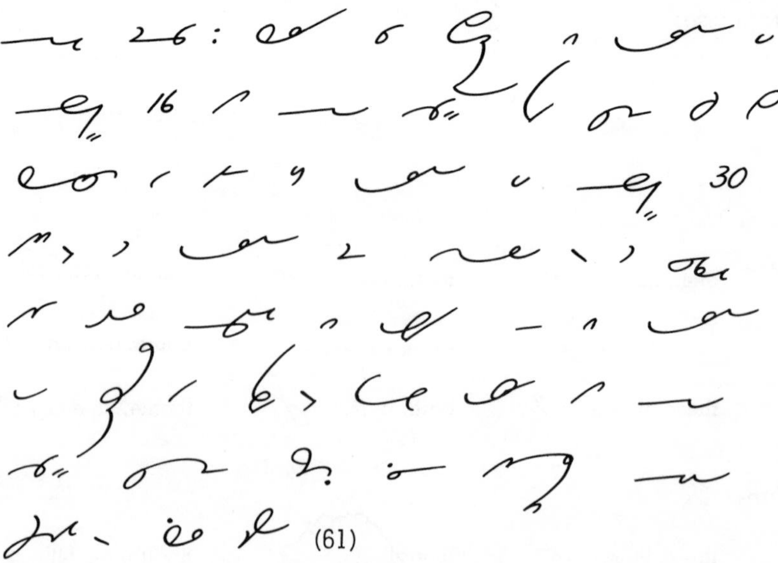

29

30

31

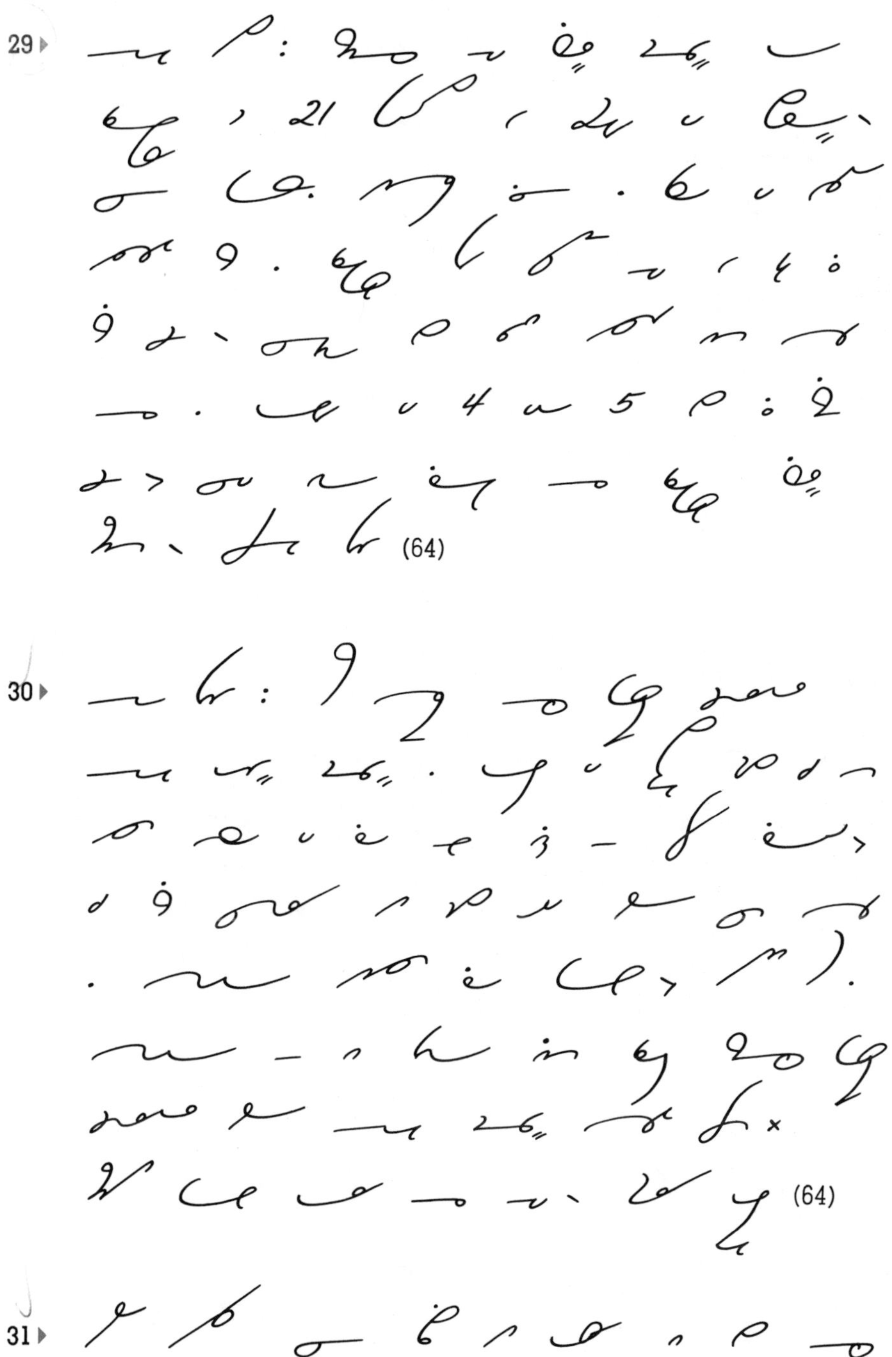

(66)

32

(63)

33

(49)

34 (48)

35 (42)

RECALL

Lesson 6 is a "breather"; it contains no new shorthand principles for you to learn. In this lesson you will find an Alphabet Recall, a simple explanation of the principles that govern the joining of the strokes you studied in Lessons 1 through 5, a Recall Chart, and a Reading Practice employing the shorthand devices of Lessons 1 through 5.

36 **Alphabet Recall**

PRINCIPLES OF JOINING

As a matter of interest, you might like to know the principles by which the words you have already learned are written. The joinings of the shorthand strokes are so simple that it hardly seems necessary to give rules or explanations; however, notice the groups into which the joinings naturally fall.

37 Circles are written outside angles and inside curves.

a

b

a Needs, teams, van, meal, same, leave.
b Appearing, east, even, lay, sale, straight, able, fee.

38▸ Circles are written clockwise on a straight line and between two straight strokes in the same direction.

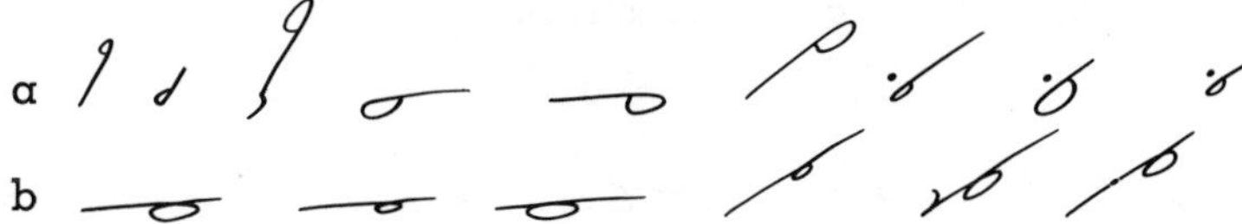

a Each, she, ages, aim, may, day, head, hat, heat.
b Main, mean, name, deed, stayed, date.

39▸ Between two curves written in opposite directions, the circle is written on the back of the first curve.

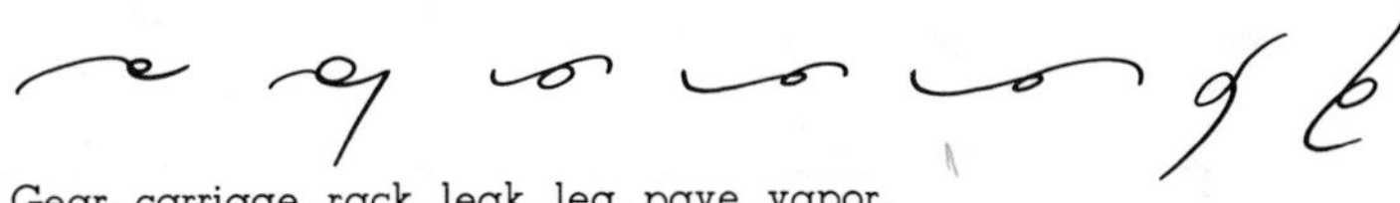

Gear, carriage, rack, leak, leg, pave, vapor.

40▸ The o hook is written on its side before *n, m* unless a downward stroke comes before the hook.

Own, loan, home, stone; shown, bone, zone.

41▸ The oo hook is written on its side after *n, m.*

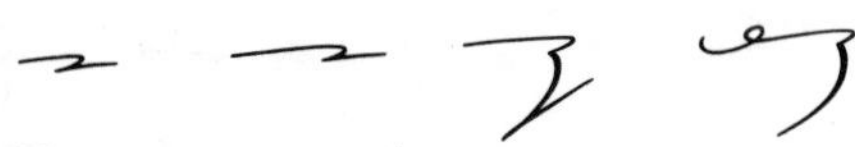

Noon, moon, moved, remove.

42▸ The under *th* is used when it is joined to o, *r, l;* in other cases, the over *th* is used.

BUT

Three, thorough, though, earth, health; these, thick, then.

43 ▸ **Recall Chart** • The following chart reviews all the shorthand devices you studied in Lessons 1 through 5. It contains 84 words and phrases. Can you read the entire chart in 9 minutes or less?

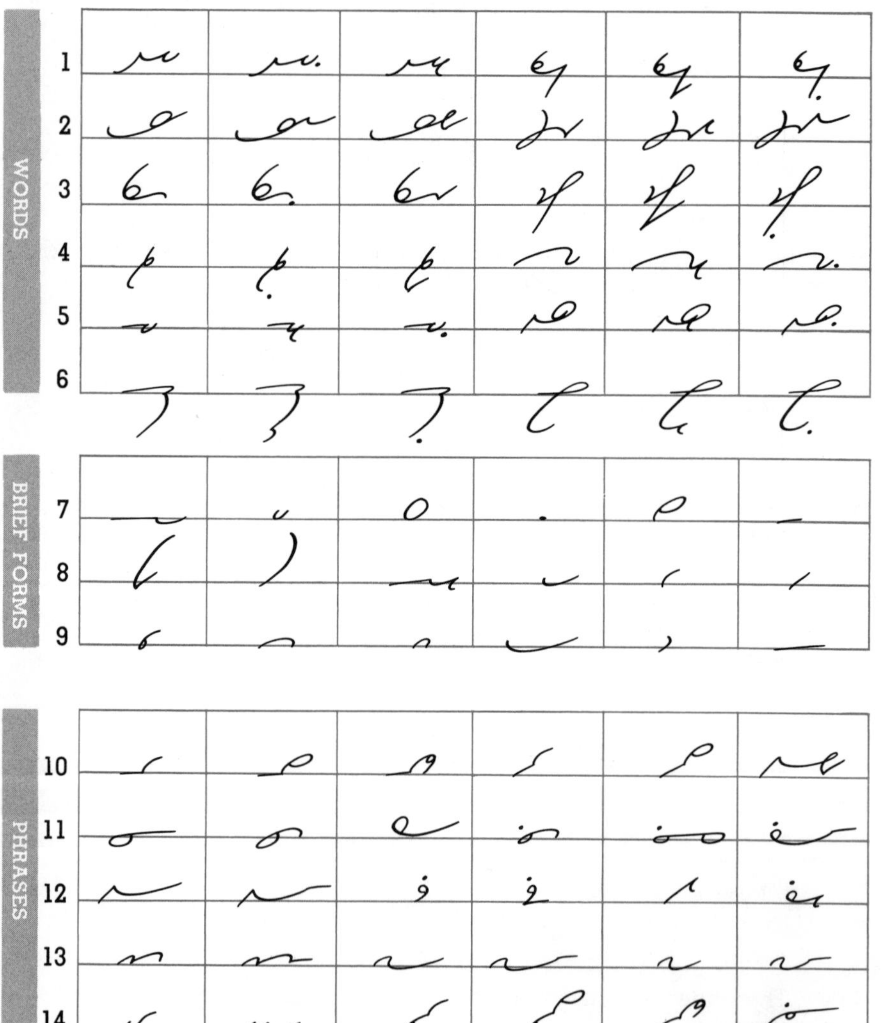

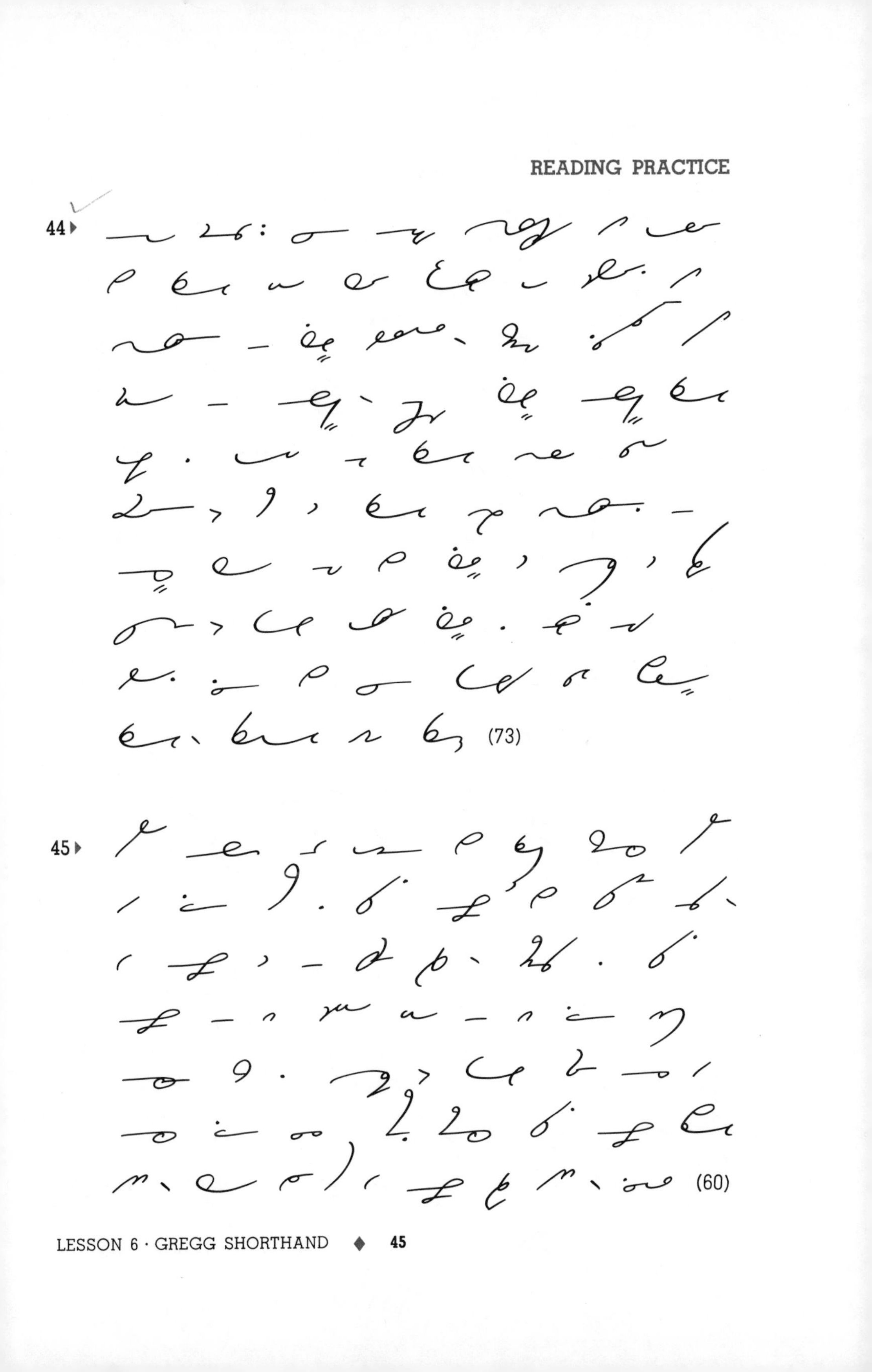

READING PRACTICE

44 (73)

45 (60)

46 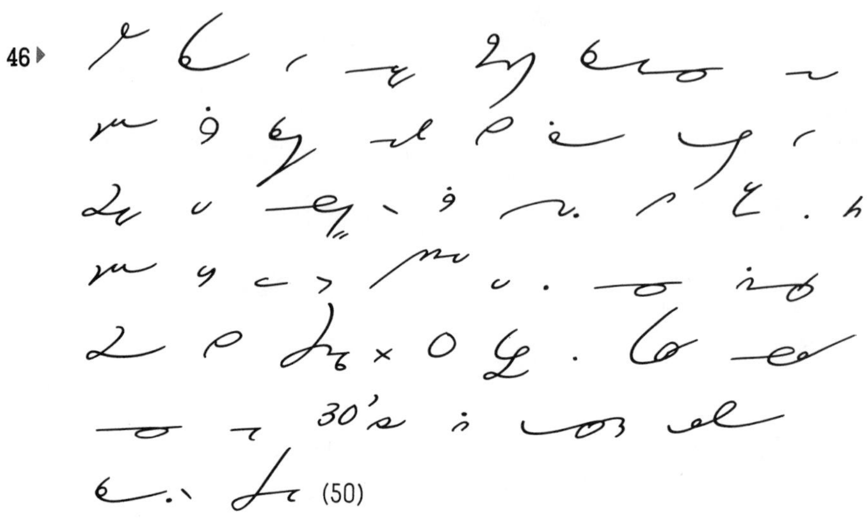

(50)

47

(67)

48

(73)

49 10

418-4414

(81)

It stands to reason that the more education and training you have, the more you have to offer an employer. Employers prefer as secretaries those who have pursued their education beyond high school, and they are willing to pay considerably more for this additional training. This does not mean that you have to have a college degree in order to better your competitive position, though it is certainly an advantage in many positions.

College-trained secretaries enter an organization holding at least three aces:

1▸ They command better starting pay.

2▸ They work for higher-level executives.

3▸ They are tagged for promotion more rapidly.

Of course, having college training in itself does not automatically entitle one to a free ride. You have to display the ability to do the job, and even a Ph.D. won't help you if you don't have competence. The point is, though, that college is often a proving ground that separates you from the also-rans. If you are successful in your college work, the chances are very good that you will be an effective employee. You bring to the job a higher level of skill, more maturity, and a more sophisticated attitude.

Of course, more comprehensive shorthand training is not the only reason why college-trained secretaries are preferred. They usually have more skill in English, vocabulary, typewriting, and office machines. College-trained secretaries are also likely to have a better understanding of business structure, economics, and finance.

Get as much education and training in college as you can. Don't settle for a "quickie" course that gives you minimum preparation. And if you can possibly do so, don't leave college until you have actually completed the prescribed course. College is a good investment — not only because it makes you a bigger person but also because it puts money in your pocket.

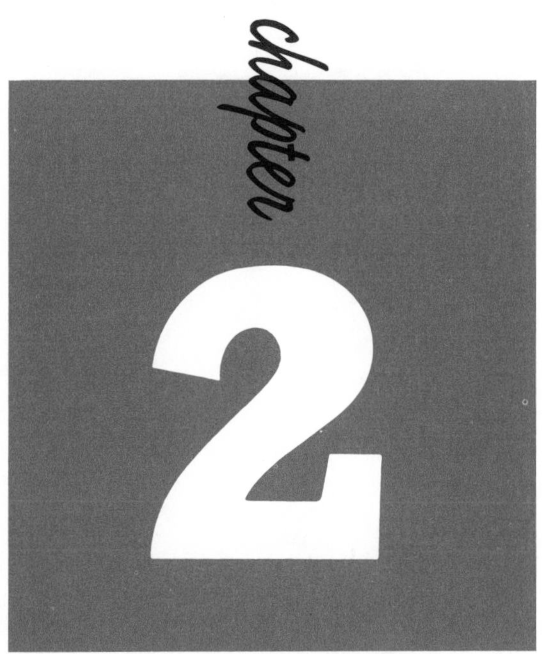

THE COLLEGE-TRAINED SECRETARY

PRINCIPLES

50 **O, Aw** • The small deep hook that represents ō, as in *row*, also represents the vowel sounds heard in *hot* and *draw*.

O	hot	copy	stock
	top	job	sorry
	drop	doctor	body
	lock	proper	occur
Aw	draws	all	taught
	ought	call	thought
	fall	small	brought
	bought	tall	cause

51 **Common Business-Letter Salutations and Closings**

Dear Sir	Sincerely yours	Very truly yours
Dear Madam	Yours truly	Yours very truly

NOTE: While the expressions *Dear Sir*, *Dear Madam*, and *Yours truly* are considered too impersonal by experts in letter writing, they are still used by many businessmen. Therefore, special abbreviations are provided for them.

READING AND WRITING PRACTICE

SUGGESTION: Take a few moments to read the suggestions for reading and writing shorthand given on pages 11 through 14. By following those suggestions, you will be able to complete this Reading and Writing Practice rapidly and efficiently.

52 ▸ (58)

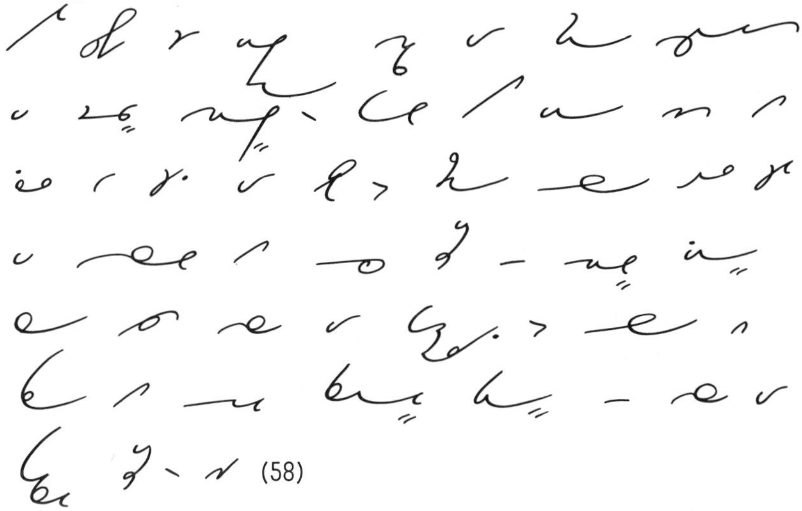

53 ▸

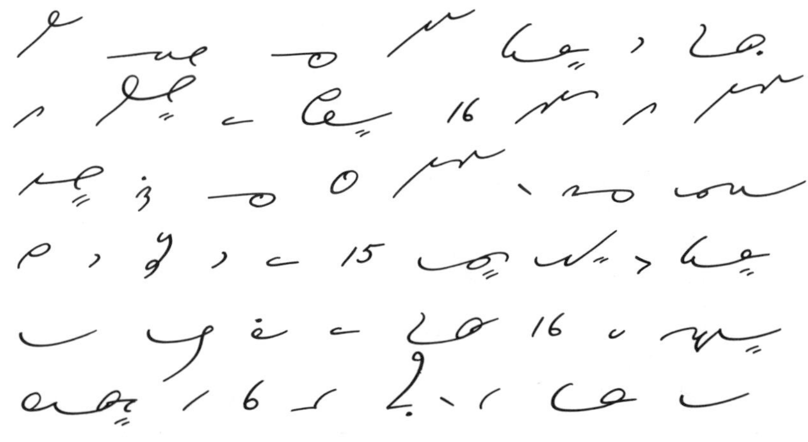

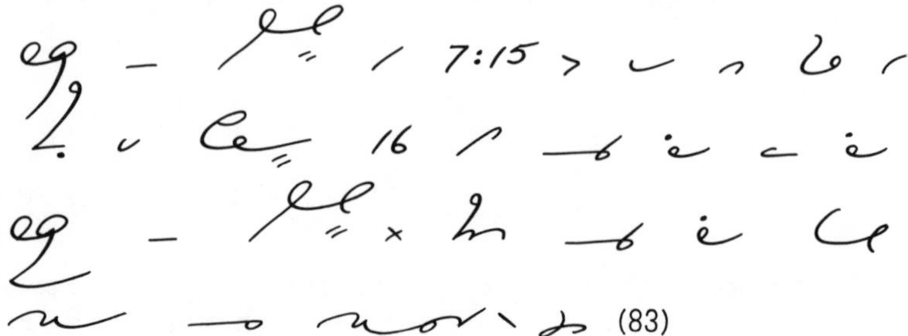

(83)

54 (81)

55

30's (115)

56 (61)

PRINCIPLES

57▸ Brief Forms • Here is another group of nine brief forms for frequently used words.

put	which	good
be, by	their, there	would
shall	this	for

58▸ Frequent Phrases • The following useful phrases are built on the brief forms in paragraph 57.

in this	I would	by the
for this	you will be	by this
for which	there is	I shall

59▸ Word Ending -ly • The very common ending *-ly* is represented by the e circle.

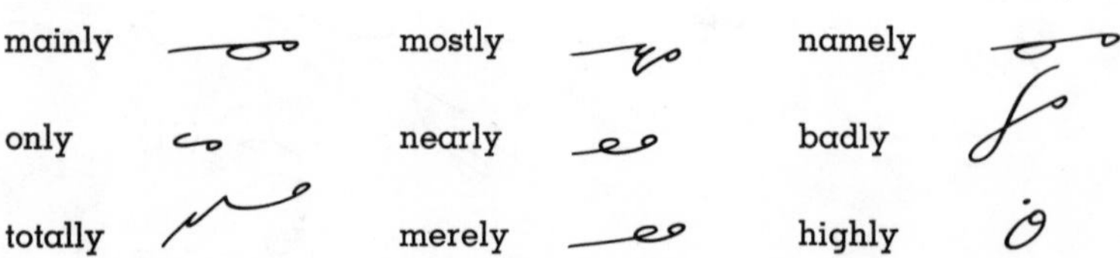

finally lately daily

NOTE: The circle for *-ly* in *daily* is added to the other side of the *d* after the *a* has been written.

60▸ Amounts and Quantities • In business you will frequently have to write amounts and quantities in your dictation. Here are some devices that will help you write them rapidly.

700	$8	four o'clock
7,000	$8,000	$4.50
700,000	$800,000	4 percent

NOTE: The *n* for *hundred* and the *th* for *thousand* are placed underneath the figure.

READING AND WRITING PRACTICE

61▸ Brief-Form Letter • The following letter contains one or more illustrations of the brief forms you studied in this lesson.

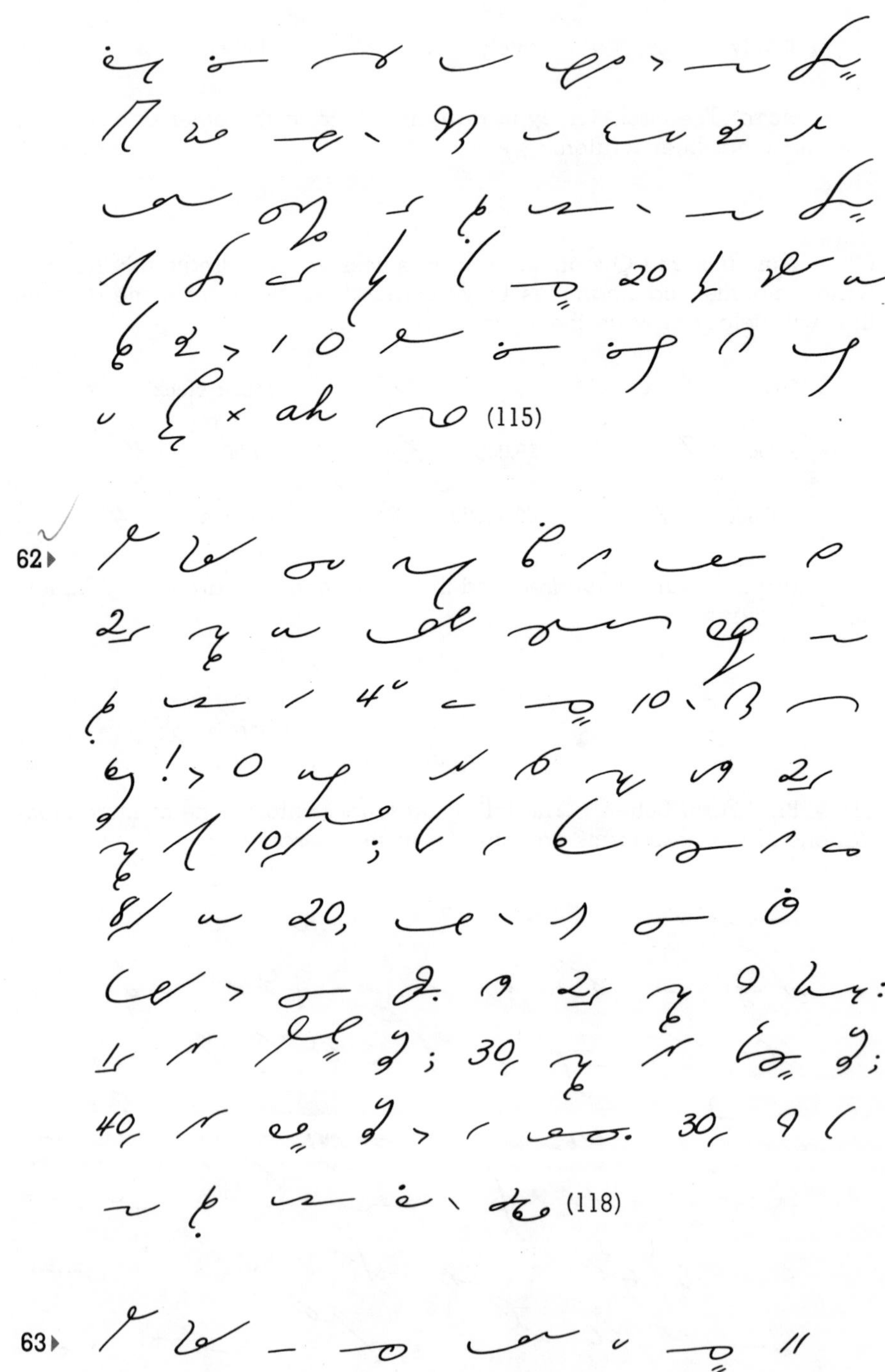
(115)
62
(118)
63

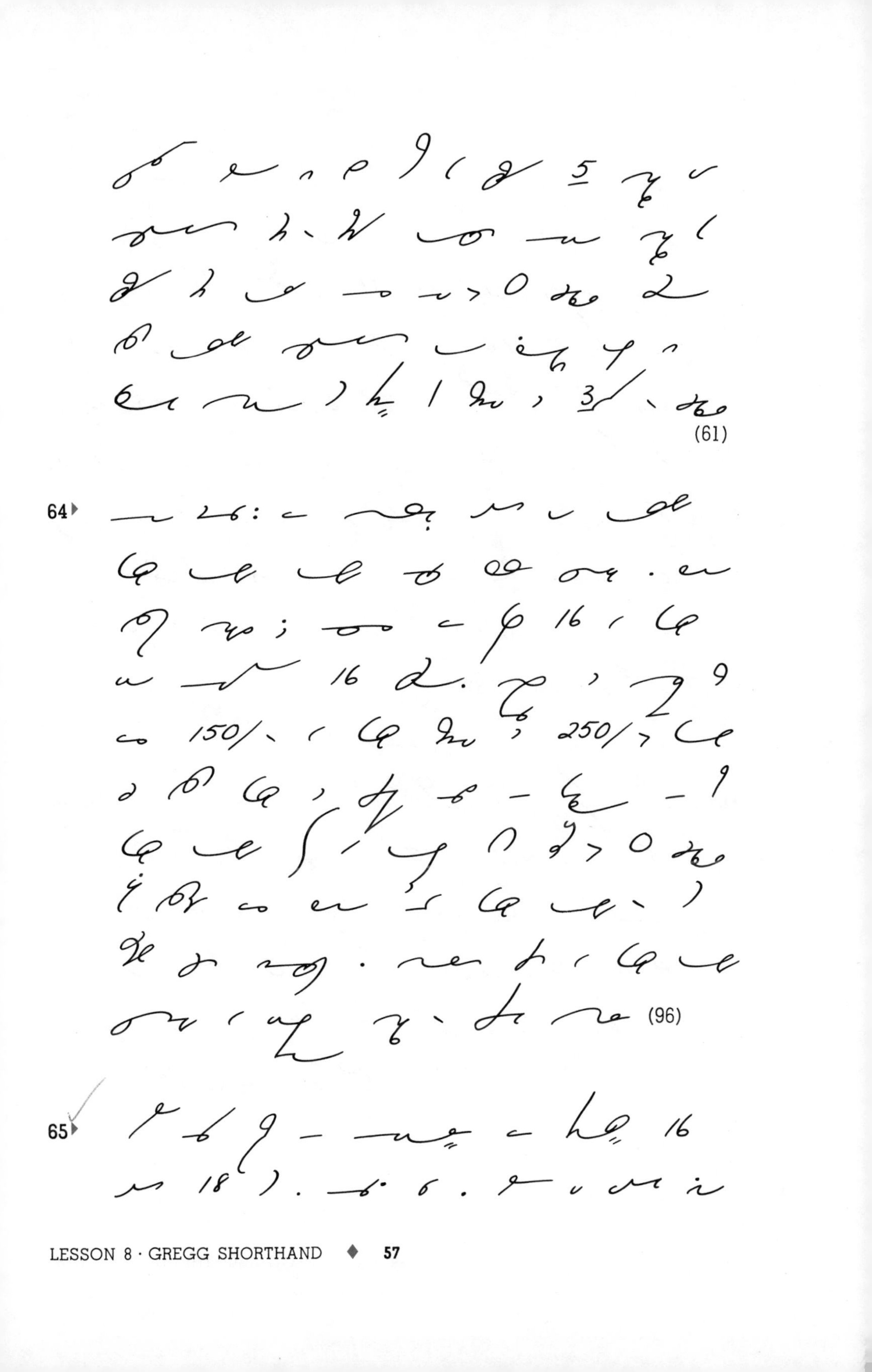

(61)

64

(96)

65

(103)

66 ▸

(49)

PRINCIPLES

67▸ Word Ending -tion • The word ending *-tion* (sometimes spelled *-sion, -cian,* or *-shion*) is represented by *sh.*

operation, position, nation, portion, physician, national, occasion, fashions, cautioned

68▸ Word Endings -cient, -ciency • The word ending *-cient* (or *-tient*) is represented by *sh-t; -ciency,* by *sh-s-*e.

patient, efficient, efficiency

69▸ Word Ending -tial • The word ending *-tial* (or *-cial*) is represented by *sh.*

special, social, initialed, official, initials, initially

70▸ T for To in Phrases • In phrases, *to* is represented by *t* when it is followed by a downstroke.

to have, to buy, to sell

to see		to fill		to which	
to be		to pay		to ship	
to put		to plan		to change	

READING AND WRITING PRACTICE

71 (113)

72

(80)

73

(124)

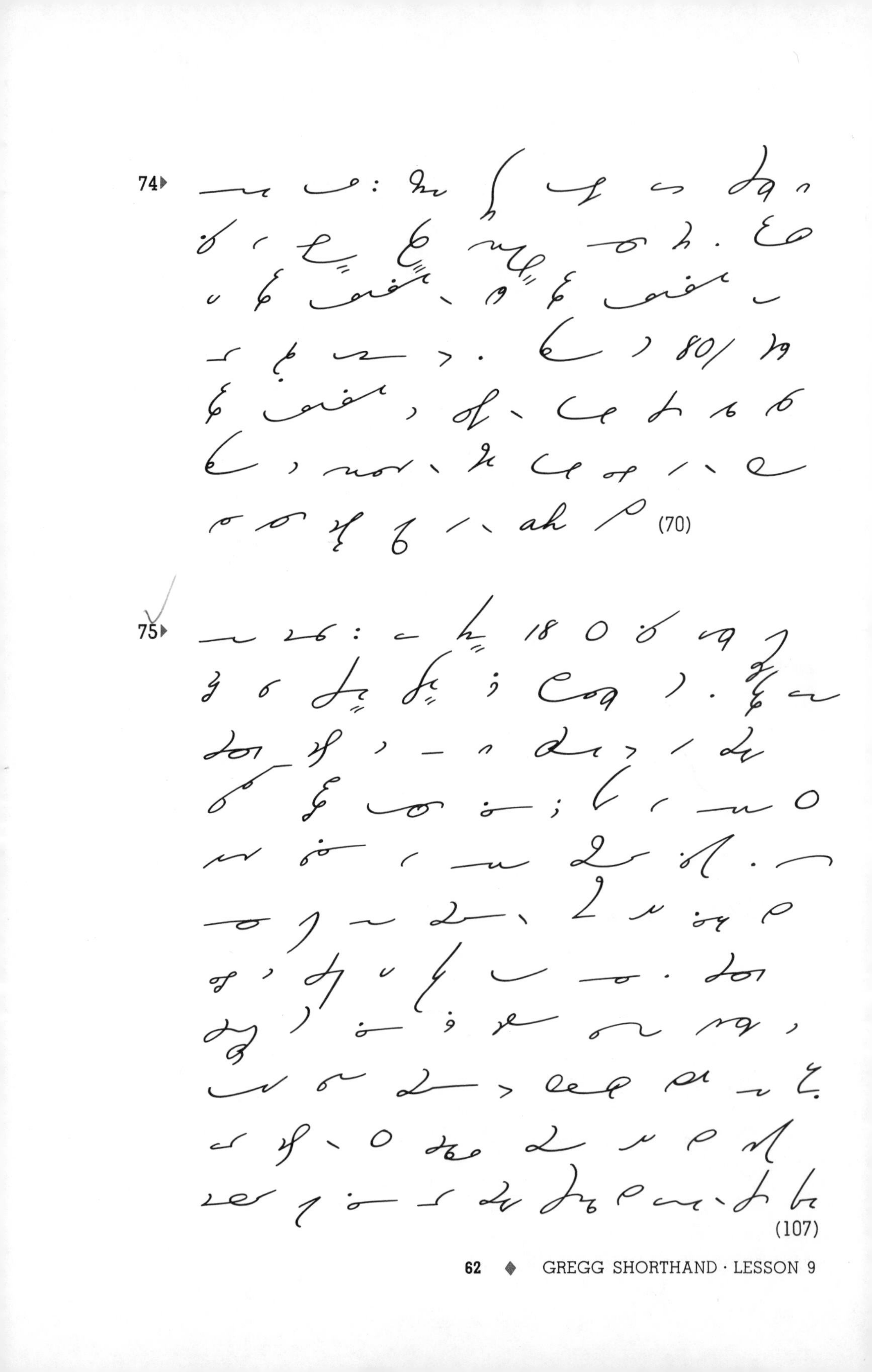

74 (70)

75 (107)

76 ▸ 26 Mets (67)

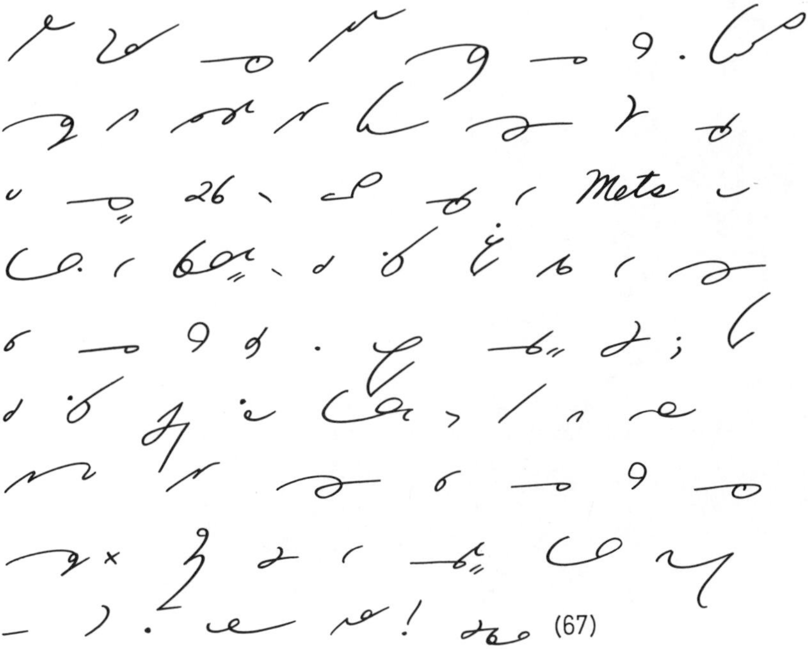

STUDY-HABIT CHECK LIST

No doubt as a conscientious student you do your home assignments faithfully. Do you, however, derive the greatest benefit from the time you devote to practice?

You do if you practice in a quiet place that enables you to concentrate.

You don't if you practice with one eye on the television and the other on your practice work!

You do if, once you have started your assignment, you do not leave your desk or table until you have completed it.

You don't if you interrupt your practice from time to time to call a friend or raid the refrigerator!

PRINCIPLES

77▸ Nd • The shorthand strokes for *n-d* are joined without an angle to form the *nd* blend, as in *trained.*

Nd

COMPARE: **train** **trained**

signed	friendly	brand
owned	spend	find
phoned	kind	mind

78▸ Nt • The stroke for *nd* also represents *nt,* as in *rent.*

rent	prevent	into
painted	agent	entirely
printer	urgent	entry

79▸ Ses • The sound of *ses,* as in *causes,* is represented by joining the two forms of *s.* The similar sounds of *sis,* as in *sister,* and *sus,* as in *versus,* are represented in the same way.

COMPARE: **cause** **causes**

face **faces**

losses		pleases		necessary	
addresses		prices		sister	
offices		closes		basis	
cases		classes		versus	

READING AND WRITING PRACTICE

80 ▸ 15 (99)

81 ▸

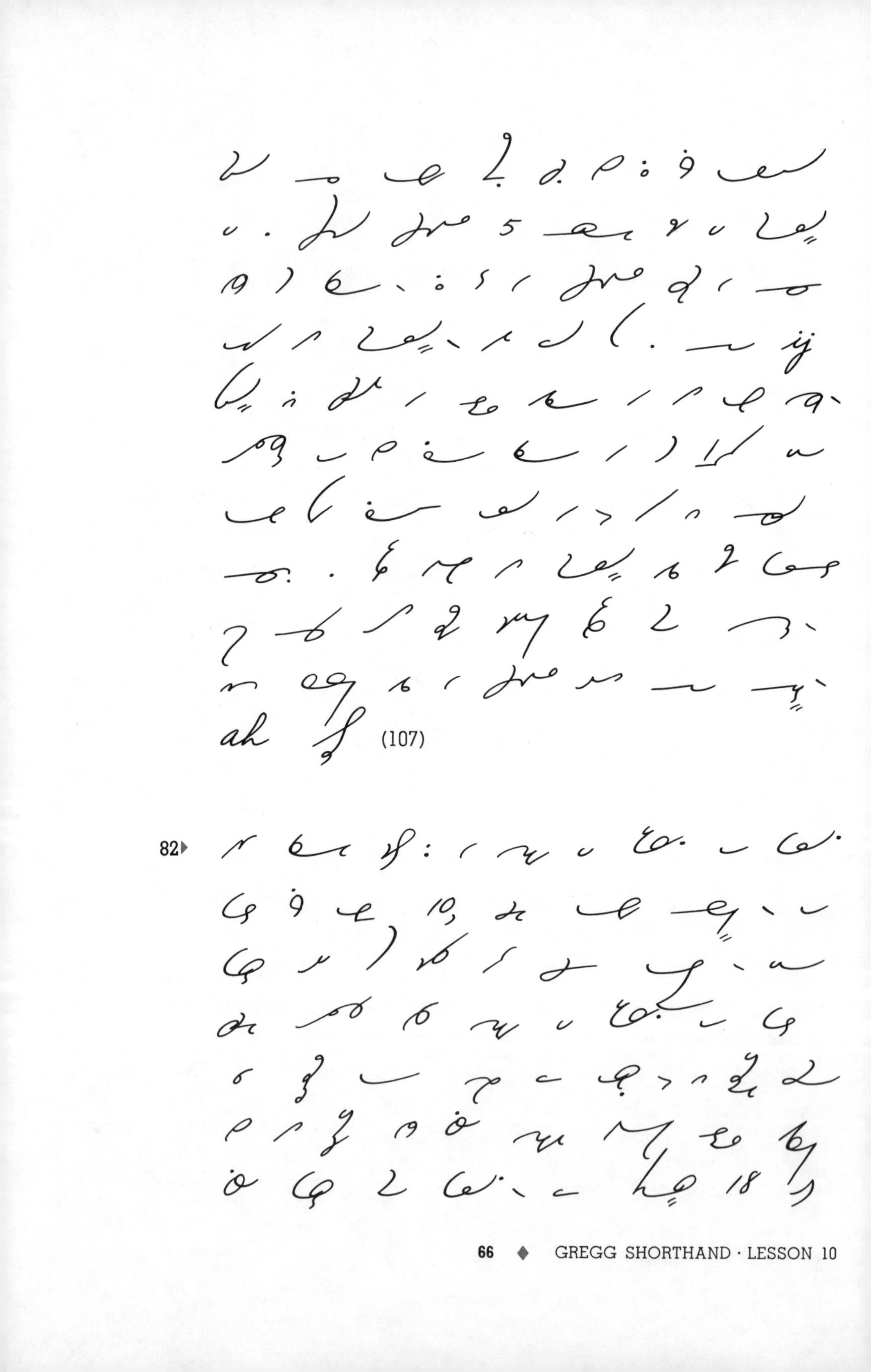

(107)

82

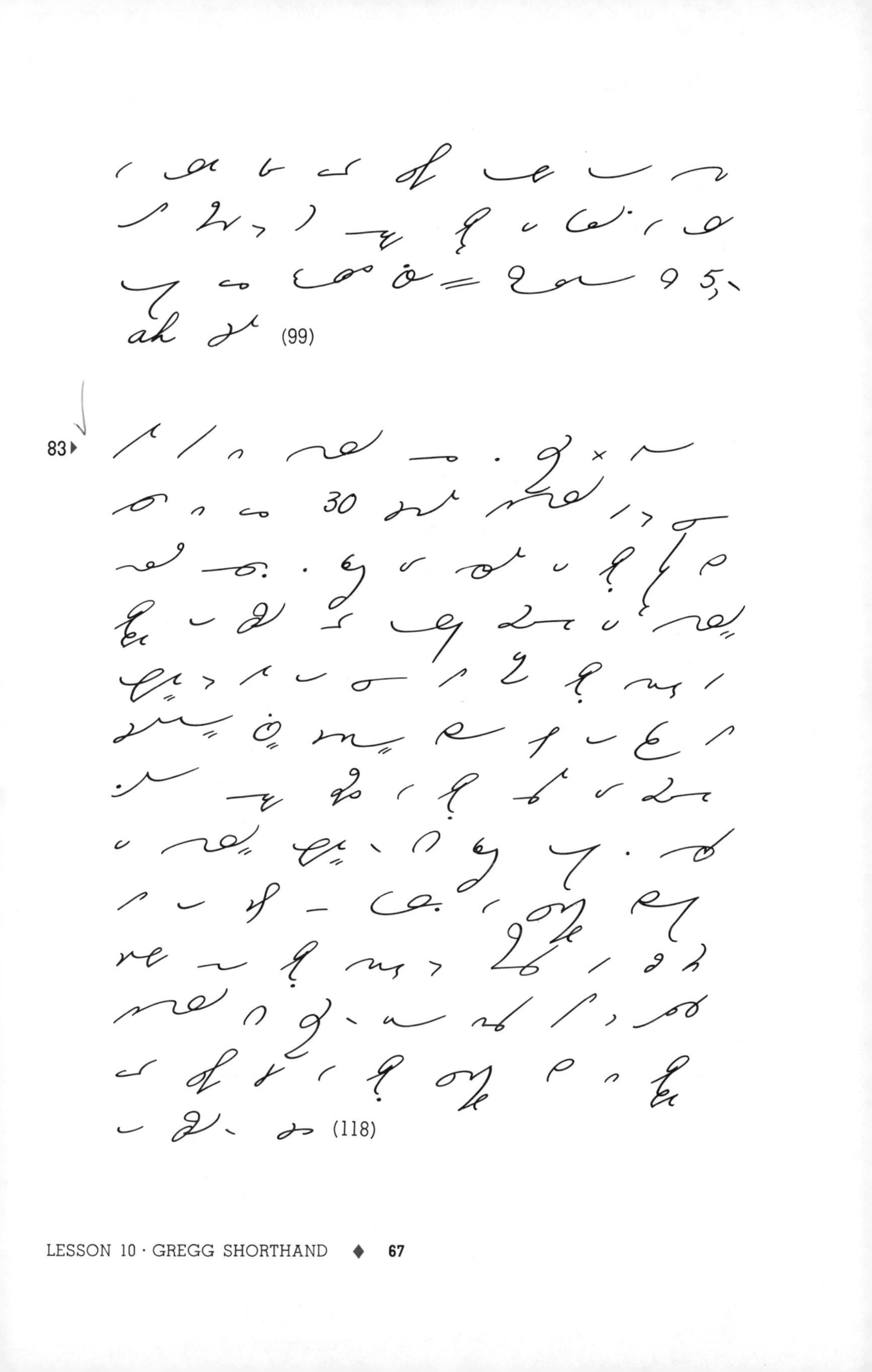

(99)

83

30

(118)

PRINCIPLES

84▸ **Brief Forms** • Here is another set of brief forms for common words.

should — could — was — send — from — and — them — they — when

85▸ **Rd** • The combination *rd* is represented by writing *r* with an upward turn at the finish.

COMPARE: **store** — **stored**

hired — appeared — hard — heard — tired — toward — record — harder — guarded

86▸ **Ld** • The combination *ld* is represented by writing the *l* with an upward turn at the finish.

COMPARE: **fail** — **failed**

87▸ Been in Phrases • The word *been* is represented by *b* after *have, has, had.*

88▸ Able in Phrases • The word *able* is represented by *a* after *be* or *been.*

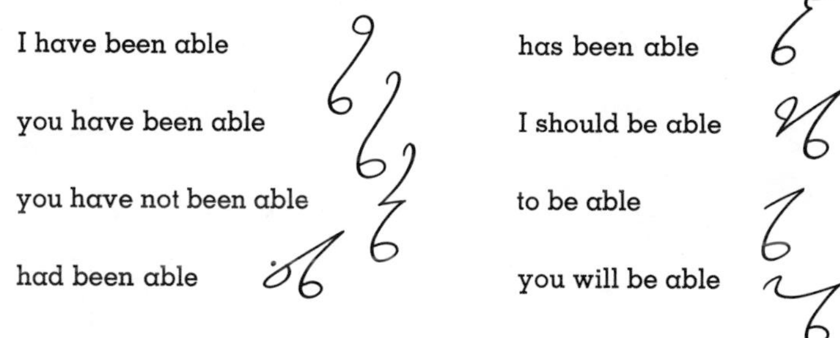

READING AND WRITING PRACTICE

89▸ Brief-Form Letter • The following letter contains at least one illustration of every brief form presented in paragraph 84.

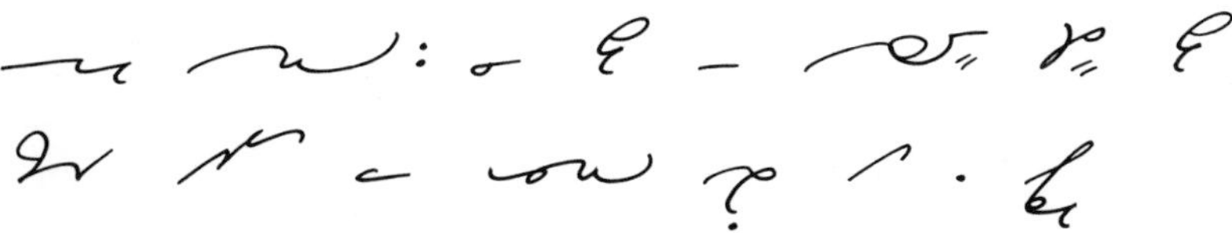

(89)

90

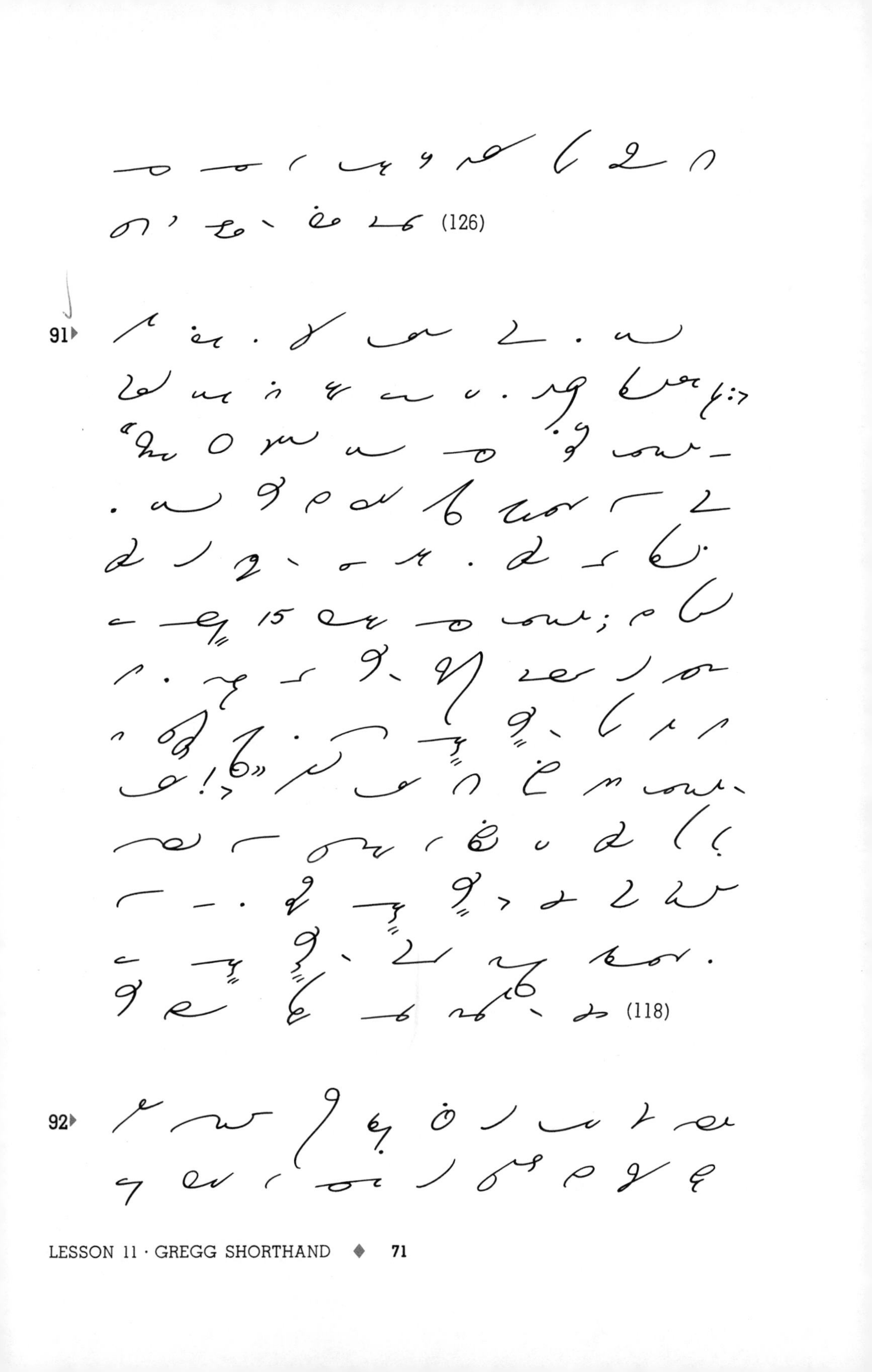

(126)

91 ... 15 ... (118)

92

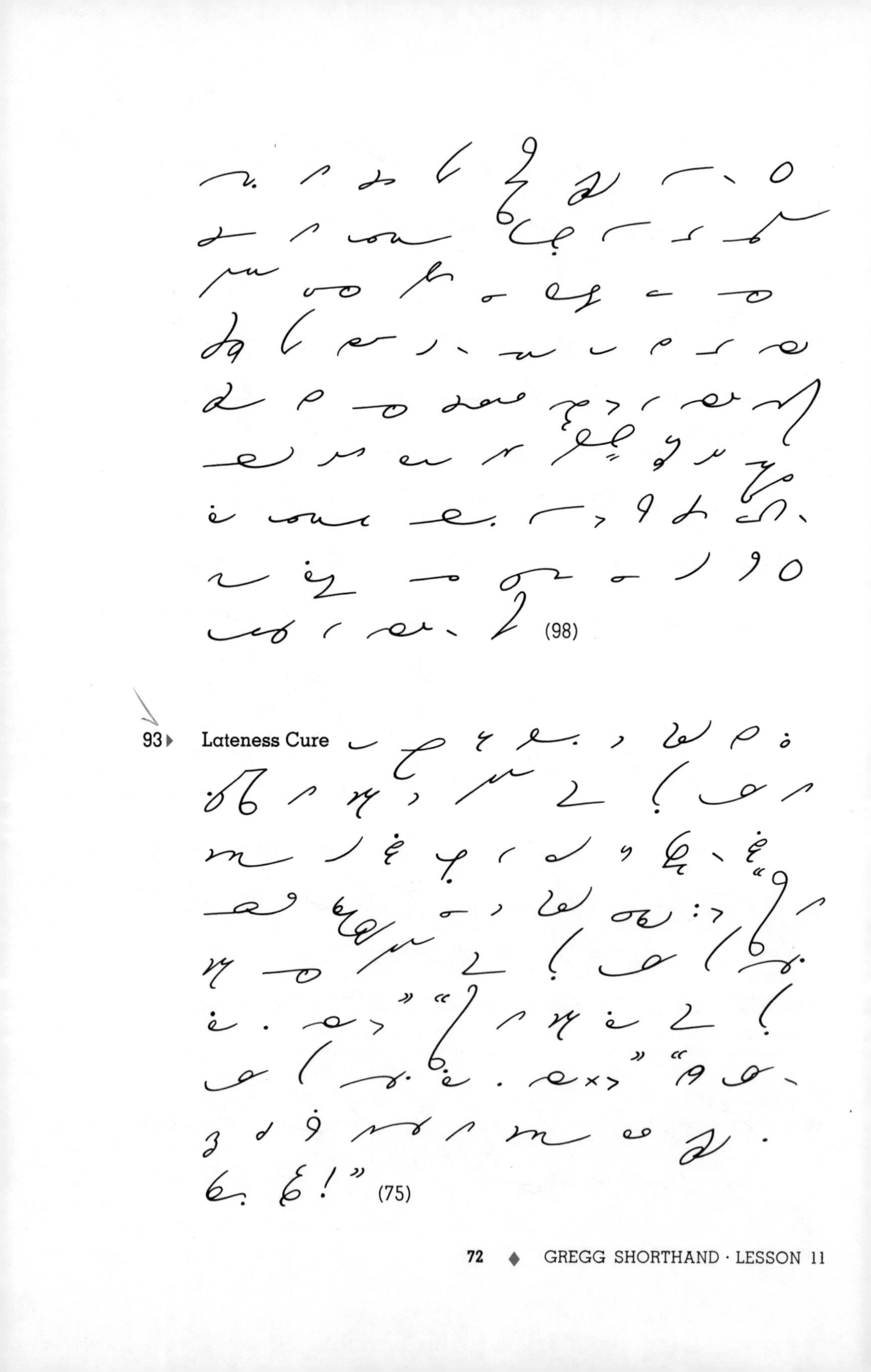

(98)

93 Lateness Cure

(75)

Lesson 12 contains no new principles for you to learn; it reviews the shorthand devices you studied in Lessons 1 through 11.

PRINCIPLES OF JOINING

The following principles deal with the joinings of the two forms of *s*.

94▸ At the beginning and ending of words, the comma *s* is used before and after *f, v, k, g;* the left *s*, before and after *p, b, r, l.*

Safes, saves, seeks, sags, sips, saber, robs, series, sales.

95▸ The comma *s* is used before *t, d, n, m, o;* the left *s* is used after those characters.

Seats, seeds, since, seems, solos, meets, needs.

96▸ The comma *s* is used before and after *sh, ch, j.*

Sessions, cashes, reaches, teaches, rages, pages, sieges, sages.

97 ▸ The comma *s* is used in words consisting of *s* and a circle vowel and *th* and a circle vowel.

See, say, these, seethe.

98 ▸ Gregg Shorthand is equally legible whether it is written on ruled or unruled paper; consequently, you need not worry about the exact placement of your outlines on the printed lines in your notebook. The main purpose that the printed lines in your notebook serve is to keep you from wandering uphill and downhill as you write.

However, so that all outlines may be uniformly placed in the shorthand books from which you study, this general rule has been followed:

The base of the first consonant of a word is placed on the line of writing. When *s* comes before a downstroke, however, the downstroke is placed on the line of writing.

Names, dealer, say, special, large, siege.

99 ▸ **Recall Chart** • The following chart reviews the principles you studied in Chapters 1 and 2.

Can you read the entire chart in 9 minutes or less?

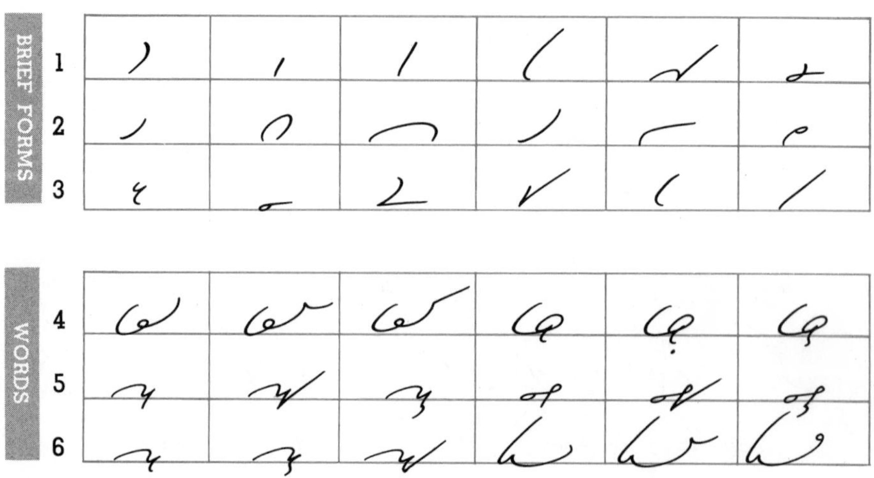

WORDS

7

8

9

10

11

PHRASES

12

13

14

15

READING AND WRITING PRACTICE

100

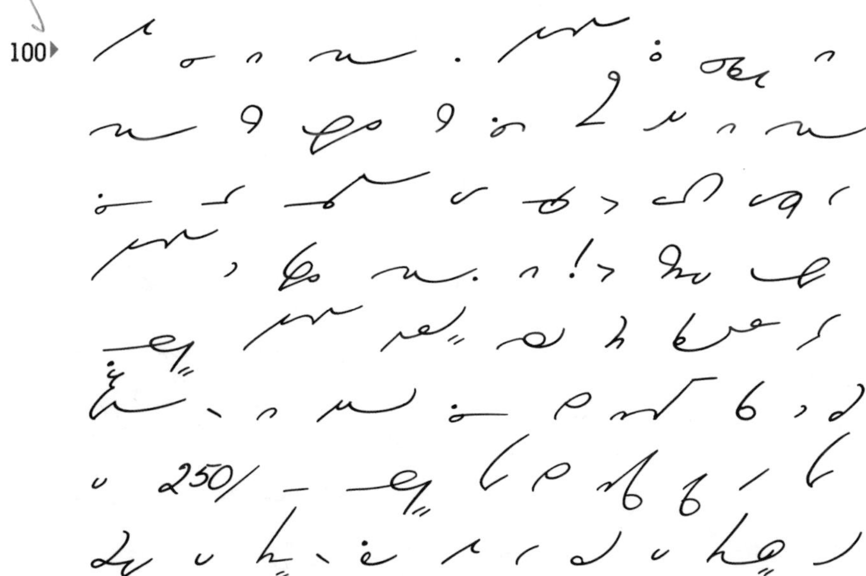

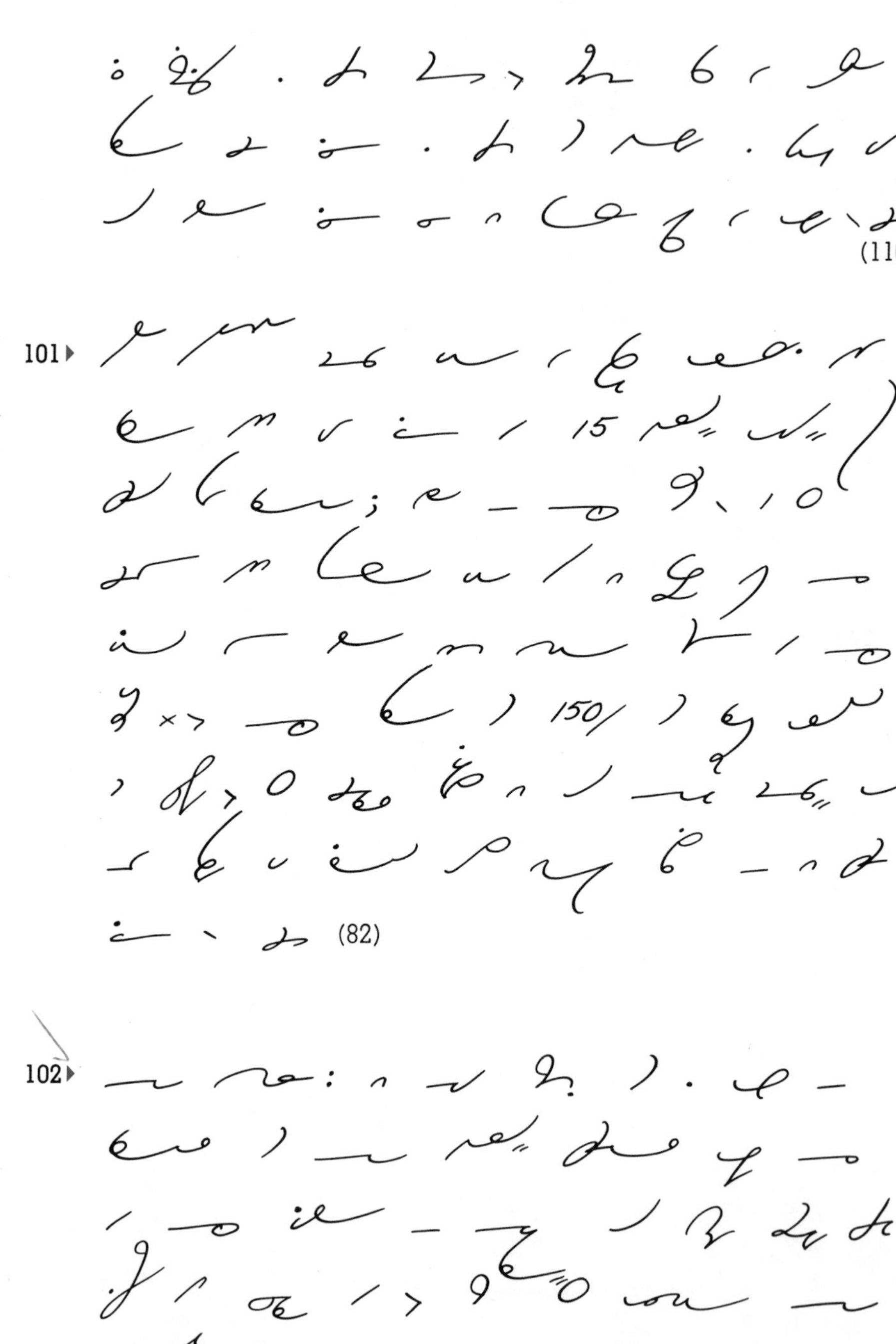

(110)

101

(82)

102

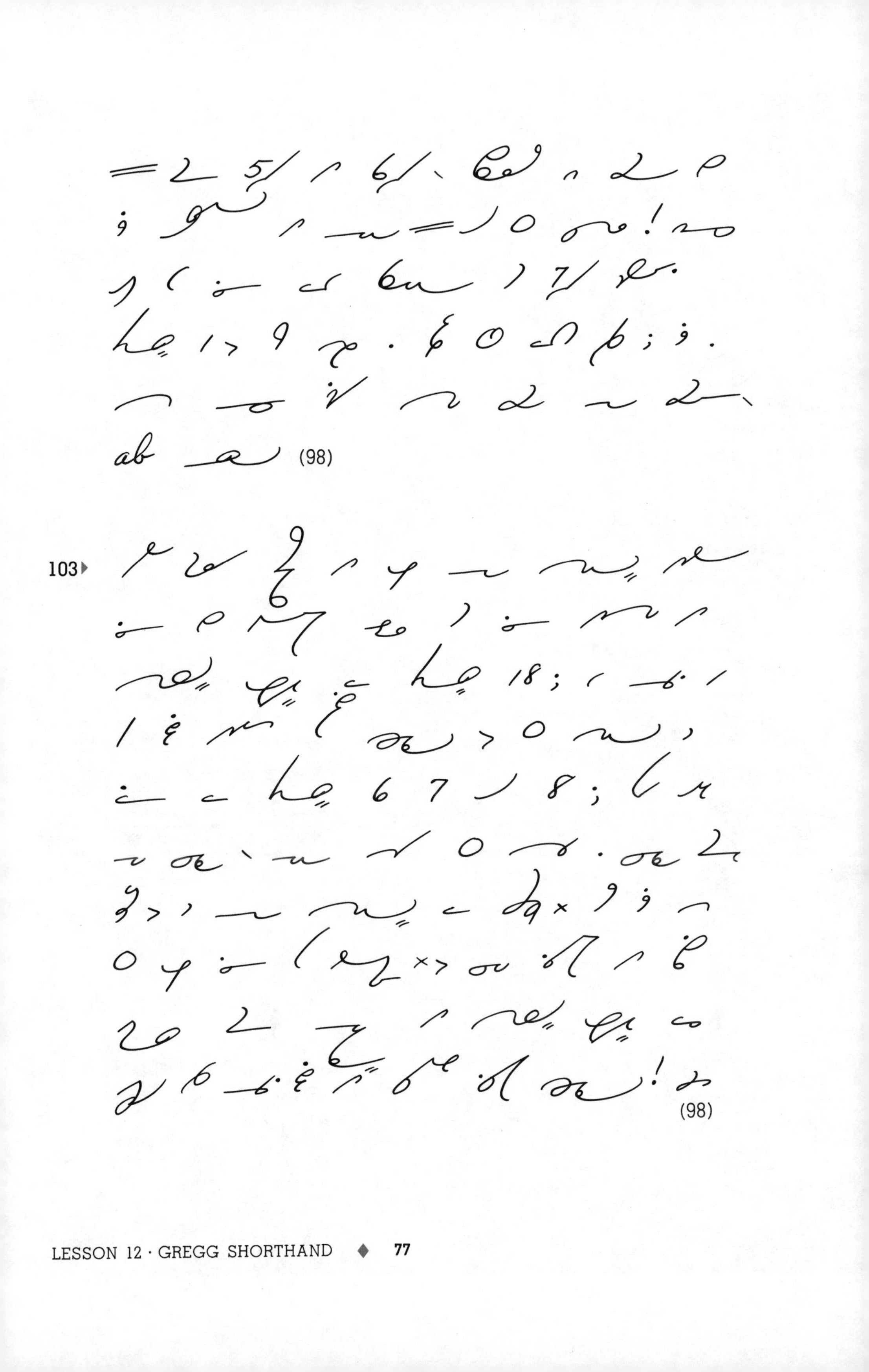

(98)

103

(98)

There are many reasons for learning shorthand, but there are very special ones why college students do so. Of course, the greatest incentive for learning shorthand is to obtain a secretarial job in a business or government office; and it is no secret that college-trained secretaries are in greater demand than ever before.

But there are other important ways in which shorthand is a valuable ally to the college woman. Whether she is taking a "business course" with a secretarial job as her objective or not, shorthand is a valuable skill to list among her achievements. Shorthand is a natural companion to the liberal arts. Shorthand provides the "extra" that puts the liberal arts major a good distance ahead of her counterpart who is not so equipped when the job search begins.

If you have chosen journalism as your career, imagine how helpful shorthand can be to you in making notes of interviews and in making a record of important events that you witness. Perhaps you have decided to major in history, government, or political science. Business often prefers this type of college training for those who work in research. But how do you "market" your particular knowledge in a business or government organization? Regardless of your grades, it will not be easy to obtain the job you want, especially when there is competition, unless you bring an extra something to the job. And one of the best "extra somethings" is shorthand!

The person with abilities in art, music, or drama is faced with keen competition in selling these talents to a commercial enterprise—there are more people seeking jobs in these areas than there are jobs to be filled. Shorthand can be the key that opens the door to these hard-to-enter fields. The English major who wants to work in business often finds it difficult to emphasize a specific skill on her qualification sheet; but when she adds shorthand to the list, the picture changes immediately.

And so it goes. Each year thousands of women who have obtained liberal arts degrees enroll in private business schools to obtain secretarial skills, for without these skills their chances of getting that ideal job are greatly lessened.

What is your major? Regardless of what it is, your chances of getting a running start in it will be greatly brightened because you are adding shorthand to your list of qualifications. Shorthand and liberal arts are a natural combination.

SHORTHAND AND THE LIBERAL ARTS

Photographed in the Museum of Modern Art, New York

Lesson 13

PRINCIPLES

104▸ Brief Forms

soon — work — order

enclose — glad — were, year

yesterday — very — thank*

*In phrases, the dot is omitted from *thank*. *Thanks* is written with a disjoined left *s* in the dot position.

thank you — thank you for — thanks

105▸ U, U̇ · The hook that expresses the sound of oo, as in *too*, also represents the vowel sounds heard in *drug* and *pull*.

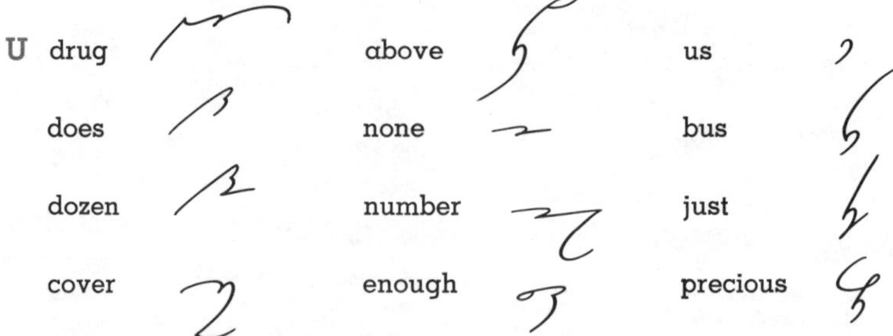

U drug
above
us
does
none
bus
dozen
number
just
cover
enough
precious

NOTE: The hook is placed on its side after *n* in *none, number, enough*; oo-s are joined without an angle in *us, bus, just, precious*.

U̇ pull — look — foot

full	book	cook
push	took	stood

106▸ W, Sw · At the beginning of words, the sound of *w* is represented by the oo hook; *sw*, by *s*-oo.

W	we	wear	wood
	way	watch	week, weak
	wait	wash	wants
Sw	sweet	swim	sweater

BUILDING TRANSCRIPTION SKILLS

107▸ BUSINESS VOCABULARY BUILDER

As a stenographer or secretary you will constantly be dealing with words. Consequently, the larger the vocabulary at your command, the easier will be your task of taking dictation and transcribing.

To help you build your vocabulary at the same time that you are learning shorthand, a Business Vocabulary Builder is provided in Lesson 13 and in many of the lessons that follow. The Business Vocabulary Builder consists of brief definitions of business words and expressions, selected from the Reading and Writing Practice of the lesson, that may be unfamiliar to you.

Be sure to read each Business Vocabulary Builder before you begin your work on the Reading and Writing Practice that follows it.

shuffle (noun) Confused movement.

testify To make a statement or declaration under oath to establish some fact.

plight Difficulty.

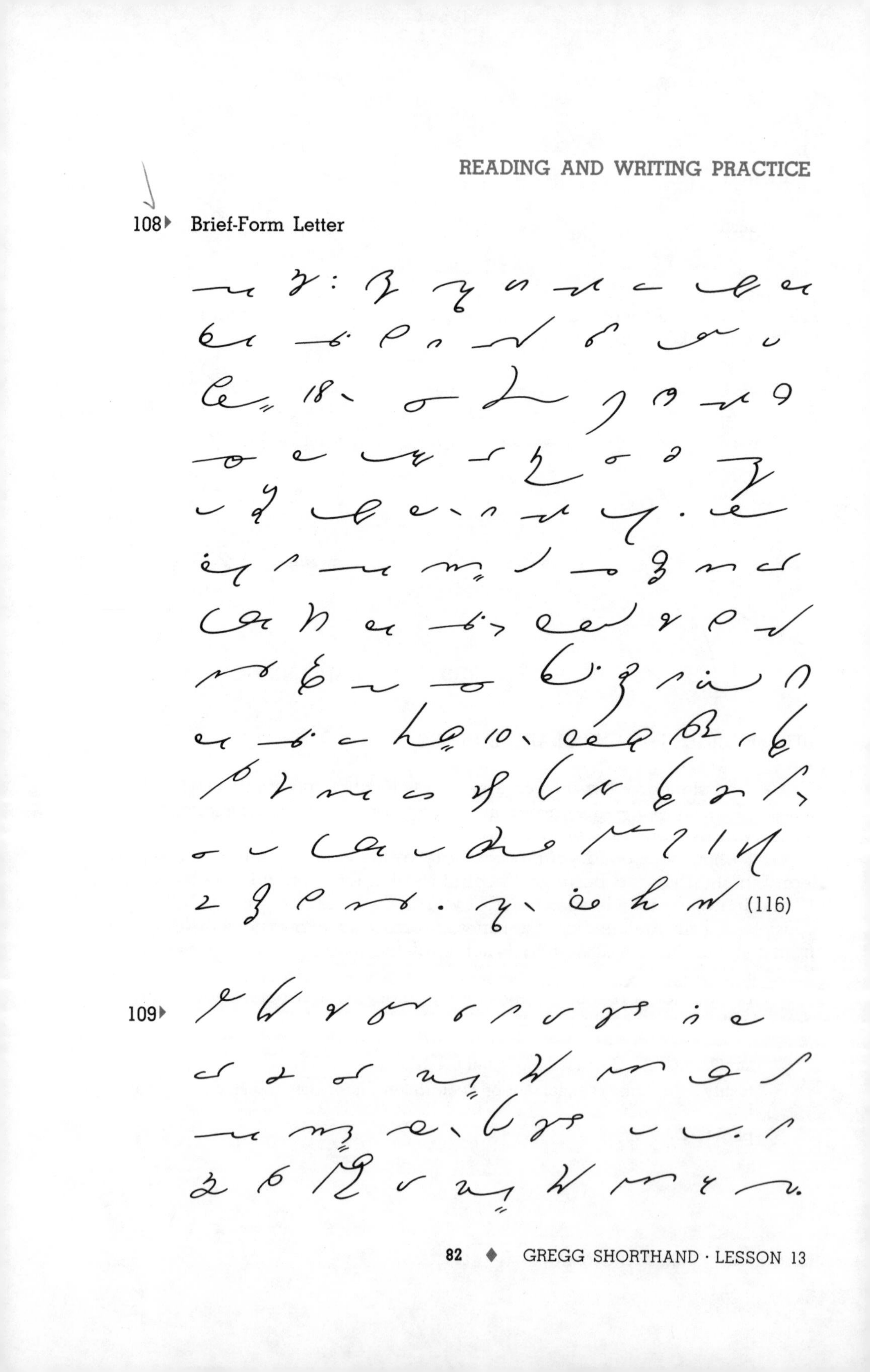

108 Brief-Form Letter

(116)

109

(101)

110

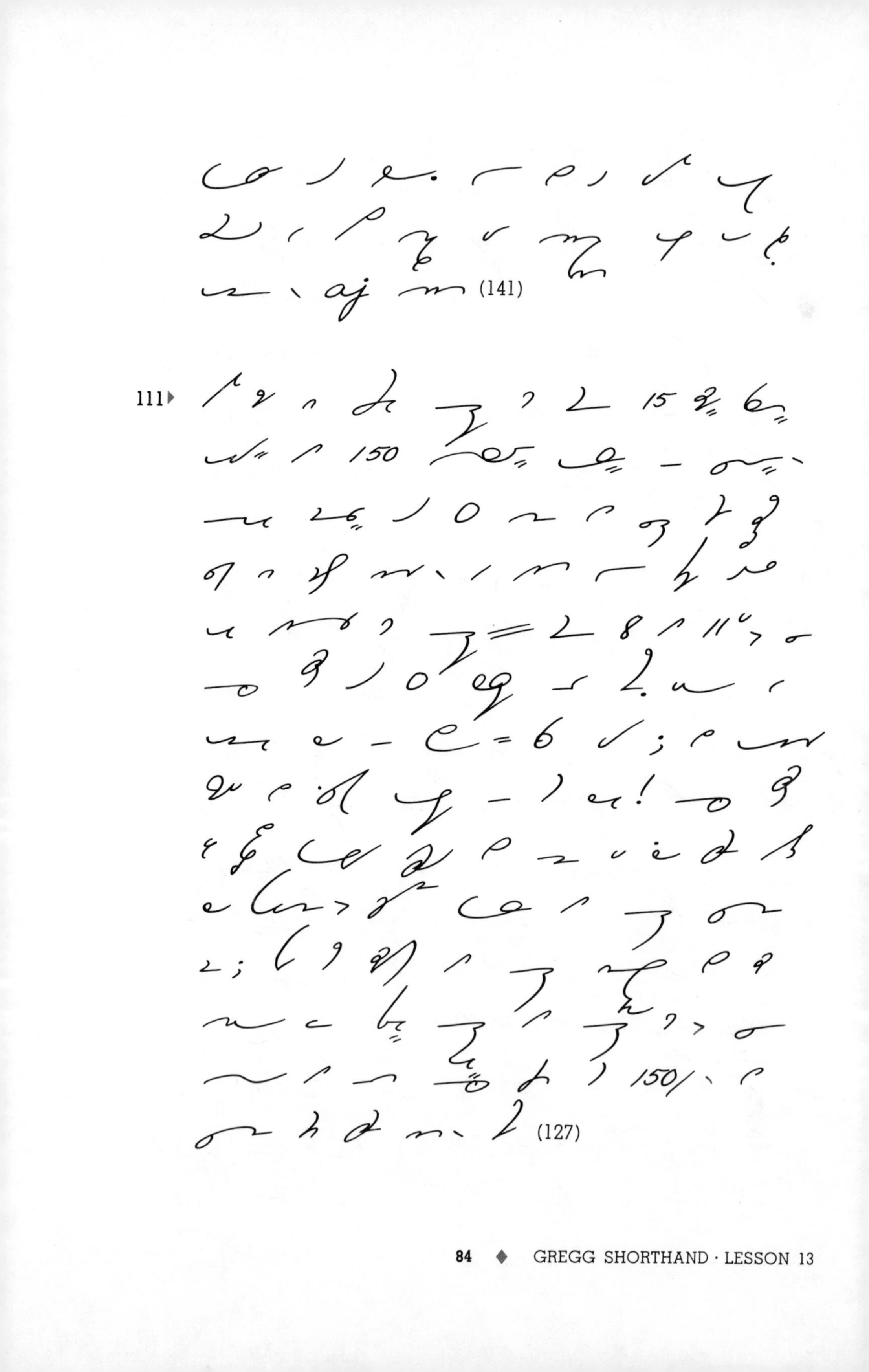

(141)

111

(127)

PRINCIPLES

112 ▸ **Wh** • *Wh*, as in *white*, is pronounced *hw* – the *h* is pronounced first. Therefore, in shorthand, we write the *h* first.

white	wheel	whip
while	whale	wheat

113 ▸ **W in the Body of a Word** • When the sound of *w* occurs in the body of a word, as in *quite*, it is represented by a short dash underneath the vowel following the *w* sound. The dash is inserted after the rest of the outline has been written.

quite	equipped	always
quick	twice	roadway
quit	square	Broadway

114 ▸ **Ted** • The combination *ted* is represented by joining *t* and *d* into one long upward stroke.

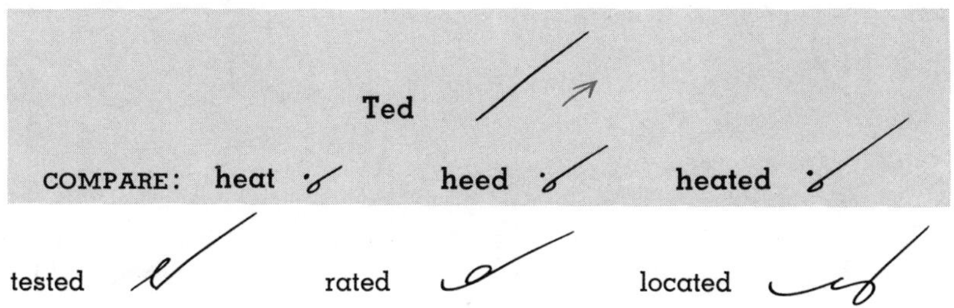

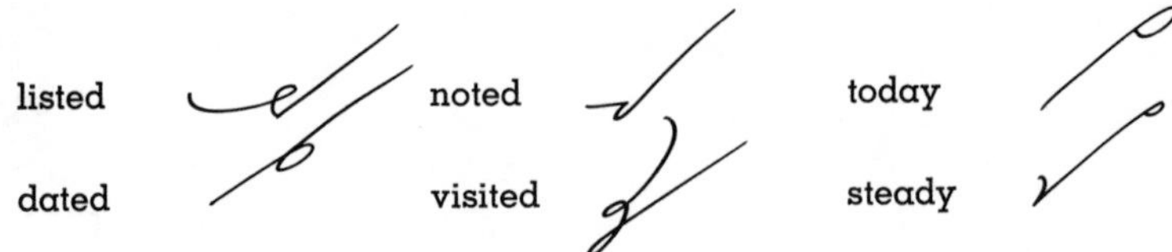

115▸ Ded, Det, Dit • The long stroke that represents *ted* also represents *ded, dit, det.*

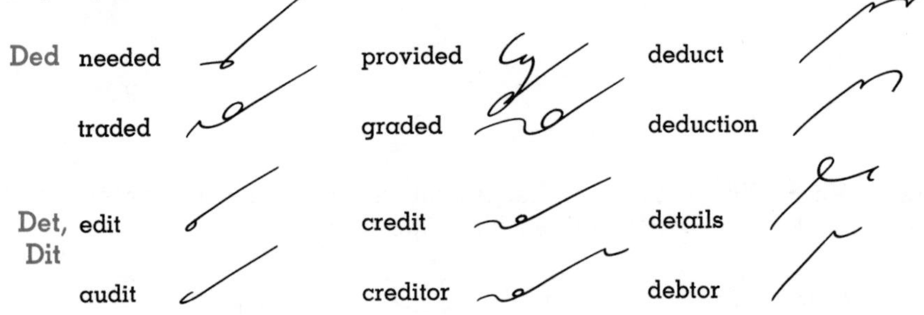

BUILDING TRANSCRIPTION SKILLS

116▸ BUSINESS VOCABULARY BUILDER

graded Made even or level.
agitated Excited; stirred up.
placated Changed from bitterness to goodwill.

READING AND WRITING PRACTICE

117▸

(101)

118 (94)

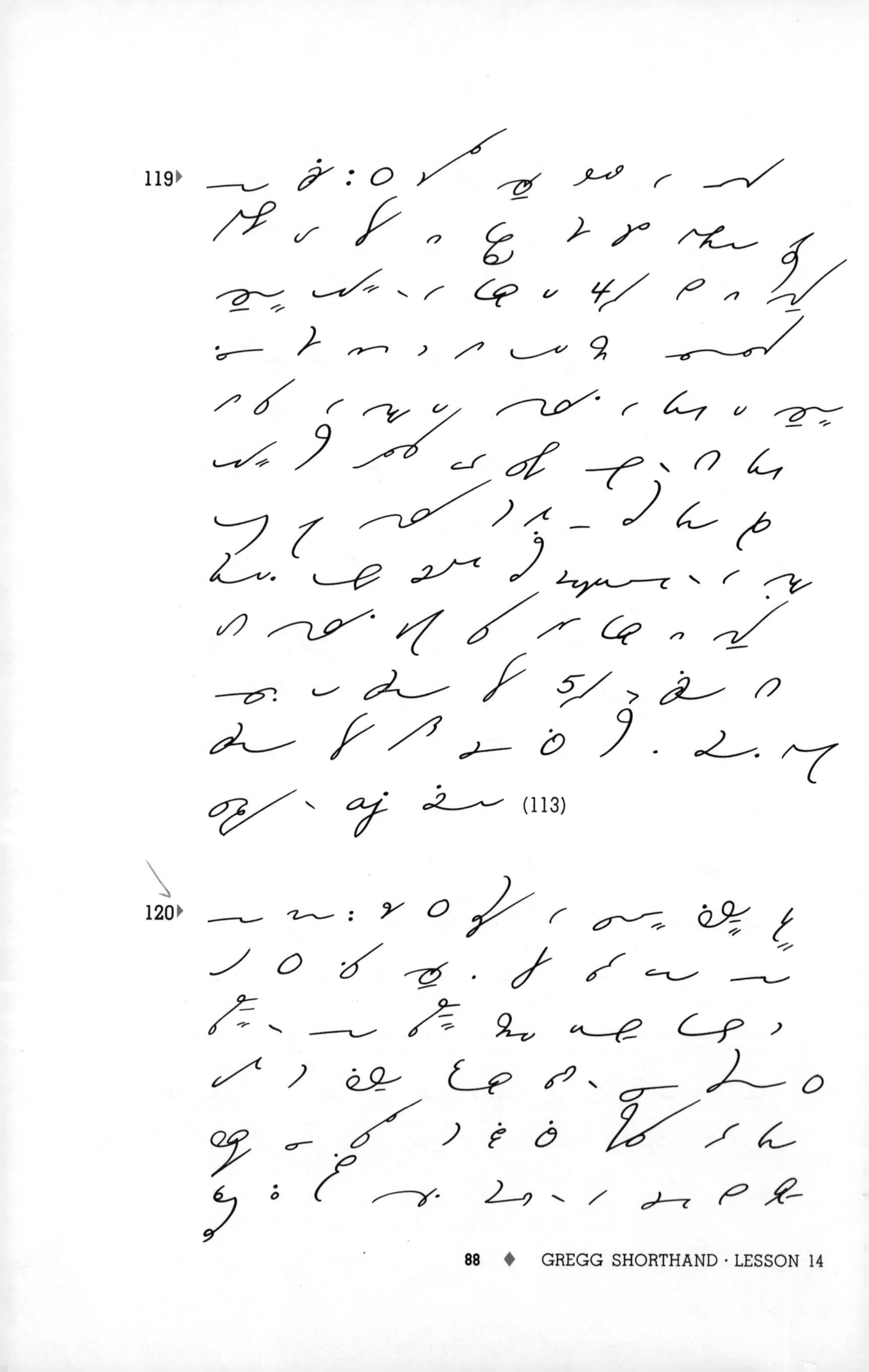

119▸

(113)

120▸

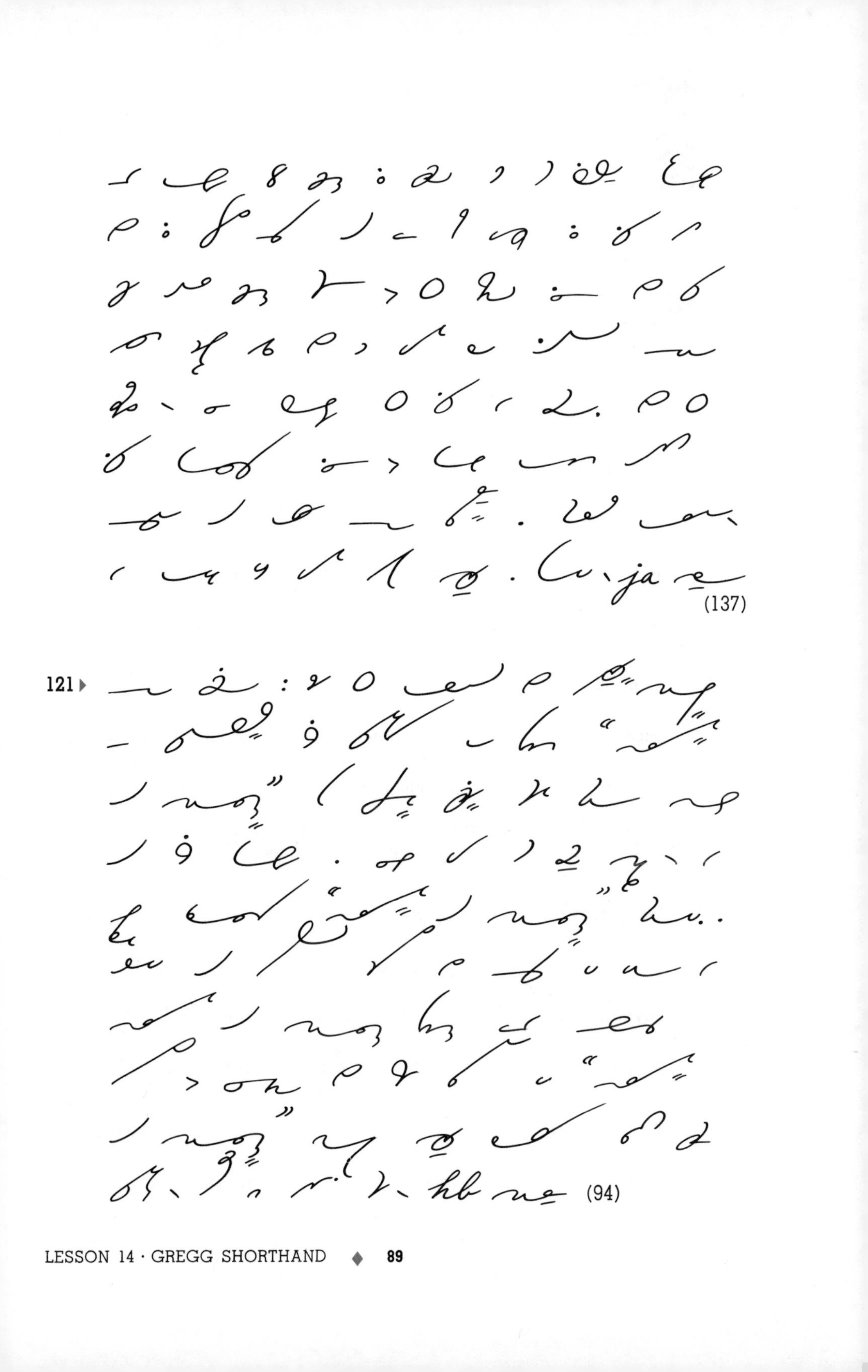

(137)

121

(94)

PRINCIPLES

122 Brief Forms

business	about	than
why	what	thing, think
great	value	one, won

123 Brief-Form Derivatives

once	things, thinks	businessman
greater	thinking	businesses

NOTE: A disjoined left *s* is used to express the plural of *thing, think;* the plural of *business* is formed by adding a second left *s*.

124 **Word Ending -ble** • The word ending *-ble* is represented by *b*.

available	profitable	tables
payable	sensible	troubled
possible	reliable	cabled

125 **Word Beginning Re-** • The word beginning *re-* is represented by *r*.

refers	received	resisted

reply		receipt		recent	
repeat		revise		reappear	
repaired		research		reopen	

BUILDING TRANSCRIPTION SKILLS

126 ▸ **BUSINESS VOCABULARY BUILDER**

resolved Settled; cleared up.
amicable Friendly.
La Scala Famous opera house in Milan, Italy.

READING AND WRITING PRACTICE

127 ▸ **Brief-Form Letter**

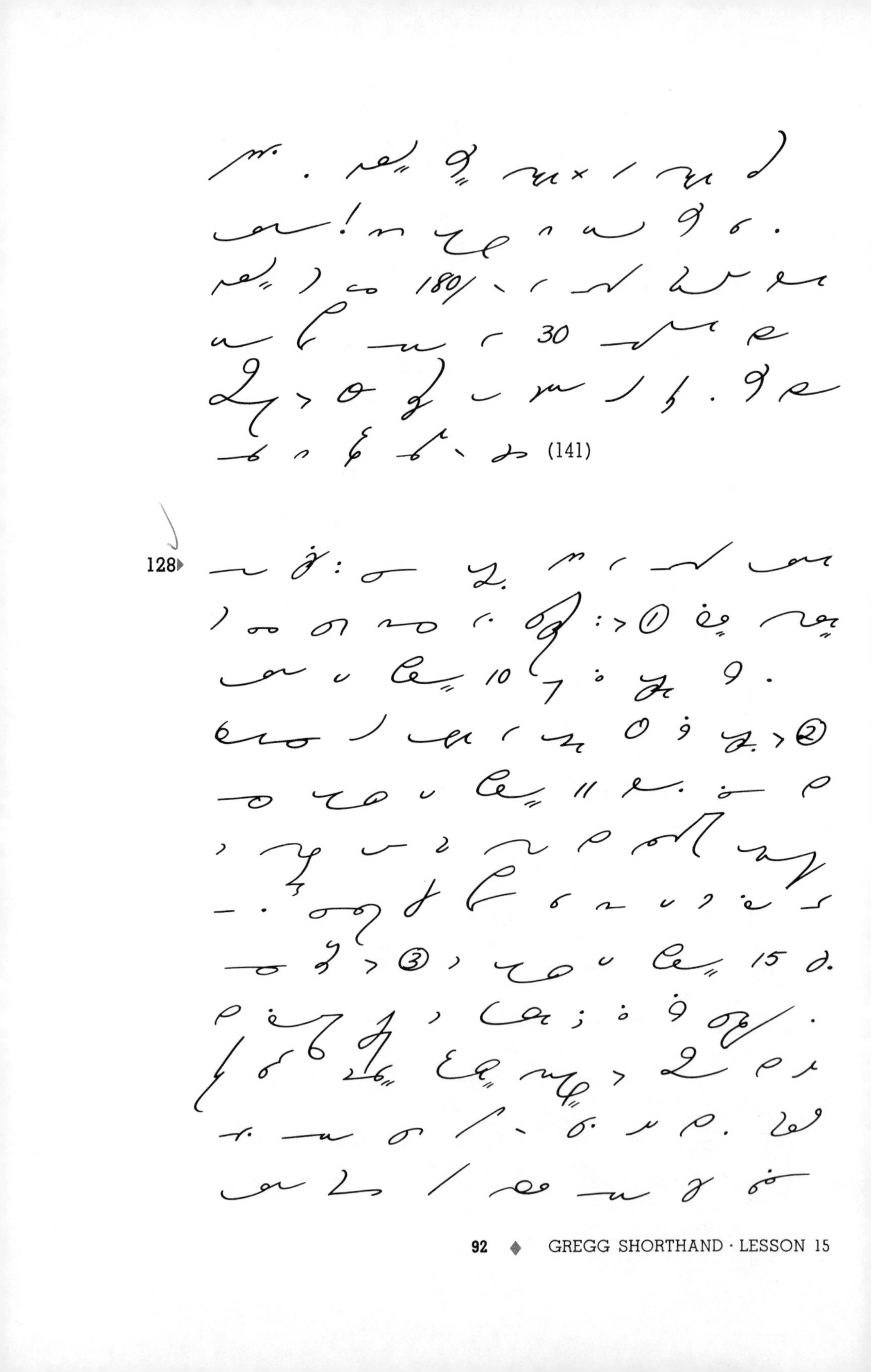

(141)

128

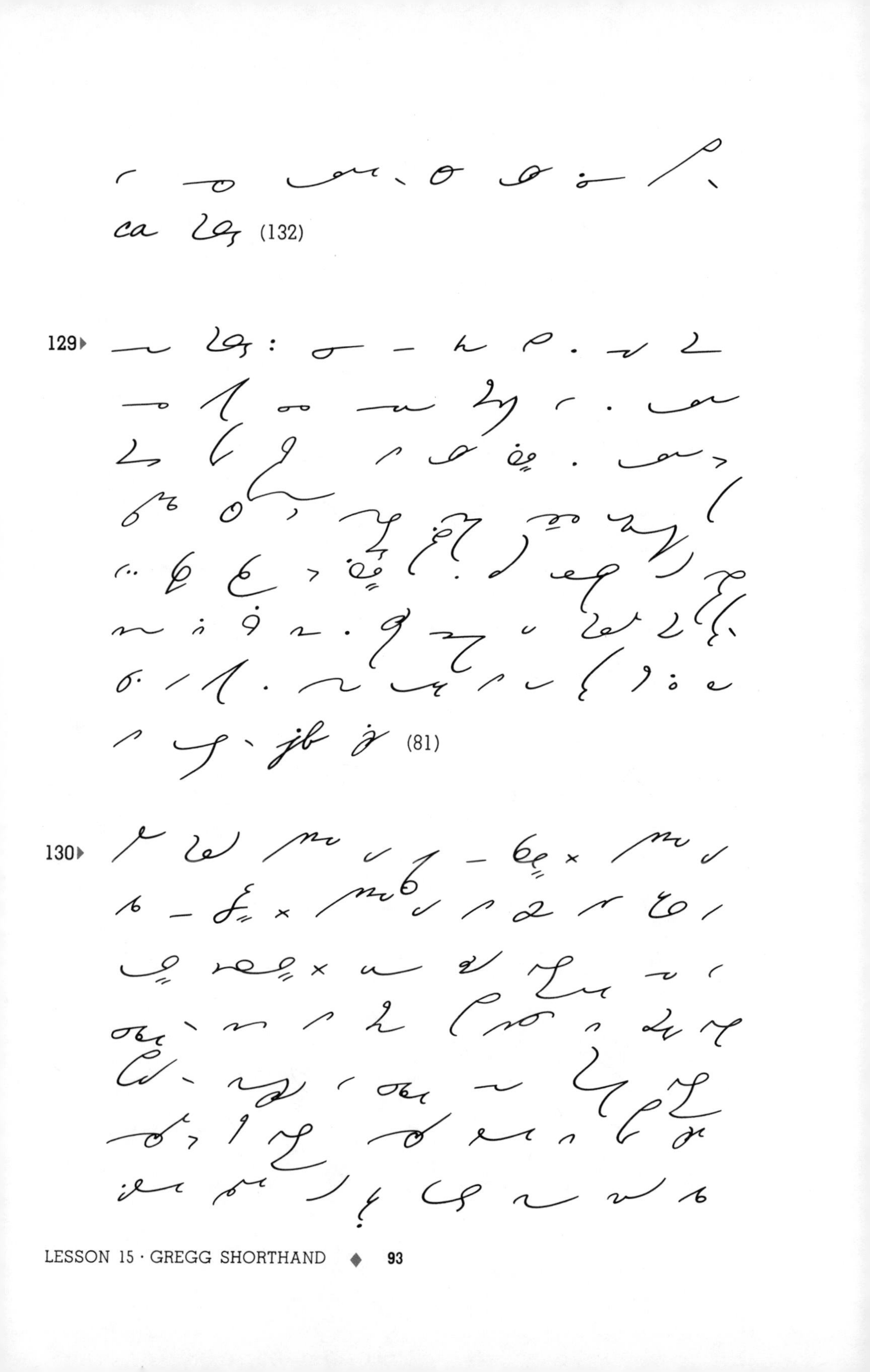

(132)

129▸ (81)

130▸

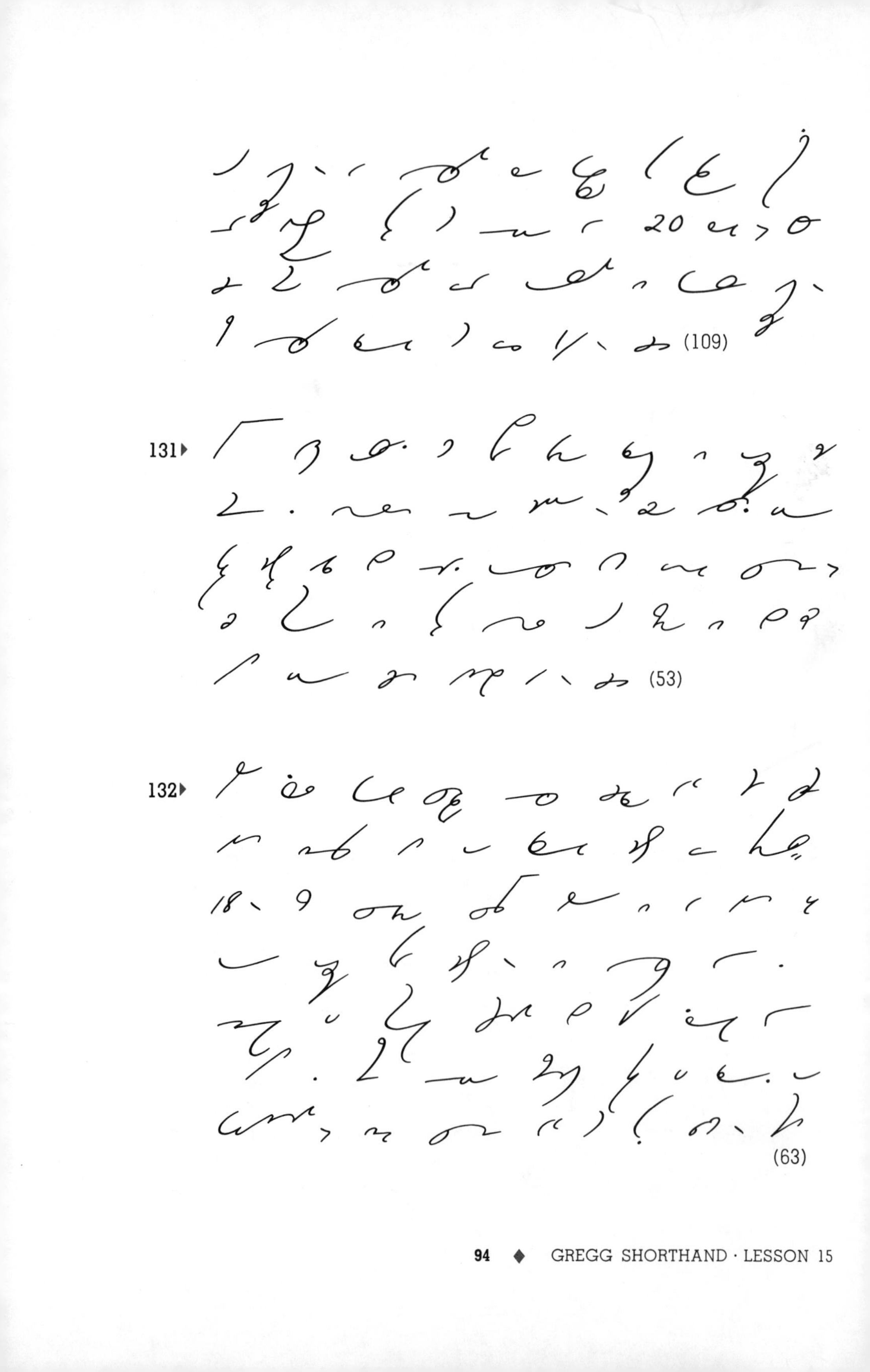

(109)

131

(53)

132

(63)

PRINCIPLES

133▸ Oi • The sound of *oi*, as in *toy*, is represented by

toy		**voice**		**choice**	
joy		**noise**		**oil**	
boy		**appointed**		**boil**	
annoy		**join**		**spoil**	

134▸ Men, Mem • The combinations *men, mem* are represented by joining *m* and *n* into one long forward stroke.

Men, Mem

COMPARE: **knee** **me** **many**

Men **men** **mental** **freshmen**

meant **mended** **women**

mentioned **salesmen** **businessmen**

Mem **member** **remember** **memorize**

members **memory** **memorable**

135▸ Min, Mon, etc. • The long forward stroke that represents *men, mem* also represents the similar sounds of *min, mon, mun*, etc.

minute	**monthly**	**lemon**
money	**managed**	**harmony**
month	**manner**	**eliminate**

136▸ Word Beginning Be- • The word beginning *be-* is represented by *b*.

begin	**because**	**became**
began	**believe**	**betray**
below	**belief**	**beyond**

BUILDING TRANSCRIPTION SKILLS

137▸ BUSINESS VOCABULARY BUILDER

immensely Greatly.

din Loud noise.

business machines Typewriters, adding machines, duplicators, etc.

eligible Qualified to be chosen. (Do not confuse with "illegible," which means "cannot be read.")

READING AND WRITING PRACTICE

138▸

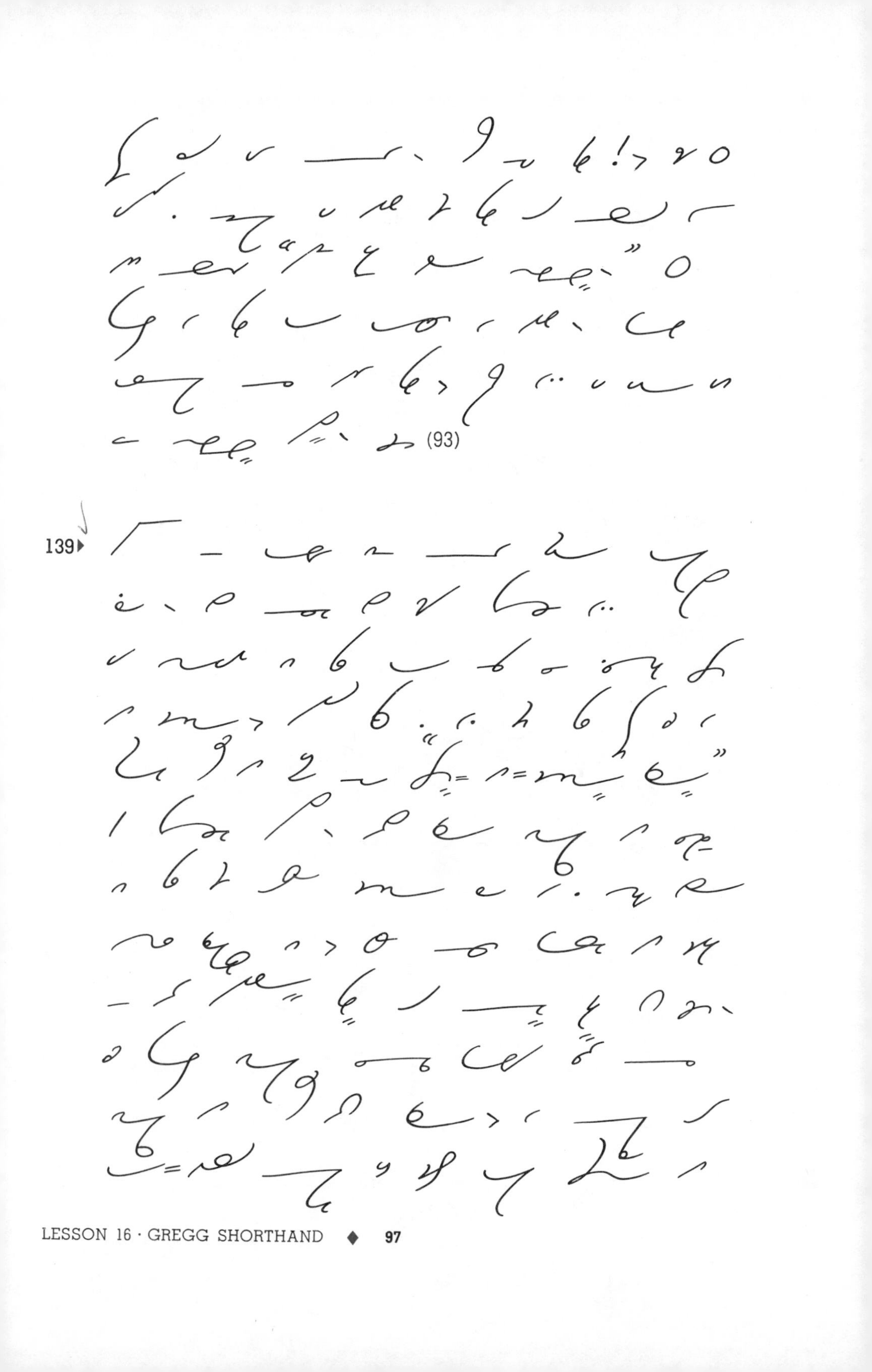

(93)

139

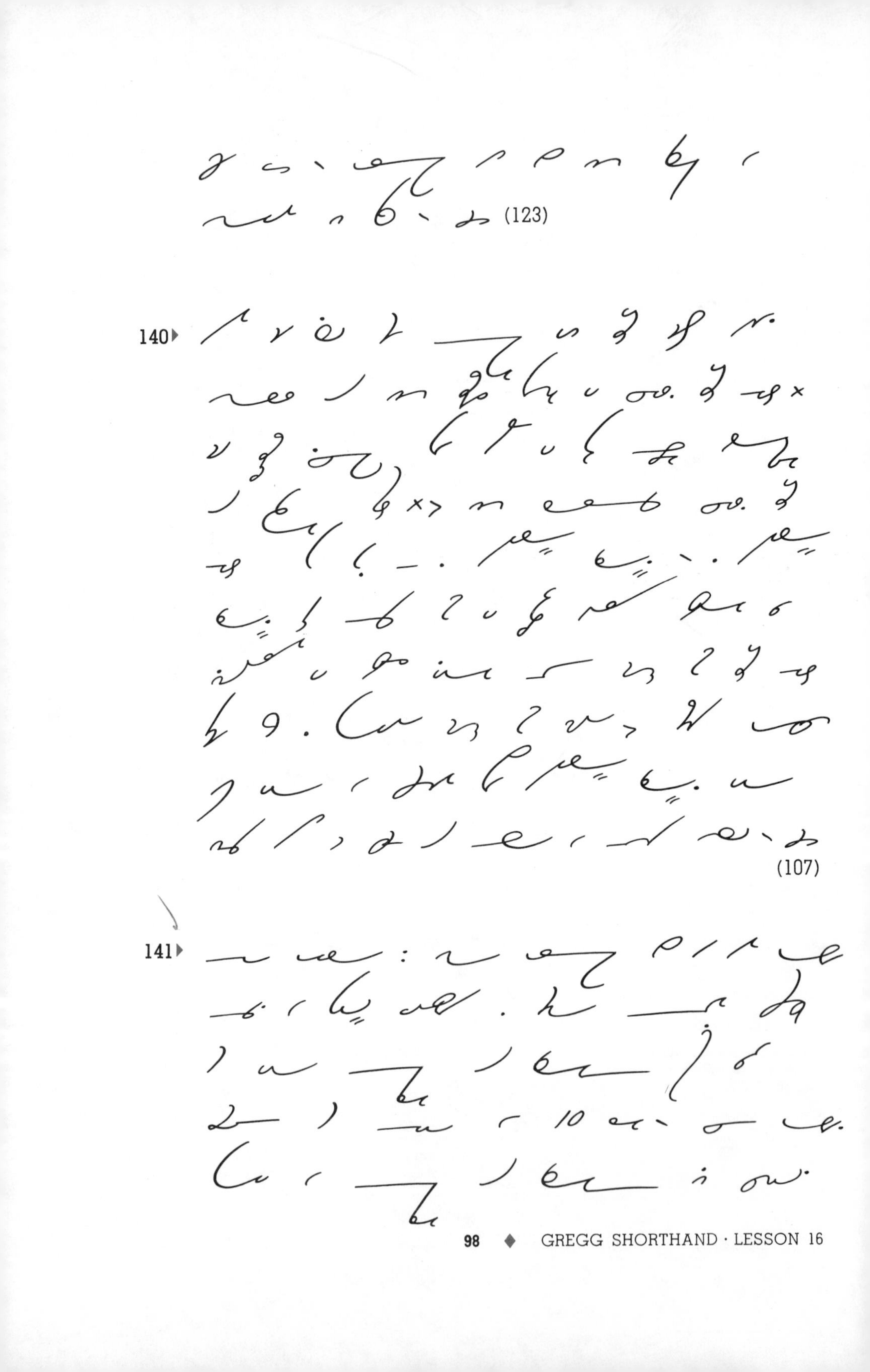

(123)

140

(107)

141

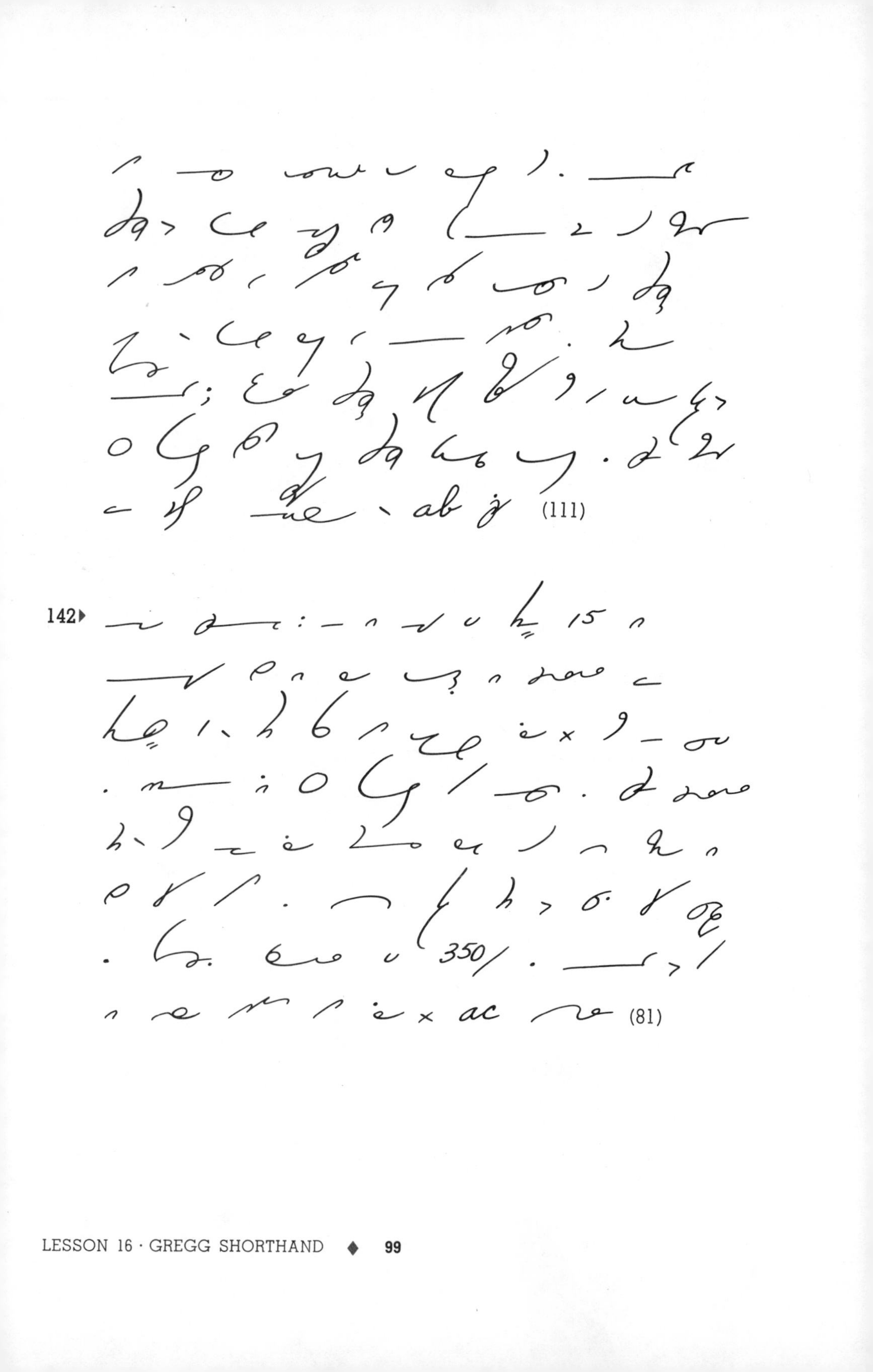

(111)

142

(81)

PRINCIPLES

143▸ Brief Forms • When you have learned the following six brief forms, you will have learned more than half the brief forms of Gregg Shorthand.

morning	**those**	**manufacture**
gentlemen	**where**	**important, importance**

144▸ Word Beginnings Per-, Pur- • The word beginnings *per-, pur-* are represented by *pr.*

Per-	**permitted**	**perfect**	**personally**
	person	**persisted**	**persuade**
Pur-	**purchase**	**purse**	**purple**

145▸ Word Beginnings De-, Di- • The word beginnings *de-, di-* are represented by *d.*

De-	**delay**	**deposit**	**deserve**
	deliver	**desired**	**derive**
Di-	**direct**	**direction**	**diploma**

146 ▸ SIMILAR-WORDS DRILL

The English language contains many groups of words that sound or look alike, but each member of the group is spelled differently and has its own meaning.

Example: **to** (toward); **too** (also); **two** (one plus one).

In addition, there are many other groups that sound or look *almost* alike:

Example: **defer** (to put off); **differ** (to disagree).

The stenographer who is not on the alert while transcribing may sometimes select the wrong member of the group, with the result that the transcript makes no sense.

In Lesson 17 and in a number of other lessons that follow, you will find a Similar-Words Drill that will call to your attention common groups of similar words on which the unwary stenographer can stumble.

Study these similar-words groups carefully so that when you transcribe you will be able to select the correct member of the group and thus avoid the embarrassment of having your letters returned for correction.

Personal, personnel

personal Individual; private; pertaining to the person or body.

Harry is a personal friend of mine.
You should watch your personal appearance with care.

personnel The people who work for a firm; the staff.

You can depend on our personnel to give you good service.
Mr. Smith is the personnel director of our firm.

147 BUSINESS VOCABULARY BUILDER

remodeling Changing the structure or design.

proceeding Advancing; moving forward. (Do not confuse with "preceding," which means "going before.")

attaché case A small suitcase used for carrying papers and documents.

READING AND WRITING PRACTICE

148 Brief-Form Letter

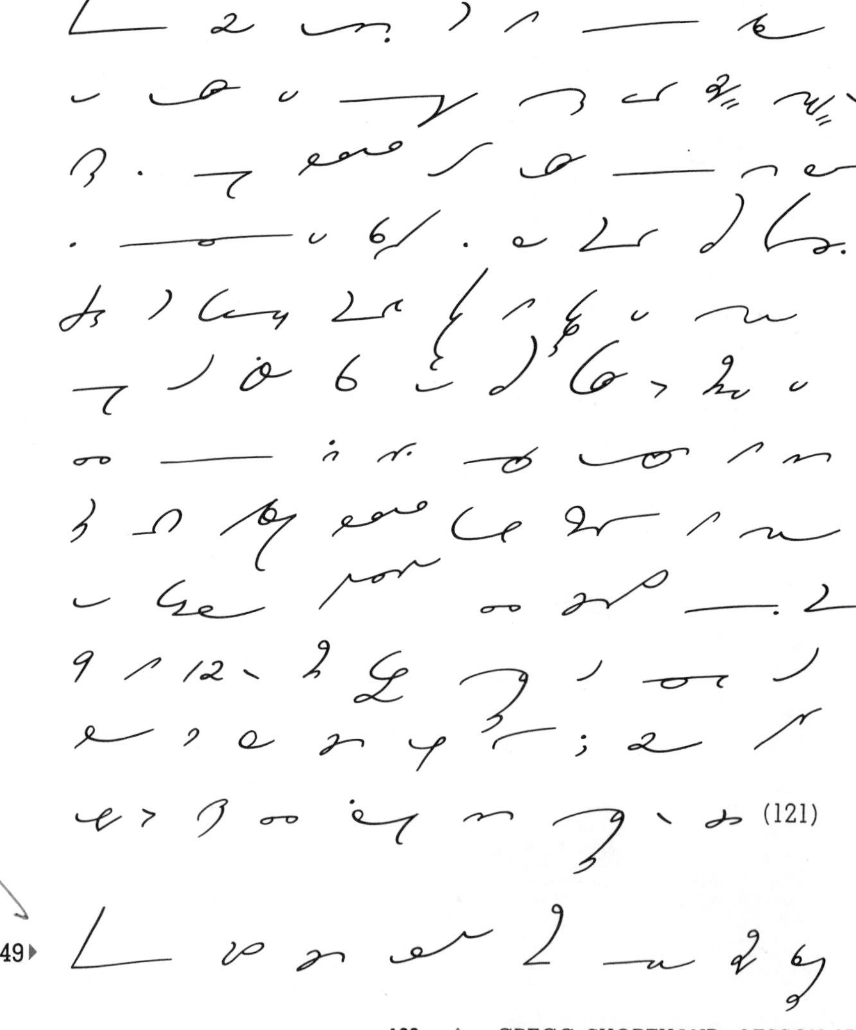

(121)

149

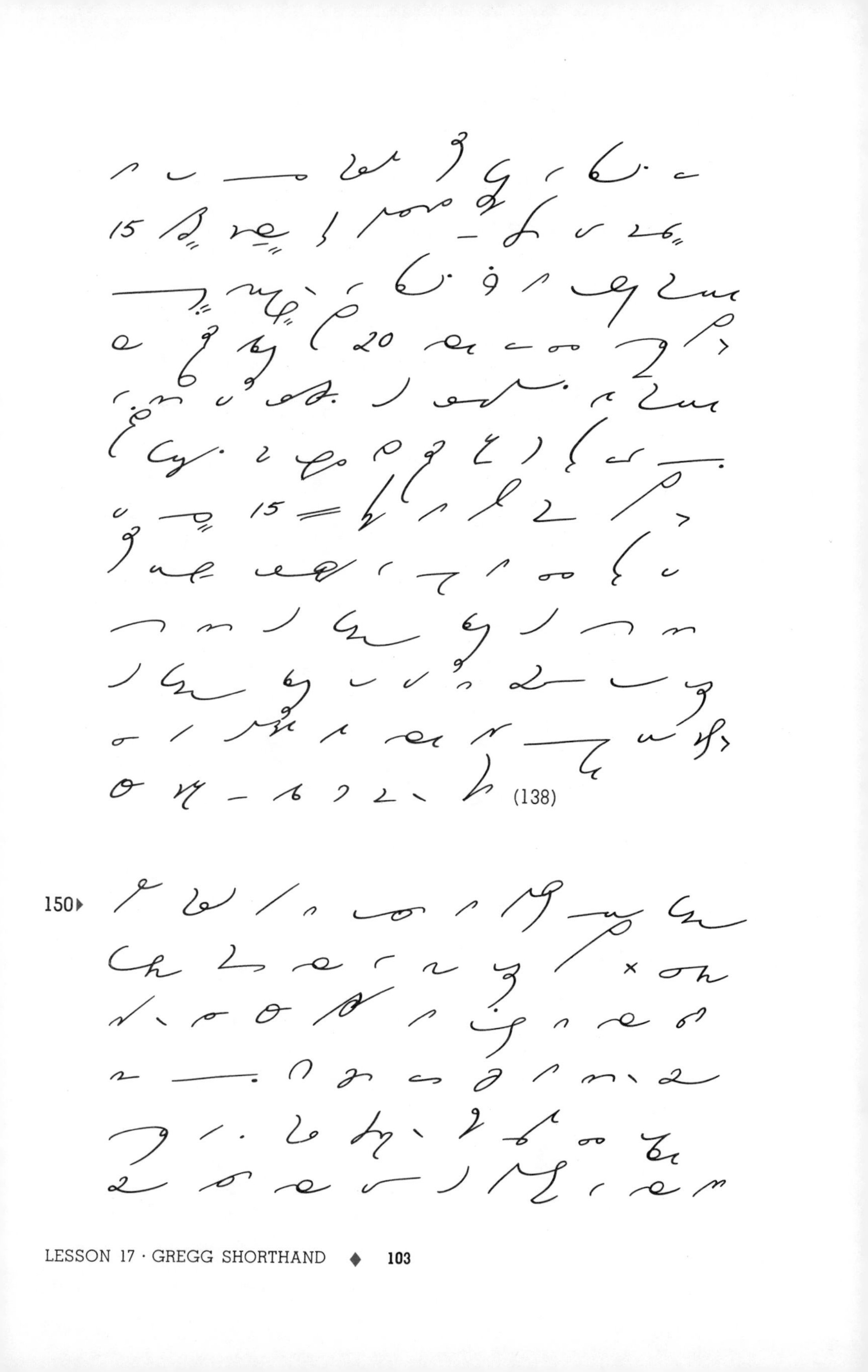

(138)

150

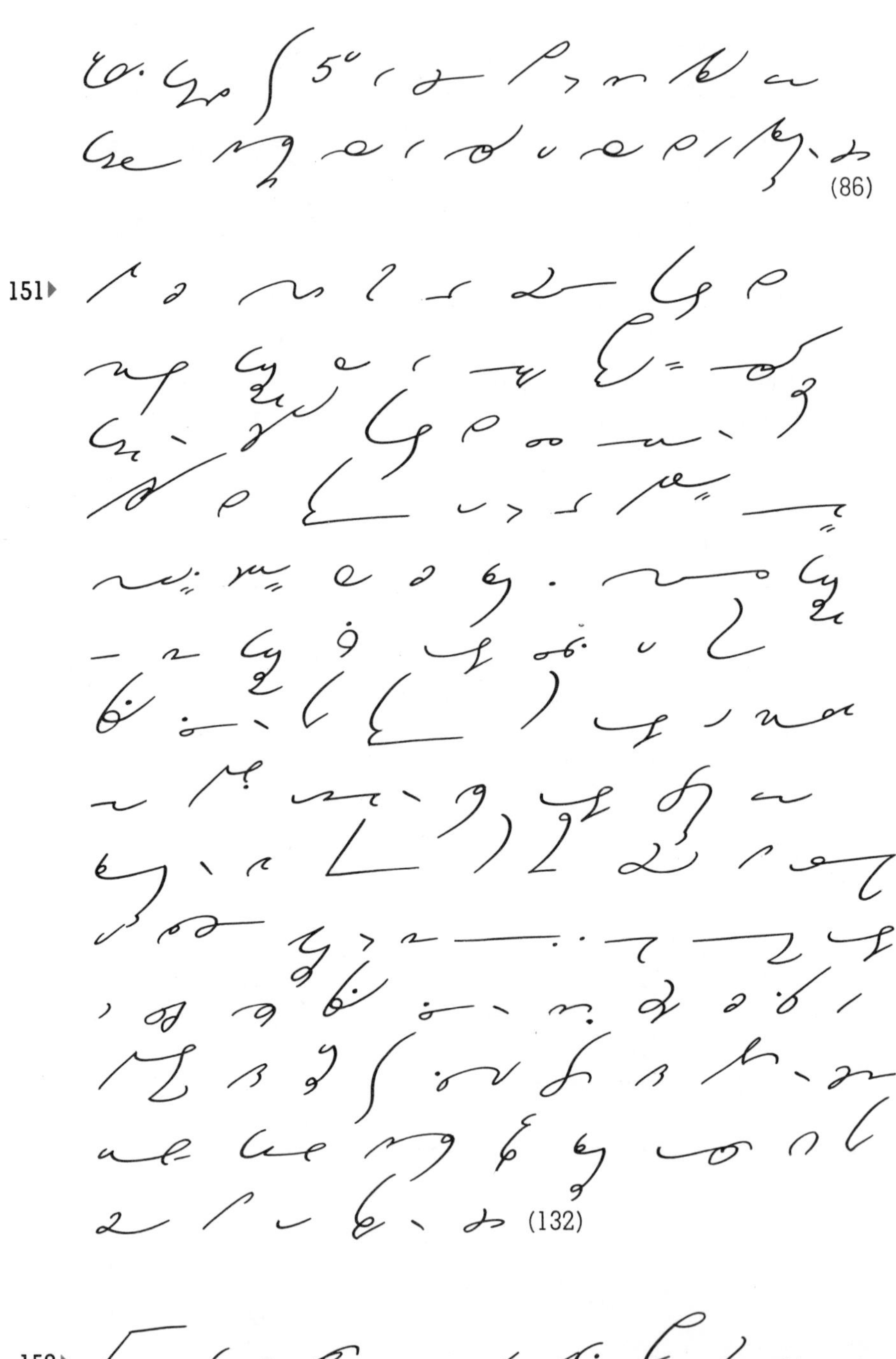
(86)

151

(132)

152

(111)

153 Woman Trouble

(72)

18 RECALL

Lesson 18 is another "breather" for you; it contains no new shorthand devices for you to learn. Lesson 18 will give you an opportunity to consolidate what you have learned in Lessons 1 through 17.

PRINCIPLES OF JOINING

154▸ At the beginning of a word and after *k*, *g*, or a downstroke, the combination *oo-s* is written without an angle.

BUT

Us, husky, gust, just; does, loose, rust.

155▸ The word beginning *re-* is represented by *r* before a downstroke or a vowel.

BUT

Research, reference, rearrange, reopen; relate, retreat, remake.

156▸ The word beginnings *de-*, *di-* are represented by *d* except before *k* and *g*.

BUT

Delivery, depressed, directs; decay, degrade, digress.

157▸ As you perhaps already noticed from your study of Lessons 1 through 17, the past tense of a verb is formed by adding the stroke for the sound that is heard in the past tense. In some words, the past tense has the sound of *t,* as in *baked;* in others, it has the sound of *d,* as in *saved.* In some words, the past tense is incorporated in a blend, as in *planned, needed, feared.*

Baked, saved, missed, faced, planned, needed, feared.

158▸ **Recall Chart** • The following chart reviews all the brief forms of Chapter 3 as well as all the shorthand devices you studied in Chapters 1, 2, and 3.

The chart contains 96 words and phrases. Can you read it in 8 minutes or less?

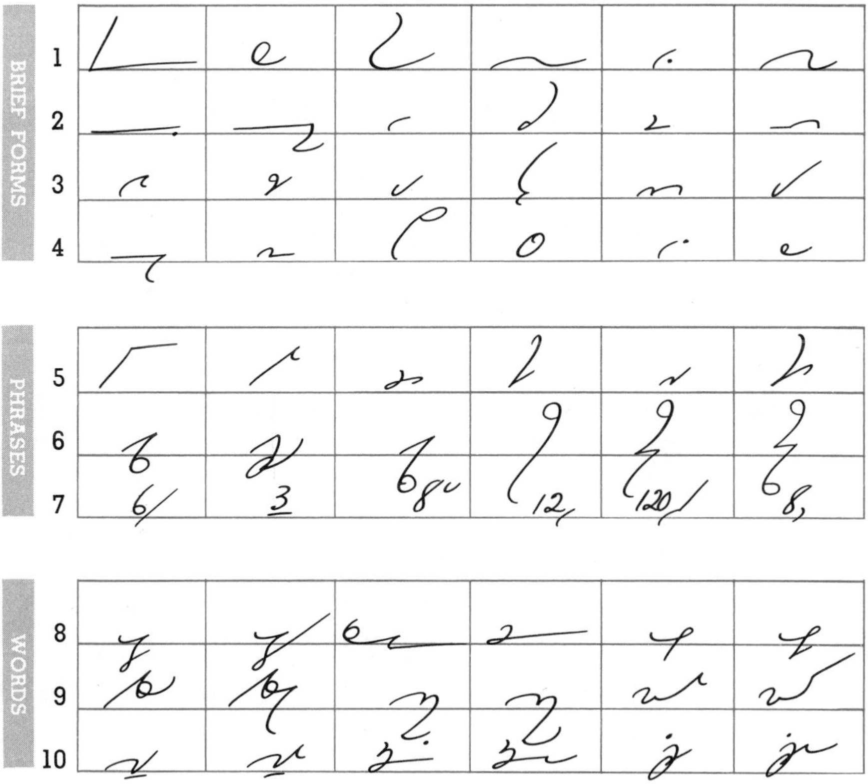

BRIEF FORMS

1
2
3
4

PHRASES

5
6
7

WORDS

8
9
10

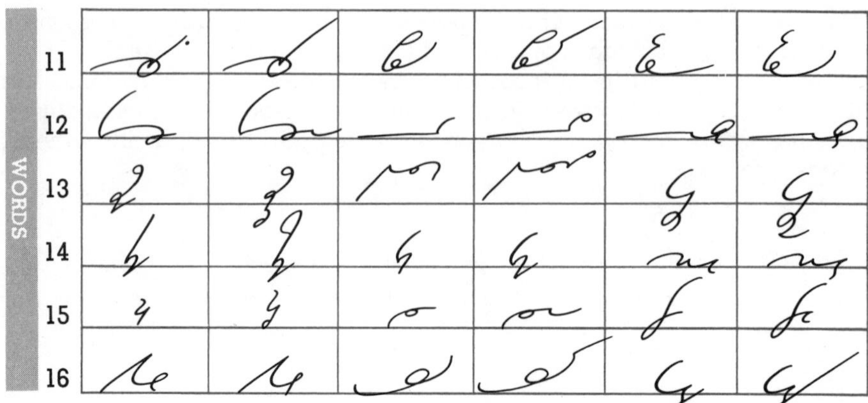

BUILDING TRANSCRIPTION SKILLS

159 ▸ **BUSINESS VOCABULARY BUILDER**

role A part played. (Do not confuse with "roll," which is a bakery item.)

chores Routine tasks or jobs.

mediocre Of moderate or low excellence.

clarify To make clear.

READING AND WRITING PRACTICE

READING SCOREBOARD • One of the factors in measuring shorthand growth is the rate at which you can read shorthand. Here is an opportunity for you to measure your reading speed on the *first reading* of the material in Lesson 18. The following table will help you determine how rapidly you can read shorthand.

LESSON 18 CONTAINS 476 WORDS

If you read Lesson 18 in:	16	17	20	22	26	32	minutes
	▼	▼	▼	▼	▼	▼	
Your reading rate is:	30	27	24	21	18	15	words a minute

If you can read Lesson 18 through the first time in less than 16 minutes, you are doing well indeed. If you take considerably longer than 32 minutes, here are some questions you should ask yourself:

1 Am I spelling each outline I cannot read immediately?

2 Am I spending too much time deciphering an outline that I cannot read even after spelling it?

3 Should I perhaps reread the directions for reading shorthand on page 11?

After you have determined your reading rate, make a record of it in some convenient place. You can then watch your reading rate grow as you time yourself on the Reading Scoreboards in later lessons.

160 **The Art of Listening**

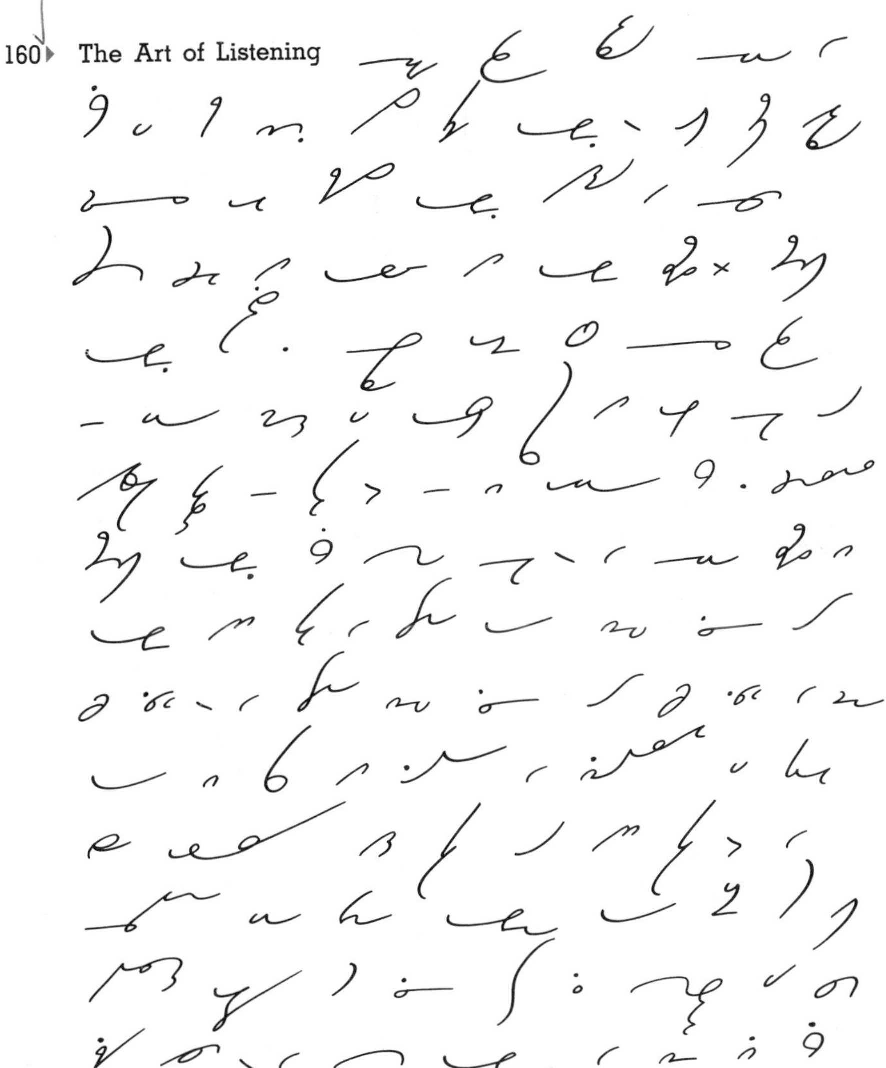

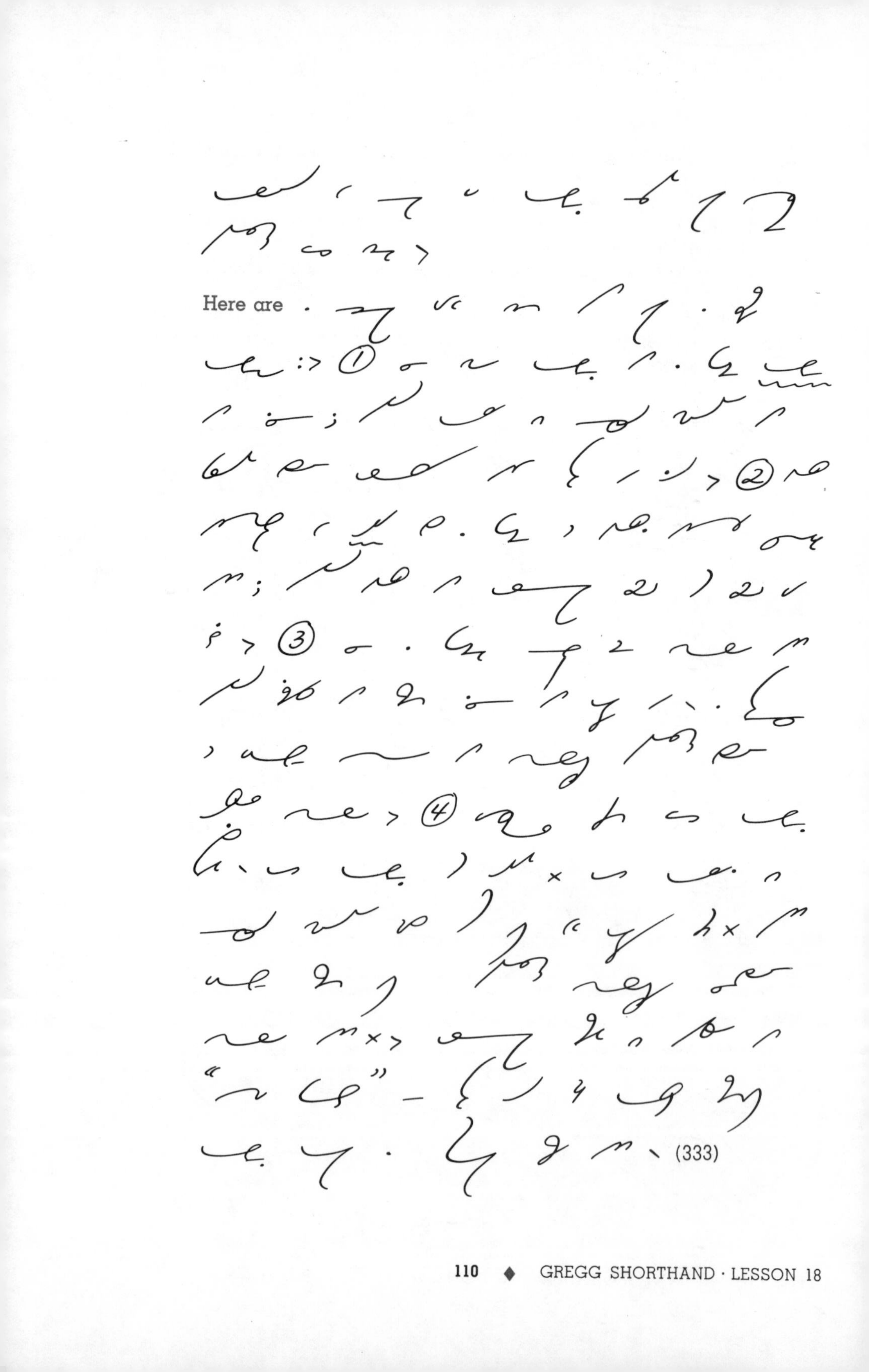

Here are

(1)

(2)

(3)

(4)

(333)

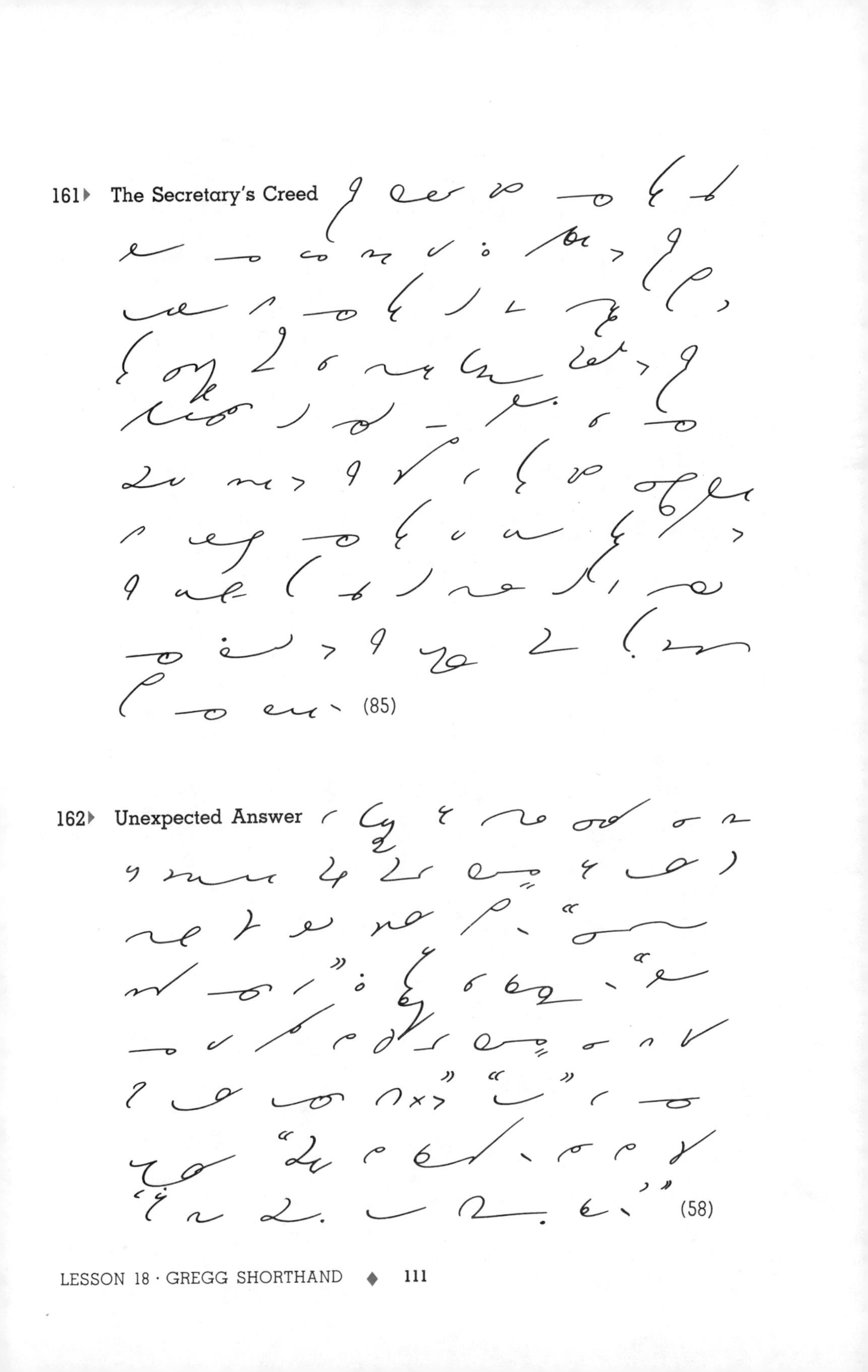

161 ▸ The Secretary's Creed

(85)

162 ▸ Unexpected Answer

(58)

Few professions offer women more opportunities to make a vital contribution to our society than does the secretarial profession. As business expanded and the need for more and better executives arose, the demand for more and better secretaries rose accordingly. It is a well-known fact that executives cannot perform their functions effectively without the help of capable secretaries.

Today's secretary is more than a person who answers the telephone and delivers coffee to her boss! Besides taking dictation and transcribing communications for her employer, the secretary keeps his appointments, organizes his daily calendar, writes letters and reports, engages in research, follows up on pending business matters, arranges and reports conferences and meetings, and performs various public relations functions for important customers and other VIPs.

The secretary is, in short, the executive's indispensable specialist in what is perhaps his most important job — communications. He depends on her to put his thoughts into type; to speak to subordinates, executives, top management, and to the public at large; to listen to the suggestions, ideas, and complaints of others; and to read business documents that cross the executive's desk.

The secretary manages an efficient records system, including letter files, so that information may be obtained at a moment's notice. The modern secretary is indeed a communications specialist!

Meeting these challenges calls for a special type of person — a *professional* — who can take her place in the inner circle of management. Actually, the secretary is an important member of the management team. She works closely with those who direct the activities of a business or government enterprise. She is in on many of the top-level decisions that are made many times a day in every American business.

The secretary plays one of the most vital roles in American business, government, and industry. To prepare for this role, she must be exceptionally well trained; and shorthand is one of the most important skill subjects that she must master.

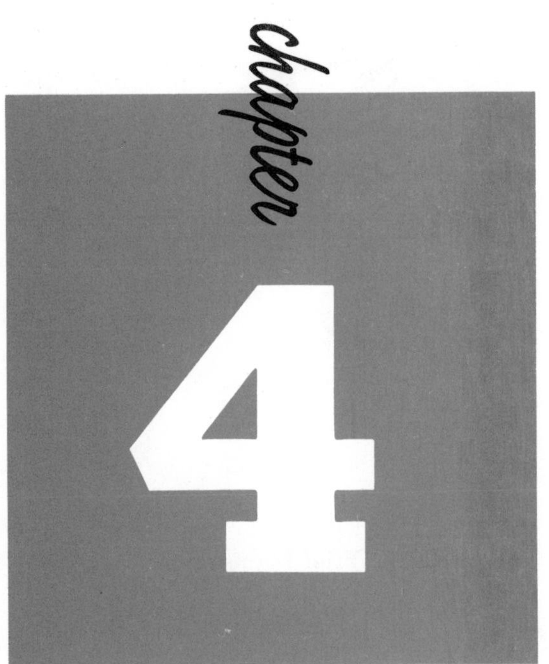

THE GROWING IMPORTANCE OF THE SECRETARY

PRINCIPLES

163▸ Brief Forms

opportunity	wish	after
must	company	part
immediate	advertise	present

164▸ U • The sound of *u*, as in *unit*, is represented by

unit	view	fewer
united	few	fuel
unique	review	cute
utilize	refuse	usual

165▸ Word Ending -ment • The word ending *-ment* is represented by *m*.

shipment	basement	settlement
payment	advertisement	equipment
moment	assignment	elementary

NOTE: In the word *assignment*, the *m* for *-ment* is joined to the *n* with a jog.

BUILDING TRANSCRIPTION SKILLS

166 ▸ BUSINESS VOCABULARY BUILDER

unique Only one of its kind. (It is, therefore, incorrect to say "most unique" or "more unique.")

caliber A degree of excellence or importance.

lose To be deprived of. (Do not confuse with "loose," which means "not fastened.")

READING AND WRITING PRACTICE

167 ▸ Brief-Form Letter

350 15

(144)

168

(147)

169

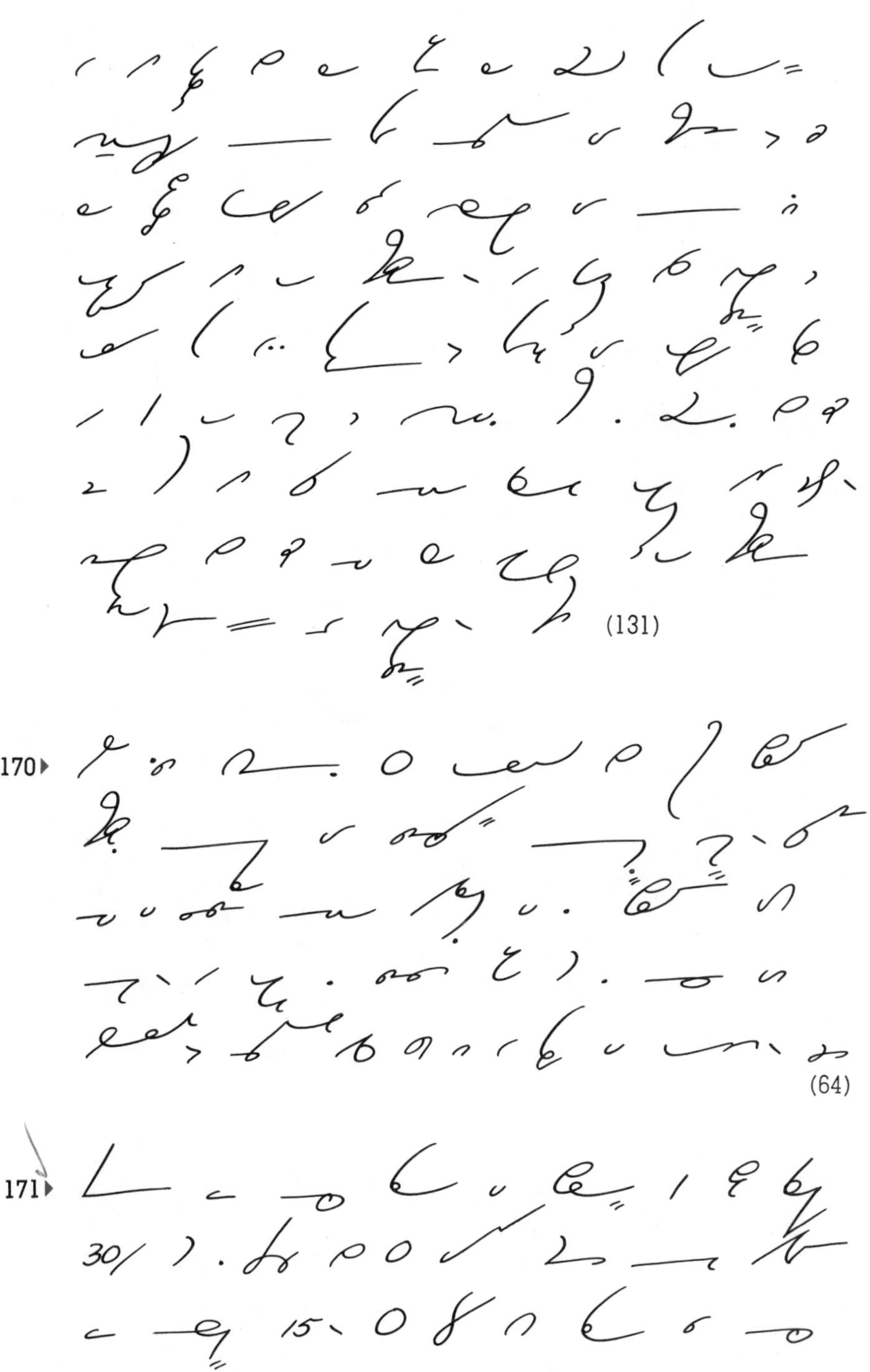
(131)

170

(64)

171

30

15

(88)

172

(113)

PRINCIPLES

173▸ Ow • The sound of *ow,* as in *now,* is written

now	sound	amount
brown	found	loud
doubt	account	ounce
allow	pound	house

174▸ Word Ending -ther • The word ending *-ther* is represented by *th.*

gather	mother	either
other	brother	rather
another	together	leather
neither	whether	bothered

175▸ Word Beginnings Con-, Com- • The word beginnings *con-, com-* are represented by *k.*

Con-	consist	conferred	controlled
	concern	considerable	contract

	concrete	confusing	confirm
Com-	complete	combine	compel
	compare	comply	accomplish
	complaint	compose	compute

176 ▸ **Con-, Com- Followed by a Vowel** • When *con-*, *com-* are followed by a vowel, these word beginnings are represented by *kn* or *km*.

connect	connote	committee
connection	commerce	commercial

BUILDING TRANSCRIPTION SKILLS

177 ▸ **BUSINESS VOCABULARY BUILDER**

competitive Relating to rivalry.

completion End.

coach seats The most inexpensive class of transportation provided by airlines or railroads.

READING AND WRITING PRACTICE

178 ▸

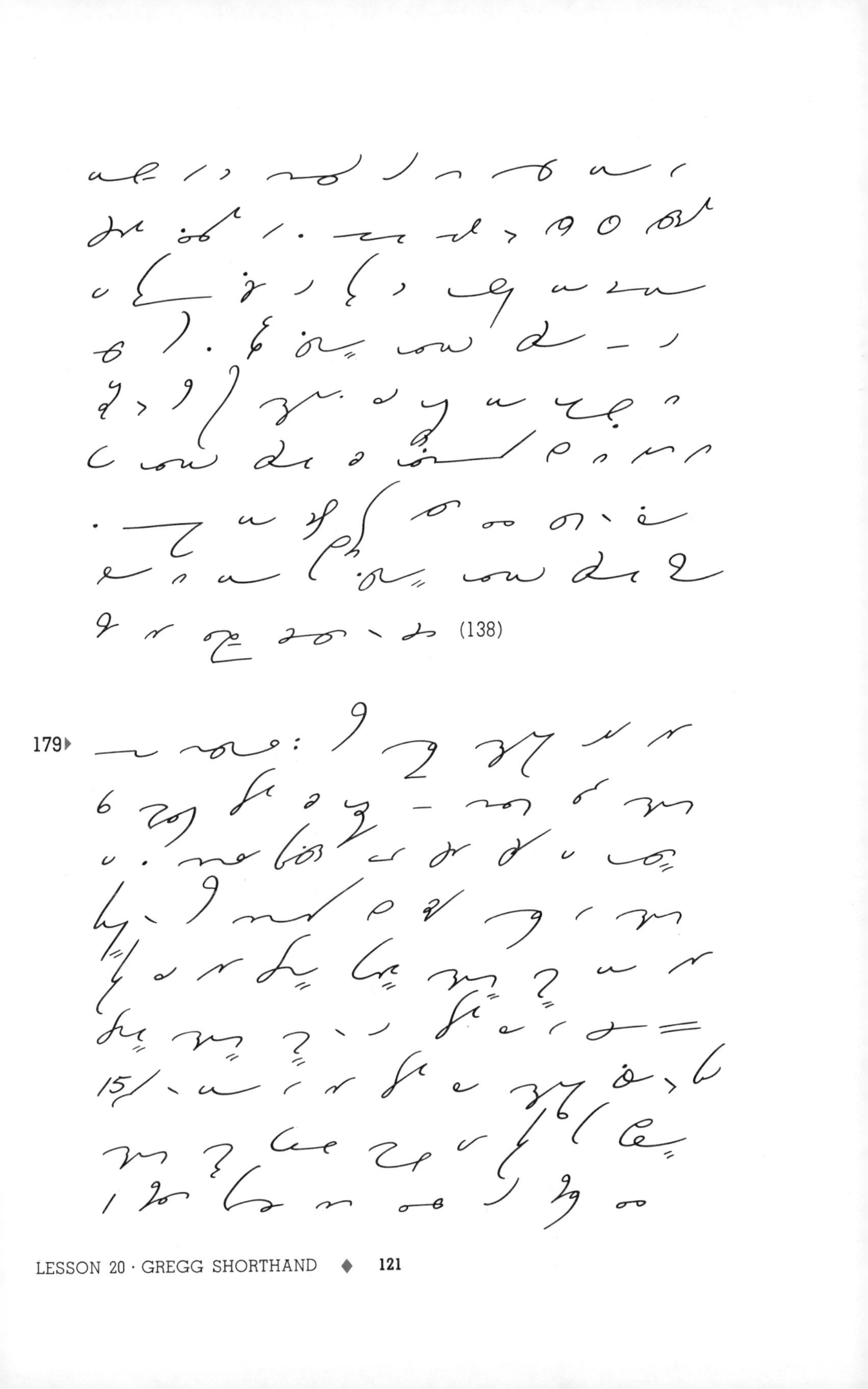

(138)

179▸

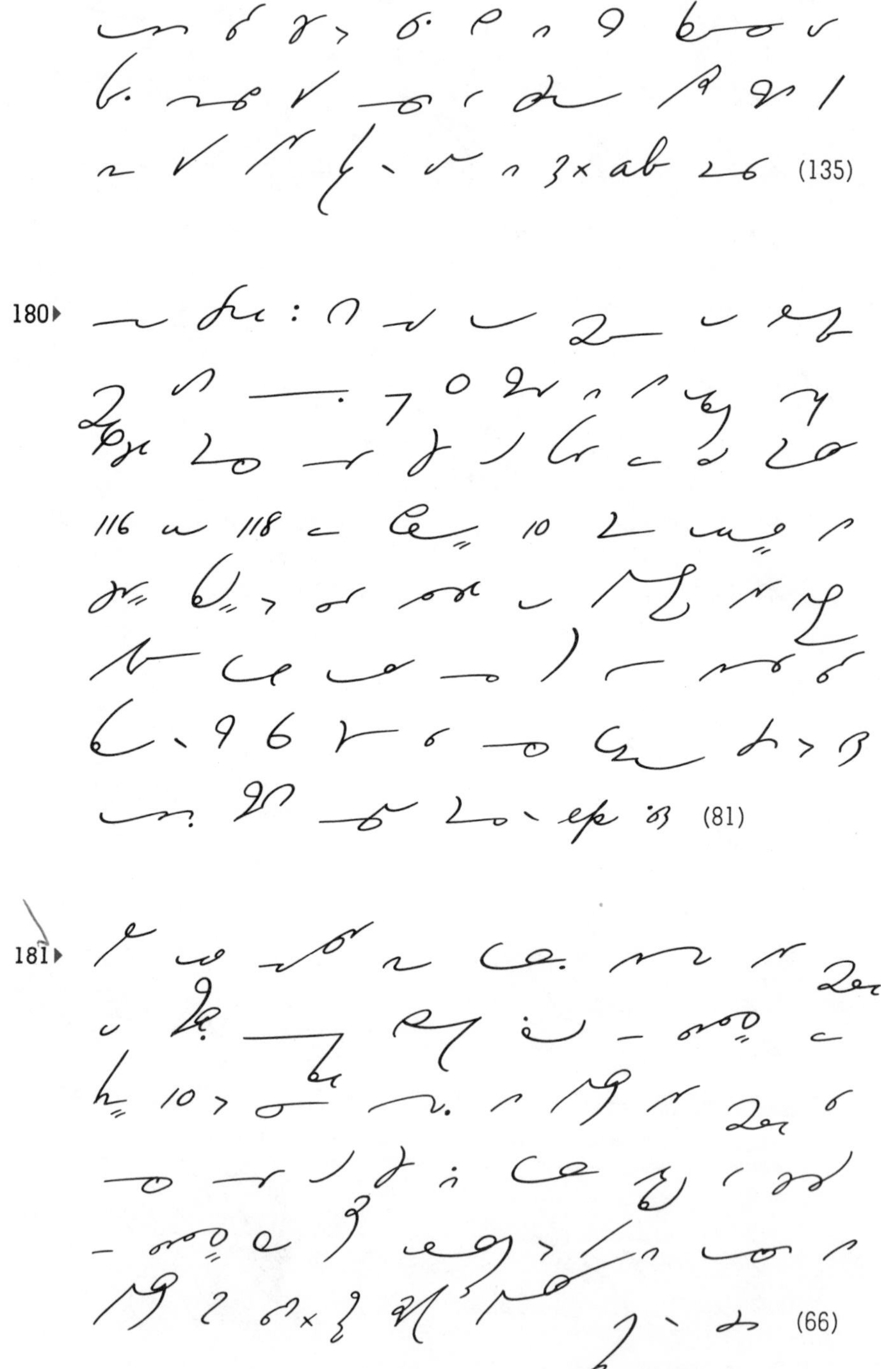
(135)
180
(81)
181
(66)

182

(121)

183

(70)

Lesson 21

PRINCIPLES

184▸ Brief Forms

suggest	big	how, out
such	use	ever, every
several	advantage	correspond, correspondence

185▸ Den • By rounding off the angle between *d-n*, we obtain the fluent blend that represents *den.*

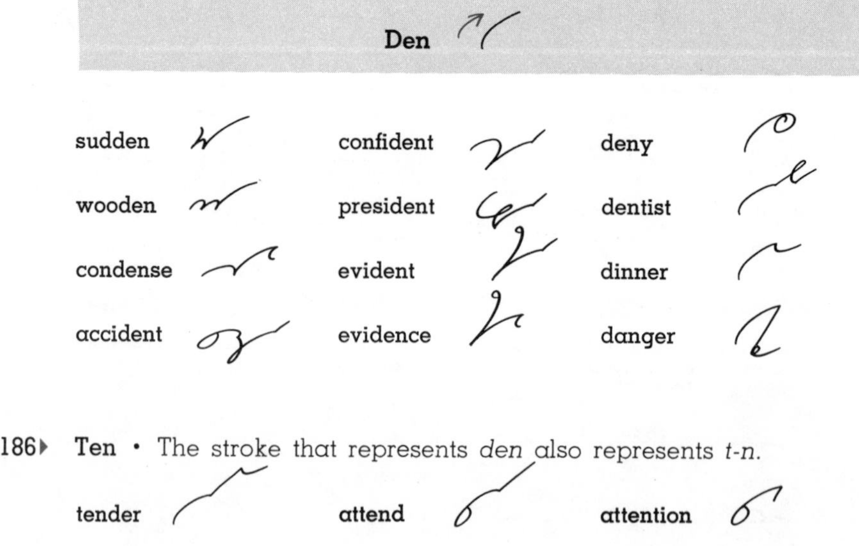

186▸ Ten • The stroke that represents *den* also represents *t-n*.

tender attend attention

sentence	written	remittances
consistent	straighten	tonight
competent	bulletin	standing

187 ▸ **-tain** • The stroke that represents *d-n, t-n* also represents *-tain.*

contain	maintain	obtainable
retain	sustain	certainly
attain	detain	container

BUILDING TRANSCRIPTION SKILLS

188 ▸ **BUSINESS VOCABULARY BUILDER**

mail-order houses Organizations that sell their products through the mails.

sturdy Strong.

opaque Not transparent; cannot be seen through.

correspondent One who writes letters for an organization.

READING AND WRITING PRACTICE

189 ▸ **Brief-Form Letter**

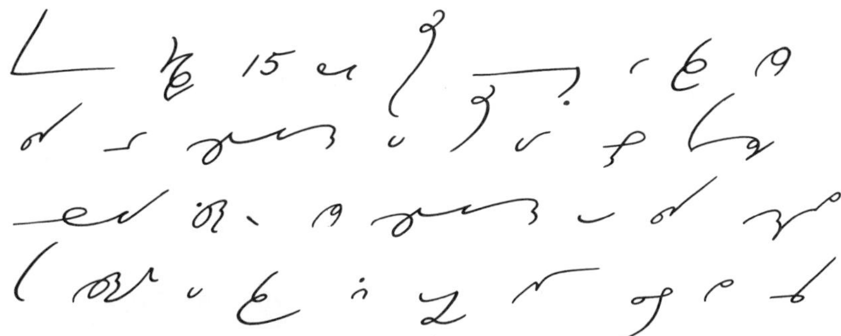

(170)

190

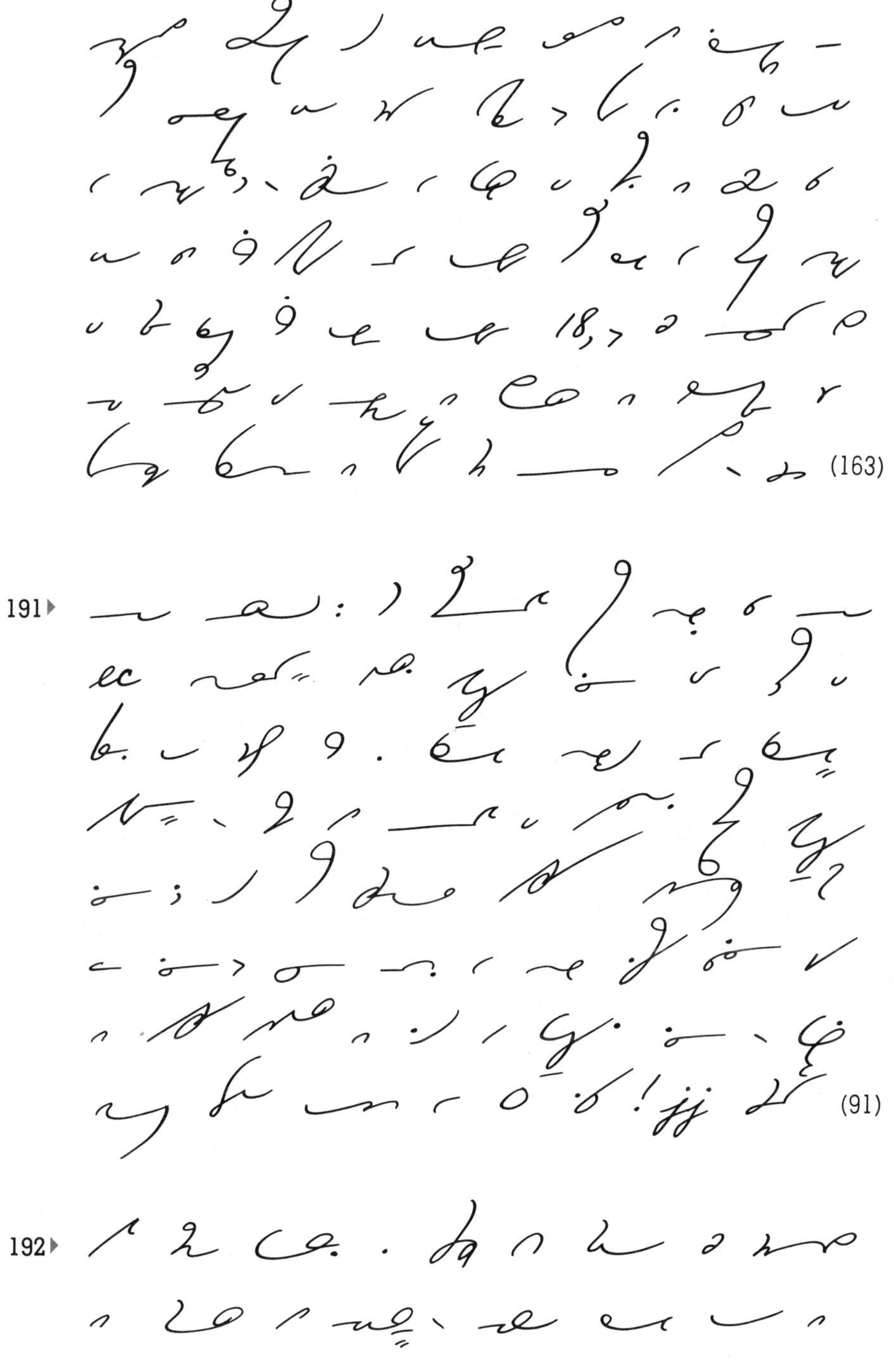
(163)

191

(91)

192

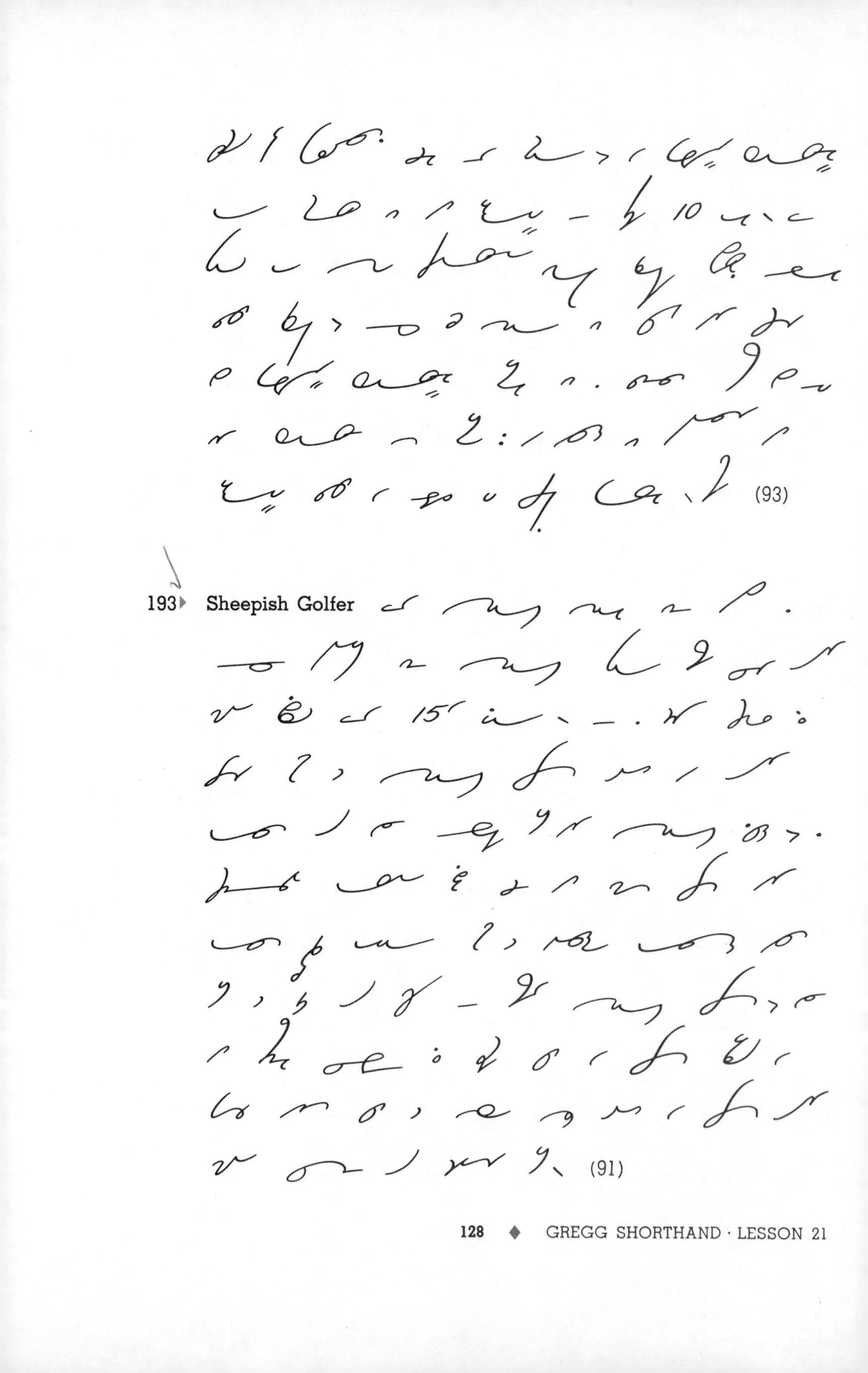

(93)

193 Sheepish Golfer

(91)

PRINCIPLES

194▸ Dem • By rounding off the angle between *d-m,* we obtain the fluent *dem* blend.

Dem

COMPARE: **den** **dem**

demand	random	domestic
demonstrate	seldom	damage
condemn	freedom	medium

195▸ Tem • The stroke that represents *d-m* also represents *t-m.*

temporary	system	automobile
attempt	item	estimate
contemplate	tomorrow	customer

196▸ Useful Phrases • The following useful phrases are formed with the *ten-tem* blends:

to know	to me	to make

197▸ Business Abbreviations • Here are additional salutations and closings that are frequently used in business letters.

Dear Mr. | Dear Miss | Cordially yours

Dear Mrs. | Yours sincerely | Very cordially yours

198▸ Days of the Week

Sunday | Wednesday | Friday

Monday | Thursday | Saturday

Tuesday

199▸ Months of the Year • You are already familiar with the shorthand outlines for several of the months, as they are written in full.

January | May | September

February | June | October

March | July | November

April | August | December

BUILDING TRANSCRIPTION SKILLS

200▸ BUSINESS VOCABULARY BUILDER

competence Ability.
temperament Frame of mind.
domestic Relating to the United States.

READING AND WRITING PRACTICE

201▸

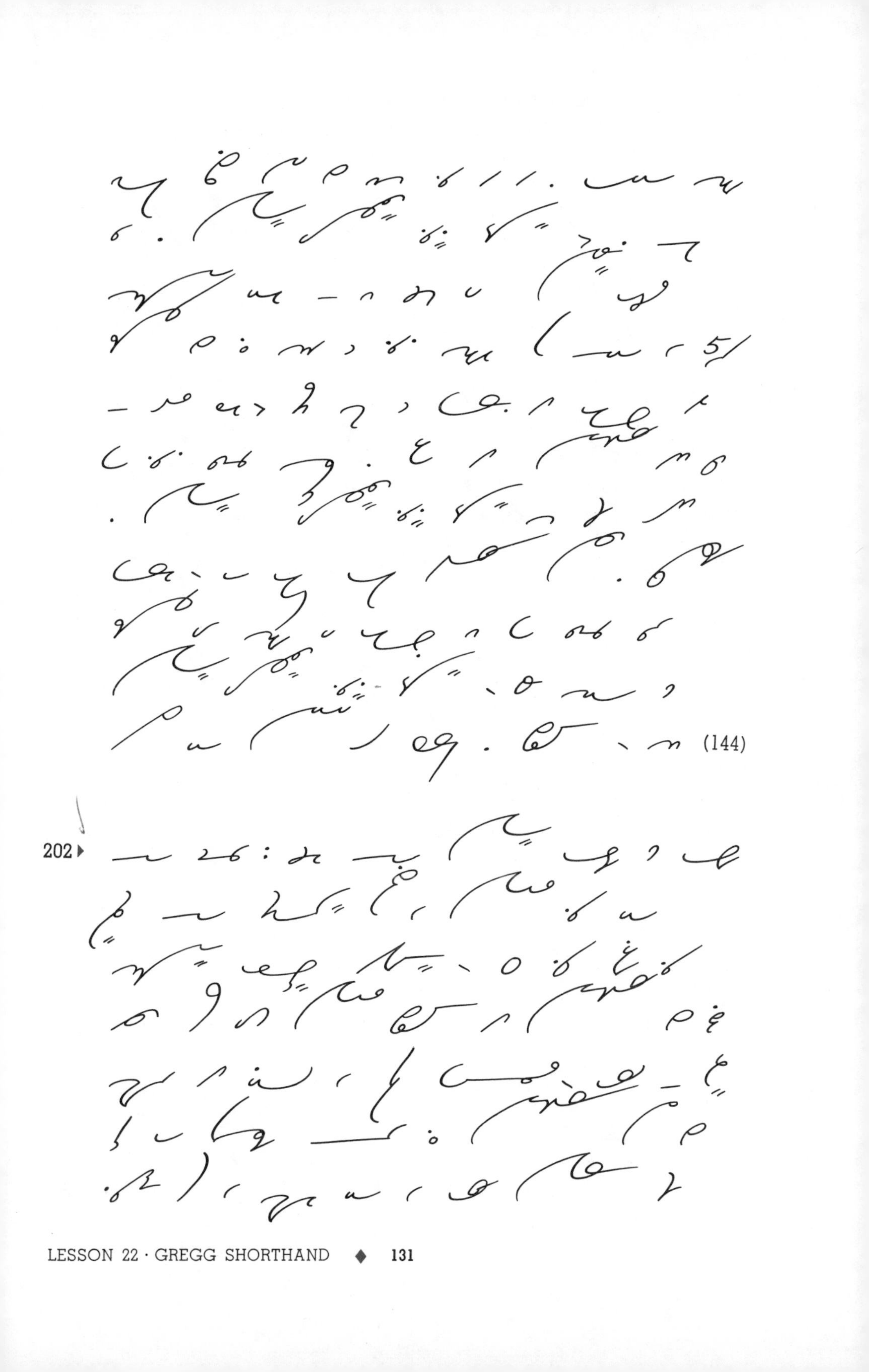

(144)

202

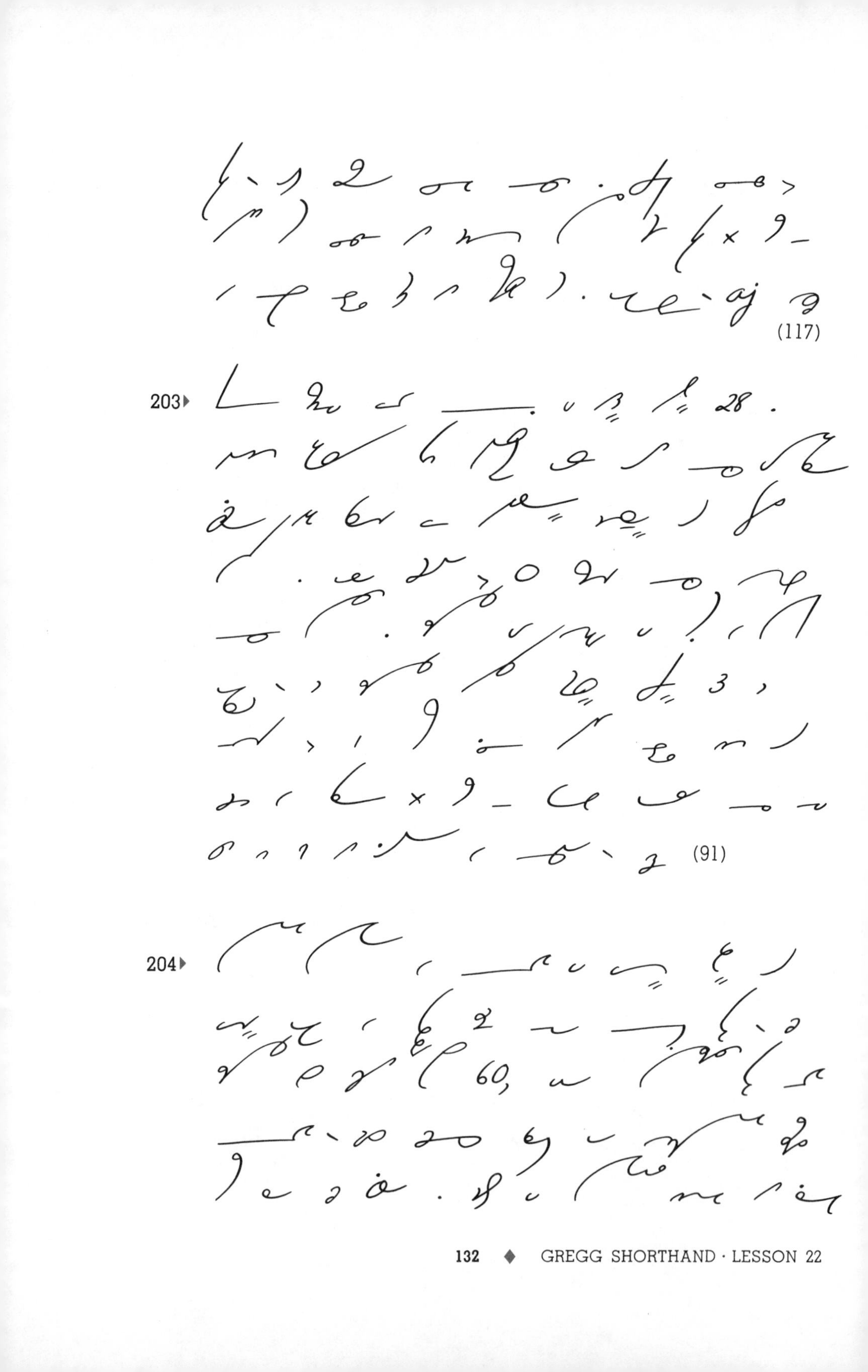

(117)

203 28. 3 (91)

204 60,

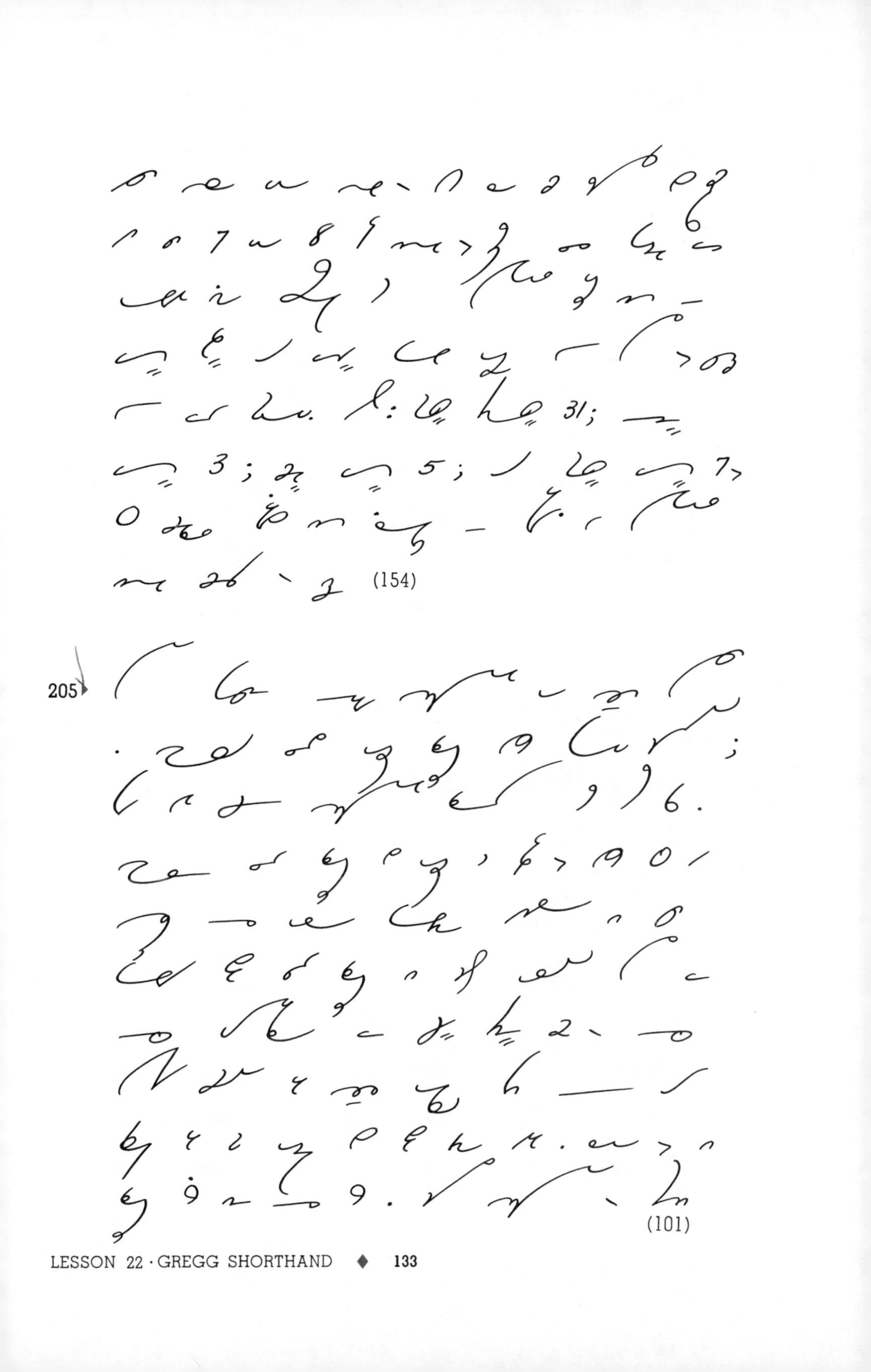

(154)

205

(101)

PRINCIPLES

206▸ Brief Forms • After you have learned the following group of nine brief forms, you will have only five more groups to learn.

worth	**time**	**gone**
yet	**acknowledge**	**during**
question	**general**	**over***

*The outline for *over* is written above the following character. It is also used as a prefix form, as in:

oversee	overcame	overdo

207▸ Def, Dif • By rounding off the angle between *d-f*, we obtain the fluent *def, dif* blend.

Def, Dif

definite	defeat	different
defy	define	differences
defense	defect	diffident

208▸ Div, Dev • The stroke that represents *def, dif* also represents *div, dev.*

divides	diversion	devices
division	devote	devised
divert	devotion	developed

209▸ U Represented by OO Hook • The *oo* hook is often used to represent the sound of *u*, as in *due.*

due	news	continue
duty	avenue	induce
issue	suit	volume

BUILDING TRANSCRIPTION SKILLS

210▸ SIMILAR-WORDS DRILL **To, too, two**

to (*preposition*) In the direction of. (*To* is also the sign of the infinitive.)

I gave the book to him.
He plans to go to the theater.

too Also; more than enough.

He, too, is a member of the team.
She receives too many telephone calls in the office.

two One plus one.

It took me two weeks to finish the job.

NOTE: The word to watch in this group is *too;* it is so easy to type *to* instead of *too!*

211 **BUSINESS VOCABULARY BUILDER**

creditors Those to whom money is owed.

manuscript A typewritten or handwritten copy of a work, such as an article or a book.

brisk Lively.

READING AND WRITING PRACTICE

212 **Brief-Form Letter**

(174)

213

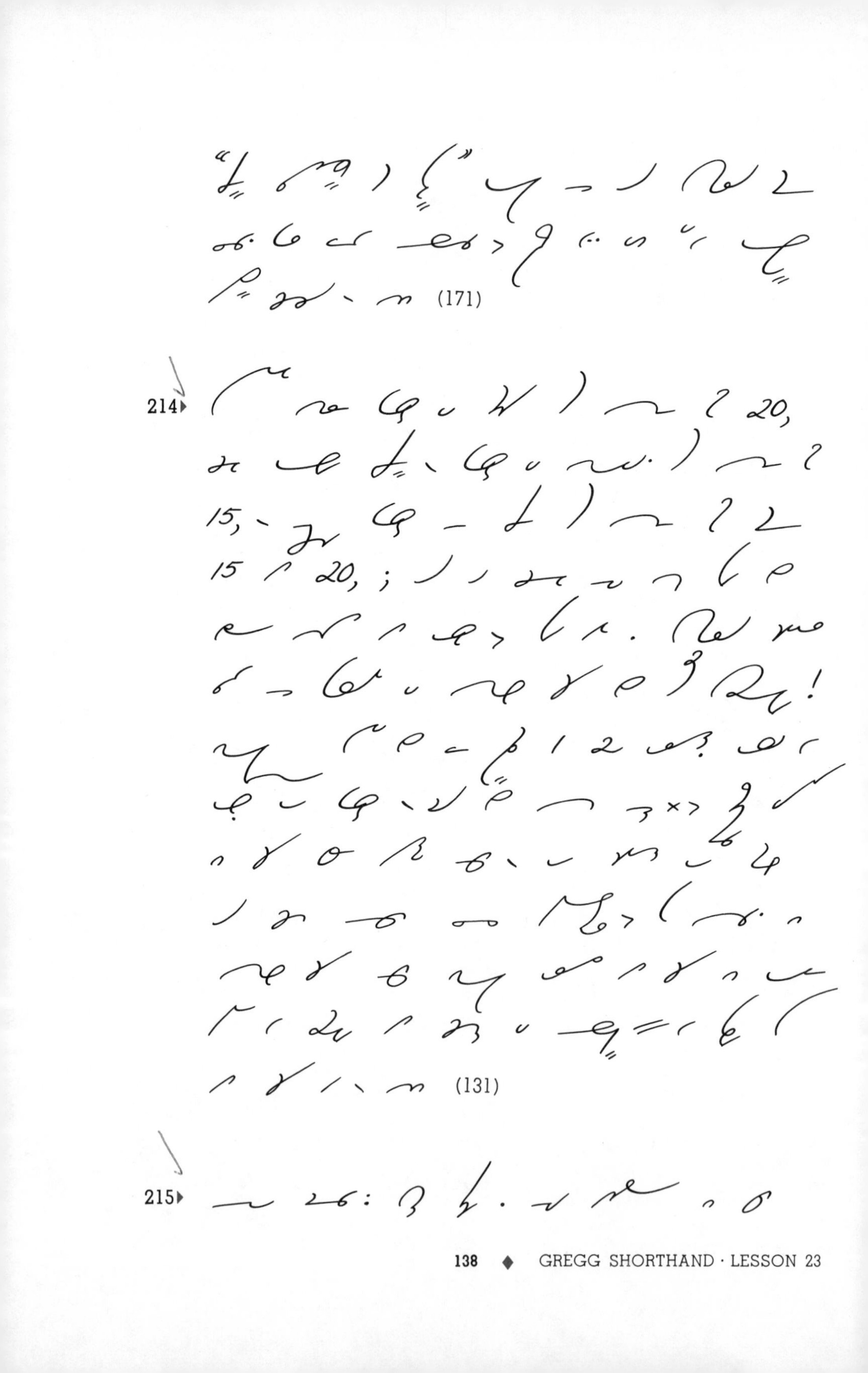

(171)

214

(131)

215

(126)

PROPORTION CHECK LIST

The writer who can read his shorthand notes fluently is the one who is careful of his proportions. In your shorthand writing, do you:

1 Make the large *a* circle huge; the small e circle tiny?

2 Make the straight strokes very straight and the curves very deep?

3 Make the o and oo hooks deep and narrow?

4 Make short strokes, such as *t* and *n*, very short and long strokes, such as *ted* and *men*, very long?

RECALL

In Lesson 24 you will have no new shorthand devices to learn; you will have a little time to "digest" the devices that you have studied in previous lessons. In Lesson 24 you will find a new feature—Accuracy Practice—that will help you improve your shorthand writing style.

ACCURACY PRACTICE

The speed and accuracy with which you will be able to transcribe your shorthand notes will depend on how well you write them. If you follow the suggestions given in this lesson when you work with each Accuracy Practice, you will soon find that you can read your own notes with greater ease and facility.

So that you may have a clear picture of the proper shapes of the shorthand strokes that you are studying, enlarged models of the alphabetic characters and of the typical joinings are given, together with a short explanation of the things that you should keep in mind as you practice.

To get the most out of each Accuracy Practice, follow this simple procedure:

a Read the explanations carefully.

b Study the model to see the application of each explanation.

c Write the first outline in the Practice Drill.

d Compare what you have written with the enlarged model.

e Write three or four more copies of the outline, trying to improve your outline with each writing.

f Repeat this procedure with the remaining outlines in the Practice Drill.

216 ▸ R L K G

To write these strokes accurately:

a Start and finish each one on the same level of writing.

b Make the *beginning* of the curve in *r* and *l* deep. Make the *end* of the curve in *k* and *g* deep.

c Make the *l* and *g* considerably longer than *r* and *k*.

Practice Drill

Are-our-hour, will-well, can, good; air, lay, ache, gay.

217▸ **Kr** **Rk** **Gl**

To write these combinations accurately:

a Make the curves rather flat.

b Make the combinations *kr* and *rk* somewhat shorter than the combined length of *r* and *k* when written by themselves.

c Make the combination *gl* somewhat shorter than the combined length of *g* and *l* when written by themselves.

Practice Drill

Cream, crate, maker, mark, dark; gleam, glean, glare, eagle.

218▸ Recall Chart • This chart contains all the brief forms in Chapter 4 and one or more illustrations of all the shorthand devices you have studied in Chapters 1 through 4.

The chart contains 90 words. Can you read the entire chart in 7 minutes or less?

WORDS

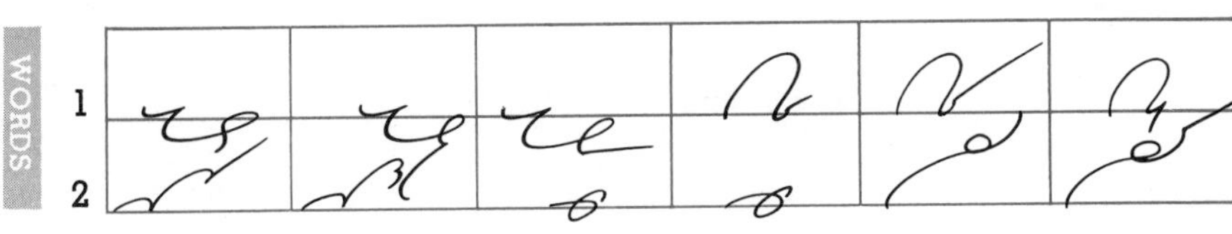

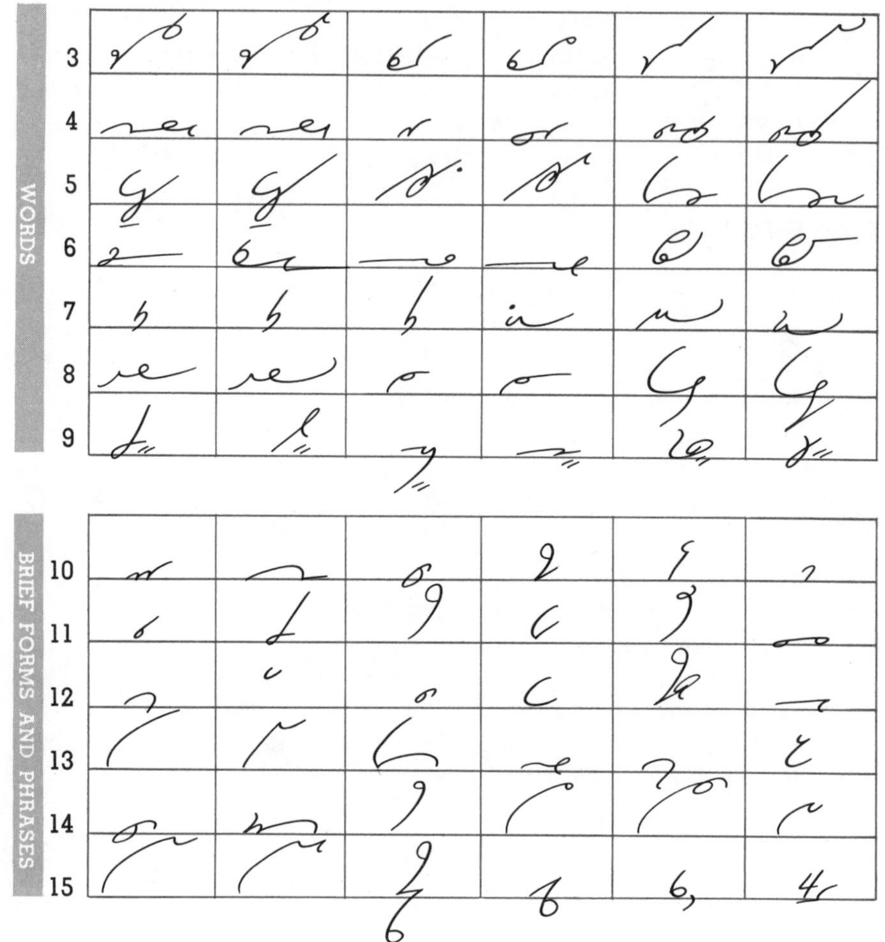

BUILDING TRANSCRIPTION SKILLS

219▸ **BUSINESS VOCABULARY BUILDER**

common knowledge Something known to everybody.

conscientious Careful.

affecting Influencing.

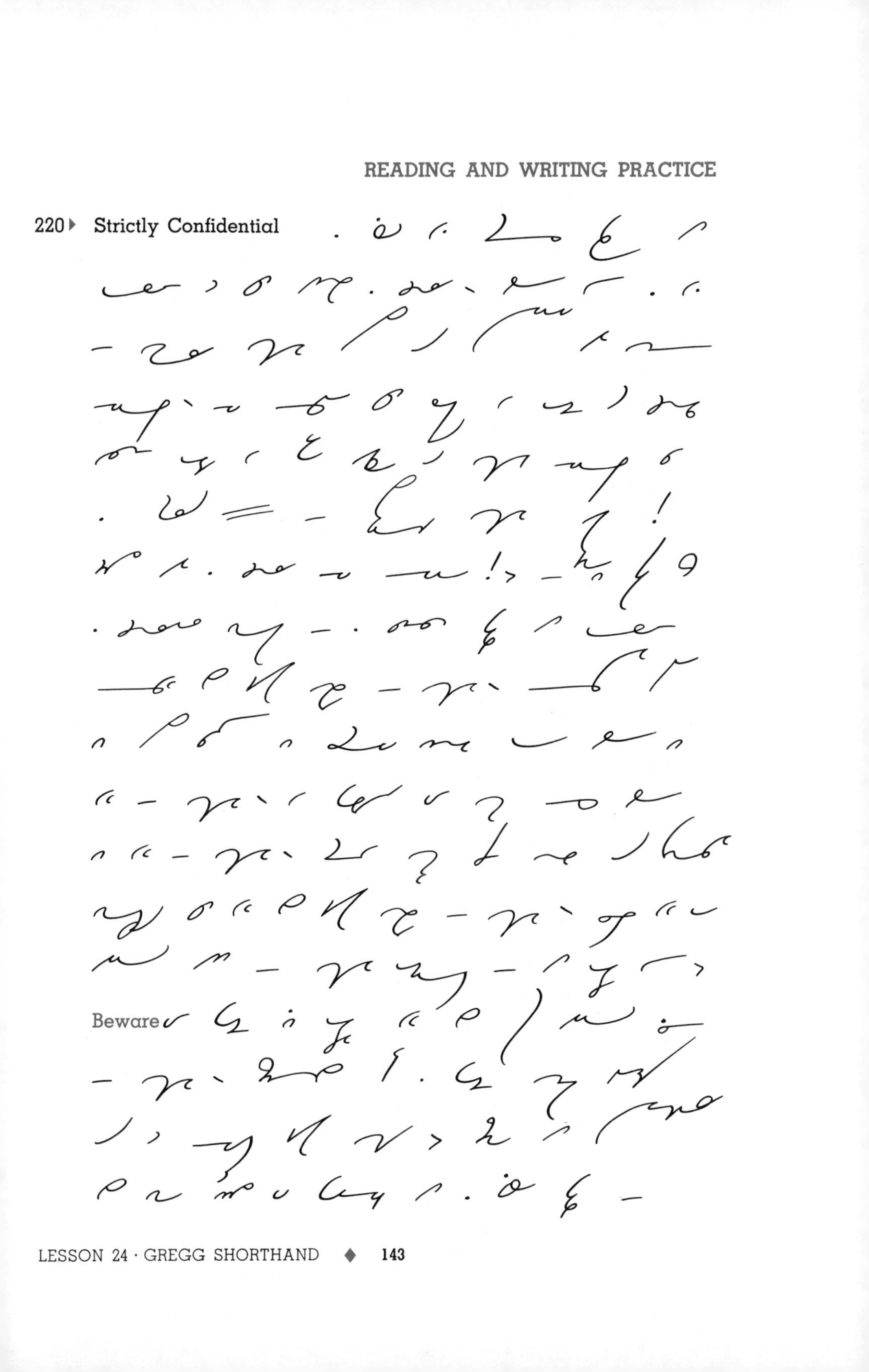

220 ▸ Strictly Confidential

Beware

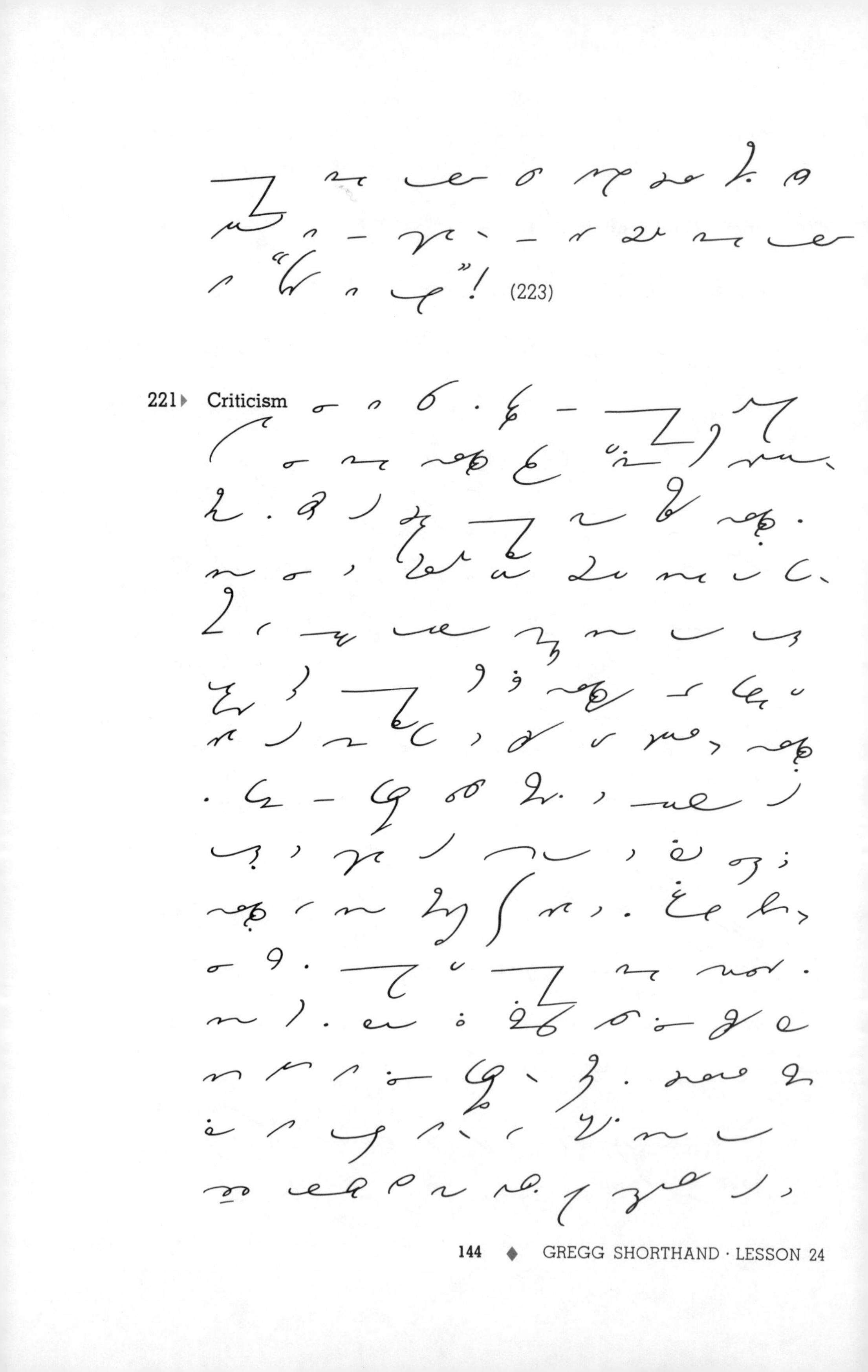

(223)

221 Criticism

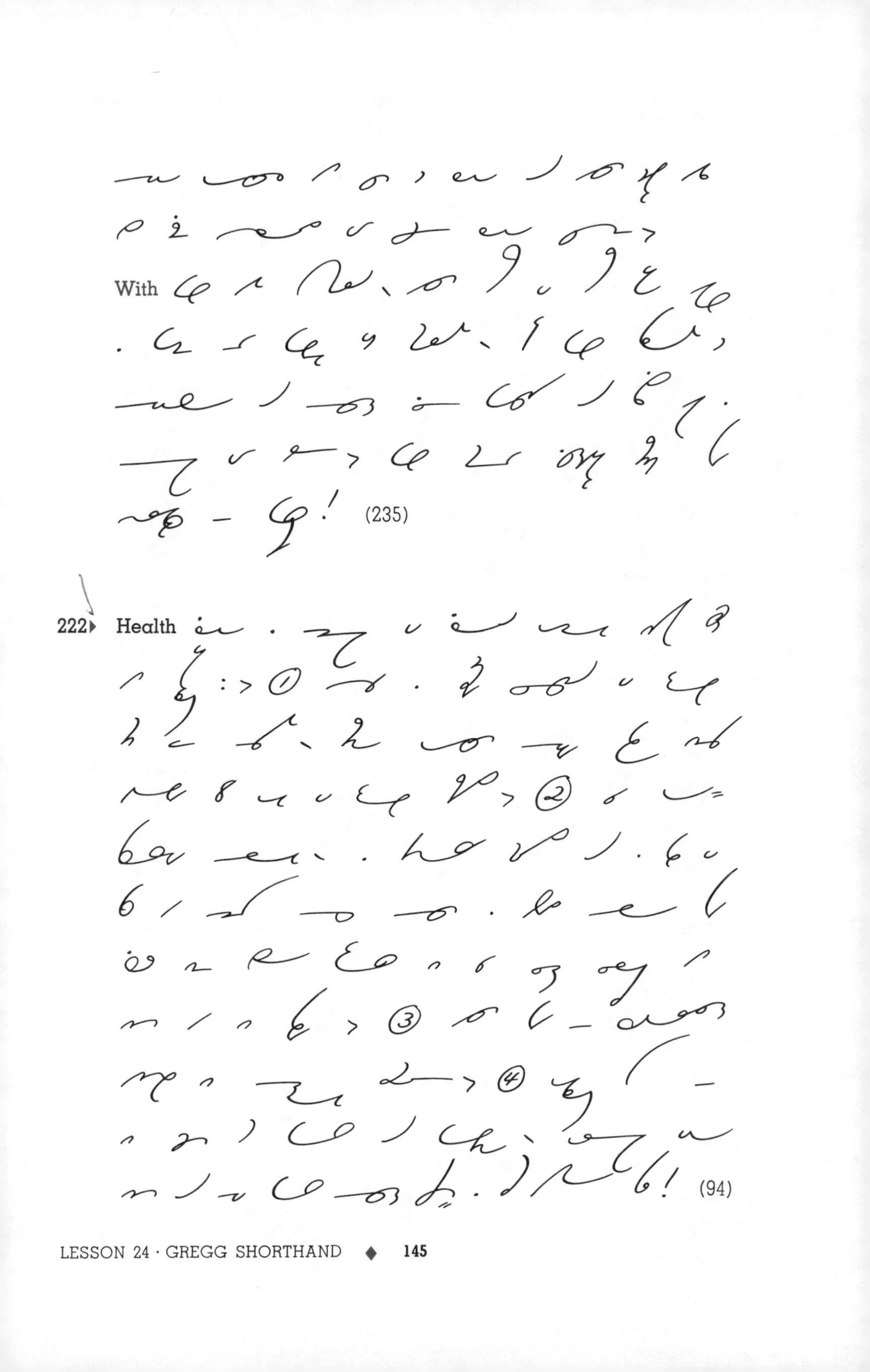

With

(235)

222 Health

(94)

The term *stenographer* is rarely heard in the business office today. Nowadays, the title *secretary* is used by most businesses to identify those who perform stenographic duties for an executive. The reason is that the term "secretary" has more prestige, and because there has long been a shortage of secretarial help, applicants could insist on a more attractive designation.

Even though the term secretary now identifies all those who act as "girl Fridays," the level of job is usually distinguished by grade – Secretary 1, Secretary 2, Secretary 5, and so on—the higher the number, the higher the grade. Of course, the grade is determined by the importance of the executive for whom the secretary works.

There have been several attempts to distinguish between levels of secretarial jobs, but it is difficult to get away from the term secretary because everyone has a pretty clear idea of what is done by the person who holds the title. Thus, the term secretary may identify the top executive assistant in a large corporation, or it may identify the newest beginner.

The term stenographer is still used in government. It is also used by some firms to designate a person who works for several executives, for another secretary, or in a pool (a group of stenographers who are on call to take dictation from any executive). The next step up from the job of stenographer is to *private secretary;* i.e., one who works for only one executive. The secretary who earns the right to work for a high-ranking executive in a business organization is often given the title executive secretary. In this case, the word "executive" does not refer to the person for whom the secretary works; it implies that the secretary is an executive in her own right, having the privilege of making important decisions and often supervising other secretaries and office employees. A more modern term for this high-level position is *administrative assistant,* and it is a job worth working for. Administrative assistants are actually executives, and they command salaries and prestige equal to those of some supervisors and department managers.

Where to from the position of administrative assistant? This depends on one's special talents and aspirations. You may become a supervisor of office personnel, an assistant department manager, a department manager, a personnel specialist, and so on. It is not as unusual as you might think for a secretary to advance into the top ranks of management.

But keep this in mind: Most secretaries progress as their bosses progress. If the boss moves up the ladder of management, his secretary moves with him. Her future, then, is very much tied in with her boss's future. The good secretary can shorten the boss's route to advancement by taking from his shoulders every assignment she can handle and by keeping him efficiently organized. When the secretary helps her boss, she helps herself.

THE ROUTE UPWARD

PRINCIPLES

223▸ Brief Forms

request	success	progress
state	difficult	satisfy, satisfactory
next	envelope	under*

*The outline for *under* is written above the following shorthand character. It is also used as a prefix, as in:

undergo	understudy	underground
underneath	underpaid	understand

224▸ Cities and States • In your work as a stenographer or secretary, you will frequently have occasion to write geographical expressions. Here are a few important cities and states.

Cities

New York	Boston	Los Angeles
Chicago	Philadelphia	St. Louis

States

Michigan	Massachusetts	Missouri
Illinois	Pennsylvania	California

225▸ Useful Business Phrases • The following phrases are used in business letters so frequently that special forms have been provided for them. Study these phrases as you would study brief forms.

I hope		as soon as		let us	
we hope		as soon as possible		to us	
your order		of course		to do	

BUILDING TRANSCRIPTION SKILLS

226▸ BUSINESS VOCABULARY BUILDER

collection agency An organization that, for a fee, collects overdue bills.

adversely Unfavorably.

lucrative Profitable.

READING AND WRITING PRACTICE

227▸ Brief-Form Letter

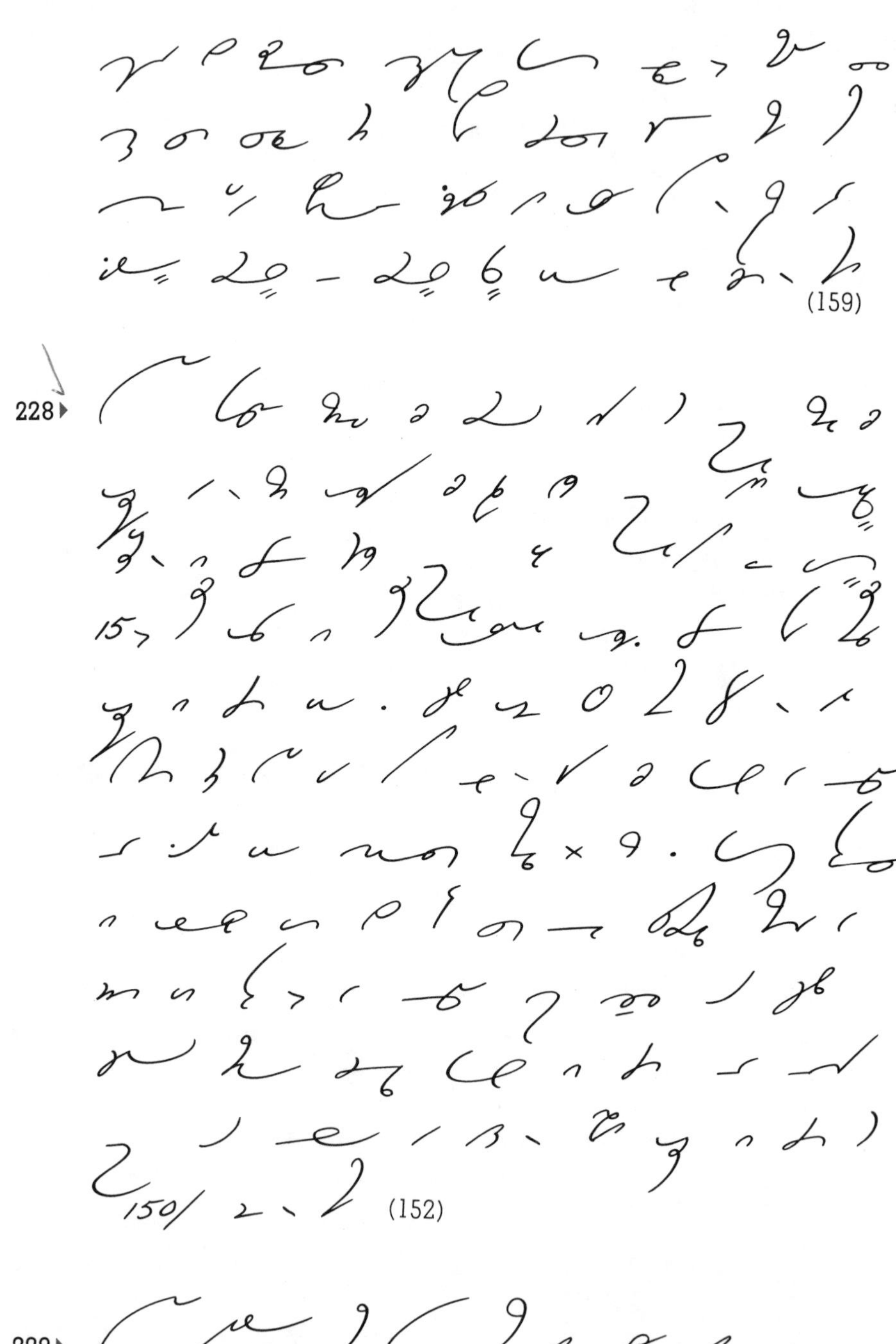
(159)

228

(152)

229

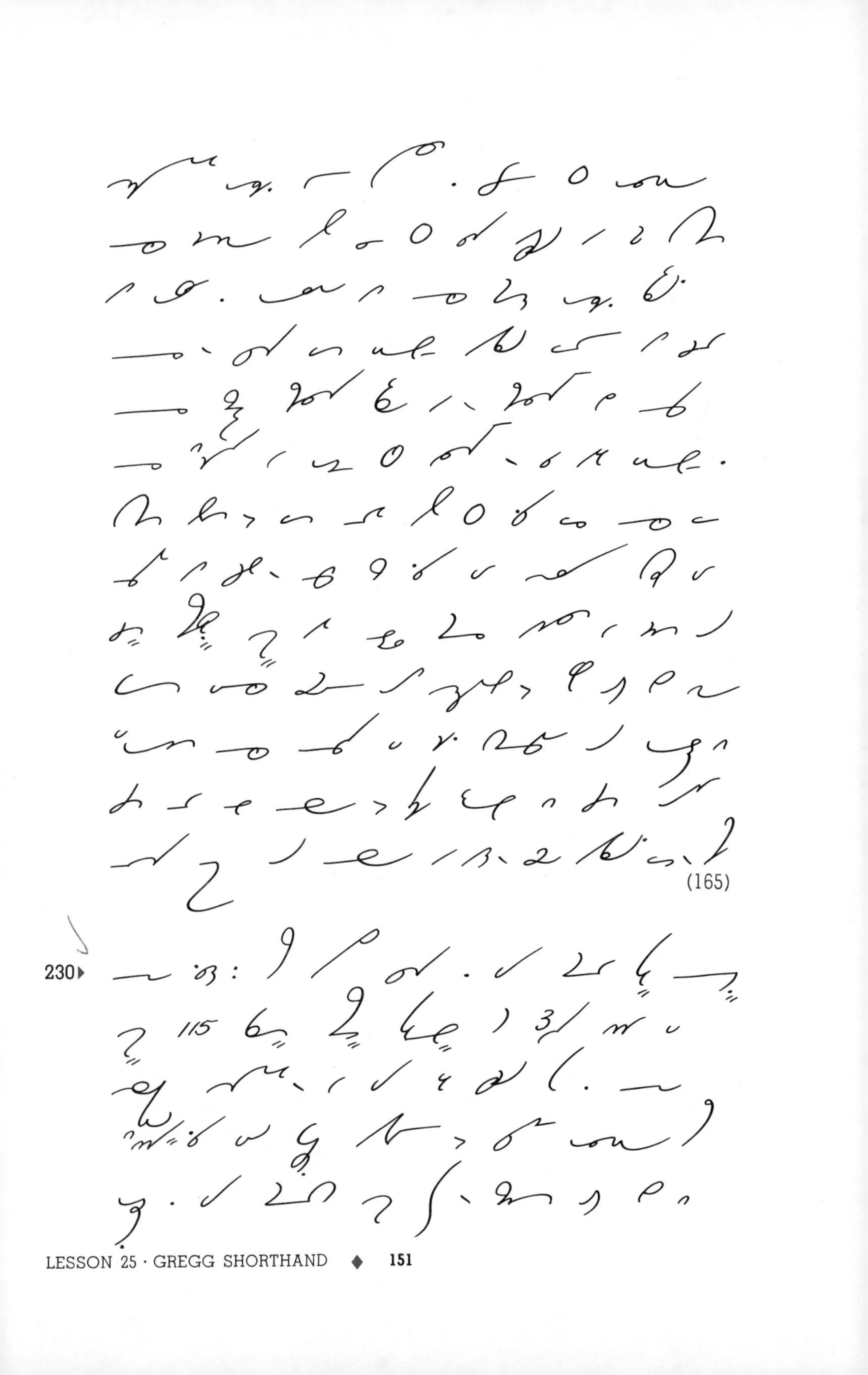

(165)

230

(111)

231 Thought for the Day

(115)

PRACTICE SUGGESTION: Turn to page 407 of the Appendix and review the word beginnings, endings, and phrases you have studied through Lesson 25. This review will help to keep the word beginnings and endings and phrases fresh in your mind.

PRINCIPLES

232▸ Long I and a Following Vowel • Any vowel following long *i* is represented by a small circle within the large circle.

COMPARE: **line** **lion**

trial **prior** **appliance**
dial **drier** **reliance**
client **quiet** **compliance**

233▸ Ia, Ea • The sounds of *ia*, as in *piano*, and *ea*, as in *create*, are represented by a large circle with a dot placed within it.

piano **appropriate** **brilliant**
area **appreciate** **radiate**
create **initiate** **variation**

234▸ Word Beginnings In-, Un-, En- • The word beginnings *in-*, *un-*, *en-* are represented by *n* before a consonant.

In **increase** **insist** **injured**
instead **instance** **insure**

Un	unless	unpack	uncertain
	unfair	until	unsettled
En	endeavor	encouragement	engage
	enjoy	enlarge	encounter

235 ▸ **In-, Un-, En- Followed by a Vowel** • When *in-, un-, en-* are followed by a vowel, they are written in full.

innovation unable enact

BUILDING TRANSCRIPTION SKILLS

236 ▸ **BUSINESS VOCABULARY BUILDER**

crucial Severe; very critical.
en route On the way.
creative Productive; imaginative.

READING AND WRITING PRACTICE

237 ▸

(139)

238

31

(137)

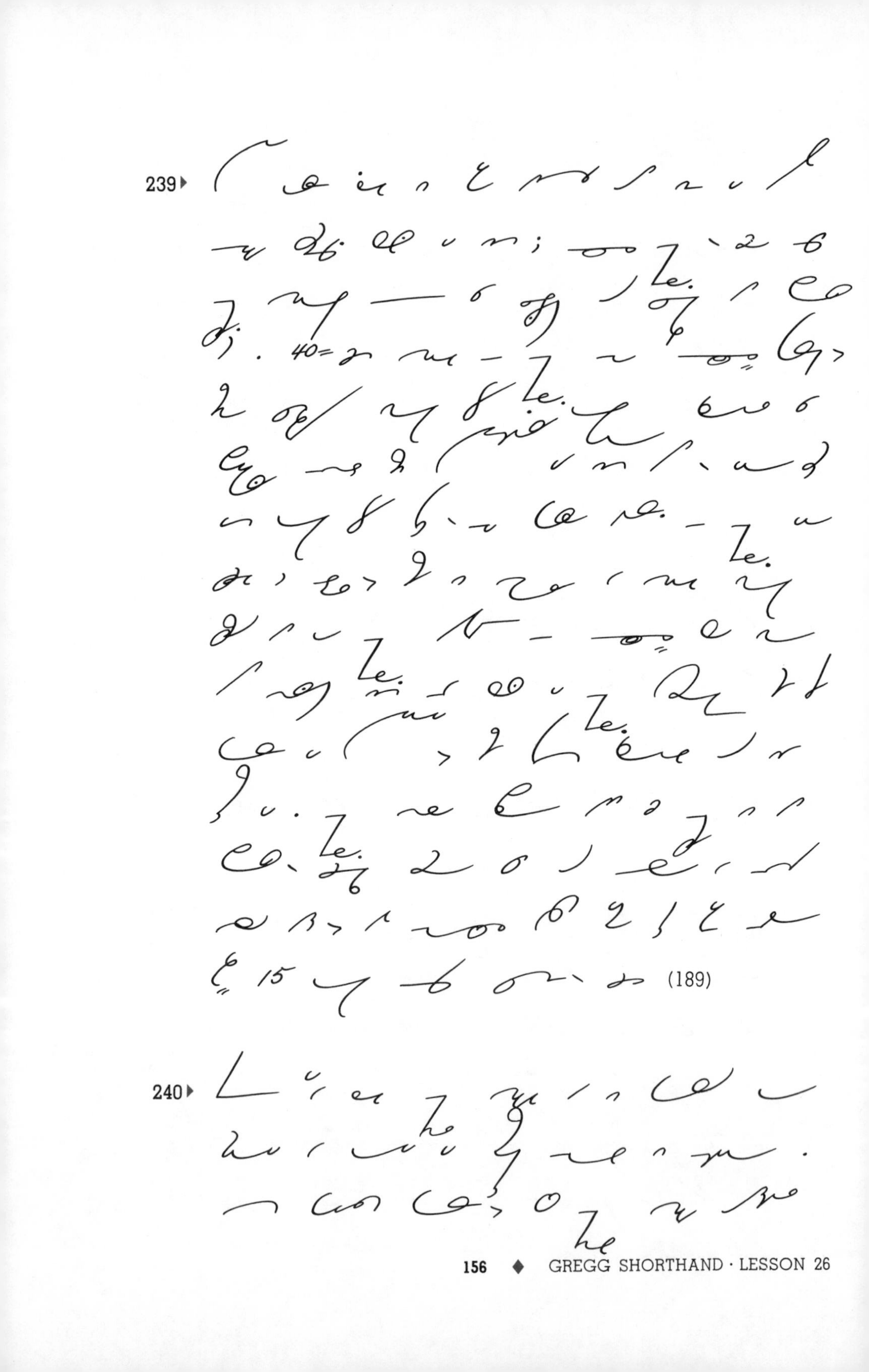

239

(189)

240

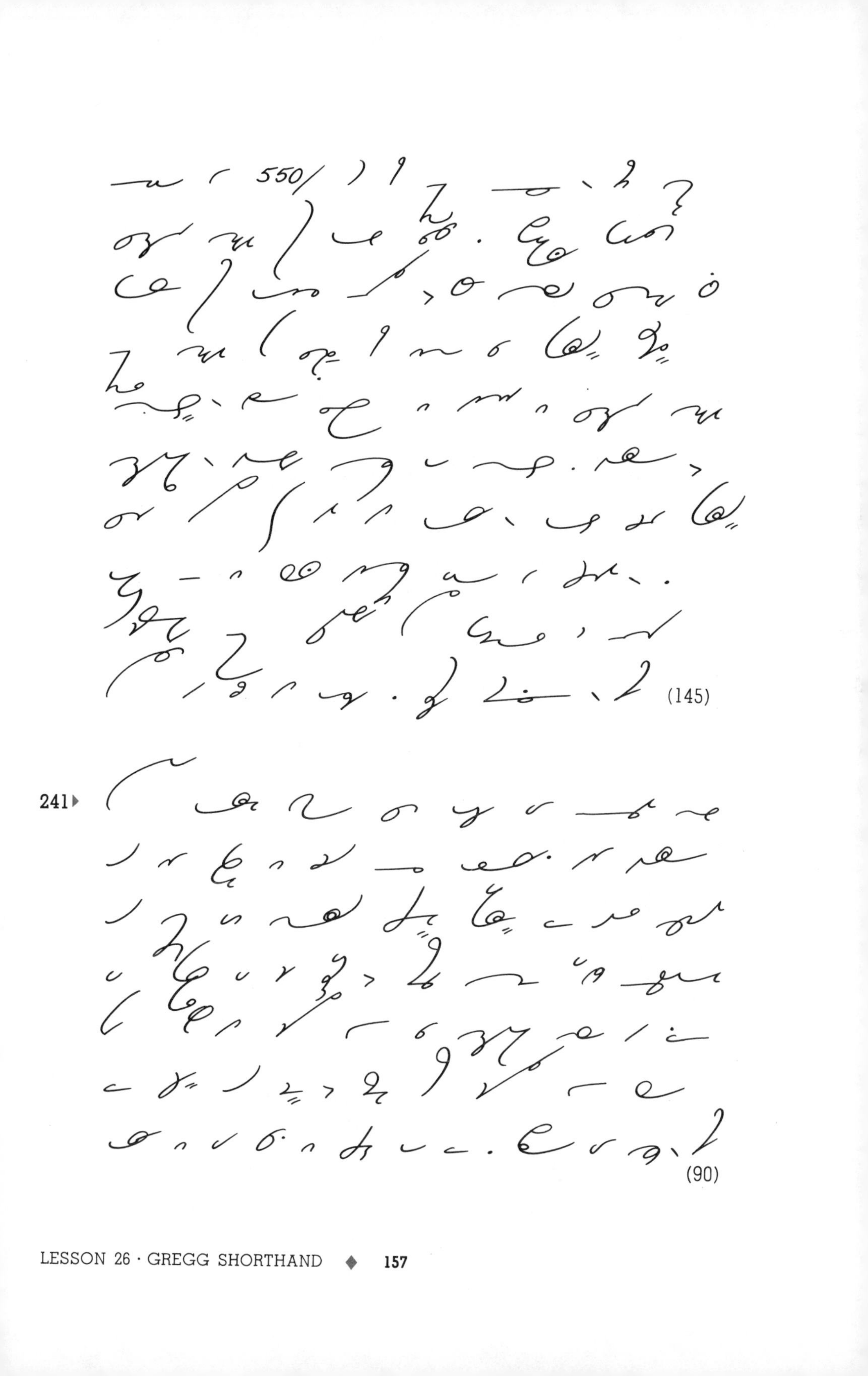

550

(145)

241

(90)

PRINCIPLES

242 ▸ **Brief Forms** • After this group, only three more to go!

newspaper	subject	regular
street	idea	probable
upon	speak	particular

243 ▸ **Ng** • The sound of *ng* is written

COMPARE: seen sing

sing	long	spring
sang	wrong	length
song	strong	strength
ring	bring	single

244 ▸ **Ngk** • The sound of *ngk* (usually spelled *nk*) is written

frank	bank	shrink
blank	banquet	drinking

rank ink anxious

tank link uncle

245▸ Omission of Vowel Preceding -tion • When *t, d, n,* or *m* is followed by *-ition, -ation,* the circle is omitted.

notation reputation commission

addition condition additional

donation combination quotations

permission admission stationed

BUILDING TRANSCRIPTION SKILLS

246▸ BUSINESS VOCABULARY BUILDER

mutilated Badly cut up.
hazards Sources of danger.
quotations Bids or prices offered.

READING AND WRITING PRACTICE

247▸ Brief-Form Letter

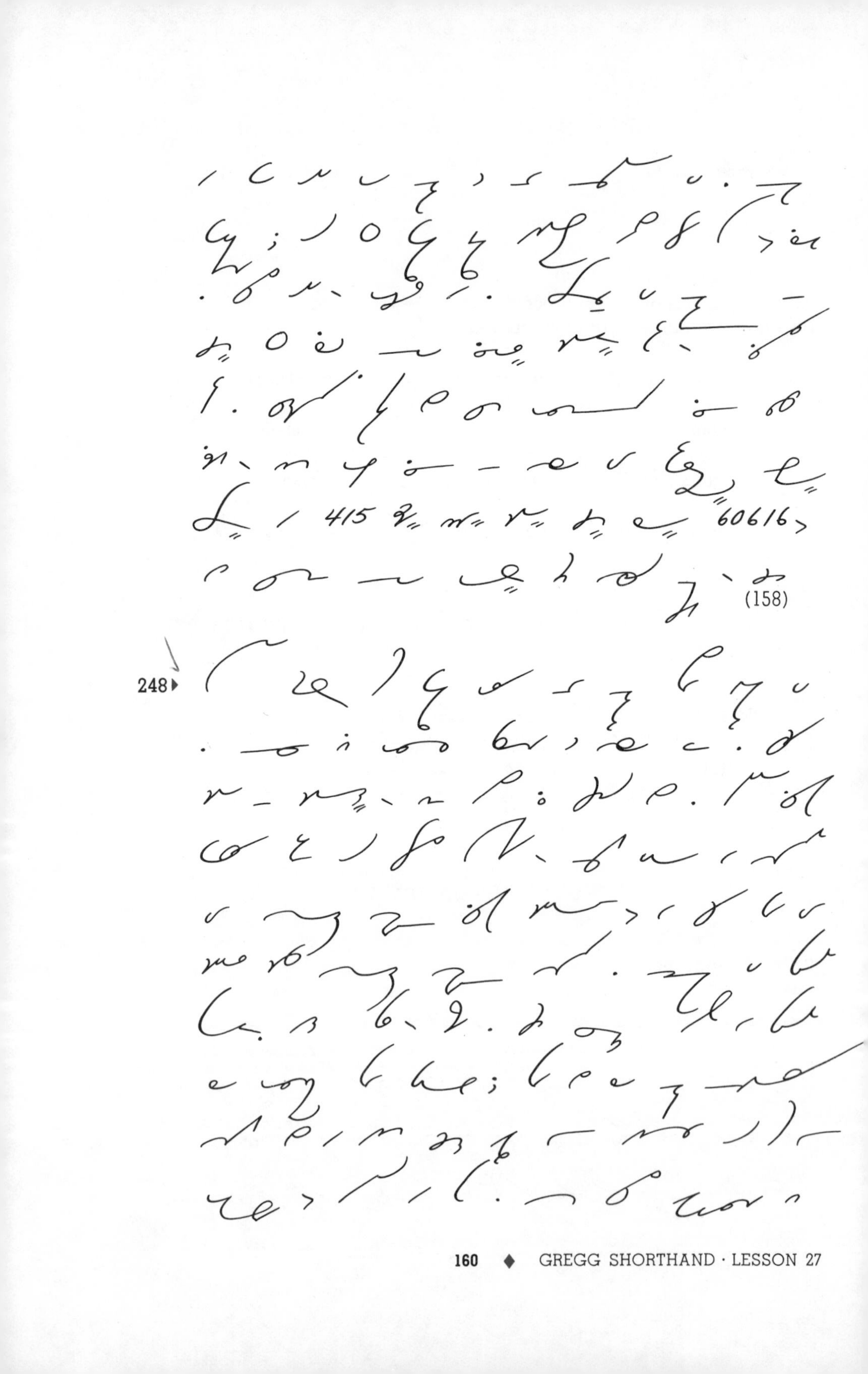

415 60616

(158)

248

(147)

249 10 12 16 10 (83)

250

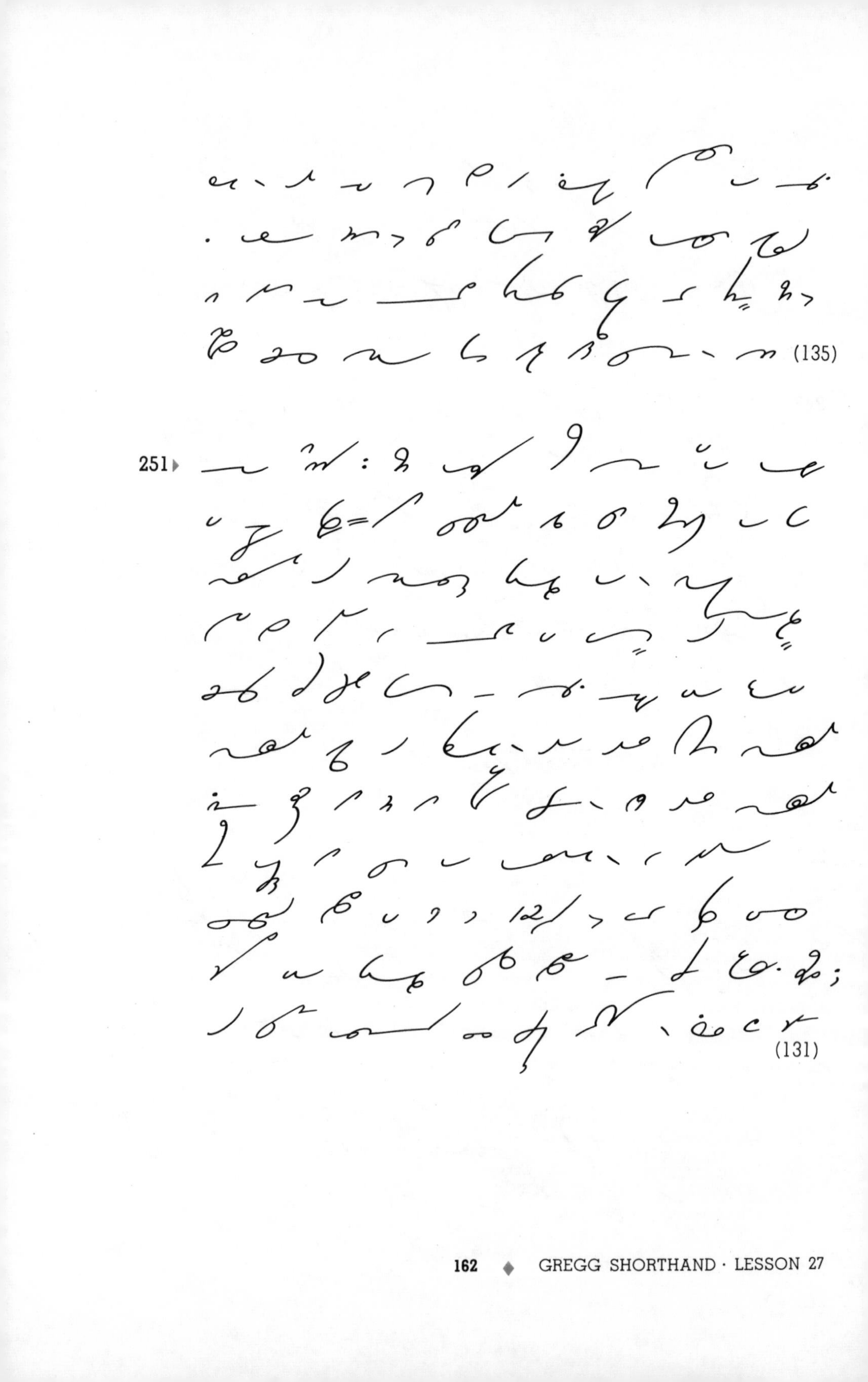

(135)

251

(131)

PRINCIPLES

252▸ Ah, Aw • A dot is used for *a* in words that begin *ah* and *aw*.

ahead · await · awoke
away · awake · aware

253▸ Y • Before o and oo, *y* is expressed by a small circle, as *y* is pronounced e. *Ye* is expressed by a small loop; *ya*, by a large loop.

youth · yellow · yard
yawn · yield · yarn

254▸ X • The letter *x* is usually represented by an *s* written with a slight backward slant.

COMPARE: miss · mix
fees · fix

tax · indexes · box
taxes · relax · boxes
index · relaxes · perplex

255▸ Omission of U • In the body of a word, the sound of *u*, as in *fun*, is omitted before *n*, *m*, or a straight downstroke.

Before N

fun	**done**	**lunch**
begun	**son**	**front**

Before M

sum, some	**come**	**income**
summer	**become**	**column**

Before a Straight Downstroke

rush	**much**	**judged**
brushed	**touch**	**budget**

BUILDING TRANSCRIPTION SKILLS

256▸ BUSINESS VOCABULARY BUILDER

wither To become dry.
complex Involved; difficult.
flexible Yielding to influence; can be changed.

READING AND WRITING PRACTICE

257▸

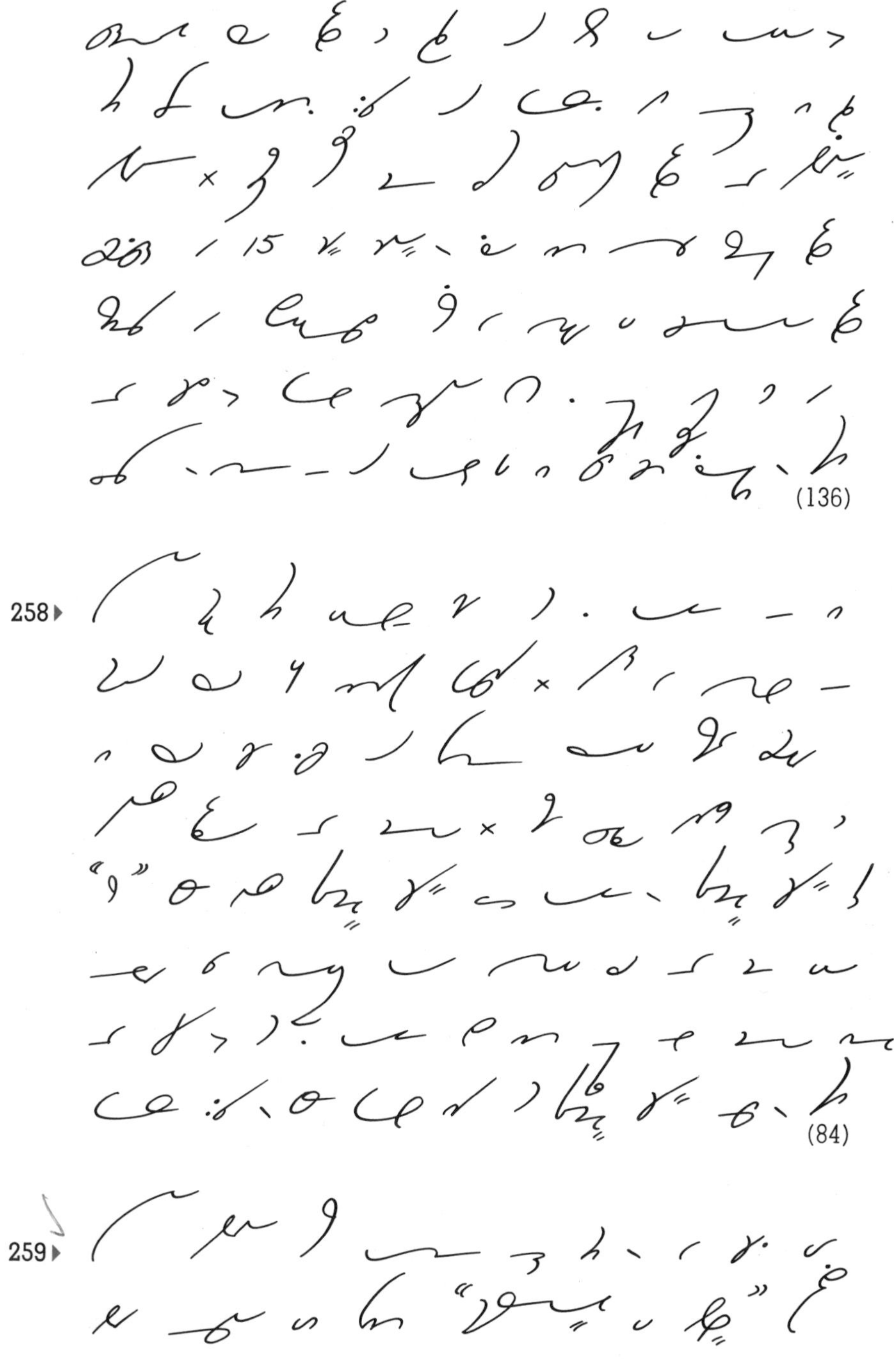

(136)

258

(84)

259

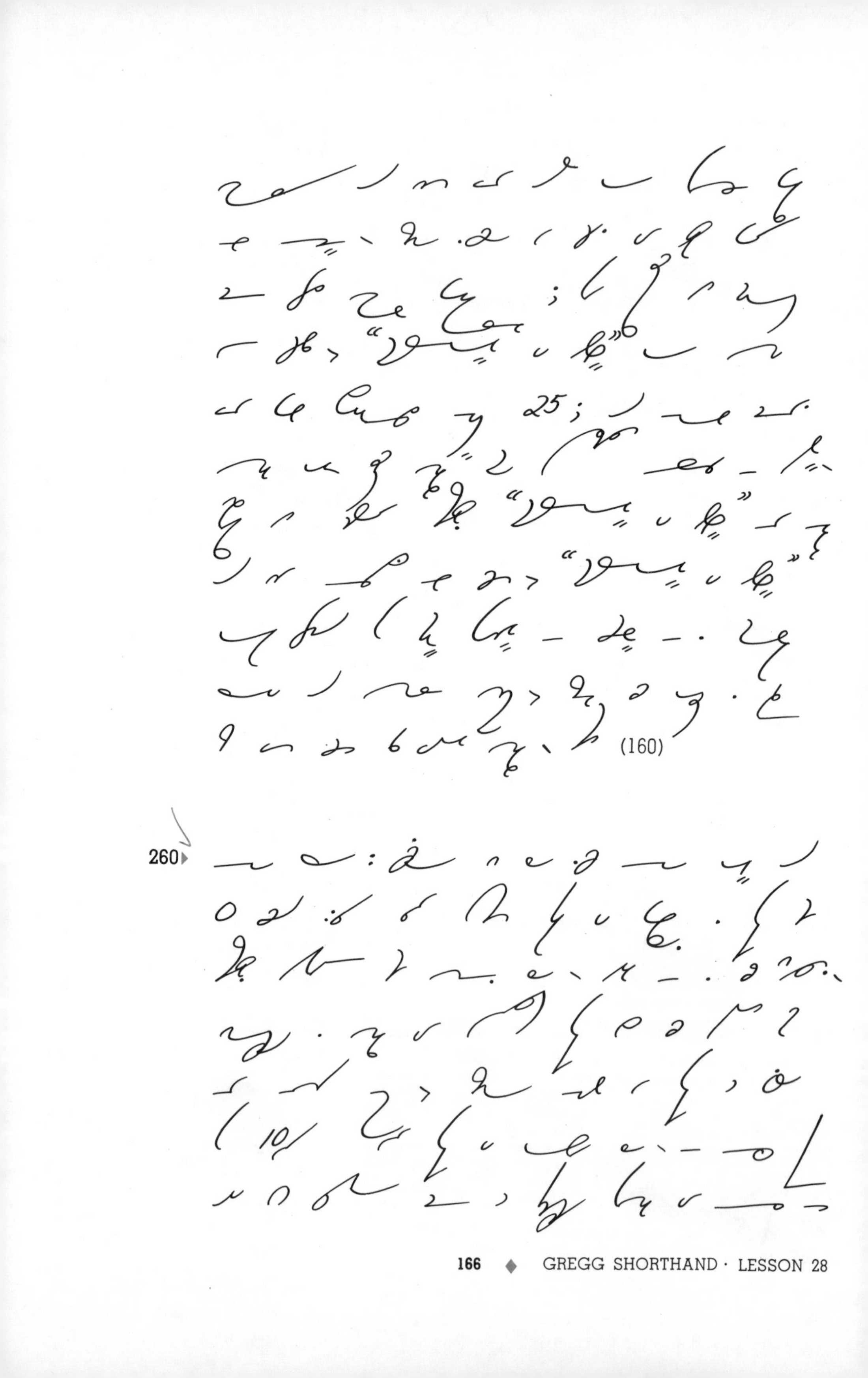

25;

(160)

260

10

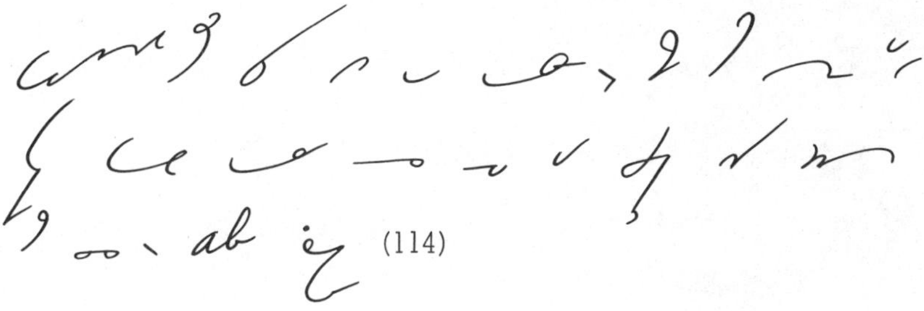

(114)

261 ▸

(84)

262 ▸

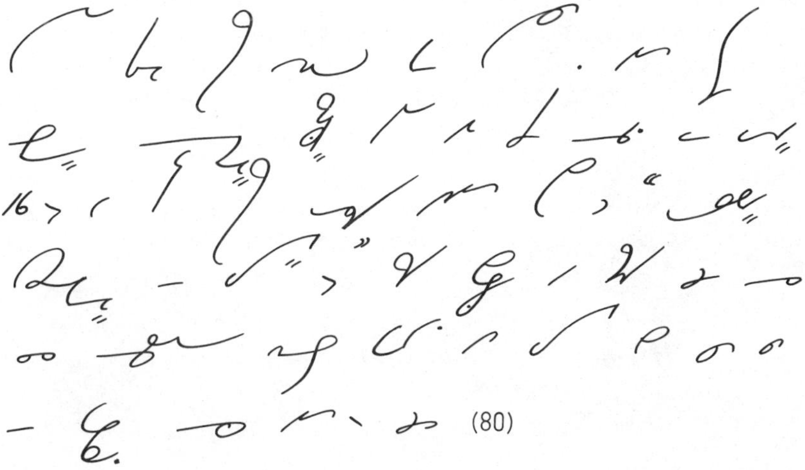

(80)

PRINCIPLES

263▸ Brief Forms

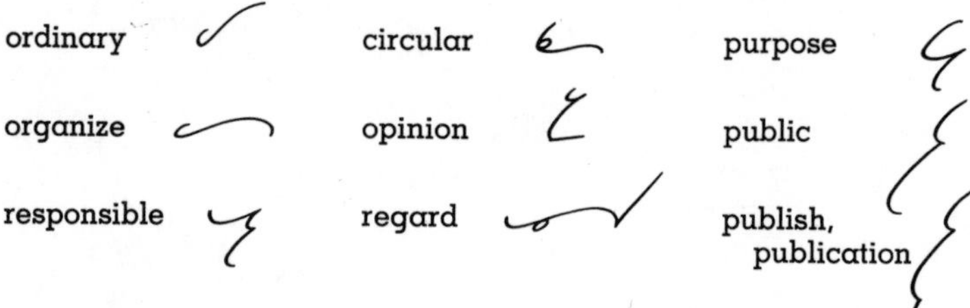

264▸ Word Beginning Ex- • The word beginning *ex-* is represented by *e-s*.

explained	examine	expect
expression	extend	expired
expenses	example	excuse
except	extra	exist

265▸ Md, Mt • By rounding off the angle between *m-d*, we obtain the fluent *md* blend. The same stroke also represents *mt*.

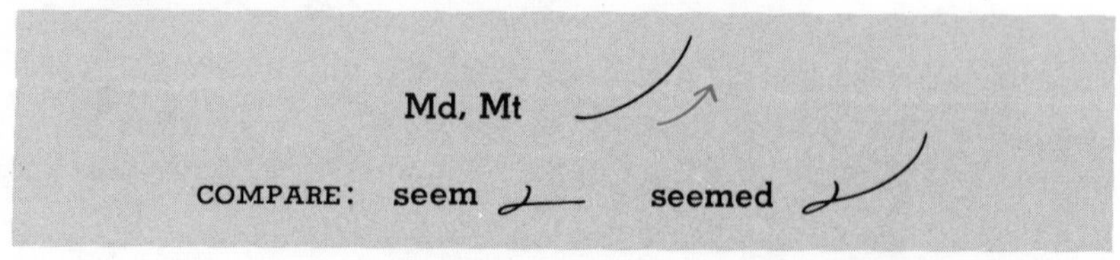

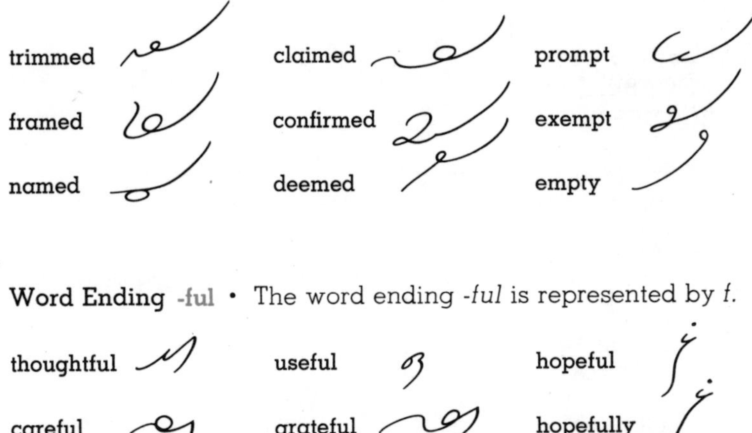

266 ▸ **Word Ending -ful** • The word ending *-ful* is represented by *f*.

thoughtful
useful
hopeful
careful
grateful
hopefully
doubtful
powerful
helpful
delightful
beautiful
helpfulness

BUILDING TRANSCRIPTION SKILLS

267 ▸ **SIMILAR-WORDS DRILL** write, right

write To put words on paper.

I will write you about our problems.

right *(noun)* Something to which one has a just claim; *(adjective)* correct; *(adverb)* directly.

You have a right to expect good service from us.
I do not have the right time.
John is going right home after the meeting.

268 **BUSINESS VOCABULARY BUILDER**

in excess of More than.
sole Only.
phase Stage. (Do not confuse with "faze," which means "to disturb.")

READING AND WRITING PRACTICE

269 Brief-Form Letter

(176)

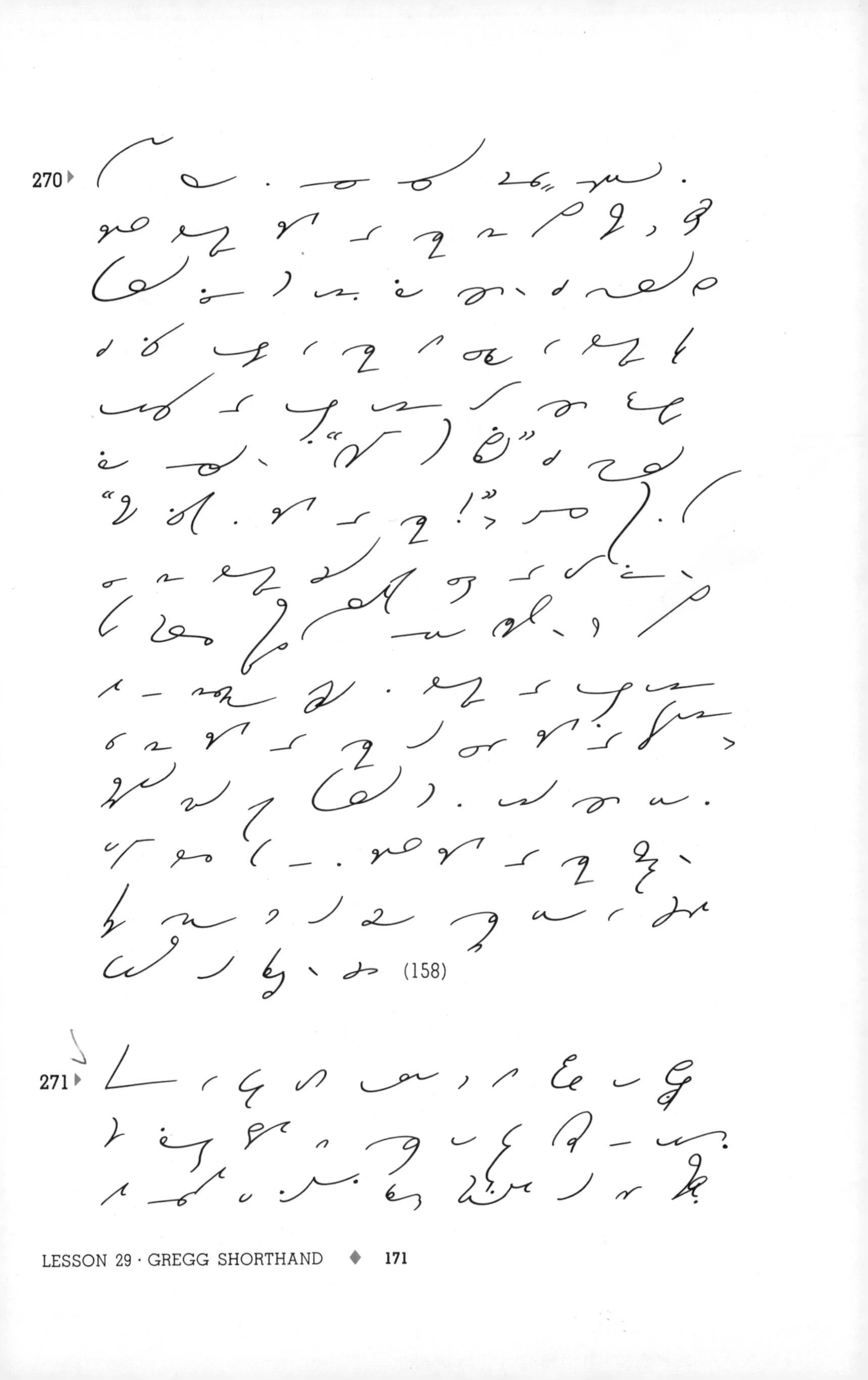

270

(158)

271

(147)

272

(107)

273 (96)

274 (79)

RECALL

There are no new shorthand strokes or principles in Lesson 30. In this lesson you will find an Accuracy Practice devoted to the curved strokes of Gregg Shorthand, a Recall Chart, and a Reading and Writing Practice.

ACCURACY PRACTICE

To get the most benefit from the Accuracy Practice, be sure to follow the procedures suggested on page 140.

275 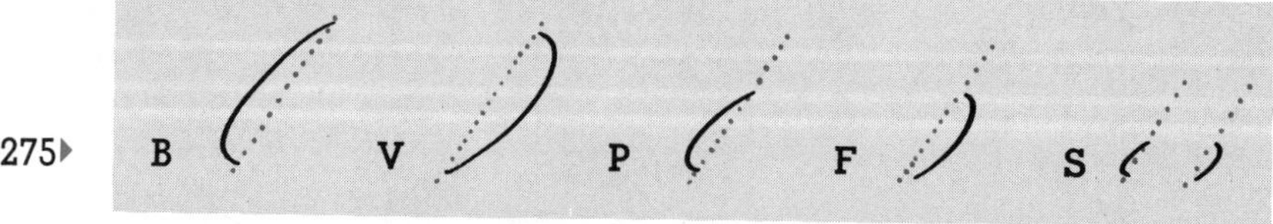

To write these strokes accurately:

a Give them approximately the slant indicated by the dotted lines.

b Make the curve deep at the beginning of *v, f,* comma *s;* make the curve deep at the end of *b, p,* left *s.*

Practice Drill

Puts, spare, business, bears, stairs, sphere, leaves, briefs.

276 Pr Pl Br Bl

To write these combinations accurately:

a Write each without a pause between the first and second letter of each combination.

b Watch your proportions carefully.

Practice Drill

Press, pray, prim, plan, plate, place.
Brim, brief, bread, blame, blast.

277 Fr Fl

To write these combinations accurately:

a Write them with one sweep of the pen, with no stop between the *f* and *r* or *l*.

Practice Drill

Free, freeze, frame, flee, flame, flap.

278 Recall Chart • This chart contains all the brief forms in Chapter 5 and one or more illustrations of the word-building principles you studied in Chapters 1 through 5.

As you read through the words in this chart, be sure to spell each word that you cannot read immediately.

Can you read the 90 words in the chart in 6 minutes or less?

BRIEF FORMS

1
2
3
4
5

WORDS

6
7
8
9
10
11
12
13
14
15

BUILDING TRANSCRIPTION SKILLS

279 ▸ **BUSINESS VOCABULARY BUILDER**

emotion One of the states termed fear, anger, love, happiness, etc.

decisive Conclusive; definite.

debased Lowered in dignity or value.

READING SCOREBOARD • The previous Reading Scoreboard appeared in Lesson 18. If you have been studying each Reading and Writing Practice faithfully, you have no doubt increased your reading speed. Measure that increase on your first reading of the material in Lesson 30. The following table will help you:

LESSON 30 CONTAINS 460 WORDS

If you read Lesson 30 in:	13	15	17	19	21	23	minutes
	▼	▼	▼	▼	▼	▼	
Your reading rate is:	35	32	27	25	22	20	words a minute

If you can read Lesson 30 in 13 minutes or less, you are doing well. If you take considerably longer than 23 minutes, perhaps you should review your homework procedures. For example, are you:

1 Practicing in a quiet place at home?
2 Practicing without the radio or television set on?
3 Spelling aloud any words that you cannot read immediately?

280 ▸ **Time for Decision**

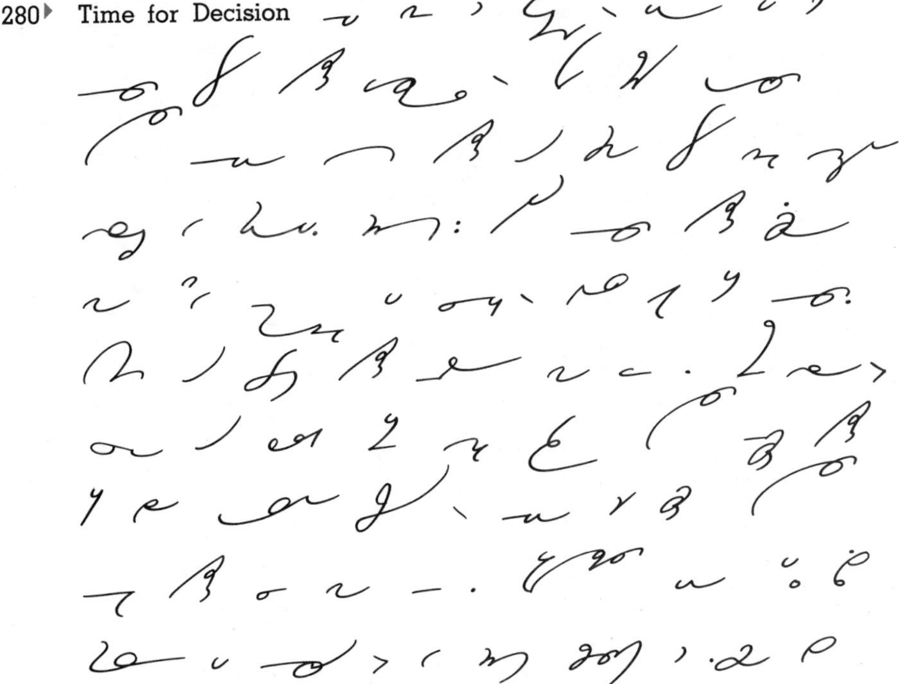

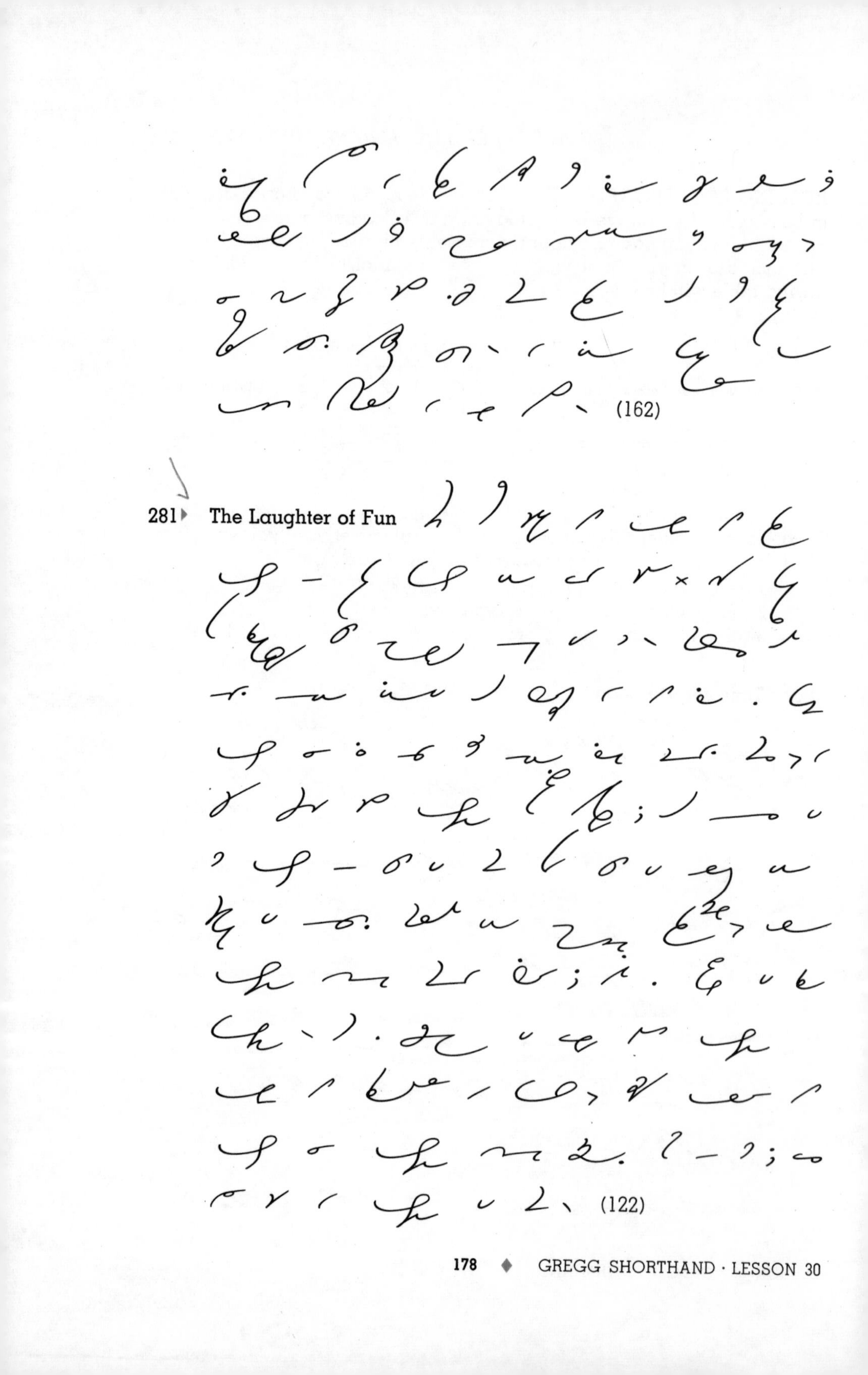

(162)

281 The Laughter of Fun

(122)

282 Thought for the Day

(77)

283 Grammar Expert

(99)

▶ To say that this is an age of specialization would be repeating a trite expression. Still, it's true. You know that many professional people specialize. A doctor may be a heart specialist, lung specialist, radiologist, or neurologist. Lawyers specialize in criminal law, corporation law, tax law, and international law. Accountants specialize, too – in tax matters, internal auditing, public accounting, and so on. Engineers have always specialized – electrical, mechanical, civil, chemical, and aeronautical, to mention a few areas.

This age of specialization has also affected secretarial work. Today we have secretaries who specialize in such areas as medicine, law, education, and various scientific and technical fields. The tendency has become so widespread that there are several national organizations of specialized secretaries.

Why specialize? There are wonderful opportunities for the secretary who goes beyond the general secretarial curriculum to take special courses in vocabulary, procedures, and dictation in a special field. A popular college curriculum is the medical secretarial area. Many private secretarial schools and colleges offer complete curricula in medical secretarial training. Such courses include laboratory techniques, principles of anatomy and physiology, medical vocabulary, and medical dictation and transcription. A growing number of colleges are offering similar programs for legal secretaries.

Perhaps the fastest growing field of secretarial specialization is the scientific and technical field. This includes a wide variety of careers with engineering firms, textile manufacturers, chemical manufacturing enterprises, and various business and government installations that deal in aeronautical engineering, rocket engineering, and electronics.

Obviously, specialization for secretaries has the same appeal as specialization for those in other areas. Specialists do a better job because they bring more training to their work, and they earn more for the same reason.

Should you specialize after you have completed your general training? The advantages are many—and there is a growing prestige in the "specialist" designation.

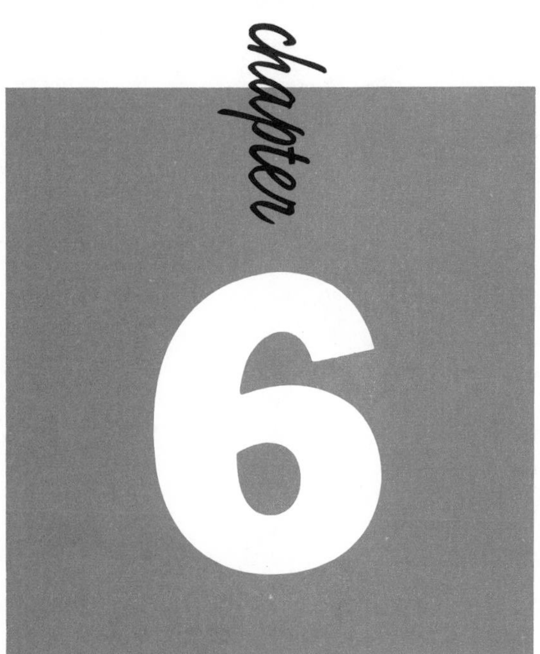

THE SPECIALIZED SECRETARY

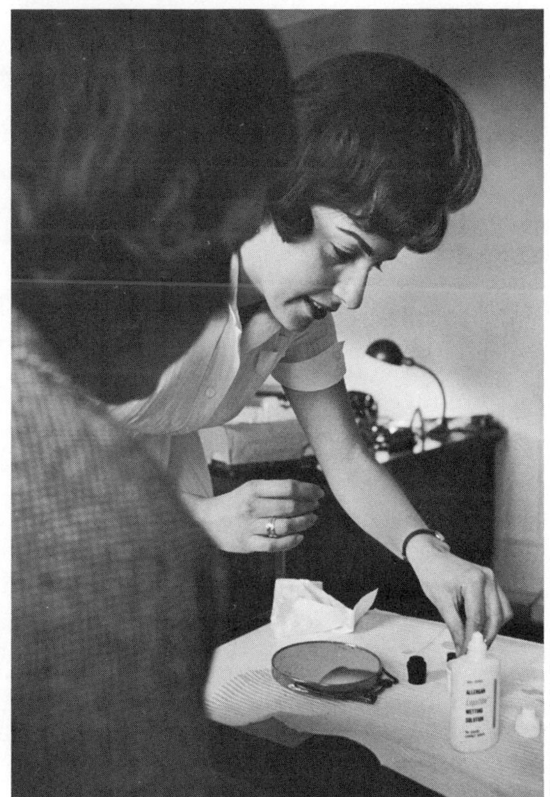

Photographed by Lionel Crawford

PRINCIPLES

284 **Brief Forms** • Only one more group to learn after this one!

situation		between		never	
quantity		experience		merchant	
short		recognize		merchandise	

285 **Word Ending -ure** • The word ending *-ure* is represented by *r.*

figure		lecture		nature	
failure		procedure		naturally	

286 **Word Ending -ual** • The word ending *-ual* is represented by *l.*

equal		mutual		annual	
gradual		eventual		annually	

BUILDING TRANSCRIPTION SKILLS

287 **PUNCTUATION PRACTICE**

Take a few moments to examine the letter on page 183. The letter makes a good first impression, doesn't it? It is nicely placed on the page,

WILLIAM BLAKE & SONS

MANUFACTURERS OF FARM EQUIPMENT AND SUPPLIES

211 North Canal Street, Chicago, Illinois • 60606

November 16, 196-

Mr. J. C. Green, President
Baker Products Company
161 Fifth Avenue
New York, New York   10056

Dear Mr. Green,

Perhaps you have been meeting business problems that have prevented you from taking care of your past-due account but surly you have not been so occupied that you could not answer our many requests for payment.

We know thet there are periods in the year when your business is slow and cash is scarse. That is ocasinally the case with our business. If your balanse is low we are willing to wait for settlement of our account, even though it is past do. The thing that worries us however is that you completely ignore all our communcations.

All we ask is that you do one of two things either send us your check for $222 or write us a note telling us when we may expect payment.

Is that asking to much.

Yours very truely,

James C. Graham
Credit Manager

JCG:RE

Can you find all the errors in this letter?

the right margin is fairly even, and all the parts of the letter are in their proper places. If you scan through the letter quickly, you find that it makes good sense and apparently represents what the employer dictated.

When you read the letter carefully, however, you quickly realize that the employer will never sign it. In fact, he will probably have a few sharp words to say to the stenographer who transcribed it about the importance of proofreading! The letter contains many errors in spelling and punctuation—all of which the stenographer should have corrected before submitting the letter for signature.

When you complete your stenographic training and accept your first position as a stenographer or secretary, your employer will, of course, expect you to record his dictation faithfully and to produce an accurate transcript of what he said. But he will expect more! He will expect to have the transcript of his dictation correctly punctuated and free of spelling errors. He realizes—as you, too, must—that letters that contain spelling and punctuation errors make a poor impression on the person receiving them.

To make sure that you can spell and punctuate accurately when you complete your stenographic training, you will, from this point on, give special attention to spelling and punctuation in each Reading and Writing Practice.

In the lessons ahead you will review ten of the most common uses of the comma. Each time one of these uses occurs in the Reading and Writing Practice, the comma will be encircled in the shorthand, thus calling it forcefully to your attention.

In the Reading and Writing Practice you will also find the shorthand outlines for some words printed in color. These words have been selected for special spelling study; they are words that stenographers and secretaries often misspell. The correct spelling and word division for these words are given in the left margin of the shorthand page.

Practice Suggestions • Your ability to spell and punctuate will improve rapidly if in your homework practice hereafter you follow these simple practice suggestions:

1 Read carefully the explanation of each comma usage (for example, the explanation of the parenthetical comma on page 185) to be sure that you understand it. You will encounter many illustrations of each comma usage in the Reading and Writing Practice exercises, so that eventually you will acquire the knack of applying it correctly.

2 Continue to read and copy each Reading and Writing Practice as you have always done. However, add these three important steps:

a Each time you see an encircled comma, note the reason for its use, which is indicated directly above the encircled comma.

b As you copy the Reading and Writing Practice, insert the commas in your shorthand notes, encircling them as in the textbook.

c When you encounter a shorthand word in *color*, finish reading the sentence in which it occurs. Then glance at the left margin of the shorthand, where the word appears in type. Spell the word, aloud if possible, pausing slightly after each word division. (The word divisions indicated are those given in Webster's Seventh New Collegiate Dictionary.)

, parenthetical

A word or a phrase or a clause that is used parenthetically (that is, a word or a phrase or a clause that is not necessary to the grammatical completeness of the sentence) should be set off by commas.

If the parenthetical expression occurs at the end of a sentence, only one comma is needed.

It is my opinion, therefore, that you should take the job.

I do not think, Mr. Green, that the typewriter is in the best of condition.

We shall send you a copy of it, of course.

par ⊙ Each time a parenthetical expression occurs in the Reading and Writing Practice, it will be indicated in the shorthand as shown in the left margin.

288 BUSINESS VOCABULARY BUILDER

prophets Those who predict future events.

draw on To take money out of.

accommodate To take care of.

READING AND WRITING PRACTICE

289 Brief-Form Letter

par ⊙ ⊙

ex·cept
ex·pe·ri·ence
proph·ets

par ⊙

par

quan·ti·ties
mer·chan·dise
pur·chased

550

15

par

(146)

290

par

15

par

per·mit·ted
or·ga·ni·za·tion

par

(101)

291

As·so·ci·a·tion
its

sched·uled
ban·quet

par

par

par

ut·most
ac·com·mo·date

26

15

praise
re·ceived

par

(190)

292 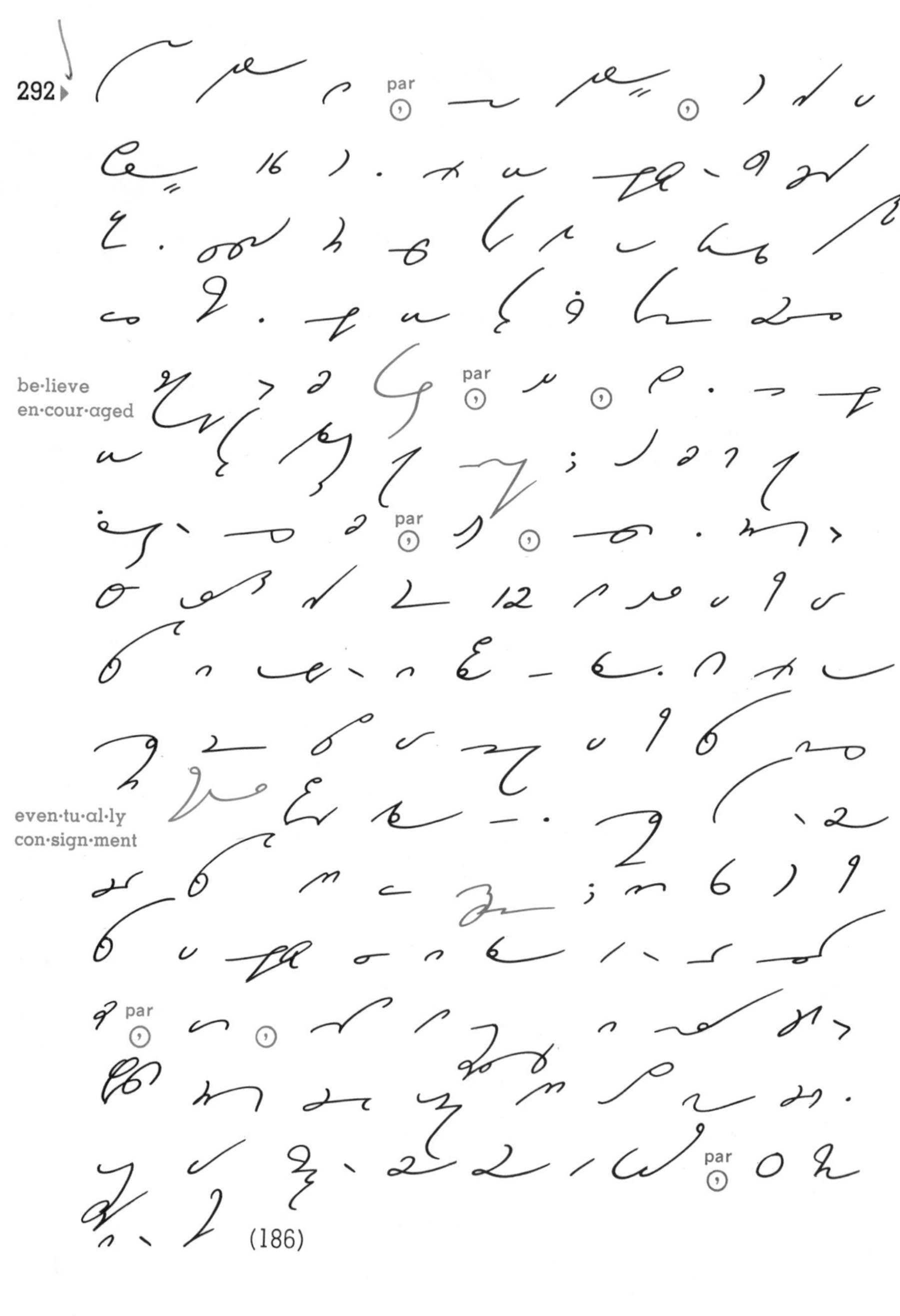

par
be·lieve
en·cour·aged
eventu·al·ly
con·sign·ment
(186)

293

lec·ture
prac·tic·es

par

par

(101)

UP-AND-DOWN CHECK LIST

Do you always write the following strokes upward?

1 and — their-there

2 it-at — would

Do you always write the following strokes downward?

1 is-his — for — have

2 shall — which

PRINCIPLES

294 **Word Ending** -ily • The word ending *-ily* is expressed by a narrow loop.

COMPARE: **steady** **steadily**

readily	hastily	temporarily
easily	speedily	heartily
necessarily	heavily	family

295 **Word Beginning** Al- • The word beginning *al-* is expressed by o.

almost	already	alter
also	although	altogether

296 **Word Beginning** Mis- • The word beginning *mis-* is represented by *m-s*.

misplace	mistake	mislead
misplaced	mistaken	misunderstood
misprint	misery	mystery

297 **Word Beginnings** Dis-, Des- • The word beginnings *dis-*, *des-* are represented by *d-s*.

Dis-	distance	discourage	discount
	discussion	discover	dispute
	dismiss	discontinue	display
Des-	describe	despite	destroy
	description	destination	destroys

BUILDING TRANSCRIPTION SKILLS

298 **PUNCTUATION PRACTICE** **, apposition**

An expression in apposition (that is, a word or a phrase or a clause that identifies or explains other terms) should be set off by commas. When the expression in apposition occurs at the end of a sentence, only one comma is necessary.

Her employer, Mr. Smith, is out of town.

I have an appointment for Friday, June 12, at twelve o'clock.

His book, "Accounting Principles and Practice," is out of stock.

I gave the report to Mr. Smith, our sales manager.

ap (,) Each time an expression in apposition appears in the Reading and Writing Practice, it will be indicated in the shorthand as shown in the left margin.

299 **BUSINESS VOCABULARY BUILDER**

unblemished Without defects or imperfections.
humid Moist; damp.
gradually A little at a time.

READING AND WRITING PRACTICE

300

re·ferred

ap

par

150/ ap

par

(115)

301

dis·cour·aged
re·cent·ly

mis·man·aged
loss

par

tem·po·rar·i·ly
qui·et·ly
look·out

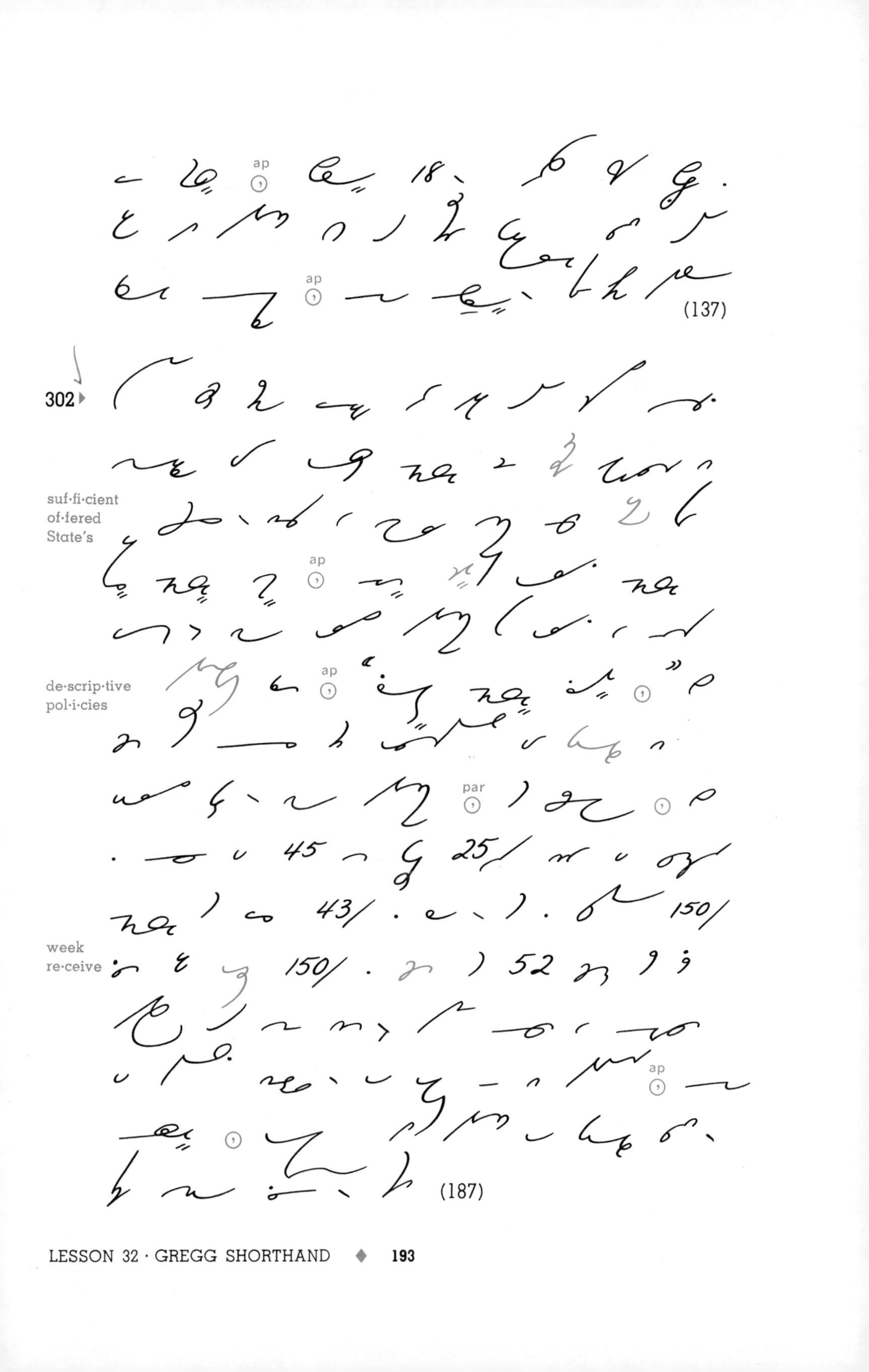

ap

ap

(137)

302

suf·fi·cient
of·fered
State's

ap

de·scrip·tive
pol·i·cies

ap

par

45 25

43 150

week
re·ceive

150 52

ap

(187)

303

an·swer
mys·tery

grad·u·al·ly
de·spite
out·side

par

par

ap

ap·pli·ance
in·stalled

(168)

304

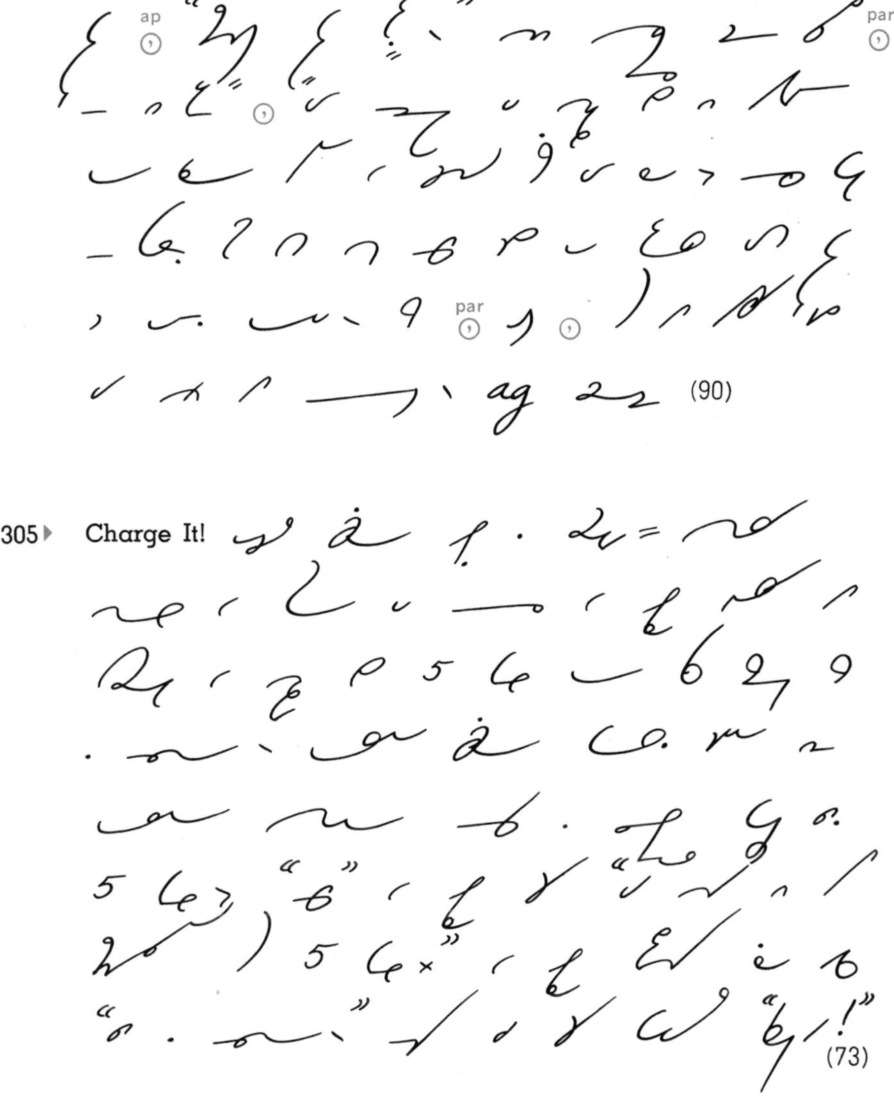

PRACTICE SUGGESTION: Turn to the brief-form chart on the back inside cover of your textbook and review all the brief forms you have studied through Lesson 31. If possible, try to spend a few minutes each day reading from this chart. This will help you to fix the brief forms firmly in your mind.

PRINCIPLES

306▸ Brief Forms • This is the last group of brief forms that you will have to learn.

govern	railroad	object
character	world	throughout

307▸ Word Beginnings For-, Fore- • The word beginnings *for-, fore-* are represented by *f*. The *f* is joined with an angle to *r* or *l* to indicate that it represents a word beginning. The *f* is disjoined if the following character is a vowel.

forgive	informed	forerunner
forget	force	forlorn
foreman	forth	forever
foremen	effort	forewarn

308▸ Word Beginning Fur- • The word beginning *fur-* is also represented by *f*.

furnish	further	furnace
furniture	furthermore	furlough

309▸ Ago in Phrases • In expressions of time, *ago* is represented by *g*.

weeks ago years ago long ago

days ago minutes ago months ago

BUILDING TRANSCRIPTION SKILLS

310▸ PUNCTUATION PRACTICE , series

When the last member of a series of three or more items is preceded by *and, or,* or *nor,* place a comma before the conjunction as well as between the other items.

For his birthday he received a shirt, a tie, and a pair of cuff links.

I saw him on July 18, on July 19, and again on July 30.

I need a girl to take dictation, to answer the telephone, and to greet callers.

ser ⊙ Each time a series occurs in the Reading and Writing Practice, it will be indicated in the shorthand as shown in the left margin.

311▸ BUSINESS VOCABULARY BUILDER

commuter One who travels back and forth regularly.

harassed Annoyed continually; worried.

maintenance Upkeep.

READING AND WRITING PRACTICE

312▸ Brief-Form Letter

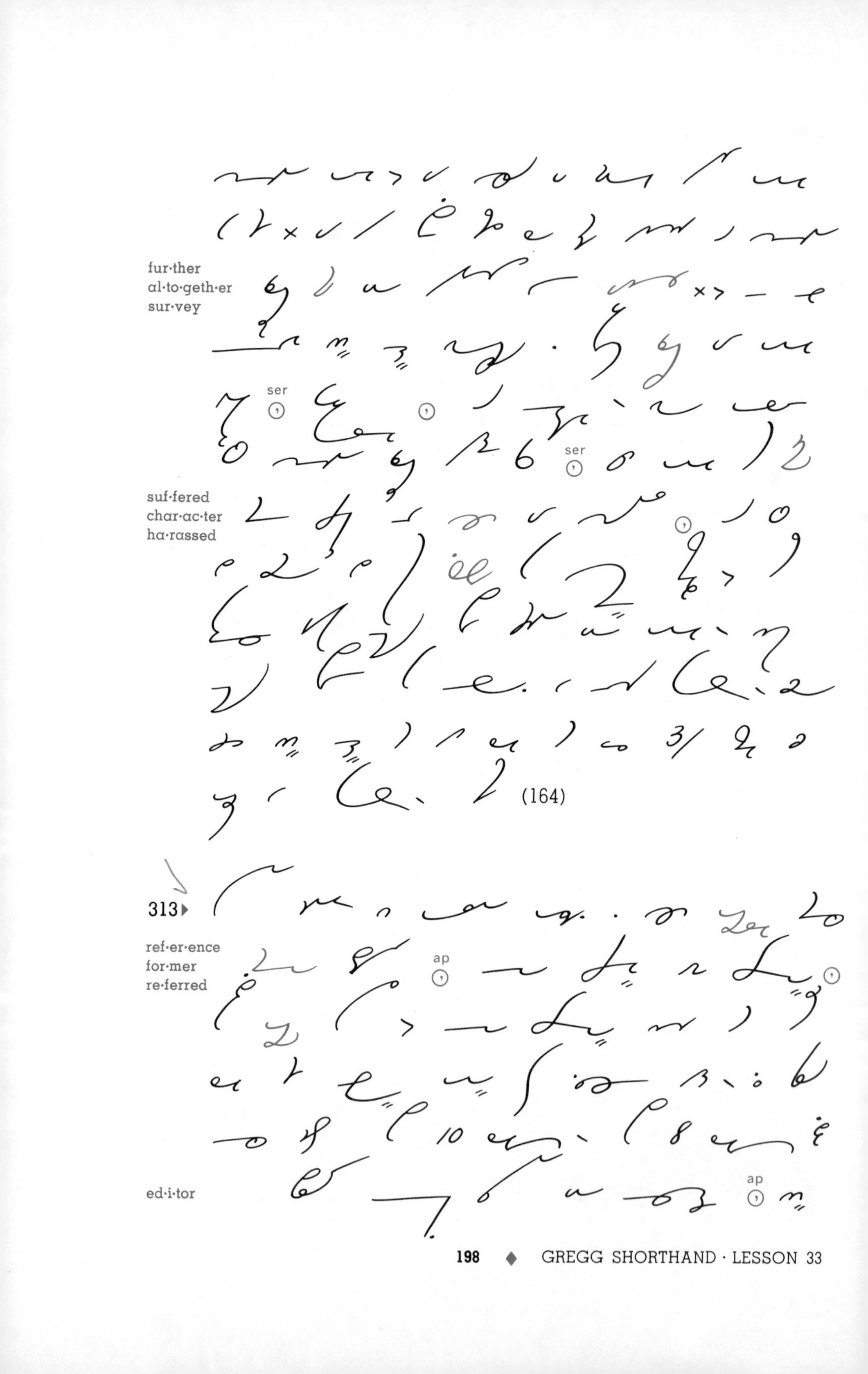

fur·ther
al·to·geth·er
sur·vey

ser

ser

suf·fered
char·ac·ter
ha·rassed

(164)

313▸

ref·er·ence
for·mer
re·ferred

ap

ed·i·tor

ap

ser

ser

ser

(163)

314

par

per·for·mance
stead·i·ly

par

par

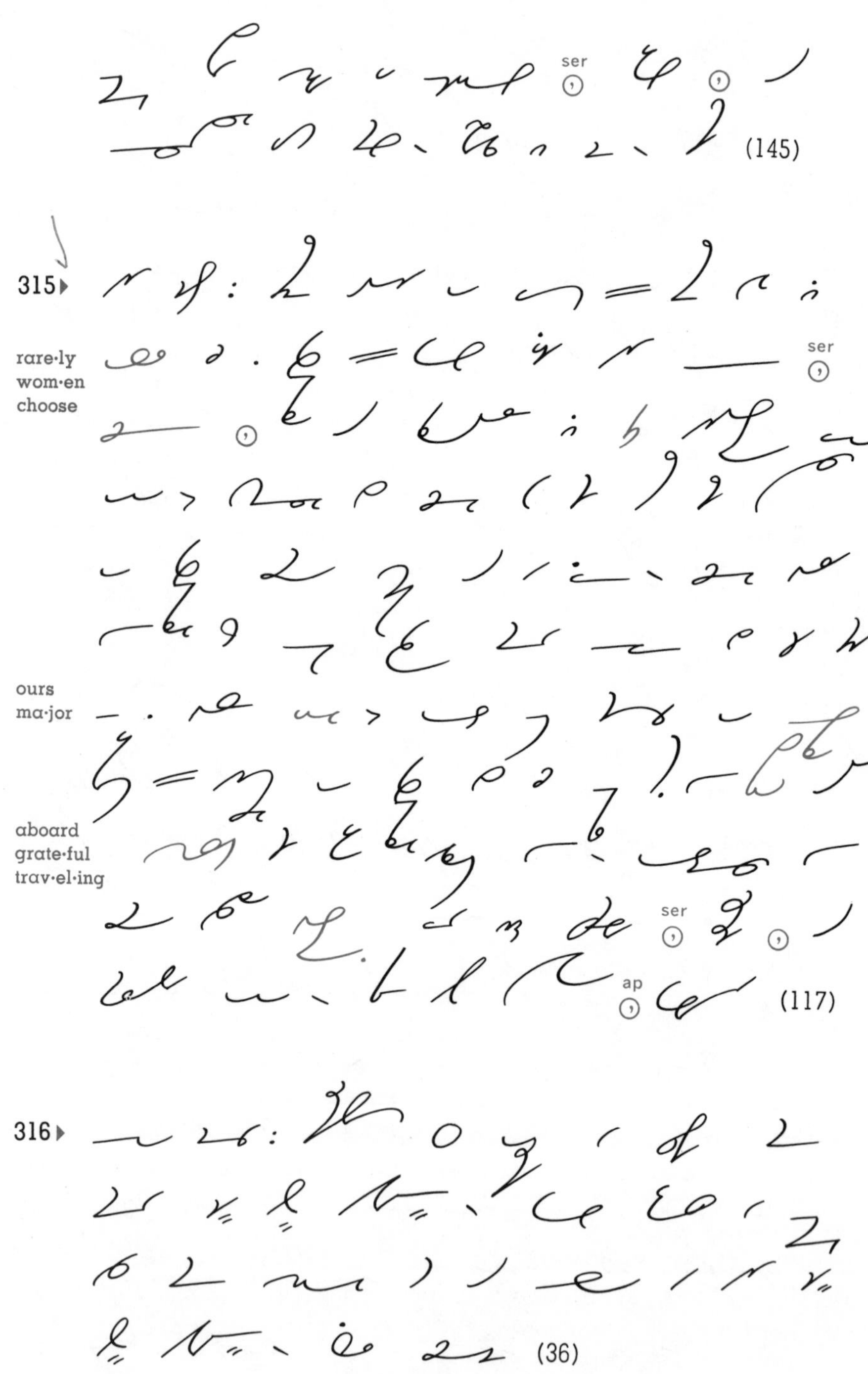

ser
(145)
315
rarely
women
choose
ser
ours
major
aboard
grateful
traveling
ser
ap
(117)
316
(36)

PRINCIPLES

317▸ Want in Phrases • In phrases, *want* is represented by the *nt* blend.

you want — I wanted — do you want
if you want — he wanted — who wanted

318▸ Ort • The *r* is omitted in the combination *ort.*

report — portable — sort
export — quart — resort

319▸ R Omitted in -ern, -erm • The *r* is omitted in the combinations *tern, term, thern, therm, dern, derm.*

turn — term — southern
return — termed — thermometer
western — determination — modern

320▸ Word Endings -cal, -cle • The word endings *-cal, -cle* are represented by a disjoined *k.*

logical — medical — physical

practical		particle		politically	
critical		articles		musically	

BUILDING TRANSCRIPTION SKILLS

321 ▸ BUSINESS VOCABULARY BUILDER

quarterly Four times a year.

executor A person designated to carry out the provisions of a will.

inevitable Incapable of being avoided; bound to happen.

READING AND WRITING PRACTICE

322 ▸

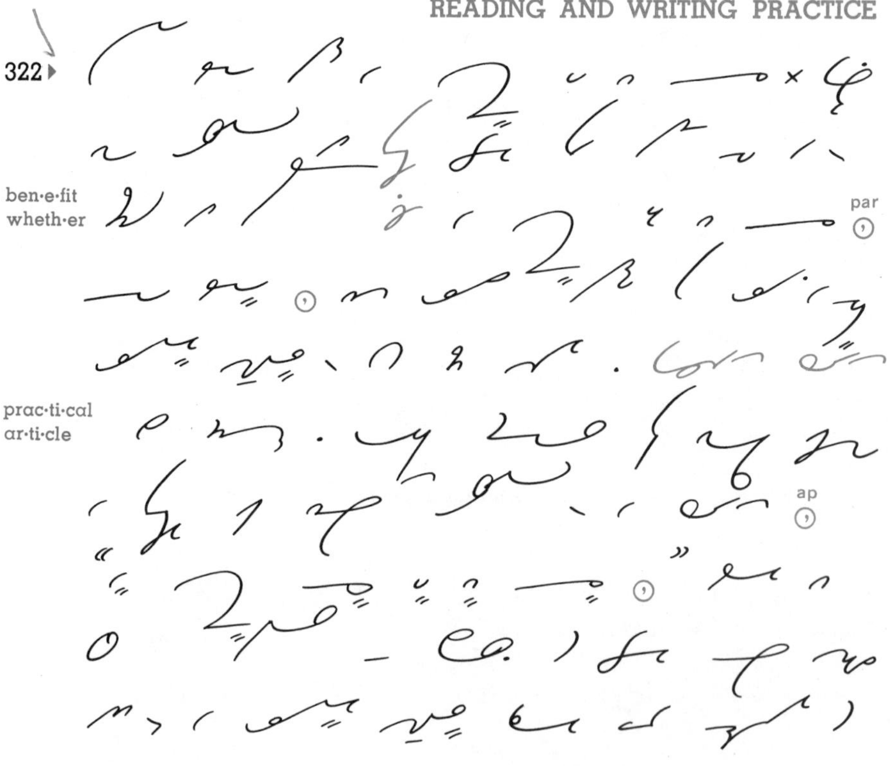

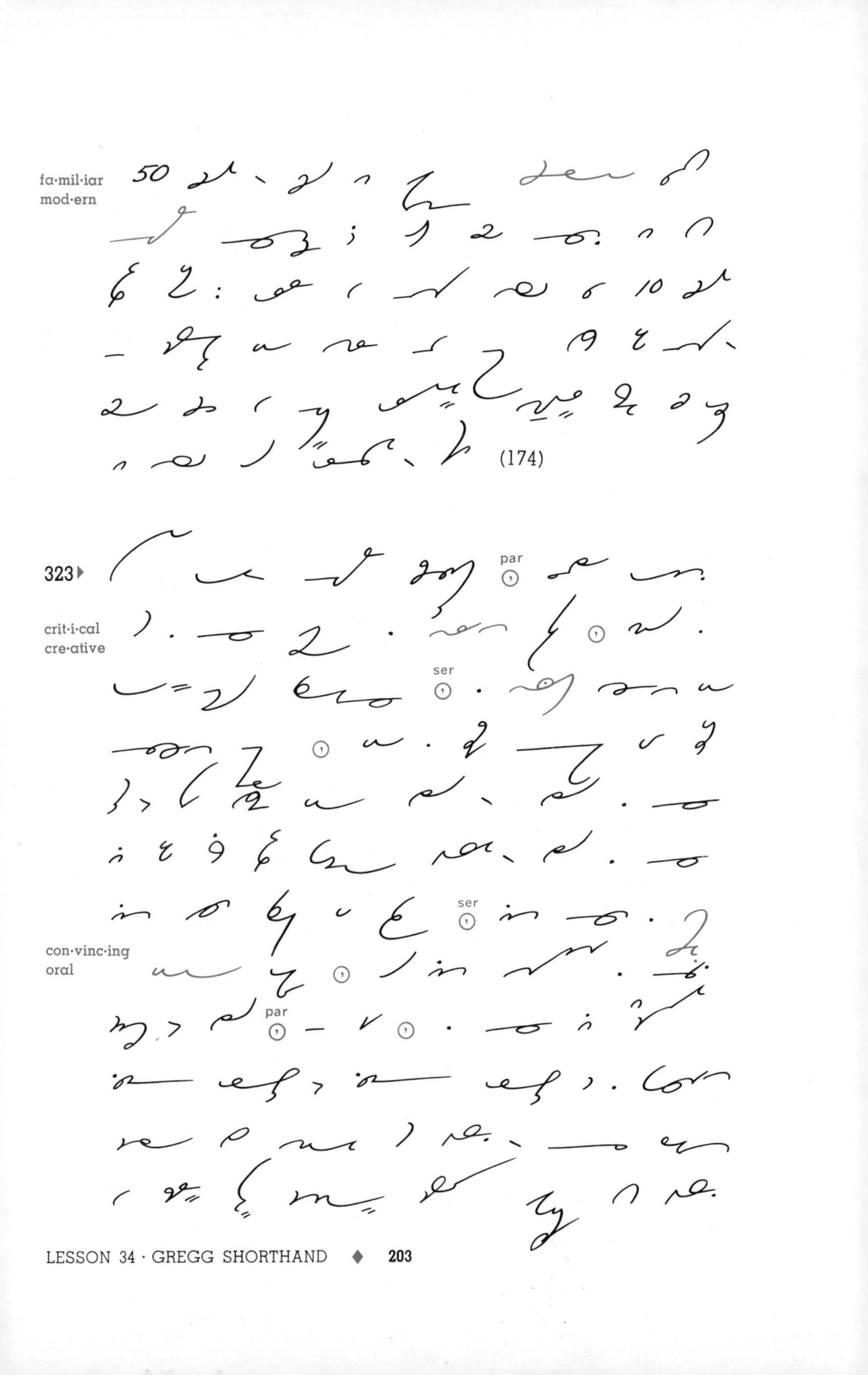

fa·mil·iar
mod·ern

(174)

323

crit·i·cal
cre·ative

par

ser

ser

con·vinc·ing
oral

par

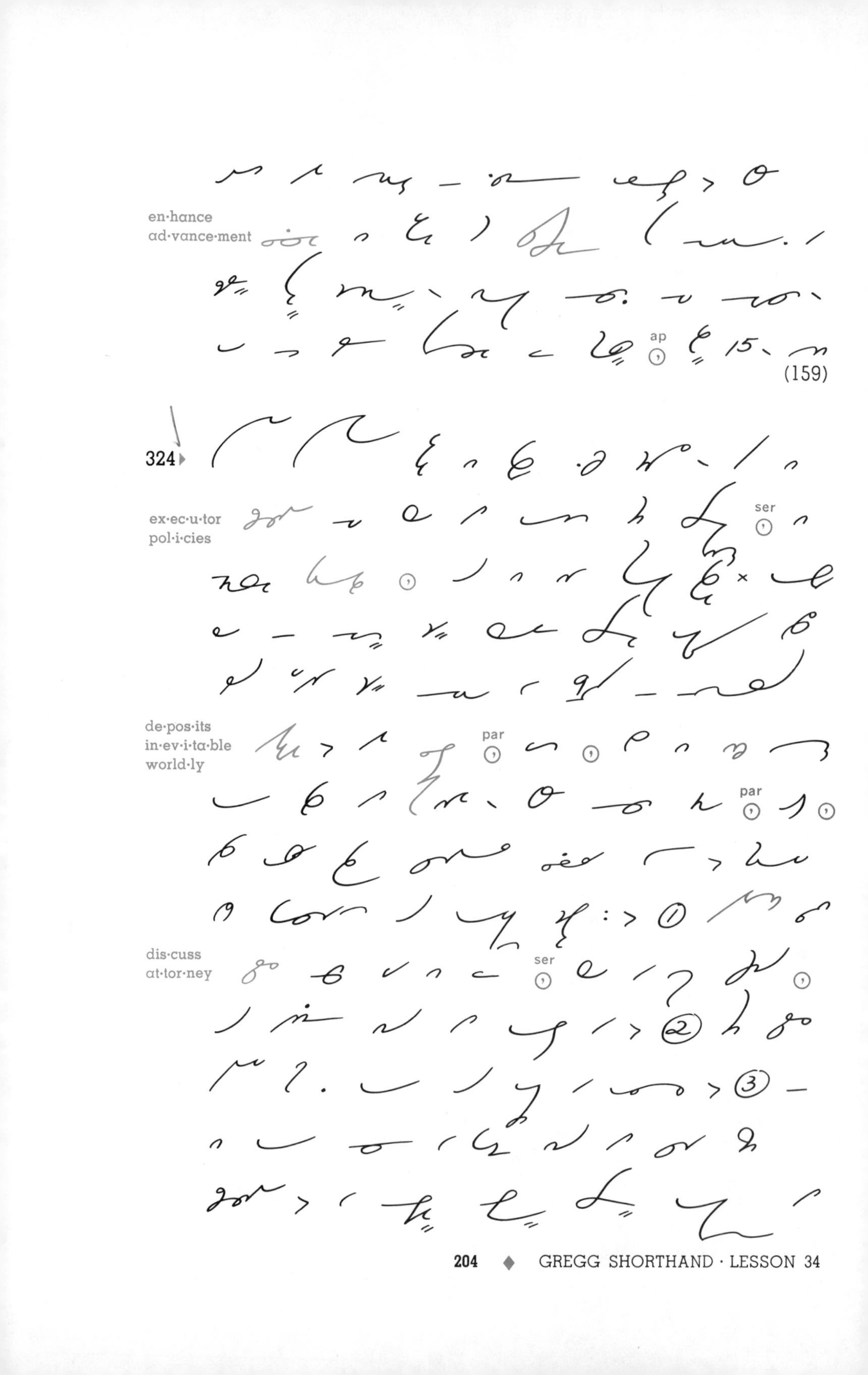

en·hance
ad·vance·ment

ap

(159)

324

ex·ec·u·tor
pol·i·cies

ser

de·pos·its
in·ev·i·ta·ble
world·ly

par

par

dis·cuss
at·tor·ney

ser

(171)

325 ap par ap

Por·ta·ble
ac·cept·ed

(144)

PERSONAL-USE CHECK LIST

Do you put your shorthand knowledge to work for you by:

1 Writing all your assignments in shorthand?
2 Making drafts of term papers and reports in shorthand?
3 Corresponding with friends in shorthand?
4 Keeping your diary in shorthand?
5 Making notes to yourself on things to do, people to see, and appointments to keep in shorthand?

PRINCIPLES

326▸ Word Beginnings Inter-, Intr-, Enter-, Entr- • The word beginnings *inter-, intr-, enter-, entr-* are represented by a disjoined *n.*

Inter-	**interests**	**interview**	**interval**
	interfere	**interrupt**	**internal**
	international	**interpret**	**intermediate**
Intr-	**introduce**	**introductory**	**intricate**
	introduction	**intruder**	**intrigue**
Enter-	**entering**	**entertain**	**enterprise**
Entr-	**entrance**	**entrances**	

327▸ Word Ending -ings • The word ending *-ings* is represented by a disjoined left *s.*

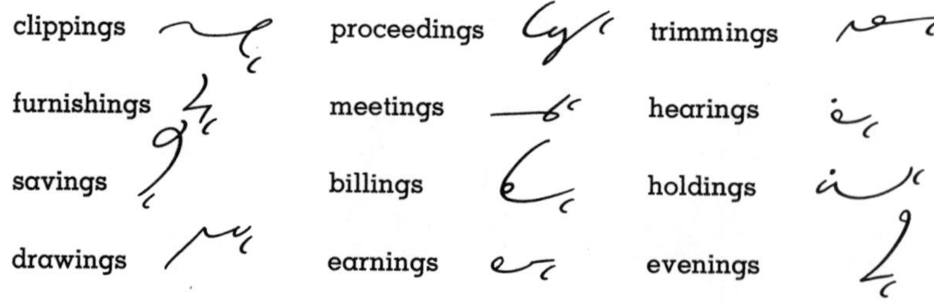

328 ▸ **Omission of Words in Phrases** • It is often possible to omit one or more unimportant words in a shorthand phrase. In the phrase *one of the*, for example, the word *of* is omitted; we write *one the*. When transcribing, the stenographer will insert *of*, as the phrase would make no sense without that word.

one of the	**some of them**	**during the past**
one of them	**up to date**	**will you please**
many of the	**able to say**	**in the future**
some of the	**in the world**	**in order to be**

BUILDING TRANSCRIPTION SKILLS

329 ▸ **SIMILAR-WORDS DRILL** **hear, here**

hear To gain knowledge of by hearing; to be informed.

I will hear his side of the story later.

here In this place.

Our staff is here to serve your needs.

330 ▸ **BUSINESS VOCABULARY BUILDER**

vandals Those who willfully destroy or damage the property of another.

intruders Those who enter by force, without permission.

misgivings Doubts.

READING AND WRITING PRACTICE

331 ▸

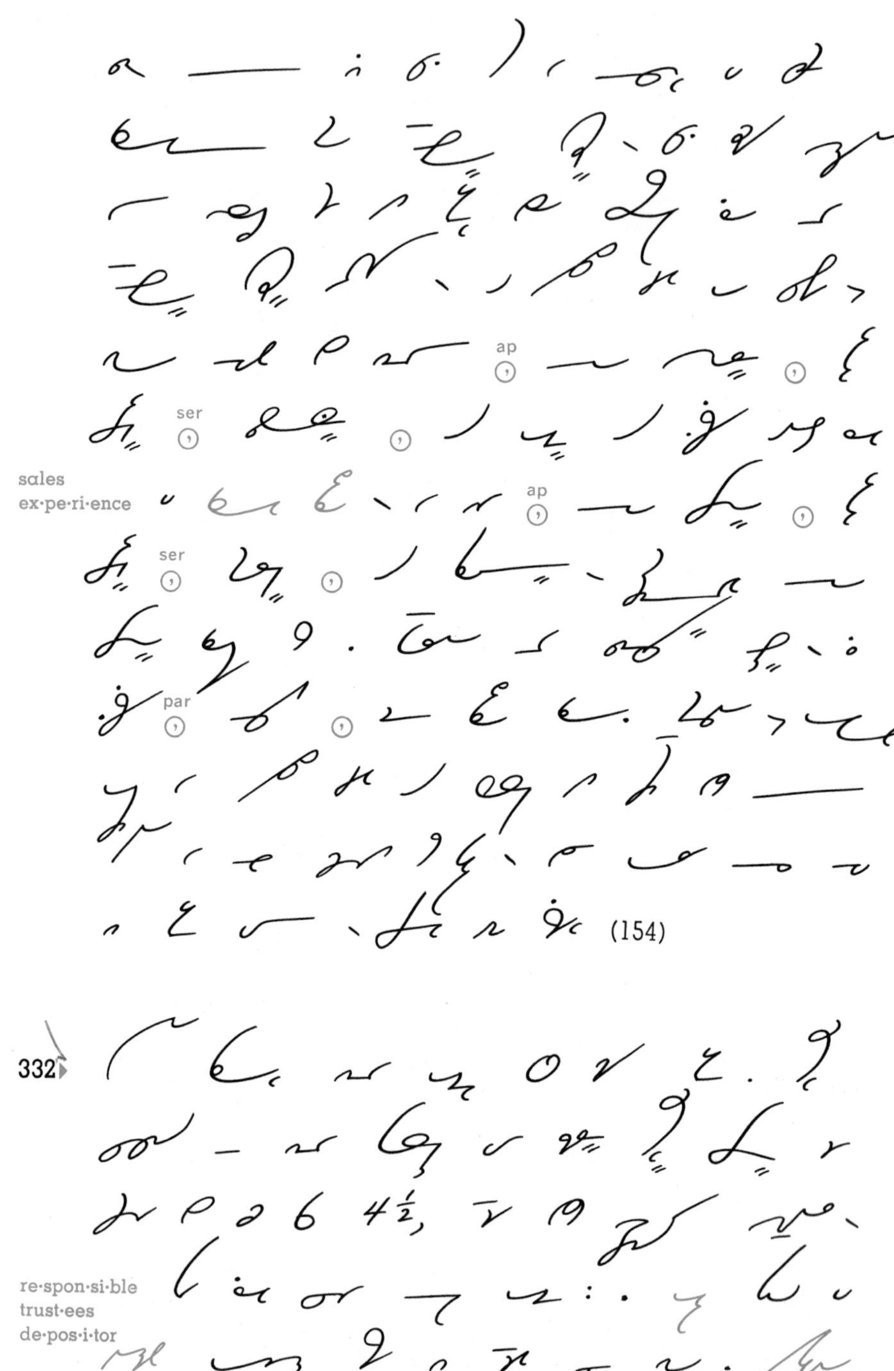

(154)

332

sales

ex·pe·ri·ence

ap

ser

par

re·spon·si·ble

trust·ees

de·pos·i·tor

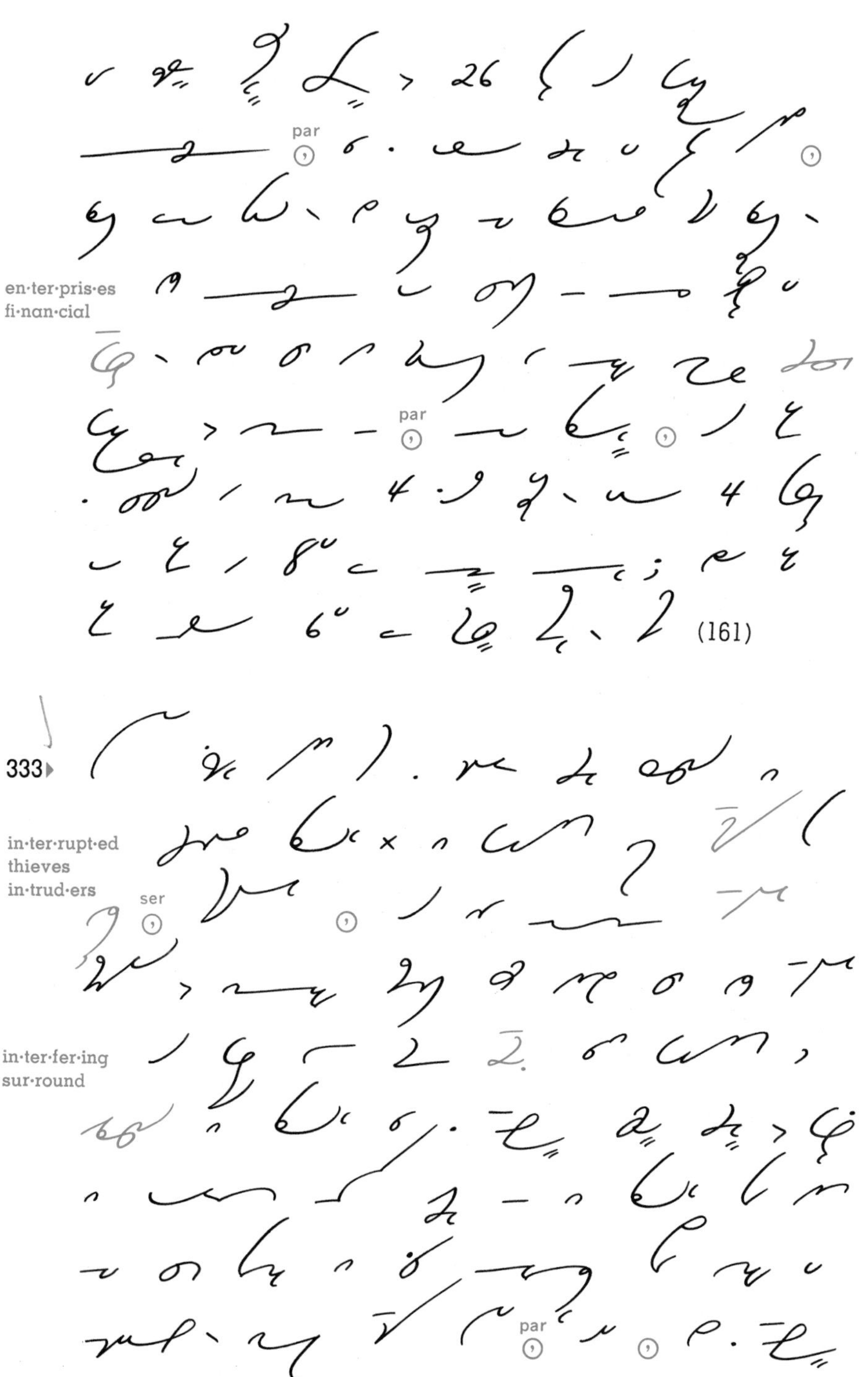
par
en·ter·pris·es
fi·nan·cial
par
(161)
333
in·ter·rupt·ed
thieves
in·trud·ers
ser
in·ter·fer·ing
sur·round
par

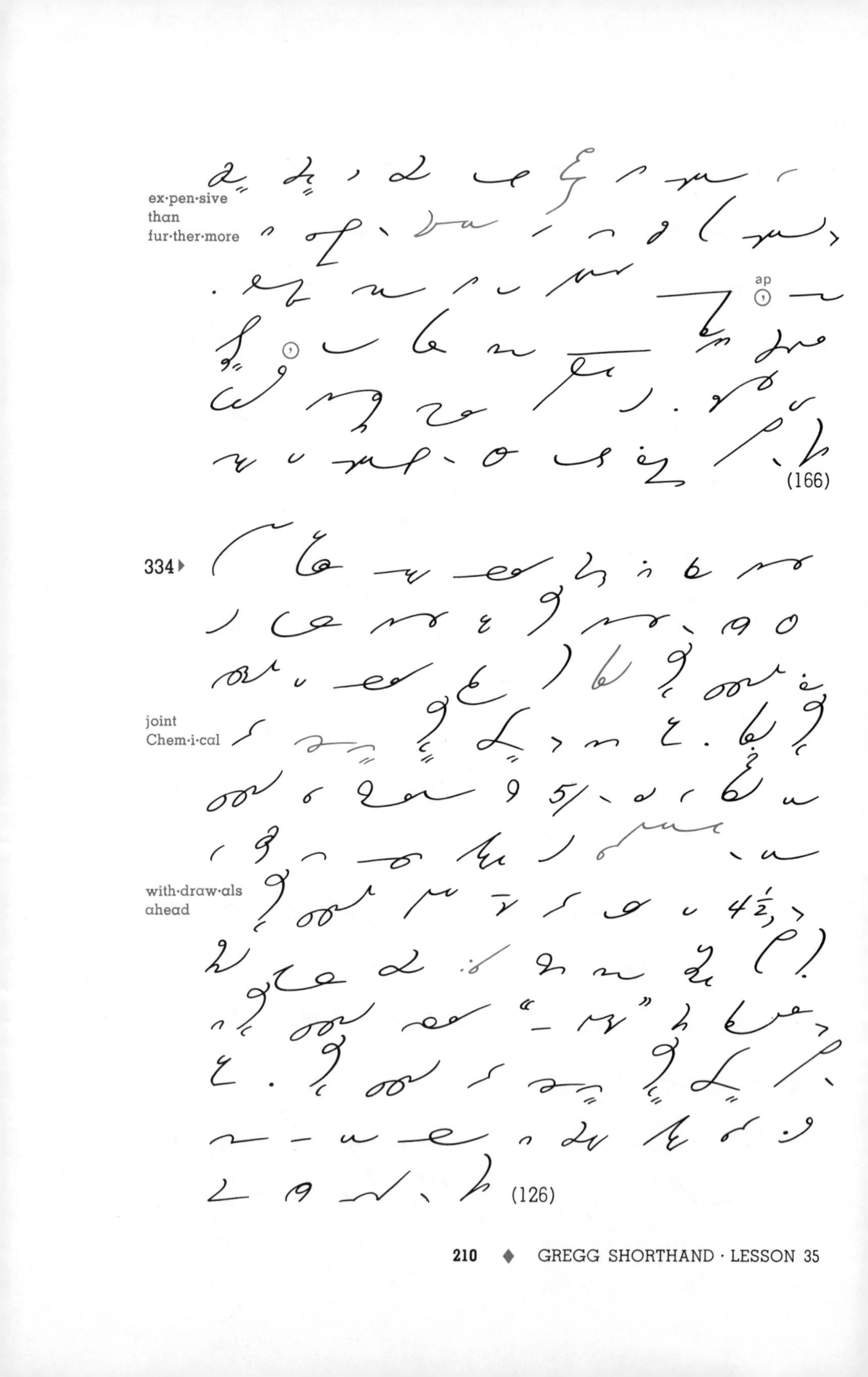

ex·pen·sive
than
fur·ther·more

ap

(166)

334

joint
Chem·i·cal

with·draw·als
ahead

(126)

335

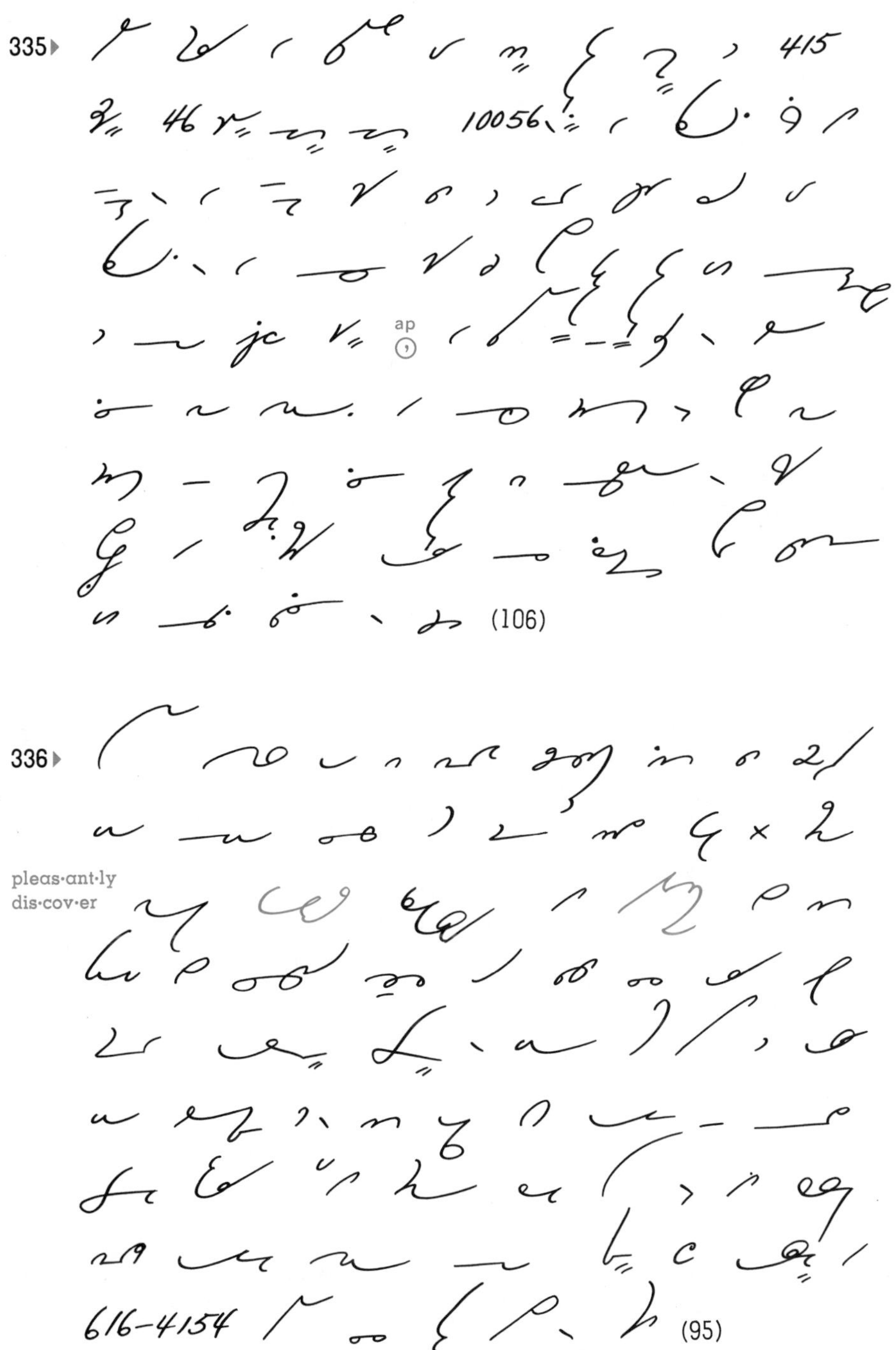
ap
415
10056
(106)
pleas·ant·ly
dis·cov·er
616-4154
(95)

336

RECALL

Lesson 36 is another breather. In Lesson 36 you will find the last principle of joining, a chart that contains a review of the shorthand devices you studied in Lessons 1 through 35, and a Reading and Writing Practice.

PRINCIPLES OF JOINING

337 The word endings *-ure* and *-ual* are represented by *r* and *l* except when those endings are preceded by a downstroke.

BUT

Nature, procedure, creature; pressure, treasure, insured.

BUT

Equal, gradual, annual; casual, usual.

ACCURACY PRACTICE

338 O On Sho Non

To write these combinations accurately:

a Keep the o hook narrow, being sure that the beginning and end are on the same level of writing, as indicated by the dotted line.

b Keep the o in *on* and *sho* parallel with the consonant, as indicated by the dotted line.

c Make the beginning of the o in *non* retrace the end of the first *n*.

d Avoid a point at the curved part indicated by the arrows.

Practice Drill

Of, know, low, own, home, hot, known, moan, shown.

339 ▸ **OO** **Noo** **Noom**

To write these combinations accurately:

a Keep the oo hook narrow and deep.

b Keep the beginning and end of the hook on the same level of writing.

c In *noo* and *noom,* keep the hook parallel with the straight line that precedes it.

d In *noom,* retrace the beginning of the *m* on the bottom of the oo hook.

e Avoid a point at the places indicated by arrows.

Practice Drill

You-your, yours truly, you would, to-too-two, do, noon, moon, mood.

340 ▸ **Hard** **Hailed**

To write these combinations accurately:

a Give the end of the *r* and the end of the *l* a lift upward.

b Do not lift the end too soon, or the strokes may resemble the *nd*, *md* combinations.

Practice Drill

Neared, feared, cheered, dared, hold, sold, bold.

341▸ Recall Chart • The following chart contains a review of the shorthand devices you studied in previous lessons. It contains 90 brief forms, words, and phrases. Can you read the entire chart in 5 minutes?

BRIEF FORMS

1

2

3

PHRASES

4

5

WORDS

6

7

8

9

10

11

12

WORDS						
13						
14						
15						

BUILDING TRANSCRIPTION SKILLS

342 ▸ BUSINESS VOCABULARY BUILDER

scores A great many; a large number.
voluminous Very big; having great bulk.
intolerable Unable to be endured.

READING AND WRITING PRACTICE

343 ▸ The Complete Treatment

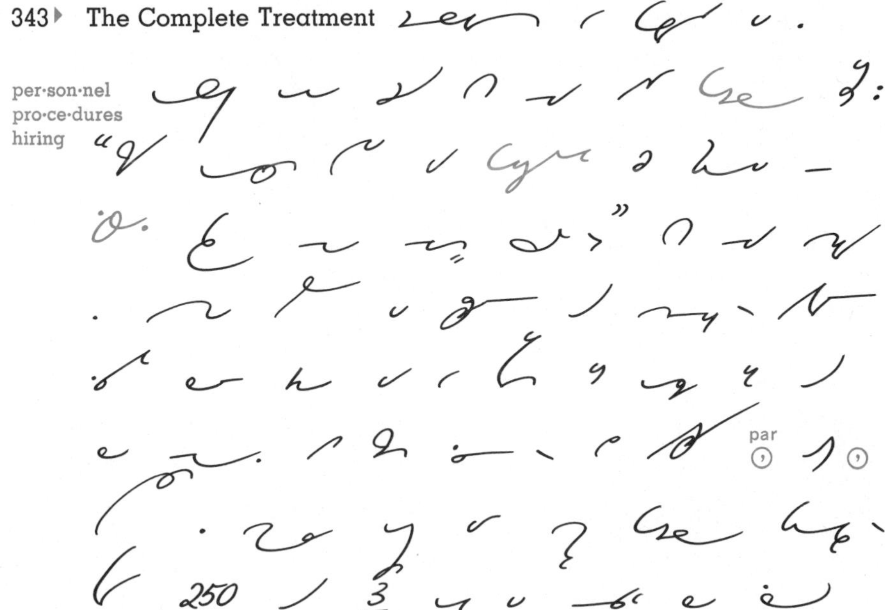

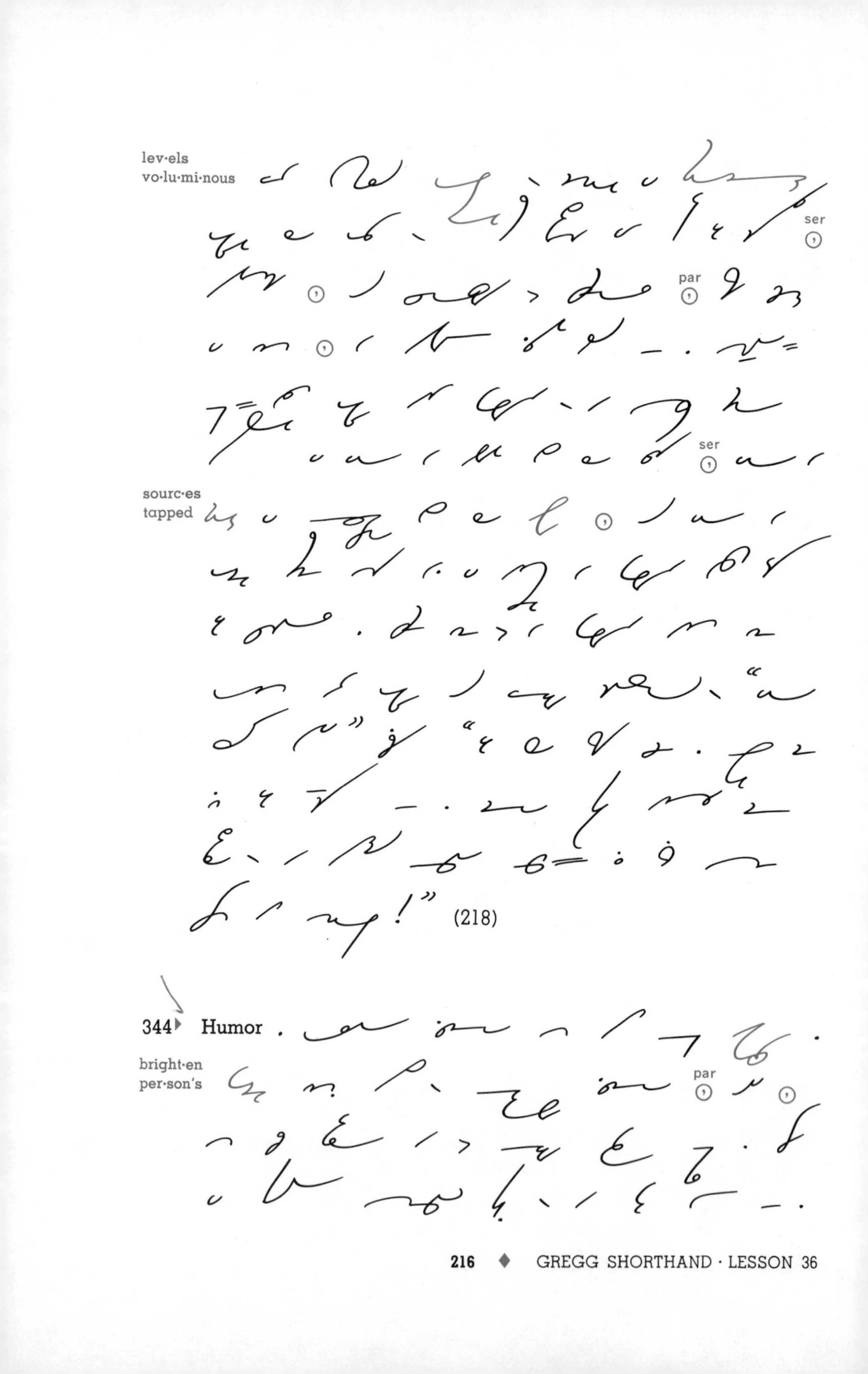

lev·els
vo·lu·mi·nous

ser

par

ser

sourc·es
tapped

(218)

344 Humor

bright·en
per·son's

par

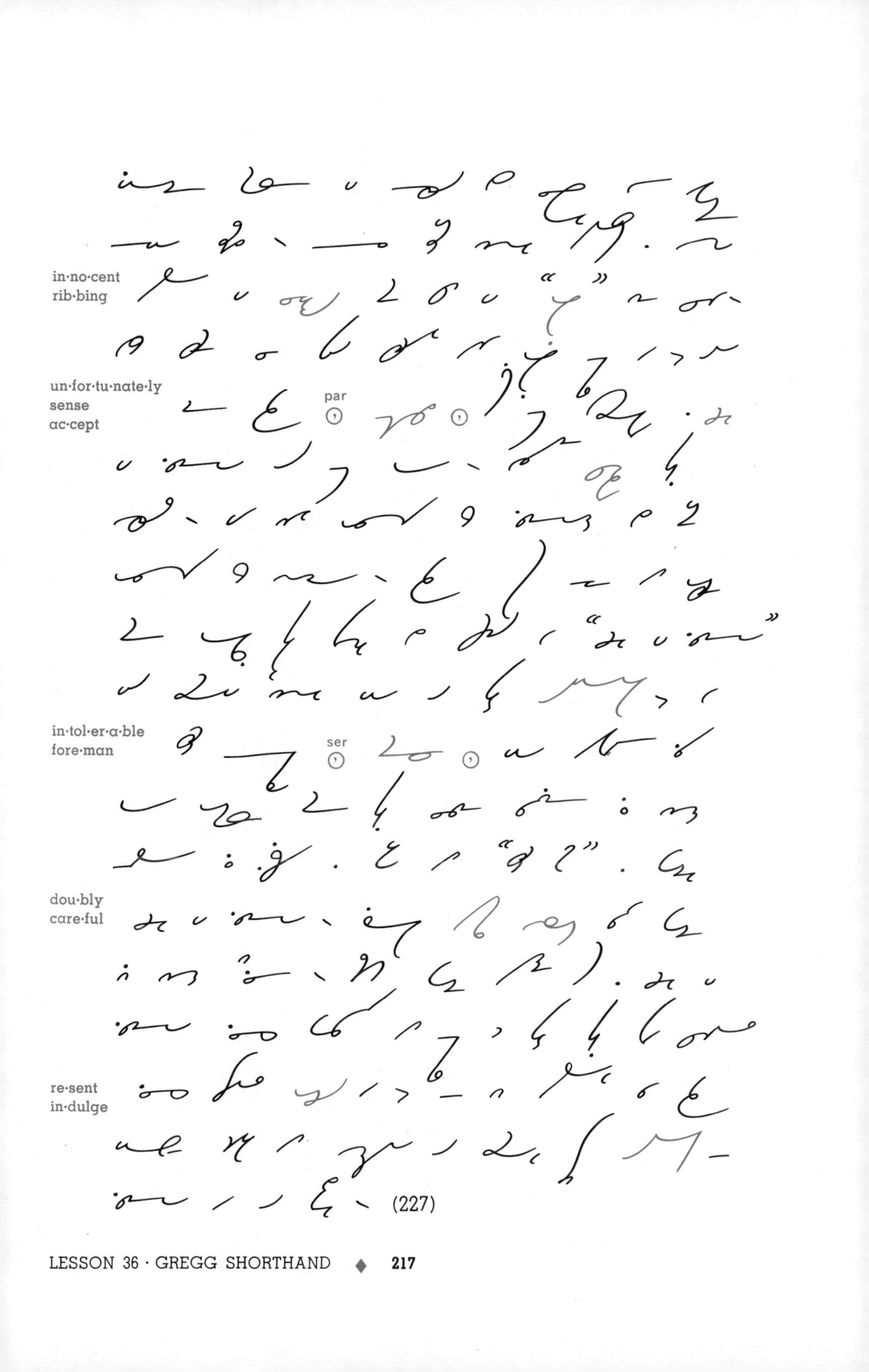

in·no·cent
rib·bing

un·for·tu·nate·ly
sense
ac·cept

par

in·tol·er·a·ble
fore·man

ser

dou·bly
care·ful

re·sent
in·dulge

(227)

▶ Some people say that if you can write 80 words a minute, you can hold a secretarial job. Others maintain that 100 words a minute is the minimum speed. Still others consider a secretary ill-trained if she cannot write 120 or 140 words a minute.

Actually, the term "words a minute" can be misleading. In order to understand what it means, we must know what kind of material was dictated and for what length of time. Simple, short business letters can be taken by the secretary at much faster speeds than long, technical ones. And the rate of 120 words a minute means little if the dictation was for only a minute and on simple material. You can say that you are a 100- or 120-word writer only if you can write for a sustained period of several minutes at that rate on average material that you have never seen before.

Why do we make such a big thing of "words a minute"? No executive sits with a stopwatch in his hand to time the dictation. He probably couldn't even guess the speed of his dictation. Actually, "words a minute" is most meaningful as a *measurement of progress* while you're in training. If you are writing 60 words a minute, you must have a goal if you are to be spurred on—a goal, say, of 80 words a minute. The 80-word writer has a goal of 100. In order to push you to greater limits, your shorthand instructor uses a stopwatch to time the dictation.

Does a speed of 80 words a minute mean that 80 actual words are dictated every 60 seconds? Not necessarily. What about short words like "a," "of," and "to" and long words like "incomprehensible" and "tintinnabulation" – should they count the same? No. In order to equalize the short and long words, the sounds uttered by the dictator are broken down into syllables and the speed is actually measured in syllables. Studies have shown that for standard dictation a typical word contains 1.4 syllables. Thus 80 words a minute is 112 syllables a minute (80 x 1.4).

Now, after all this discussion, what is an "adequate" speed for a shorthand writer? You will hear from time to time that the average dictation speed in the business office is about 80 words a minute. And studies have shown this to be true. But note the word "average." If you are going to take the dictation of an executive whose rate *averages* 80 words a minute, you will need to be able to write about 100 words a minute, because a good part of the dictation will be at more than 80. If you work for an executive whose average speed is 100 words a minute, you will need a speed of about 120 words a minute. And so on.

Studies have shown that only the secretary who can write for a sustained period at 120 words a minute can be reasonably sure that she can handle the dictation of every executive.

The point is this: Don't be satisfied with a minimum speed of 80 words a minute just because someone told you that's all you need. Continue to build your skill to the highest degree possible. Aim for a speed of 120 words a minute or more so that you can be sure of handling the dictation of any executive who might become your employer. You will never be sorry that you built this reserve power for the inevitable emergencies.

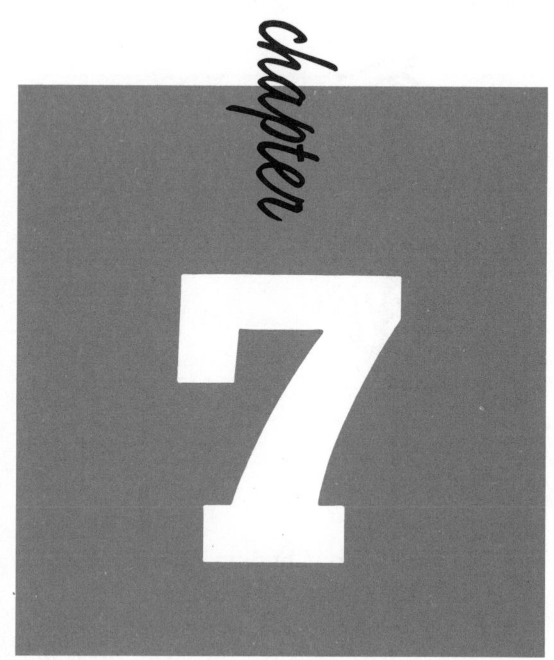

WHAT IS AN "ADEQUATE" SHORTHAND SKILL?

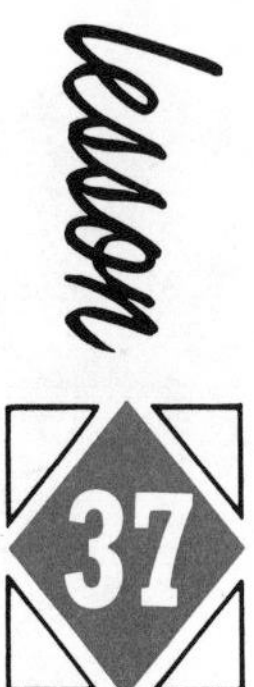

PRINCIPLES

345▸ Word Ending -ingly • The word ending *-ingly* is represented by a disjoined e circle.

knowingly **accordingly** **exceedingly**

willingly **surprisingly** **increasingly**

346▸ Word Beginnings Im-, Em- • The word beginnings *im-*, *em-* are represented by *m*.

Im- **impress** **improve** **impossible**

import **impartial** **imposing**

Em- **employ** **embrace** **emphasis**

embarrass **emphatically** **empire**

347▸ Im-, Em- Followed by a Vowel • When *im-*, *em-* are followed by a vowel, they are written in full.

immoral **emotional** **immodest**

348▸ Omission of Minor Vowel • When two vowel sounds come together, the minor vowel may be omitted.

courteous **genuine** **theory**

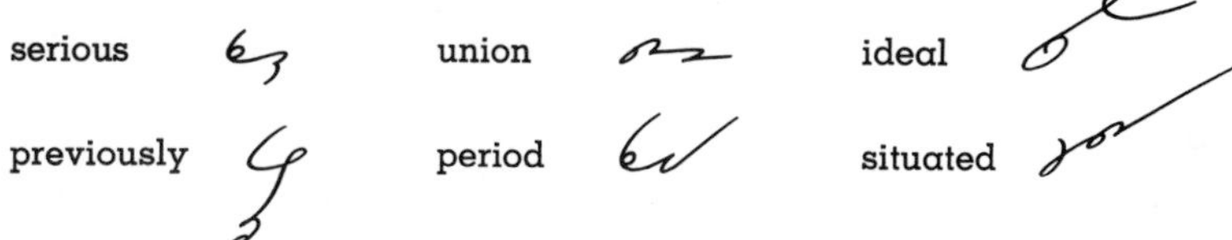

BUILDING TRANSCRIPTION SKILLS

349▸ PUNCTUATION PRACTICE , *if* clause

A frequent error made by the beginning transcriber is the failure to make a complete sentence. In most cases the incomplete sentence is a dependent or subordinate clause introduced by a word such as *if, when,* or *as.* The dependent or subordinate clause deceives the transcriber because it would be a complete sentence if it were not introduced by a word such as *if;* therefore, it requires another clause to complete the thought.

The dependent or subordinate clause often signals the coming of the main clause by means of a subordinate conjunction. The commonest subordinating conjunctions are *if, as,* and *when.* Other subordinating conjunctions are *though, although, whether, unless, because, since, while, where, after, whenever, until, before,* and *now.* In this lesson you will consider clauses introduced by *if.*

A subordinate clause introduced by *if* and followed by a main clause is separated from the main clause by a comma.

If you complete the work before five o'clock, you may leave.

If you would like to have more information about our products, please fill out and return the enclosed card.

if ⊙ Each time a subordinate clause beginning with *if* occurs in the Reading and Writing Practice, it will be indicated in the shorthand as shown in the left margin.

350▸ BUSINESS VOCABULARY BUILDER

impartially In a manner not favoring one side more than the other.

implement (verb) To carry out; to put into effect.

impair To harm.

imperative Not to be avoided; obligatory.

351

if

se·ri·ous
im·per·son·al·ly
im·par·tial·ly

ser

courte·ous
em·ploy·ee

971-1144

if

(144)

352

if

ex·er·cis·es
ide·al

ap

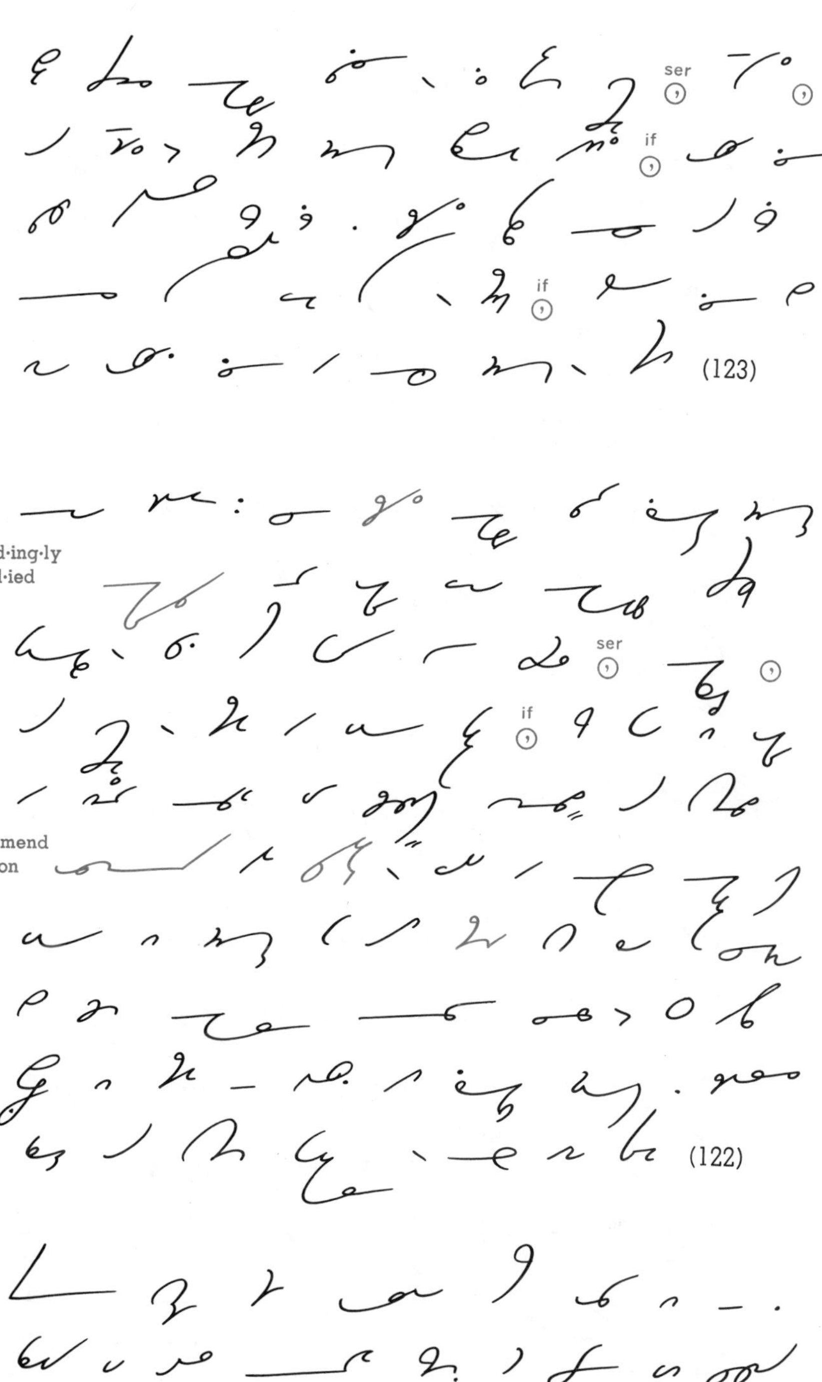

ser
if
if
(123)
353
ex·ceed·ing·ly
em·bod·ied
ser
if
rec·om·mend
adop·tion
ef·fect
(122)
354

be·com·ing
im·pa·tient
im·pair

le·gal
pro·ceed·ings
em·phat·i·cal·ly

par

if

if

law·yers
af·fect·ed

(161)

355

em·bar·rass·ing
com·plaint

par

dis·cour·te·ous
un·wit·ting·ly

par

par

re·dou·ble
cour·te·sy

ap

(164)

SHORTHAND NOTEBOOK CHECK LIST

Your shorthand notebook is another important tool of your trade. Do you:

1 Use a notebook with a spiral binding so that the pages always lie flat as you write?

2 Write on the front cover your name and the first and last dates on which you use the notebook?

3 Place a rubber band around the used portion of your notebook so that it opens automatically to the first blank page?

4 Date the first page of each day's dictation at the bottom of the page for quick and convenient reference — just as a stenographer in an office would do?

5 Check before class to see that there are sufficient pages remaining in your notebook for the day's dictation and, if not, supply yourself with a second notebook so that you will not run out of paper in the middle of dictation?

PRINCIPLES

356▸ Word Ending -ship • The word ending *-ship* is represented by a disjoined *sh*.

relationship	**membership**	**steamship**
friendship	**township**	**scholarships**

357▸ Word Beginning Sub- • The word beginning *sub-* is represented by *s*.

submit	**substantial**	**sublet**
subscribe	**subdivision**	**suburb**

358▸ Joining of Hook and Circle Vowels • When a hook and a circle vowel come together, they are written in the order in which they are pronounced.

poet	**poetry**	**folio**
poem	**radios**	**portfolio**

BUILDING TRANSCRIPTION SKILLS

359▸ PUNCTUATION PRACTICE **, *as* clause**

A subordinate clause introduced by *as* and followed by the main clause is separated from the main clause by a comma.

As you can well imagine, an effective credit letter is not an easy one to write.

As you may have read in the newspapers, Frank Smith was made president of the New York Publishing Company.

as ⊙ Each time a subordinate clause beginning with *as* occurs in the Reading and Writing Practice, it will be indicated in the shorthand as shown in the left margin.

360 ▸ **BUSINESS VOCABULARY BUILDER**

substantial Considerable; important.

suburbs A small community outside a big city.

subsidiaries Companies wholly controlled by other companies.

READING AND WRITING PRACTICE

361 ▸

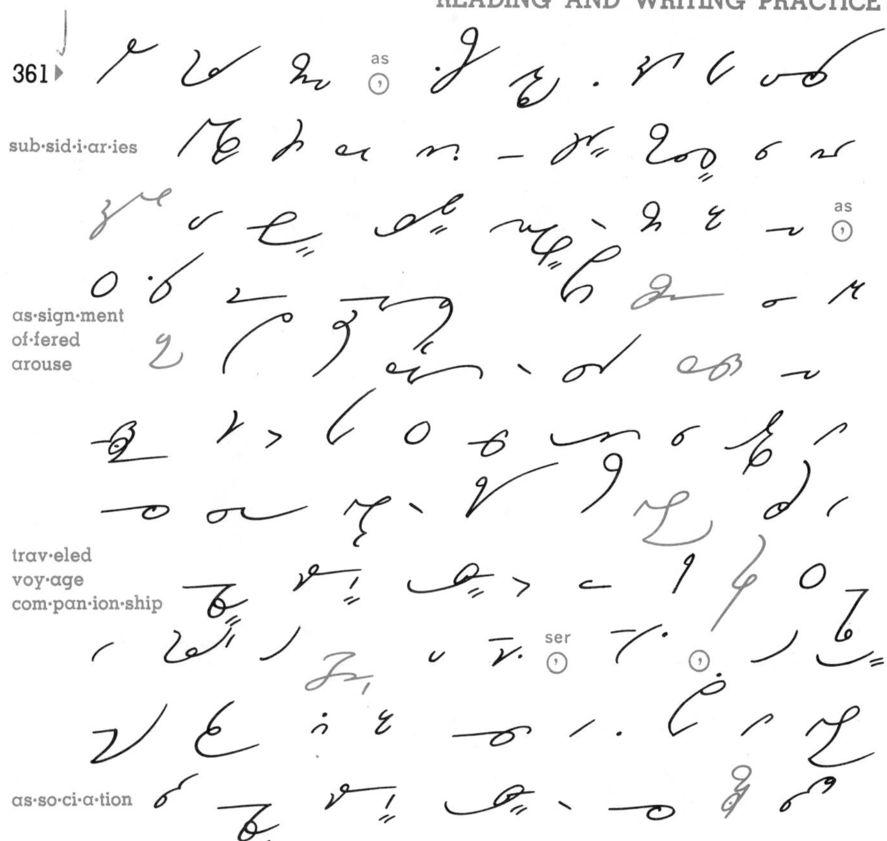

led

if

(169)

362

as

sub·urbs
de·sir·able

as

if

(162)

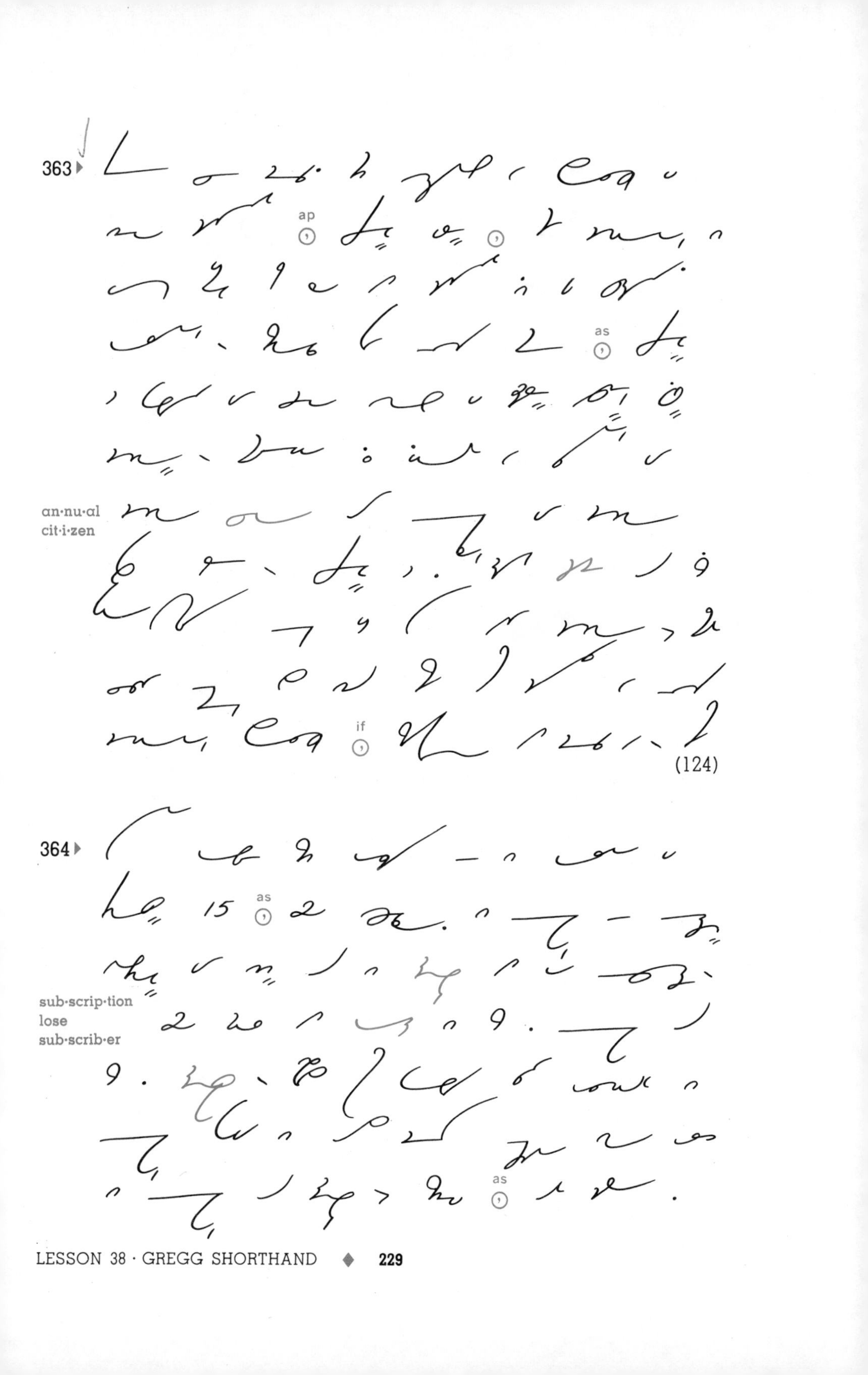

363

ap

as

an·nu·al
cit·i·zen

if

(124)

364

as

sub·scrip·tion
lose
sub·scrib·er

as

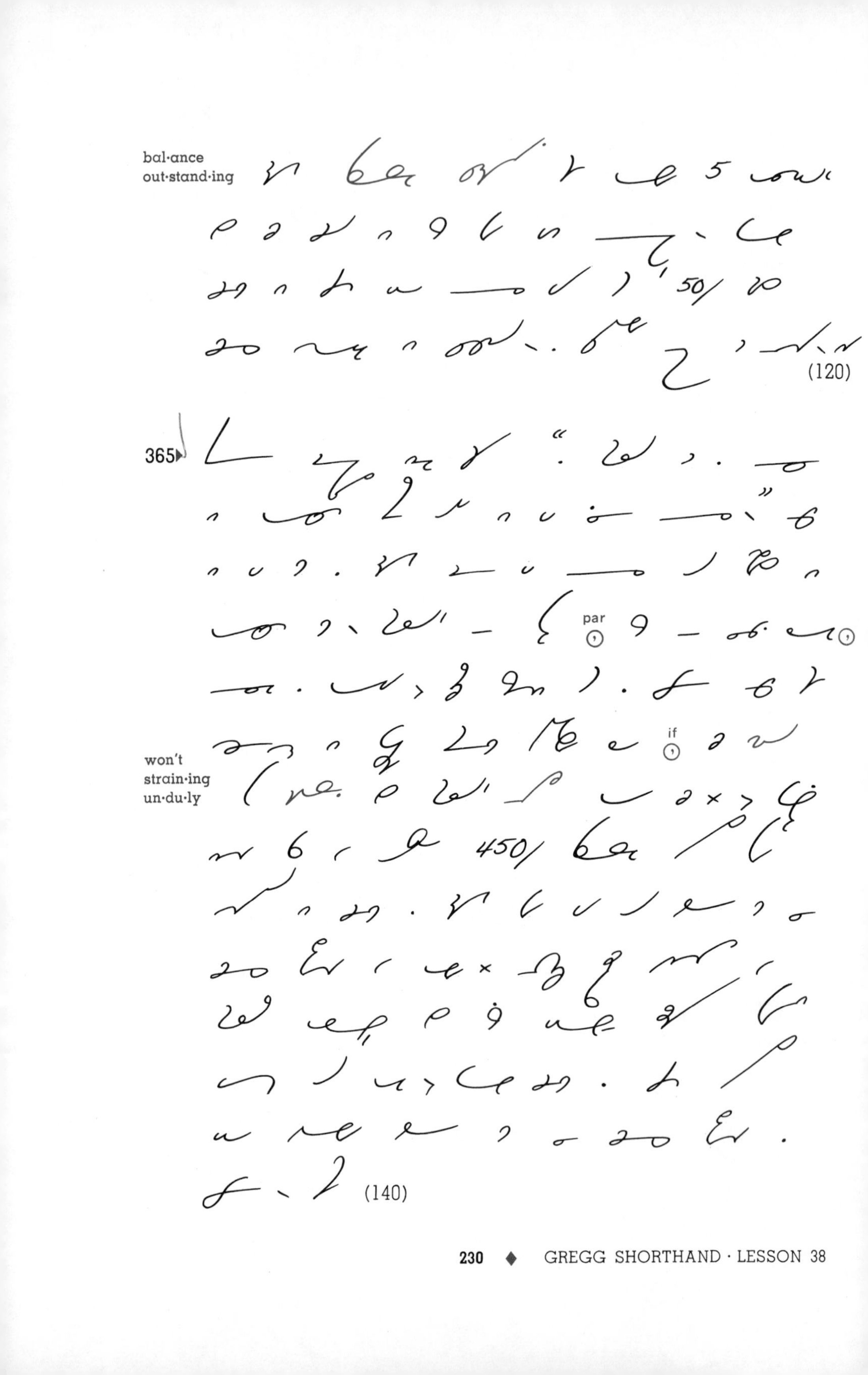

bal·ance
out·stand·ing

(120)

365

par

if

won't
strain·ing
un·du·ly

(140)

PRINCIPLES

366▸ Word Ending -rity • The word ending *-rity* is represented by a disjoined *r.*

sincerity majority celebrity
security minority prosperity
maturity popularity authorities

367▸ Word Ending -lity • The word ending *-lity* is represented by a disjoined *l.*

ability vitality quality
facility locality responsibility
utility personality reliability

368▸ Word Ending -lty • The word ending *-lty* is also represented by a disjoined *l.*

faculty loyalty penalty

369▸ Word Endings -self, -selves • The word ending *-self* is represented by *s; -selves,* by *ses.*

-self herself myself yourself

	himself		itself		oneself	
-selves	themselves		yourselves		ourselves	

BUILDING TRANSCRIPTION SKILLS

370▸ PUNCTUATION PRACTICE , *when* clause

A subordinate clause introduced by *when* and followed by the main clause is separated from the main clause by a comma.

When I was in Chicago last week, I visited your company.

When you delay paying your account after it is due, you endanger your credit standing.

when ⊙ Each time a subordinate clause beginning with *when* occurs in the Reading and Writing Practice, it will be indicated in the shorthand as shown in the left margin.

371▸ BUSINESS VOCABULARY BUILDER

casualty Victim of an accident.

precedents Similar events that took place in the past.

implicitly Without reservation; absolutely.

READING AND WRITING PRACTICE

372▸

thrown

ca·su·al·ty

when

al·ready
loss·es
em·ploy·ees

par

rea·son·ably
in·stalled

when

(160)

373

its
main·tained

par

mu·si·cians
sense

as

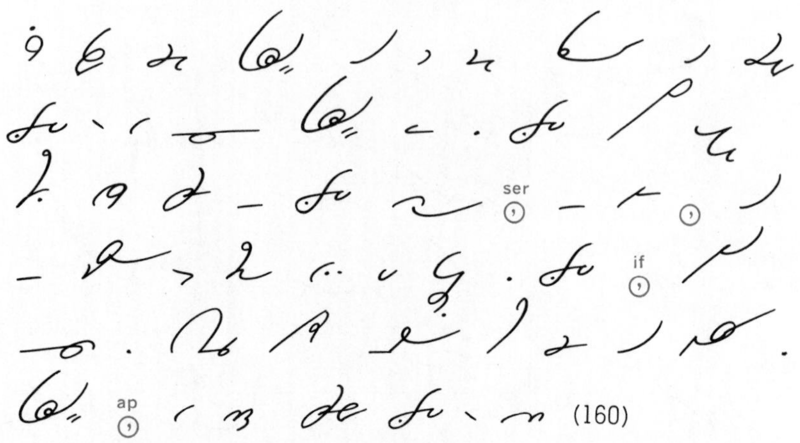

374 The Qualities of Leadership

when

de·ci·sion
prec·e·dents
pop·u·lar·i·ty

(2)

when

(3)

goal
af·fect

judg·ment
im·plic·it·ly

if

when

(284)

375 ▸ Thought for the Day

(55)

PRINCIPLES

376 ▸ Abbreviated Words—in Families • Many long words may be abbreviated in shorthand by dropping the endings. This device is also used in longhand, as *Jan.* for *January.* The extent to which you use this device will depend on your familiarity with the words and with the subject matter of the dictation. When in doubt, write it out! The ending of a word is not dropped when a special shorthand word-ending form has been provided, such as *-lity.*

Notice how many of the words written with this abbreviating device fall naturally into families of similar endings.

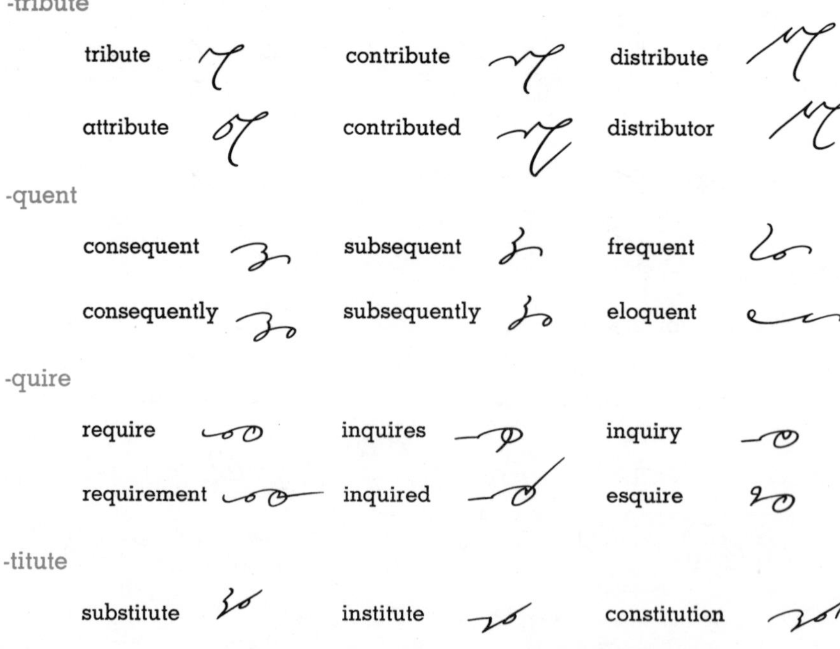

-titude

aptitude **gratitude** **latitude**

BUILDING TRANSCRIPTION SKILLS

377 ▸ PUNCTUATION PRACTICE , introductory

A comma is used to separate the subordinate clause from a following main clause. You have already studied the application of this rule to subordinate clauses introduced by *if, as,* and *when.* Here are examples of subordinate clauses introduced by other subordinating conjunctions.

Although the car cost more than he had planned to pay, he bought it.

Before you sign the contract, you should discuss it with your lawyer.

Unless I hear from you by March 18, I shall have to refer your account to a collection agency.

While I am in Chicago on business, I shall stop in to see my uncle.

A comma is also used after introductory words or phrases such as *furthermore, on the contrary,* and *for instance.*

Furthermore, the report was not prepared in the proper form.

On the contrary, you are not the one who made the mistake.

intro ⊙ Each time a subordinate (or introductory) word, phrase, or clause other than one beginning with *if, as,* or *when* occurs in the Reading and Writing Practice, it will be indicated in the shorthand as shown in the left margin.

NOTE: If the subordinate clause or other introductory expression follows the main clause, the comma is usually not necessary.

I am enclosing a stamped envelope for your convenience in sending me your check.

378 ▸ BUSINESS VOCABULARY BUILDER

subsequent Later.

aptitude tests Tests that help to determine a person's suitability for a given line of work.

constitute To make up.

READING AND WRITING PRACTICE

379 ar·ti·cle at·ti·tudes sec·re·tar·ies

ser

as

par

intro

intro

(131)

380

ap

par

intro

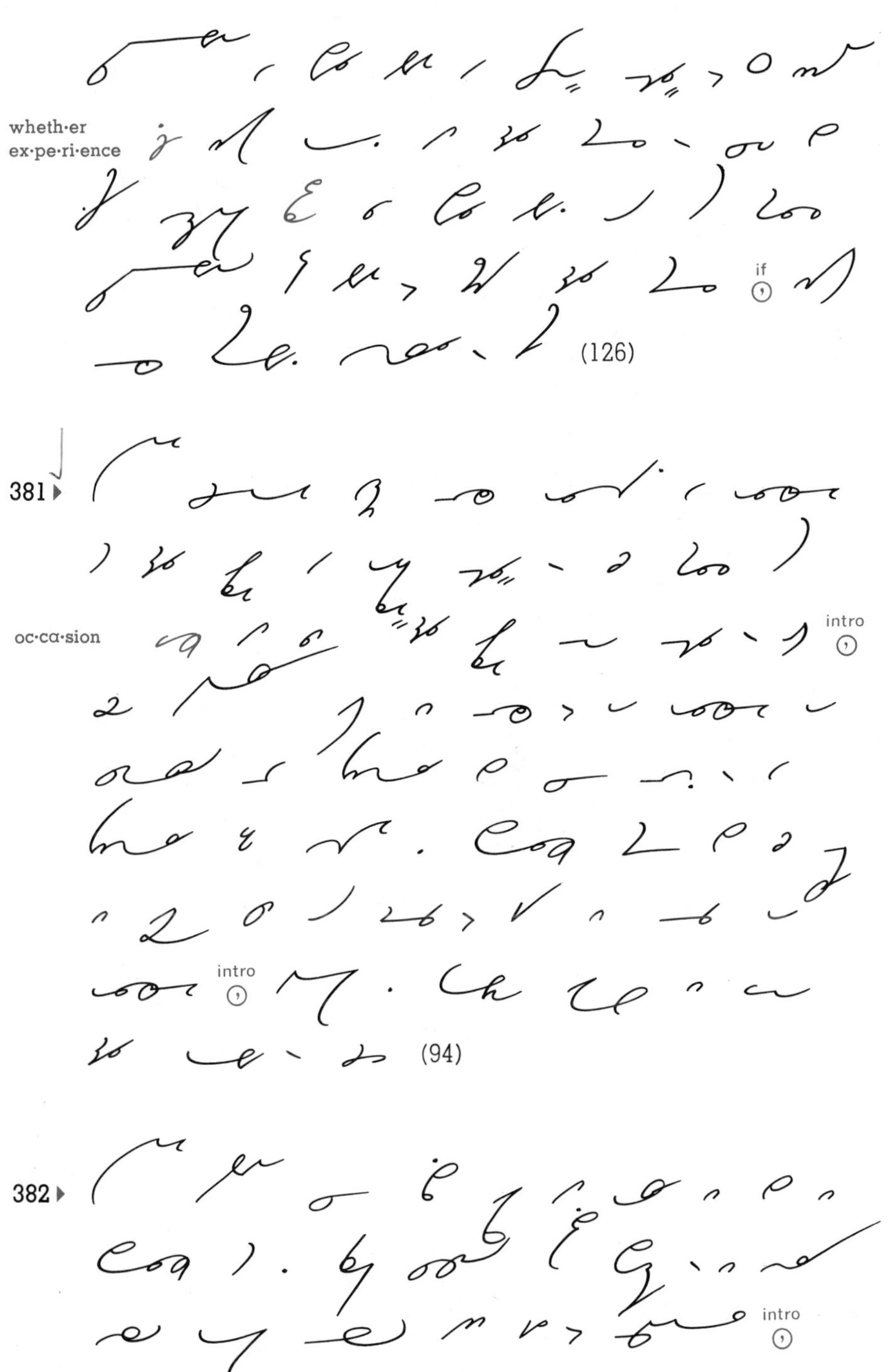
wheth·er
ex·pe·ri·ence
if
(126)
381
oc·ca·sion
intro
intro
(94)
382
intro

al·ways
cloth·ing

par

when

ap·pre·ci·ate
per·son·al·ly

(111)

383

dis·trib·u·tors
com·plain·ing

intro

em·bar·rass·ing
min·i·miz·ing

in·qui·ries
pri·or·i·ty

intro

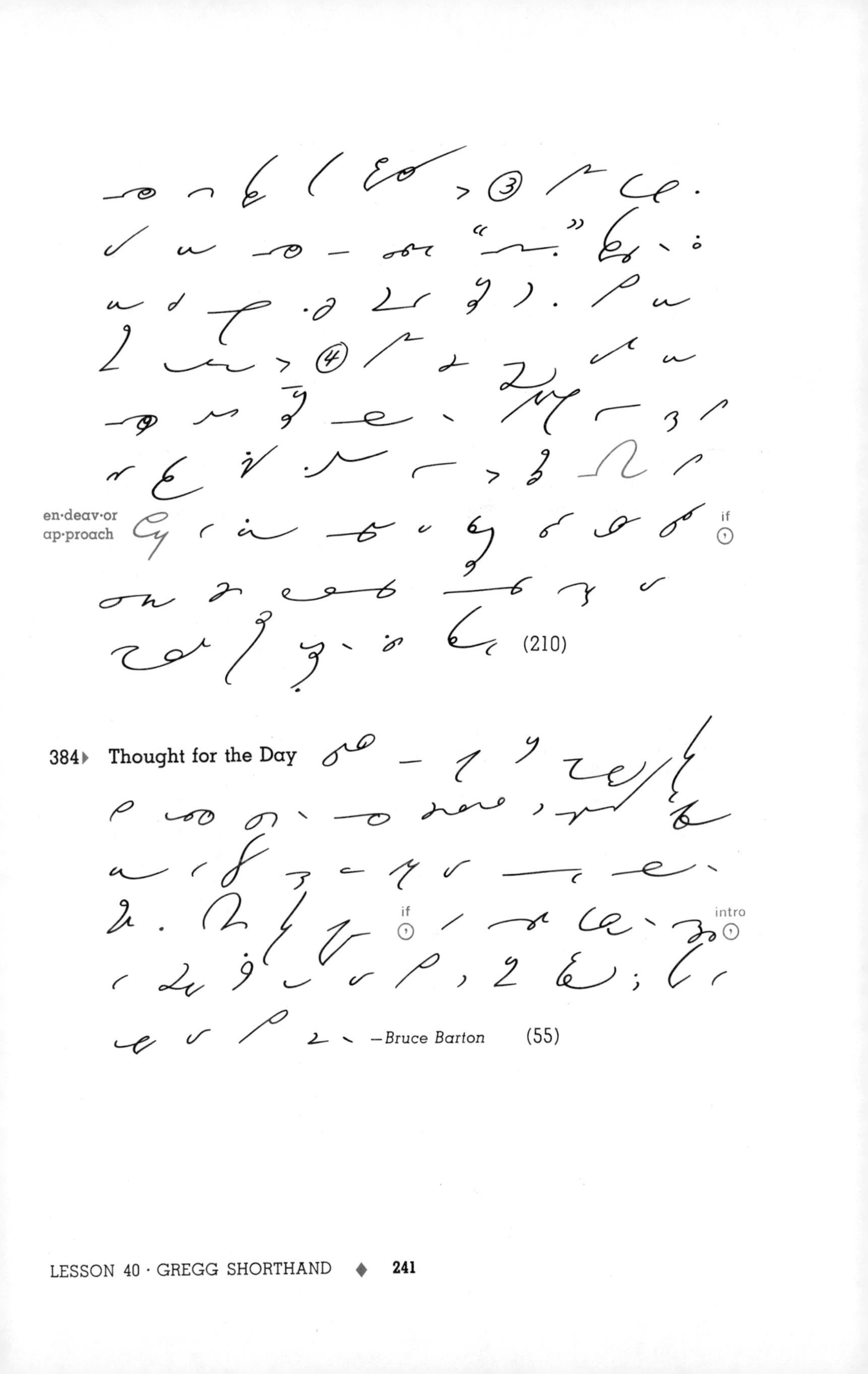

en·deav·or
ap·proach

if

(210)

384▸ **Thought for the Day**

if

intro

—*Bruce Barton* (55)

PRINCIPLES

385 ▸ Abbreviated Words—Not in Families • The ending may be omitted from some long words even though they do not fall into a family.

alphabet, philosophy, privilege, memorandum, convenient, convenience, privileges, equivalent, reluctant, reluctance, privileged

386 ▸ Word Beginning Trans- • The word beginning *trans-* is represented by a disjoined *t*.

transmit, transact, transported, transferred, translate, transplant, transcribe, transcript, transit

387 ▸ Word Ending -ification • The word ending *-ification* is represented by a disjoined *f*.

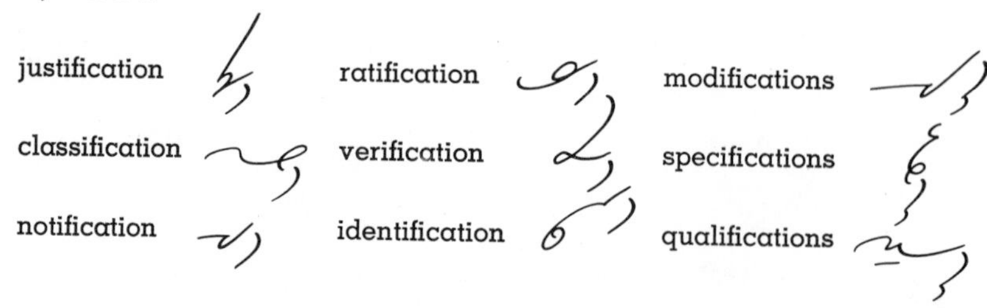

justification, ratification, modifications, classification, verification, specifications, notification, identification, qualifications

BUILDING TRANSCRIPTION SKILLS

388 SIMILAR-WORDS DRILL **assistance, assistants**

assistance Help.

If we can be of any assistance to you, please let us know.

assistants Helpers.

My assistants and I shall need more time to complete the job.

389 BUSINESS VOCABULARY BUILDER

with our compliments Free.

amplification The act of expanding, to bring out more or clearer details.

reluctance Unwillingness.

READING AND WRITING PRACTICE

390

as

par

pa·tience
source

ac·cept
com·pli·ments
priv·i·lege

(196)

391 ▸

es·pe·cial·ly
tes·ti·mo·ny

ap

as

30

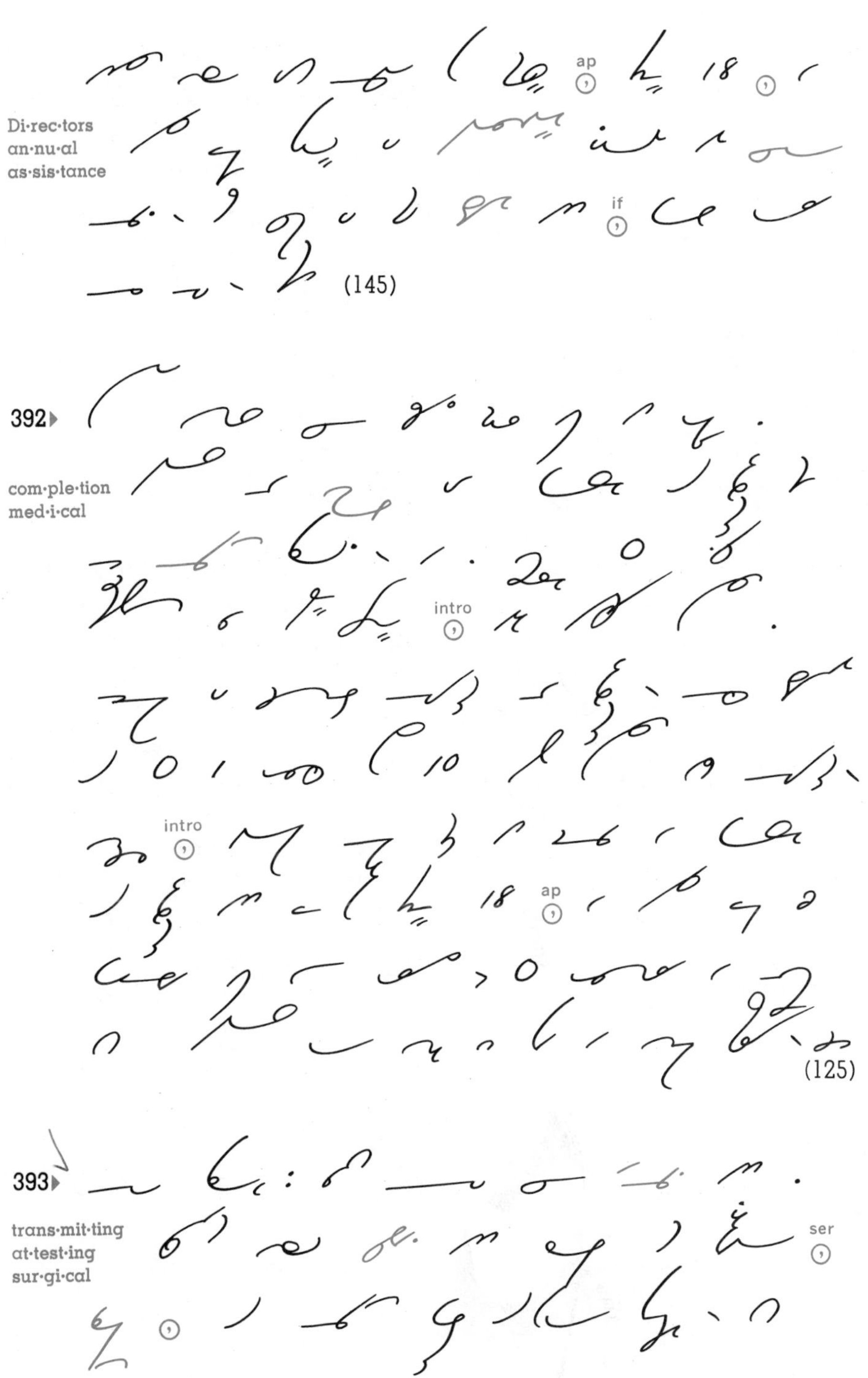
ap
18
Di·rec·tors
an·nu·al
as·sis·tance
if
(145)
392
com·ple·tion
med·i·cal
intro
intro
18
ap
(125)
393
trans·mit·ting
at·test·ing
sur·gi·cal
ser

intro

par

de·pen·dents
lose

if

(183)

394

re·luc·tance
Phi·los·o·phy

156

when

par

trans·ferred
fac·ul·ty

al·ready
en·rolled

(113)

395

wheth·er
el·i·gi·ble

ap

(170)

RECALL

There are no new shorthand devices for you to learn in Lesson 42. However, it does contain an Accuracy Practice, a review of the word beginnings and endings you have studied thus far, and a Reading and Writing Practice.

ACCURACY PRACTICE

396 ▸ **My** ... **Lie** ... **Fight** ...

To write these combinations accurately:

a Join the circle in the same way that you would join an *a* circle, but turn the end inside the circle.

b Before turning the end of the circle inside, be sure that the stroke touches the stroke to which the *i* is joined.

c Avoid making a point at the places indicated by arrows.

Practice Drill

My, night, sight, line, mile.

397 ▸ **Ow** ... **Oi** ...

To write these combinations accurately:

a Keep the hooks deep and narrow.

b Place the circles outside the hooks as indicated by the dotted lines.

Practice Drill

How-out, now, doubt, scout; toy, soil, annoy.

398▸ Th Nt, Nd Mt, Md

To write these combinations accurately:

a Slant the strokes as indicated by the dotted lines.

b Start these strokes to the right and upward.

Practice Drill

There are, and will, empty, health, lined, ashamed.

COMPARE:

Hint, heard; tamed, detailed.

399▸ Recall Chart • There are 90 word beginnings and endings in the following chart. Can you read them in 5 minutes?

WORD BEGINNINGS

1						
2						
3						
4						

WORD BEGINNINGS AND ENDINGS

5

6

7

8

9

10

11

12

13

14

15

BUILDING TRANSCRIPTION SKILLS

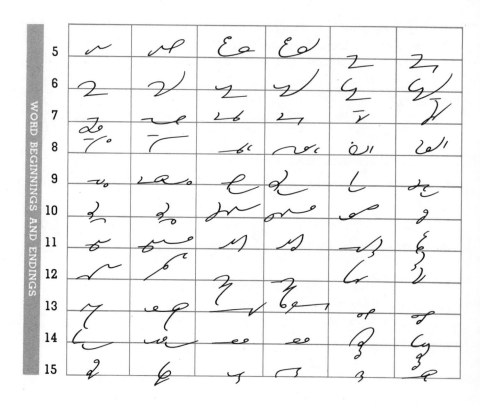

400 ▸ **BUSINESS VOCABULARY BUILDER**

transform To change the outward appearance of.
vehemently Strongly; forcefully.
irate Angry.

READING AND WRITING PRACTICE

READING SCOREBOARD • Twelve lessons have gone by since you last measured your reading speed. You have, of course, continued to do each Reading and Writing Practice faithfully; and, consequently, your reading speed will reflect this faithfulness! The following table will help you measure your reading speed on the *first reading* of Lesson 42.

LESSON 42 CONTAINS 497 WORDS

If you read Lesson 42 in:	12	14	16	18	20	22	**minutes**
	▼	▼	▼	▼	▼	▼	
Your reading rate is:	40	35	31	27	25	23	**words a minute**

If you can read Lesson 42 through the first time in less than 12 minutes, you are doing well. If you take considerably longer than 22 minutes, perhaps you should:

1 Pay closer attention in class while the shorthand devices are being presented to you.

2 Spend less time trying to decipher outlines that you cannot read.

3 Review, occasionally, all the brief forms you have studied by referring to the chart on the inside back cover of your text.

401▸ The Executive As a Salesman

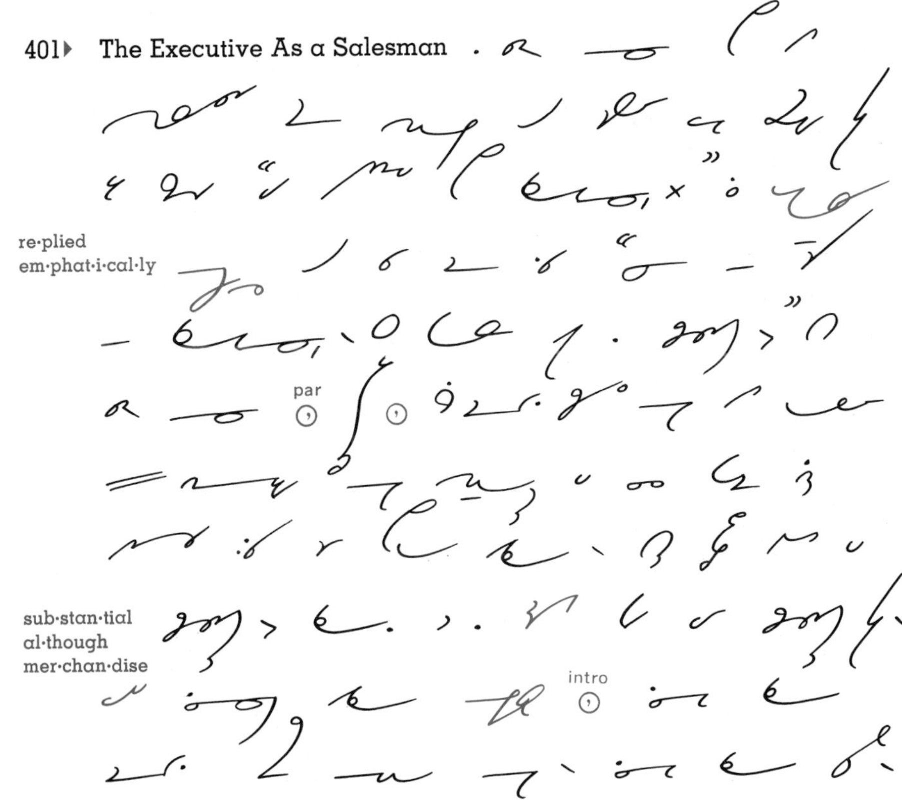

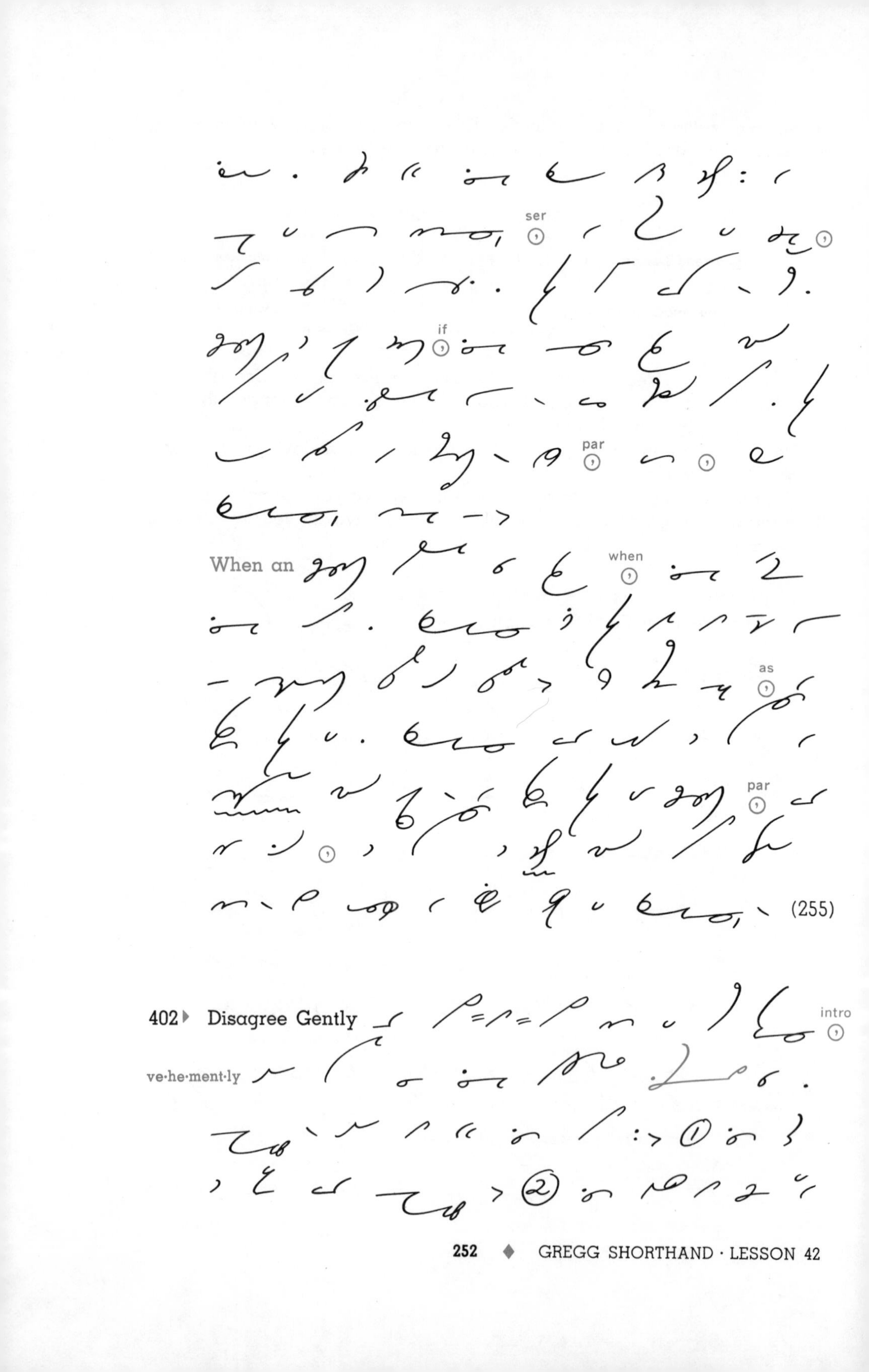

ser

if

par

When an

when

as

par

(255)

402 ▸ Disagree Gently

intro

ve·he·ment·ly

al·ways
choose

judg·ment
ab·so·lute·ly

par

par

One of the

if

if

intro

(242)

Insofar as secretarial jobs are concerned, it is still a seller's market. This means that the secretary can actually *choose* the company or organization for which she would like to work—assuming, of course, that she has the proper skills to bring to the job.

Because your first job may be your most important one, it is smart to choose it carefully. If you jump at the first opportunity, you may be forced to leave the job shortly afterwards because it wasn't what you wanted. And changing jobs is always a disagreeable chore.

How can you find out which is the right job for you? First, determine where your interests are. If you like an academic atmosphere, you might find a position in a school office or college dean's office exciting. If the advertising world fascinates you, there are plenty of jobs for secretaries in advertising agencies and in advertising departments of companies. Maybe you would like to work for a doctor, a personnel manager, or a hotel manager. Perhaps you would like a government job in Washington or on a military base, a position with a major airline, or a job in a newspaper office. Decide in what general surrounding you would probably be happiest and aim in that direction.

Another factor to be considered is the reputation of the company. Do people talk favorably about it, and do they think it has a bright future? What do the employees of the company think of it as a place to work? What fringe benefits are offered, such as insurance, vacation, hospitalization, recreation, etc.?

Location is important to some people. It may be more important to you to live within walking distance of your job than to have the ideal job in another part of town. Or you may prefer working in a big city to working in a small town.

To this point we haven't mentioned money, but of course this is enormously important. The reason it is listed last is that too many people rank it first.

Secretarial jobs in a given location do not vary greatly in beginning salaries. Find out from your college placement counselor what beginning salaries are being paid to people of your background, and don't be afraid to ask for a comparable wage. Don't raise the salary issue, however, unless it is clear that your interviewer does not intend to.

Basically, the three most important questions you should ask yourself before you accept a position are these:

1▸ Will the work be interesting and challenging?

2▸ Will I enjoy the people I work with and for?

3▸ Will I be given reasonable opportunity for financial and professional advancement?

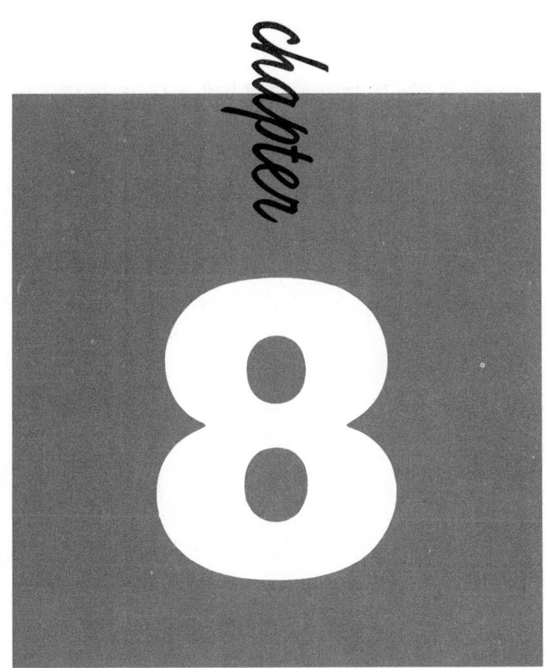

CHOOSING A JOB

Hat by Mr. John Jr.

PRINCIPLES

403 ▸ Word Ending -ulate • The word ending *-ulate* is represented by a disjoined oo hook.

circulate accumulate regulate
stipulate stimulating regulator
congratulate calculated regulates

404 ▸ Word Ending -ulation • The word ending *-ulation* is represented by disjoined *oo-tion.*

circulation accumulation calculation
stipulation stimulation regulations

405 ▸ Word Beginning Post- • The word beginning *post-* is represented by a disjoined *p.*

postcard postdate postpone
postal postmark post office

406 ▸ Word Beginning Super- • The word beginning *super-* is represented by a disjoined comma *s.*

supervise supervision superhuman

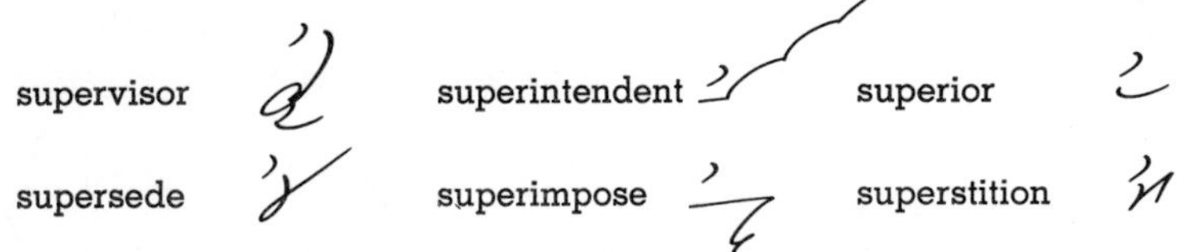

BUILDING TRANSCRIPTION SKILLS

407 ▸ PUNCTUATION PRACTICE , conjunction

A comma is used to separate two independent clauses that are joined by one of the following conjunctions: *and, but, or, for, nor.*

An independent clause (sometimes called a main or a principal clause) is one that has a subject and predicate and that could stand alone as a complete sentence.

> There are twelve men in the department, but only six of them have been with us for more than one year.

The first independent clause is:

> There are twelve men in the department

and the second is:

> only six of them have been with us for more than one year.

Both clauses could stand as separate sentences, with a period after each. Because the thoughts of the two clauses are closely related, however, the clauses were joined to form one sentence. Because the two independent clauses are connected by the coordinating conjunction *but,* a comma is used between them, before the conjunction.

conj (,) Each time this use of the comma occurs in the Reading and Writing Practice, it will be indicated in the shorthand as shown in the left margin.

408 ▸ BUSINESS VOCABULARY BUILDER

superb Excellent.

decade Ten years.

edification Instruction.

extemporaneously Without preparation.

READING AND WRITING PRACTICE

409

wait
Mod·el

conj

if

piece
de·nom·i·na·tions

conj

116

12

116

conj

loss
close

conj

conj

116

par

(238)

410

intro

intro

in·stalled fuel

40,

conj

choose then

if

if

conj

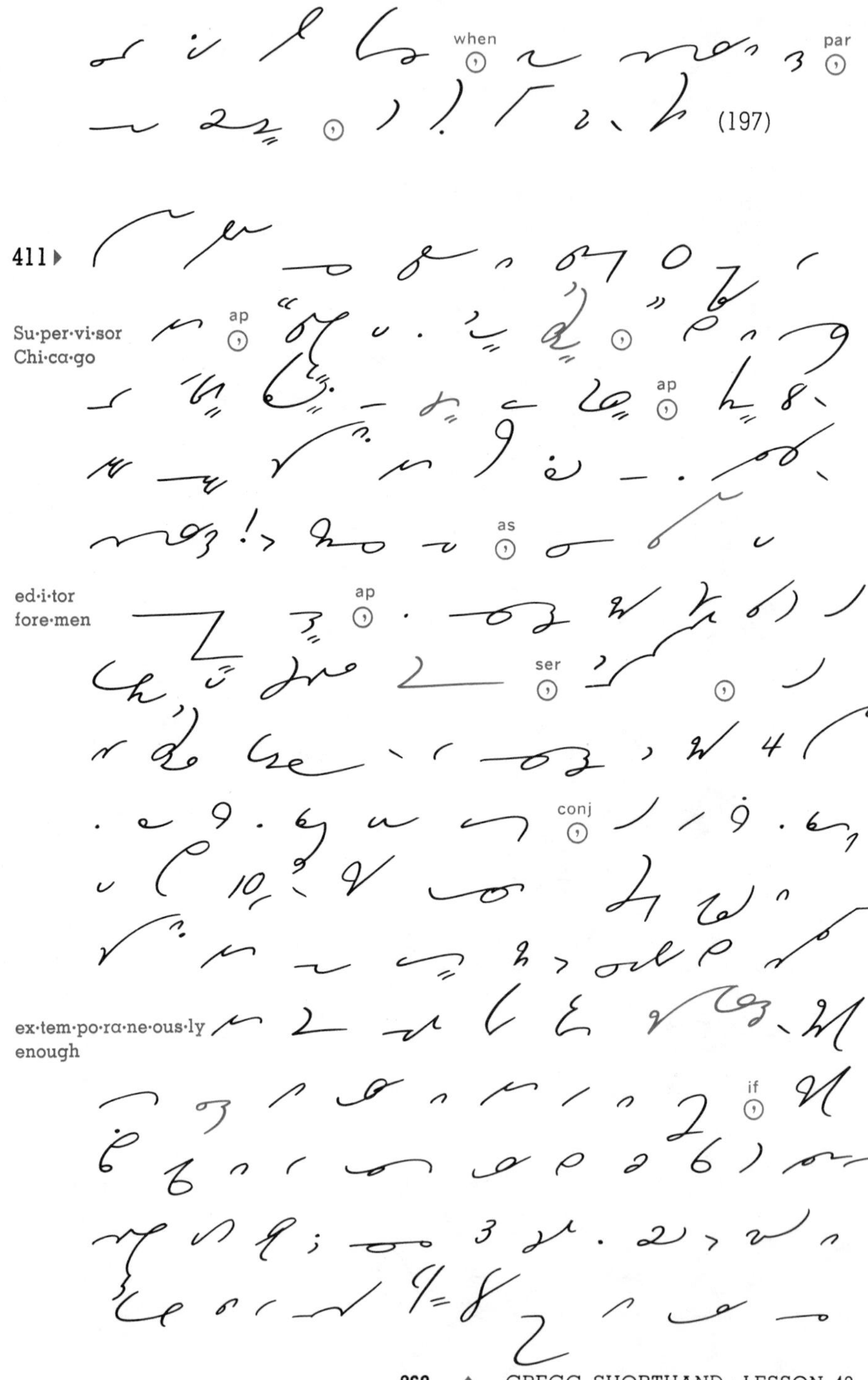
when
par
(197)
411
Su·per·vi·sor
Chi·ca·go
ap
ap
ed·i·tor
fore·men
as
ap
ser
conj
ex·tem·po·ra·ne·ous·ly
enough
if

intro

(208)

412

intro

occasion

profited

conj

intro

par

(102)

413

calculator

referred

conj

occurred

transit

intro

(82)

PRINCIPLES

414▸ Word Ending -sume • The word ending *-sume* is represented by *s-m.*

consume — presume — consumer
resume — assume — assumed

415▸ Word Ending -sumption • The word ending *-sumption* is represented by *s-m-tion.*

resumption — presumption — consumption

416▸ Word Beginning Self- • The word beginning *self-* is represented by a disjoined left *s.*

self-defense — self-supporting — self-assurance
self-confident — self-satisfied — selfish
self-reliant — self-made — selfishness

417▸ Word Beginning Circum- • The word beginning *circum-* is also represented by a disjoined left *s.*

circumstance — circumstances — circumstantial

418 PUNCTUATION PRACTICE , *and* omitted

When two or more adjectives modify the same noun, they are separated by commas.

Enclosed is a stamped, self-addressed envelope.

However, the comma is not used if the first adjective modifies the combined idea of the second adjective plus the noun.

The book was bound in an attractive brown cloth.

NOTE: You can quickly determine whether to insert a comma between two consecutive adjectives by mentally placing *and* between them. If the sentence makes good sense with *and* inserted between the adjectives, then the comma is used. For example, the first illustration would make good sense if it read:

Enclosed is a stamped and self-addressed envelope.

and o

Each time this use of the comma occurs in the Reading and Writing Practice, it will be indicated in the shorthand as shown in the left margin.

419 BUSINESS VOCABULARY BUILDER

sponsored Assumed the responsibility for.
assume To take upon oneself; to take for granted.
self-composure Calmness; poise.

READING AND WRITING PRACTICE

420

spon·sored
dis·con·tin·ued

conj

18 ser 19 20

conj

ap·pre·ci·ate
as·sump·tion

19

and o

(167)

421

self-as·sur·ance
self-com·po·sure

if par

ap

study·ing
tech·niques

intro

and o

al·ready
de·vel·op

conj

par

and o

if

if

(200)

422

car·ried
sto·ries
di·sas·trous

par

au·to·mat·i·cal·ly

cel·lar
at·tic

as

when

(175)

423

conj

par

self-con·fi·dence
les·son

if

(121)

424

self-ex·plan·a·to·ry
cir·cu·la·tion

as

grat·i·fi·ca·tion
skill·ful

and o

(110)

425

if

(71)

PRINCIPLES

426 ▸ Word Ending -hood • The word ending *-hood* is represented by a disjoined *d.*

childhood parenthood likelihood
motherhood manhood neighborhood

427 ▸ Word Ending -ward • The word ending *-ward* is also represented by a disjoined *d.*

onward backward forward
afterward awkwardly forwarded

428 ▸ Ul • *Ul* is represented by the oo hook when it precedes a forward or upward stroke.

result resulted adults
consult ultimate multiply
insulted culture culminate

429 ▸ Quantities and Amounts • Here are a number of additional helpful devices for expressing quantities and amounts.

$600 8,000,000 $7,000,000

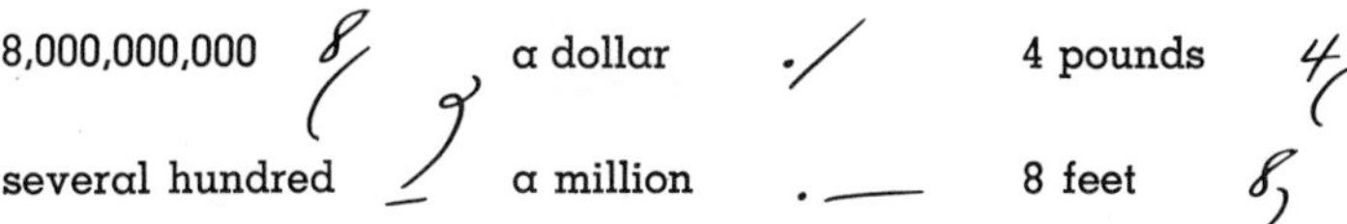

NOTE: The *m* for *million* is written beside the figure. We thus obtain a positive distinction between *million* and *hundred*, in which the *n* is written underneath the figure.

BUILDING TRANSCRIPTION SKILLS

430 PUNCTUATION PRACTICE , nonrestrictive

Nonrestrictive clauses and phrases are set off by commas. A nonrestrictive clause or phrase is one that may be omitted without changing the meaning of the sentence. The nonrestrictive clause or phrase might be classified as parenthetical. It is important that you follow the meaning of the dictation in order to be able to identify the restrictive and the nonrestrictive clauses and phrases and to punctuate them correctly.

> **RESTRICTIVE—NO COMMAS:** All persons who are old enough to vote should register.
>
> **NONRESTRICTIVE—COMMAS:** John Smith, who is old enough to vote, should register.

In the first sentence above, *who are old enough to vote* is a restrictive clause and must not be set off by commas. The expression *who are old enough to vote* identifies the persons who should register.

In the second sentence, *who is old enough to vote* is a nonrestrictive (or descriptive or parenthetical) clause that must be set off with commas. It is not needed to identify the particular person who should register; it could be omitted without changing the meaning of the sentence.

nonr ⊙ Each time the nonrestrictive use of the comma occurs in the Reading and Writing Practice, it will be indicated in the shorthand as shown in the left margin.

431 BUSINESS VOCABULARY BUILDER

adage A popular saying; a proverb.
facilitate To make easy.
multitude Many.

READING AND WRITING PRACTICE

432

pre·ven·tion
de·vel·ops

intro

en·gi·neer·ing
de·vice

nonr

intro

intro

par

then
be·lieve

un·in·ter·rupt·ed
in·ex·pen·sive

ser

when

(210)

433 as intro

re·con·di·tion·ing
re·seed
nonr

(1) (2) 40, 40 (3)

ac·cept·ing
prompt·ly
if

and o

(133)

434 ap
and o
nonr

chil·dren's
de·scribes

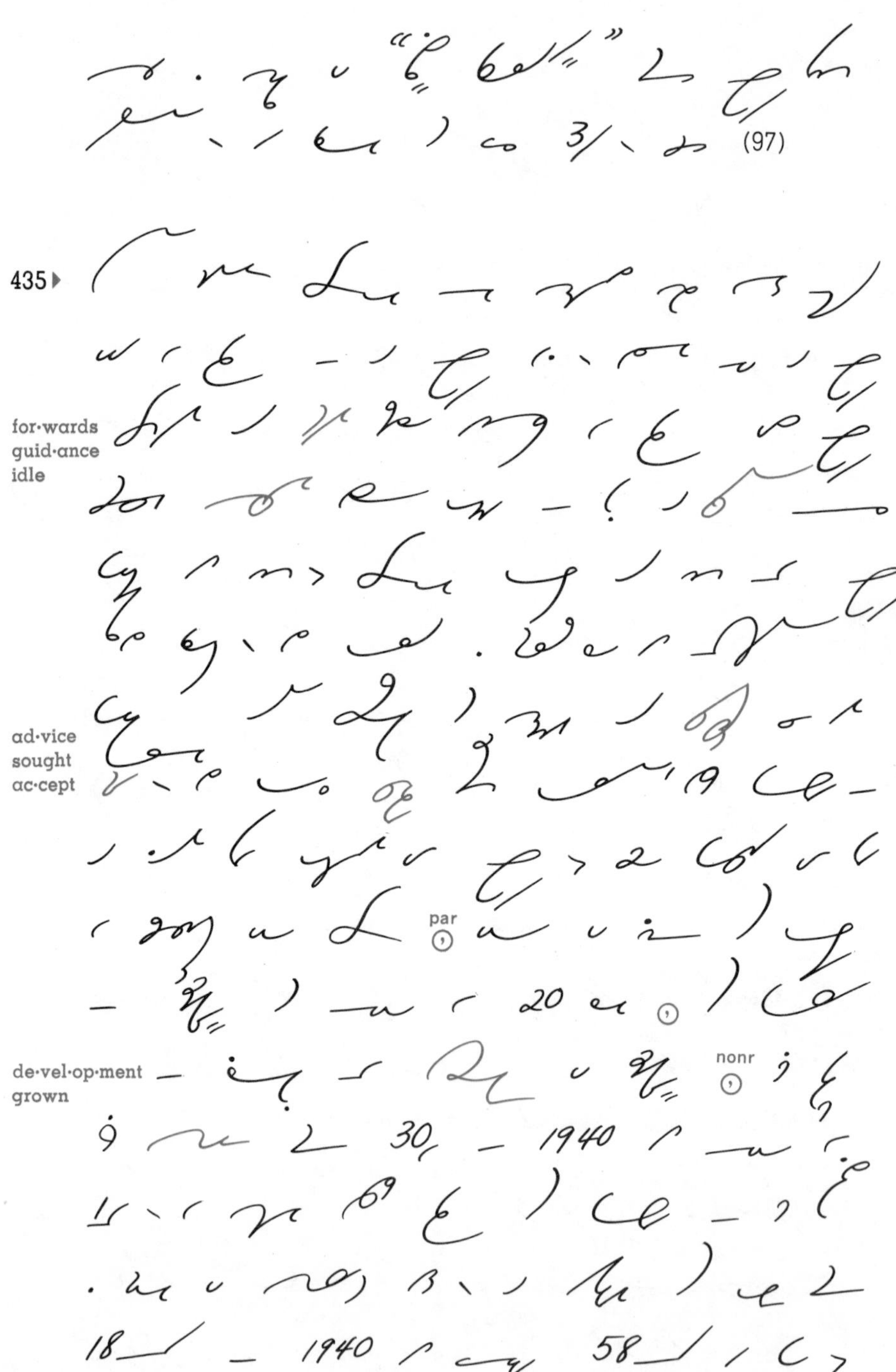
(97)

435

for·wards
guid·ance
idle

ad·vice
sought
ac·cept

par

de·vel·op·ment
grown

nonr

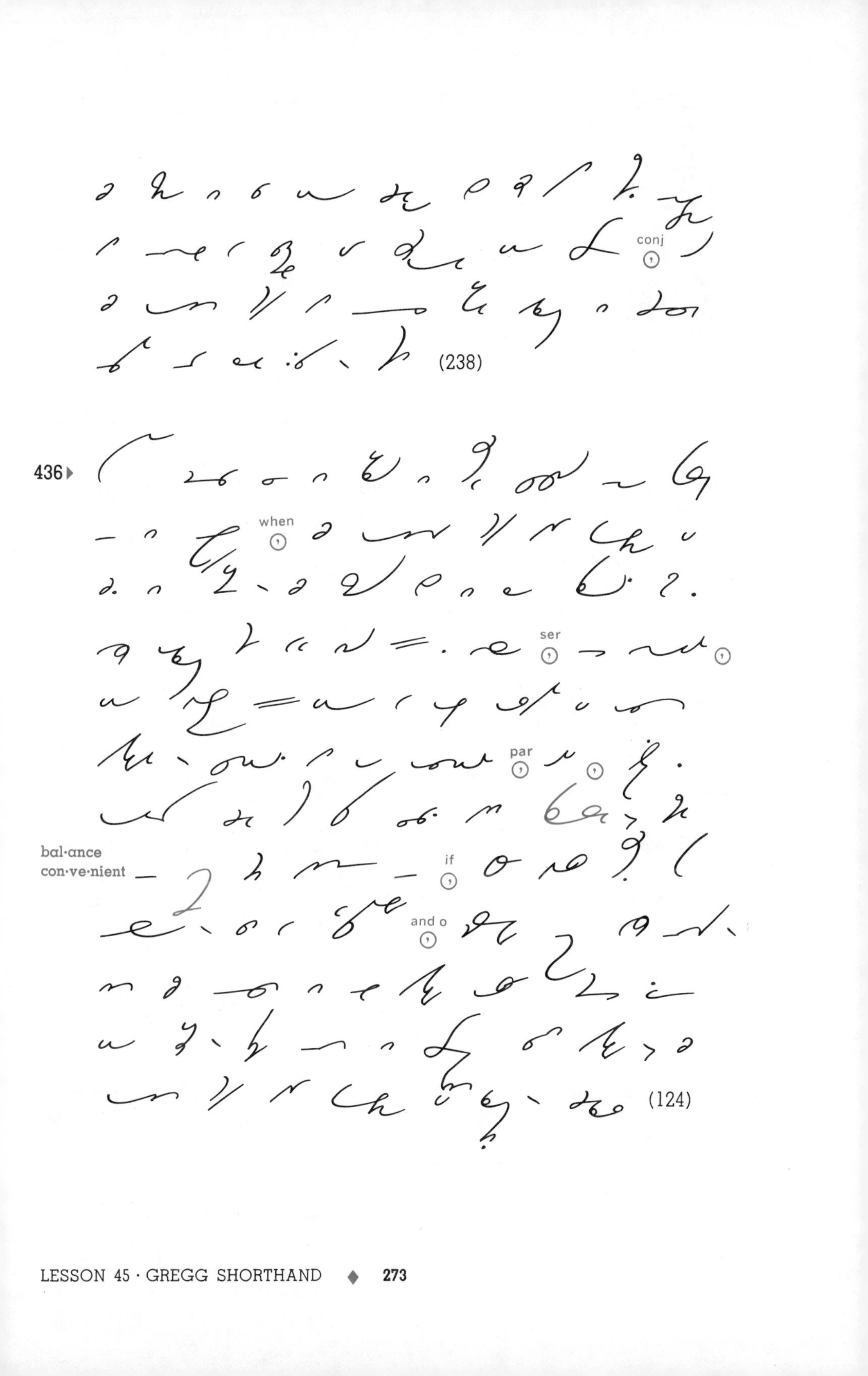

conj

(238)

436

when

ser

par

bal·ance
con·ve·nient

if

and o

(124)

PRINCIPLES

437▸ Word Ending -gram • The word ending *-gram* is represented by a disjoined *g*.

diagram | cablegram | monograms
telegram | radiogram | programmed

438▸ Electric, Electr- • The word *electric* and the word beginning *electric-* are represented by a disjoined *el*. The word beginning *electr-* is also represented by a disjoined *el*.

Electric

electric | electric motor | electrical
electric fan | electric wire | electrically

Electr-

electronic | electrotype | electricity

439▸ Compounds • Most compound words are formed by simply joining the outlines for the words that make up the compound. In some words, however, it is desirable to modify the outline for one of the words in order to obtain a facile joining.

anyhow | someone | within

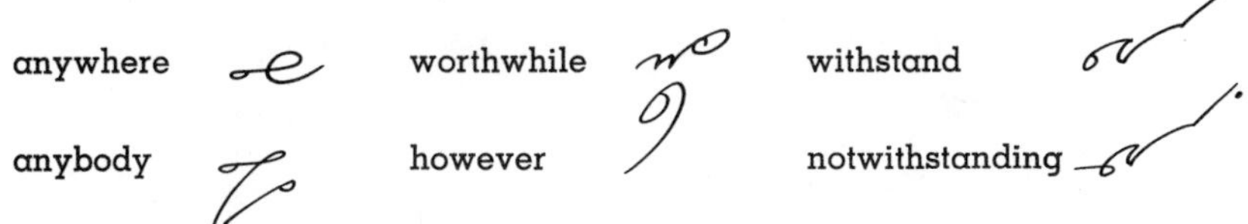

440 ▸ **Intersection** • Intersection, or the writing of one character through another, is sometimes useful for special phrases. This principle may be used when the constant repetition of certain combinations of words in your dictation makes it clearly worthwhile to form special outlines for them.

a.m. | **vice versa**

p.m. | **Chamber of Commerce**

BUILDING TRANSCRIPTION SKILLS

441 ▸ **SIMILAR-WORDS DRILL** **it's, its**

it's Contraction for *it is.*

A modern kitchen isn't a luxury; it's a convenience.

its Possessive form of *it.*

Its operating efficiency will make cooking a delight.

442 ▸ **BUSINESS VOCABULARY BUILDER**

checked out Paid one's hotel bill and left.
customary Usual.
category Class.

443

orig·i·nal·ly
of·fered

mod·ern
it's

its
ef·fi·cien·cy

nonr
nonr
and o
conj
when
ser

(221)

444 ▸ ap 15 intro par as

un·til
cus·tom·ary

35 intro and o par (138)

445 ▸ 70 intro

an·nounc·er
ra·zor
de·scrip·tion

conj

stat·ic
in·ter·fered

intro intro

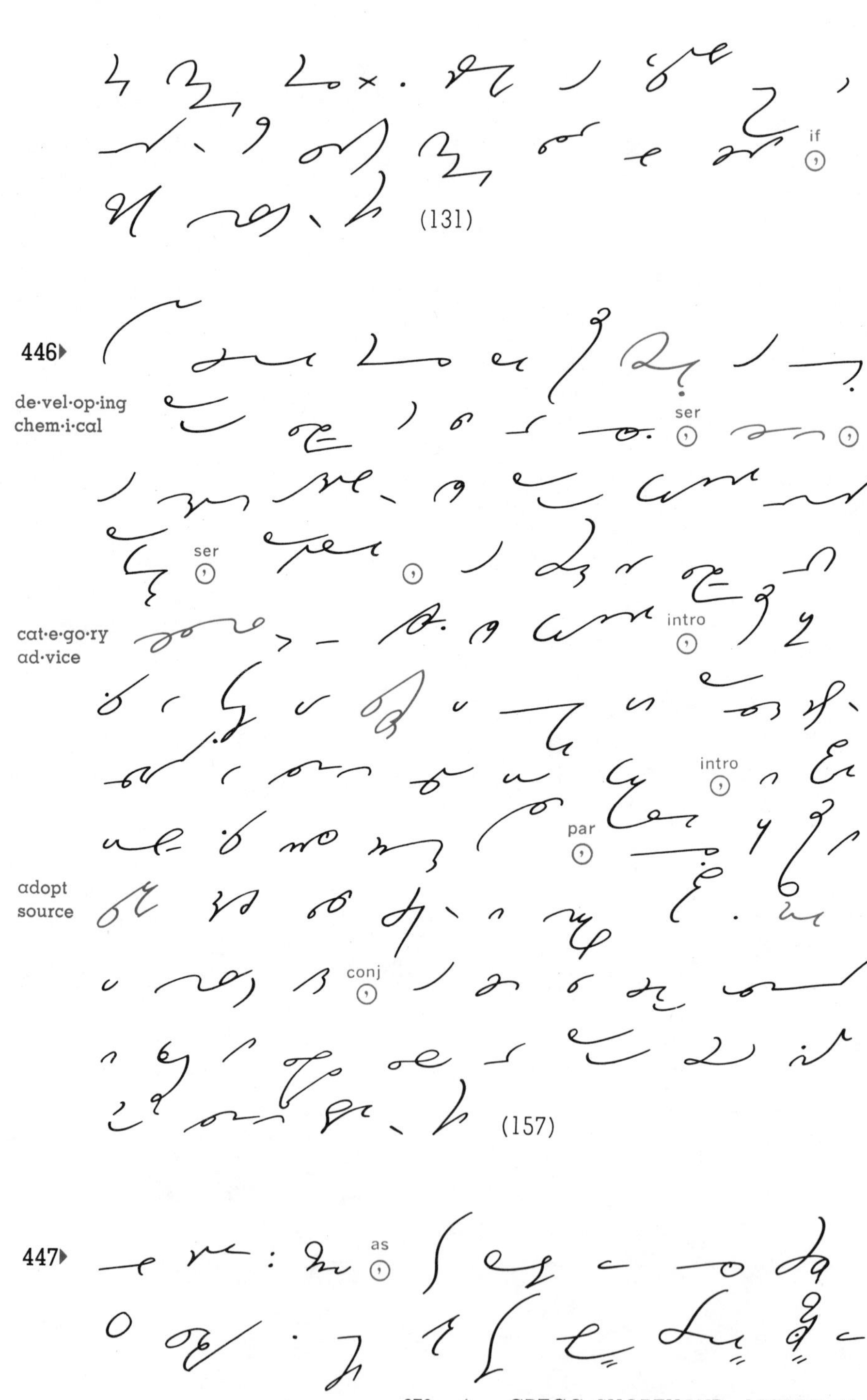
if
(131)
446
de·vel·op·ing
chem·i·cal
ser
ser
cat·e·go·ry
ad·vice
intro
intro
par
adopt
source
conj
(157)
447
as

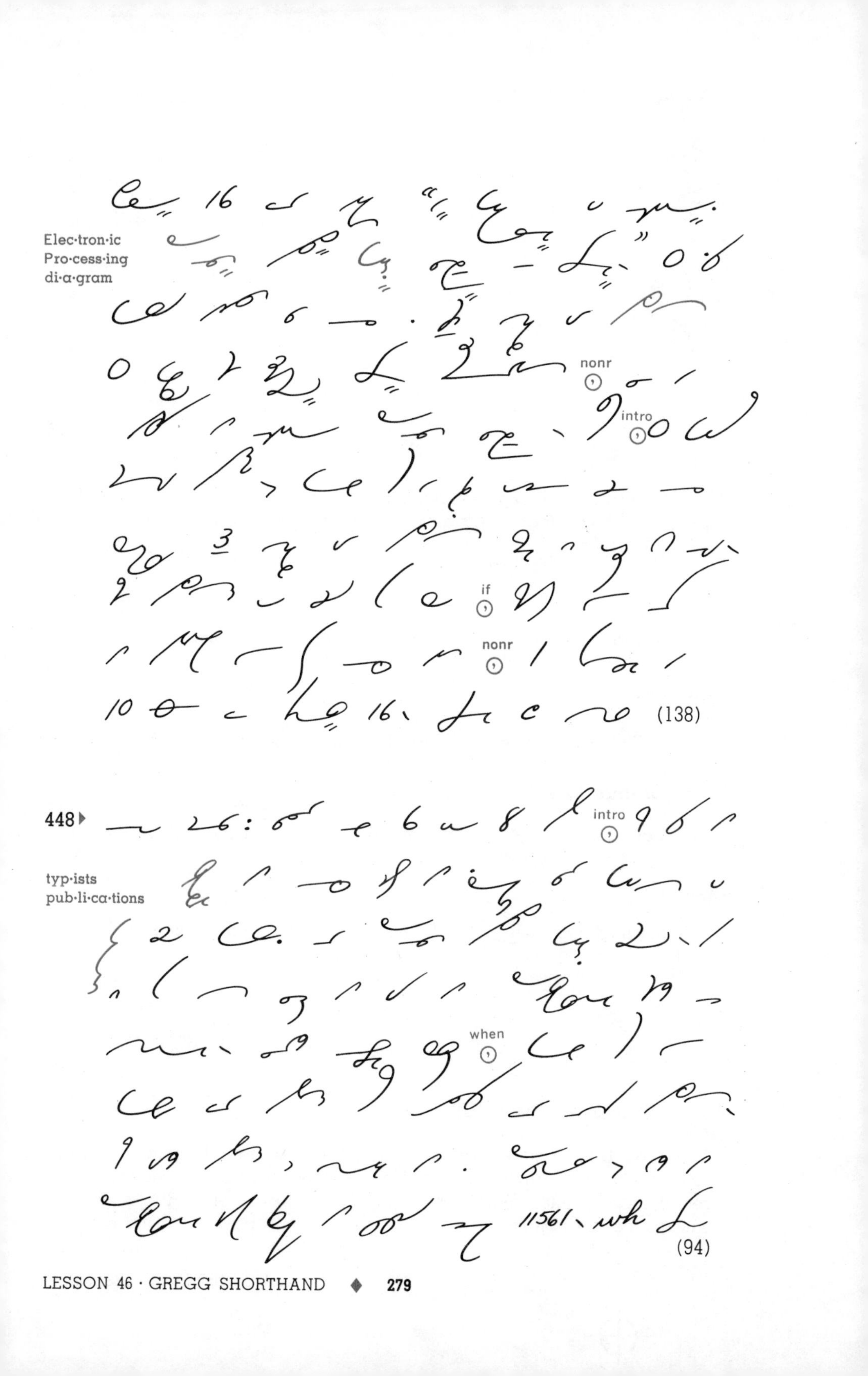

Elec·tron·ic
Pro·cess·ing
di·a·gram

nonr

intro

if

nonr

(138)

448

intro

typ·ists
pub·li·ca·tions

when

(94)

PRINCIPLES

449▸ Geographical Expressions • In geographical expressions, *-ville* is represented by *v; ington,* by a disjoined *ten* blend; *-burg,* by *b; -ingham,* by a disjoined *m.*

-ville

Jacksonville **Nashville** **Evansville**

-ington

Lexington **Wilmington** **Washington**

-burg (or *-burgh*)

Harrisburg **Pittsburgh** **Newburgh**

-ingham

Buckingham **Cunningham** **Framingham**

BUILDING TRANSCRIPTION SKILLS

450▸ GRAMMAR CHECKUP

Most businessmen have a good command of the English language. Some rarely make an error in grammar. There are times, though, when even the best dictators will perhaps use a plural verb with a singular noun or use the objective case when they should have used the nominative. They usually know better; but in concentrating intently on expressing a thought or idea, they occasionally suffer a grammatical lapse.

It will be your job, as a stenographer or secretary, to catch these occasional errors in grammar and to correct them when you transcribe.

From time to time in the lessons ahead, you will be given an opportunity to brush up on some of the rules of grammar that are frequently violated.

Subject and Verb

A verb must agree with its subject in number.

Our president is looking forward to the pleasure of serving you.
Your canceled checks are mailed to you each month.

The inclusion of a phrase such as *in addition to, as well as,* or *along with* after the subject does not affect the number of the verb. If the subject is singular, use a singular verb; if the subject is plural, use a plural verb.

Our president, as well as the members of the staff, is looking forward to the pleasure of serving you.
Your canceled checks, along with your statement, are mailed to you each month.

451 ▸ **BUSINESS VOCABULARY BUILDER**

availed themselves Took advantage of.

gratification Pleasure.

sorority A club of girls or women, especially at a college.

READING AND WRITING PRACTICE

452 ▸

ser

fur·ni·ture

and o

intro

16

intro

cus·tom·ers
sub·stan·tial

par

neigh·bor·hood
con·ve·nience

nonr

(240)

453

guests

availed

conj

intro

extensive remodeling

nonr

ser

par

intro

(170)

454

sorority planning

intro

historical sites

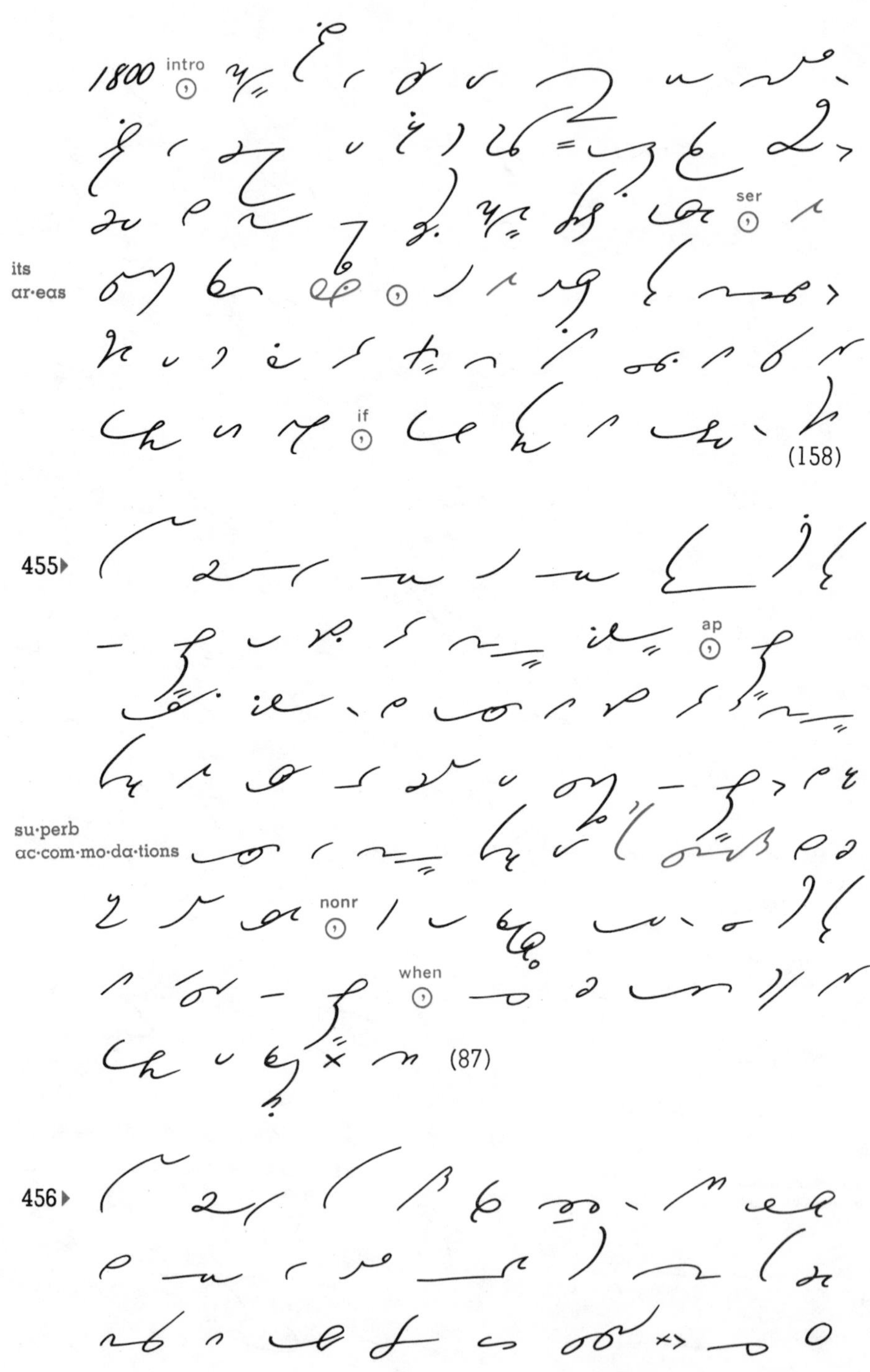
1800
intro
ser
its
ar·eas
if
(158)
455
ap
su·perb
ac·com·mo·da·tions
nonr
when
(87)
456

(53)

457

mag·nif·i·cent
as·so·ciates

ser

conj

conj

fa·cil·i·ties
de·scrip·tive

(140)

In Lesson 47 you studied the last of the new shorthand devices of Gregg Shorthand. In this lesson you will find an Accuracy Practice, a Recall Chart that reviews all the word-building principles of Gregg Shorthand, and a Reading and Writing Practice.

ACCURACY PRACTICE

458▸ **Def**

To write this stroke accurately:

a Make it large, almost the full height of your notebook line.

b Make it narrow.

c Start and finish the strokes on the same level of writing, as indicated by the dotted lines.

Practice Drill

Divide, definite, defeat, devote, differ, endeavor.

459▸ **Th** **Ten** **Tem**

To write these strokes accurately:

a Slant the strokes as indicated by the dotted lines.

b Make the beginning of the curve deep.

c Make the *tem* large, about the full height of the line; the *th* small; the *ten* about half the size of the *tem*.

Practice Drill

In the, in time, tender, teeth, detain, medium.

460▸ Recall Chart • This chart contains one or more illustrations of every word-building and phrasing principle of Gregg Shorthand.

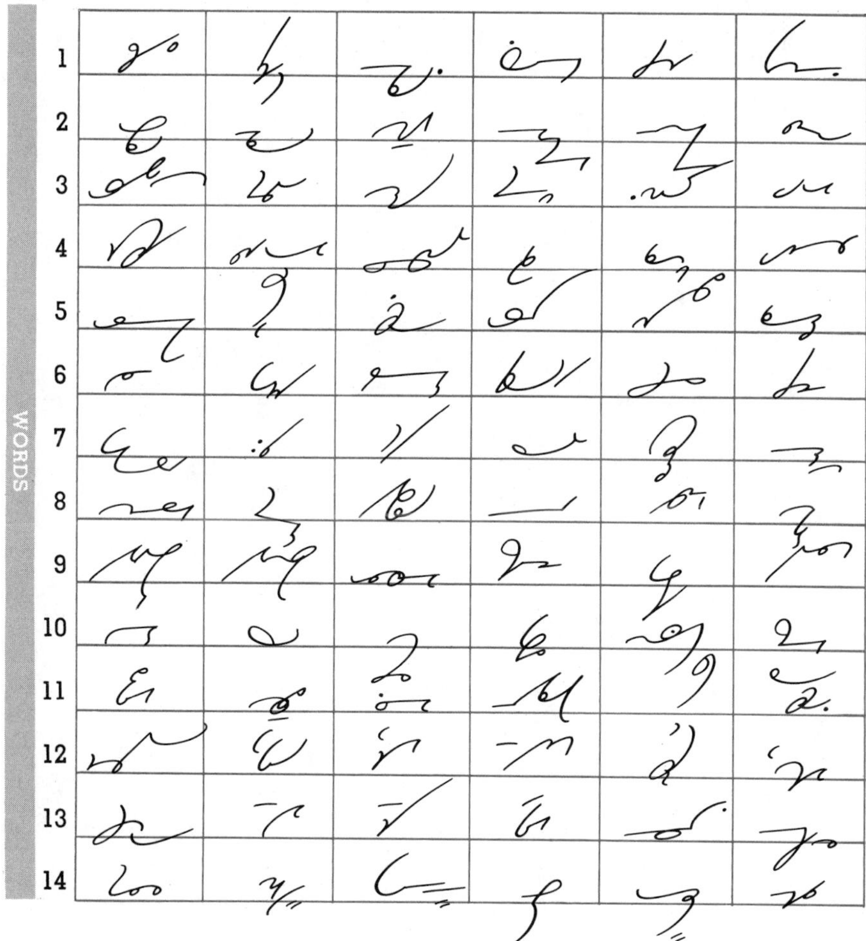

PHRASES						
15						
16						
17						

BUILDING TRANSCRIPTION SKILLS

461 ▸ BUSINESS VOCABULARY BUILDER

confidant One to whom secrets are entrusted.

accumulating Gathering.

metropolitan Pertaining to the center of activity, such as a large city.

READING AND WRITING PRACTICE

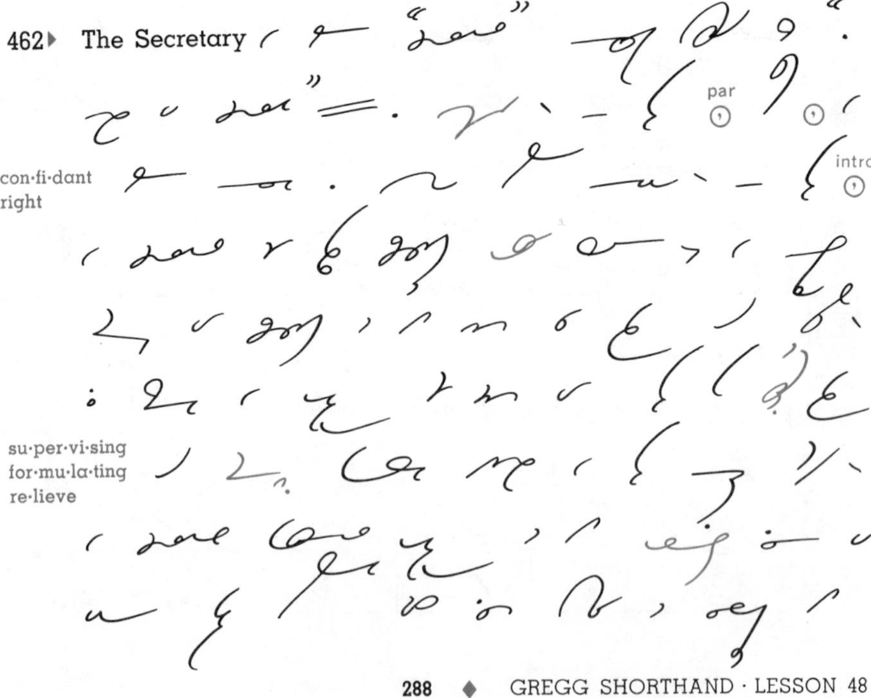

ser

intro

greet·ing
sur·vey
re·cent·ly

ser

intro

Many exciting

ser

ser

med·i·cine
me·di·um

conj

chal·leng·ing
self-sat·is·fy·ing

ser

In many

(477)

TRANSCRIPTION CHECK LIST

Are you getting the full benefit from the spelling and punctuation helps in the Reading and Writing Practice by—

1 Encircling all punctuation in your notes as you copy each Reading and Writing Practice?

2 Noting the reason for the use of each punctuation mark to be sure that you understand why it was used?

3 Spelling aloud at least once the spelling words given in the margin of the shorthand?

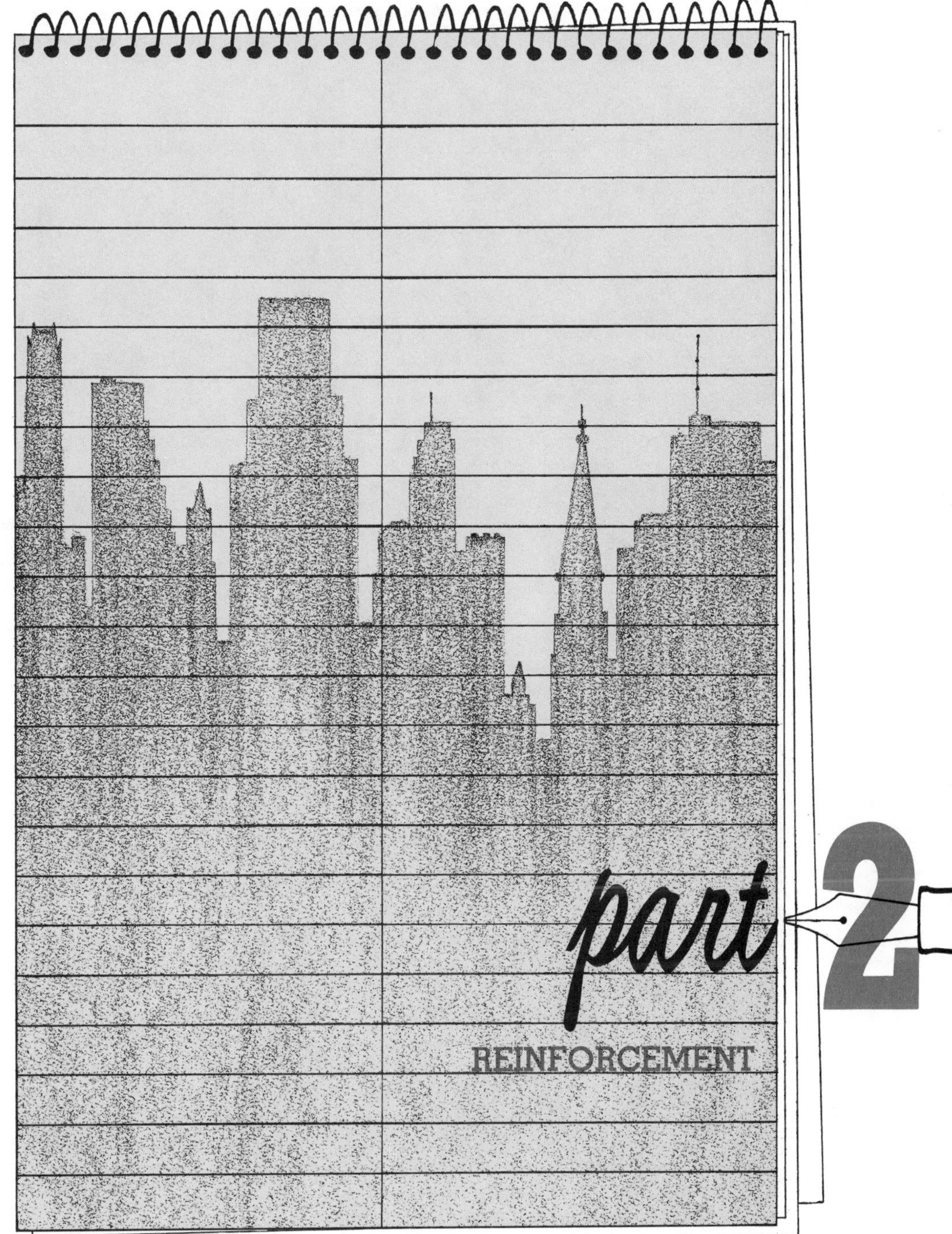

part 2

REINFORCEMENT

Today, more than ever, people are "status" conscious. They select their clothes, their food, their houses, their recreation, and their friends with the fervent hope that others will look with envy and admiration upon their good taste and their sophistication. Even the work that people do must have status — if not in *what* they do, certainly in what the job is *called*. Janitors insist on being called "custodial managers" or "maintenance engineers." The term "beauty operator" long ago gave way to the more sophisticated "beautician." Many women object to the old term "housewife" and insist that they are really "homemakers." Today's salesman is called a "service representative," "sales consultant," "product consultant," or "sales engineer."

The job of the secretary has increased in status over the years; yet the title has remained virtually unchanged. While the term "administrative assistant" is often used to identify a high-level secretarial position, it is slow in catching on. The executive is responsible in large measure for this; he finds it difficult to refer to his assistant by any other name than "secretary." But he certainly has no difficulty describing her status! The secretary is the shadow of her boss. When the executive utters the phrase "my secretary," he is, in effect, saying: "The person who runs my office and my schedule . . ." To find out the status of the secretary to an executive, you need only to eavesdrop on the boss when the secretary is on vacation or at home ill. He is very likely to use such phrases as, "My secretary isn't here this week, and I have no idea where to find . . ." or "Would you mind calling again next week when my secretary returns? She knows what we decided, but I have forgotten . . ." or "I think I'll ask the client to wait another week until my secretary returns. She has *all* the facts."

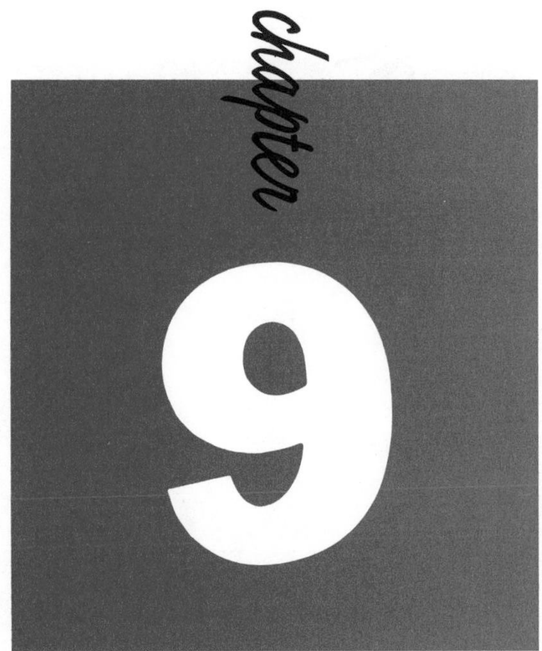

chapter 9

"STATUS" AND THE SECRETARY

Business would truly be paralyzed if the secretary were not on the job. The executive is helpless without her. He cannot retrieve the needed materials from the files; he cannot get that important report ready, because only the secretary knows where to get the facts; he cannot schedule that meeting, because he needs someone completely reliable to report the minutes. There are few jobs that have the status that the secretary enjoys.

Status is one of the reasons why secretaries enjoy their work so much. They know that they are on the firing line of executive decisions — that important reports, meetings, conferences, and decisions could not take place if they were not there to supply the information needed to "run the show."

With status, of course, go pleasant surroundings, good pay, security, and all the other hallmarks of the "ideal" position. If you want to feel needed, to make a valuable contribution to managerial performance, to sit on the front row of the drama of business—a drama that may affect the well-being and activities of thousands — become a secretary. There is no other job for a woman that has more status and that is more needed in the arena of the American economy.

And you don't have to sugarcoat the job by calling it something more dignified. The term "secretary" is fine just the way it stands.

Photographed at Revlon, Inc.

Lesson 49 provides a thorough review of the shorthand principles you studied in Chapter 1.

463 BRIEF FORMS, DERIVATIVES, AND PHRASES

a The, that, Mrs., but, Mr., have, will-well, is-his.
b Willing, wills, are-our-hour, ours, can, cannot, you-your, it-at, in-not.
c I am, I have, of the, with the, in the, in that, I will, I will not.

READING PRACTICE

464

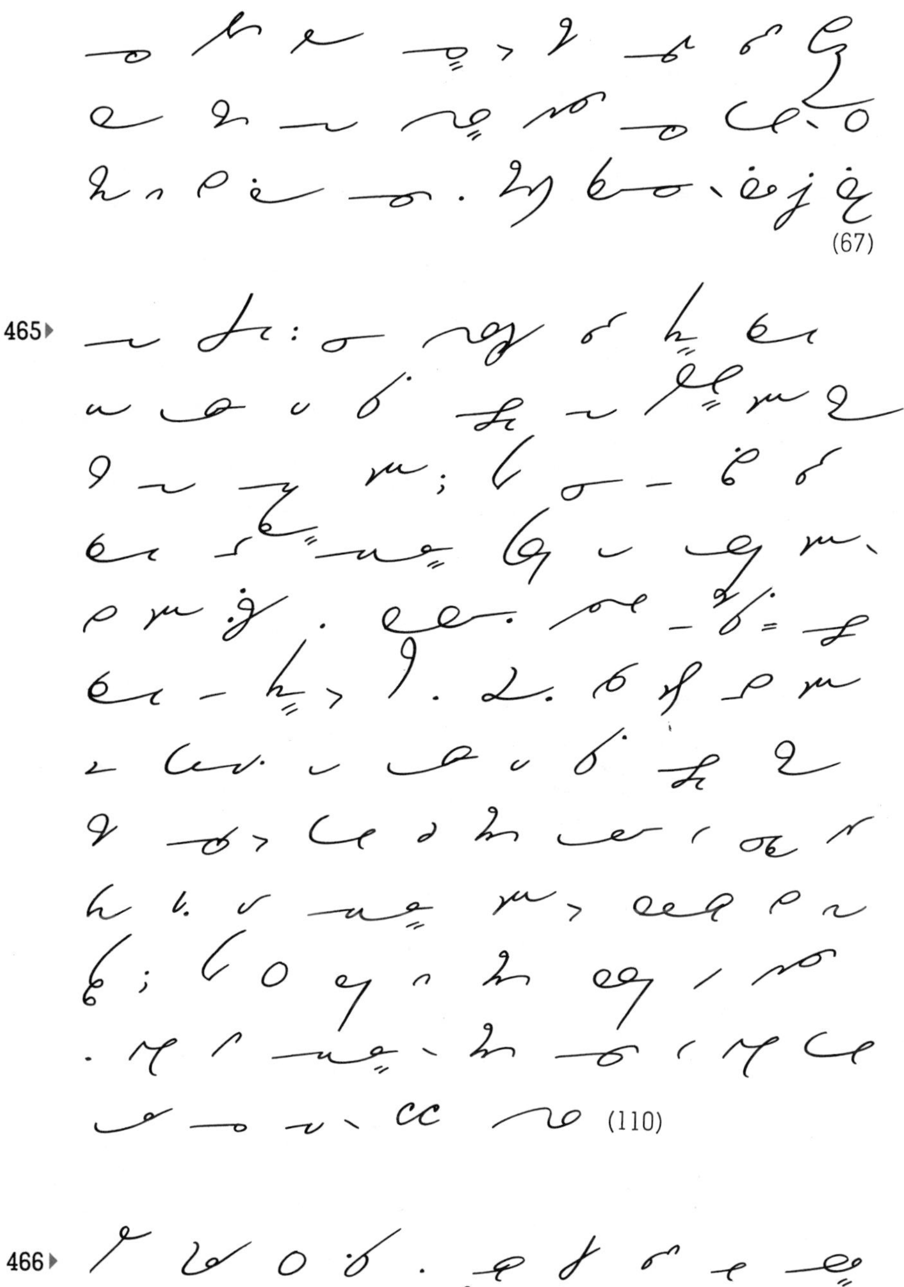

(67)
465
(110)
466

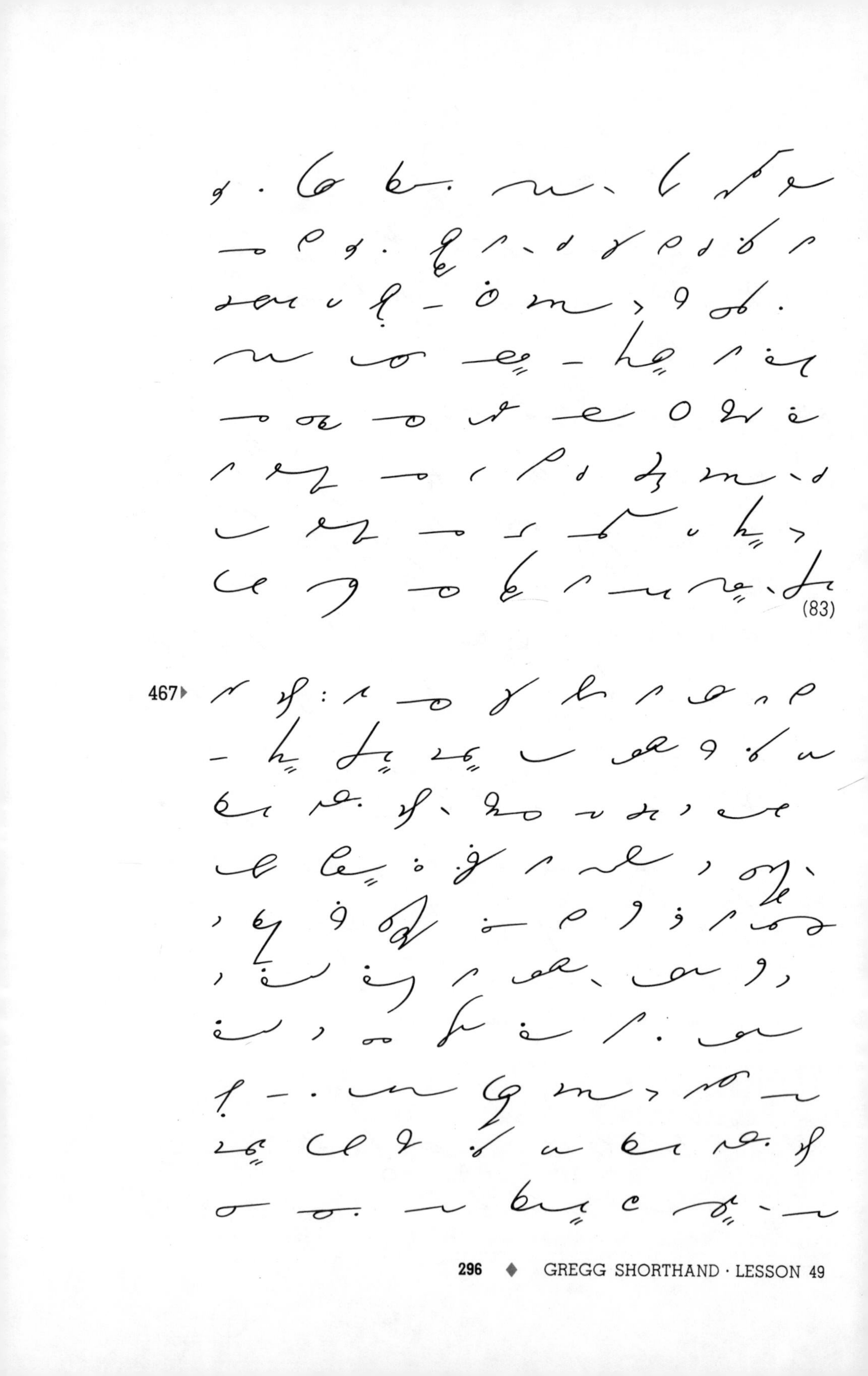

(83)

467

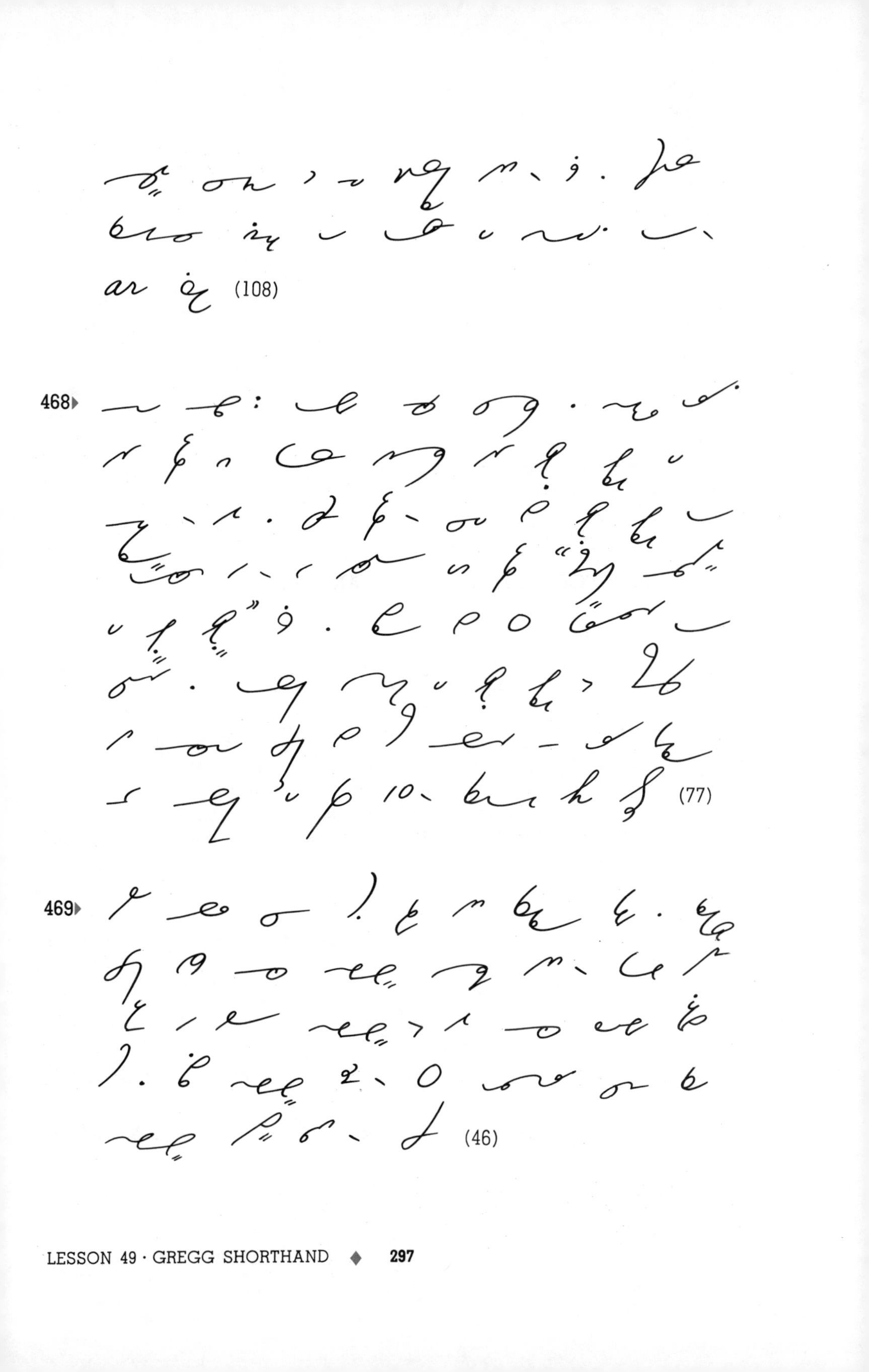

(108)

468 (77)

469 (46)

The practice material in Lesson 50 concentrates on the principles you studied in Chapter 2.

470 BRIEF FORMS, DERIVATIVES, AND PHRASES

a Put, putting, be-by, being, would, their-there, this, and, good, goods.
b And, send, sending, they, which, shall, from, should, could.
c I was, for the, which is not, this is, from them, for this, when the, I would not.

READING AND WRITING PRACTICE

471

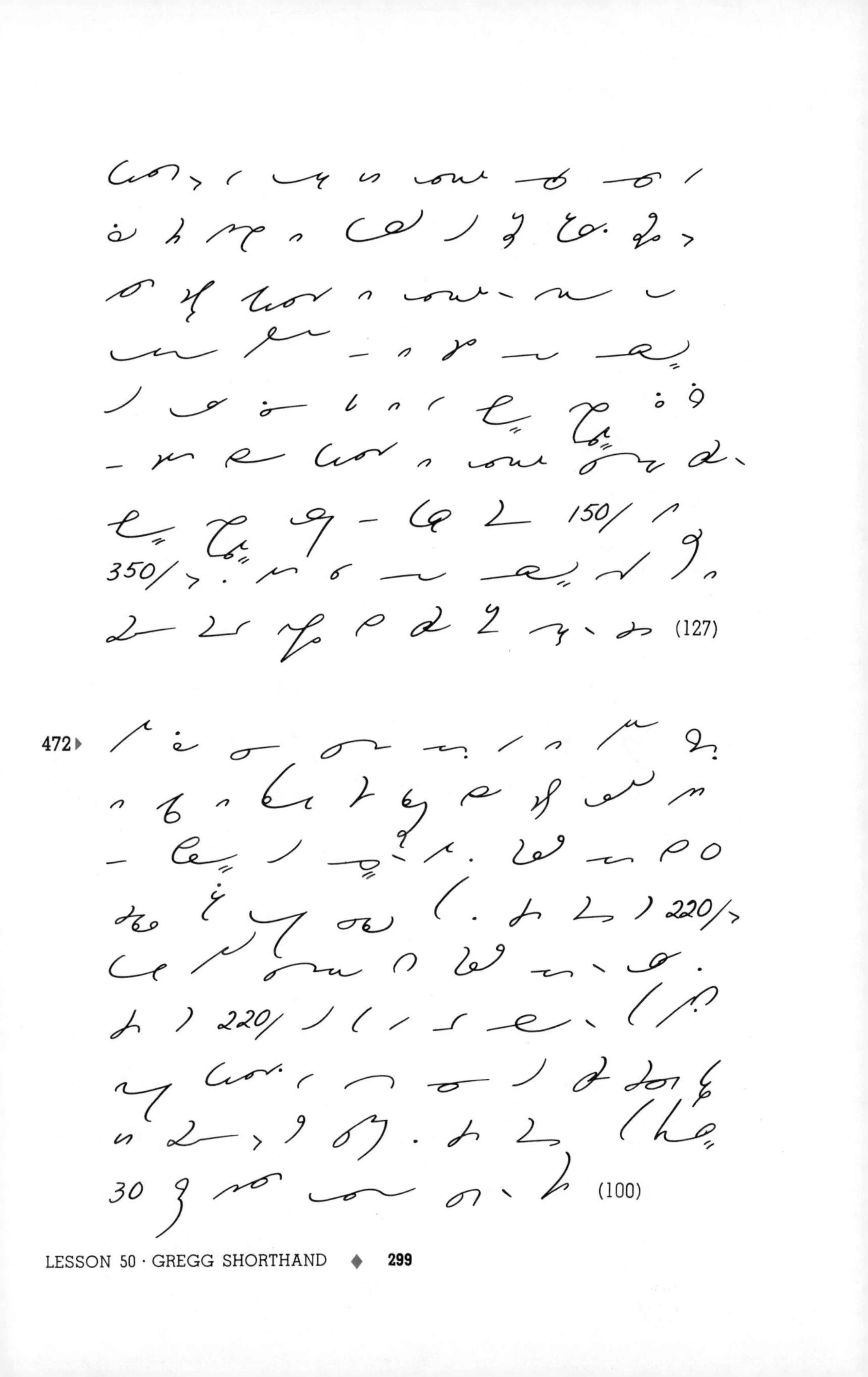

(127)

472 (100)

473 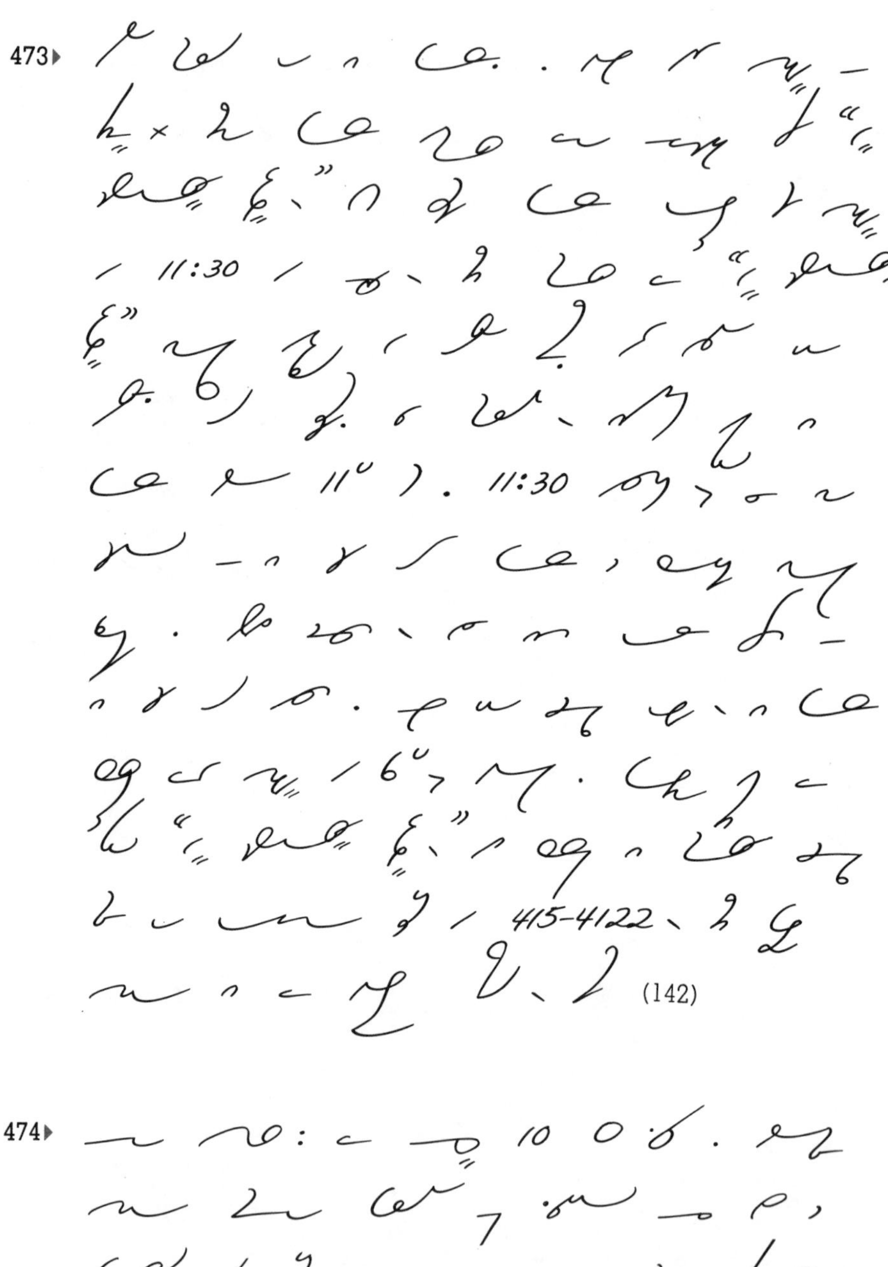

(142)

474

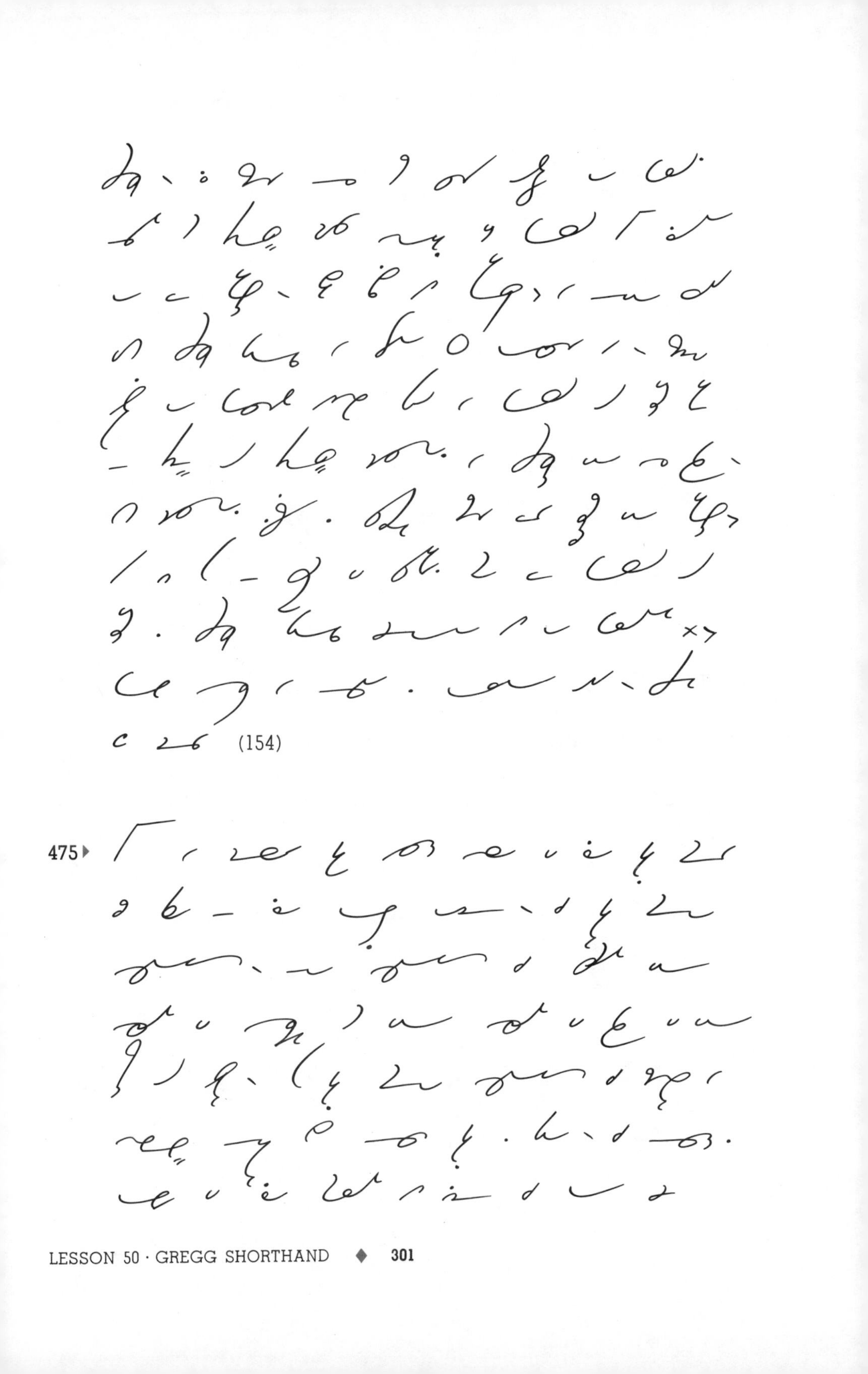

(154)

475

(134)

476

(97)

In this lesson you will review intensively the shorthand principles that you studied in Chapter 3.

477 BRIEF FORMS, DERIVATIVES, AND PHRASES

a Manufacturing, where, those, important-importance, gentlemen, businesses.
b Why, thing-think, greater, about, what, once, than, values.
c Were-year, enclose, soon, order, thank, very, yesterday, worker, gladly.
d About the, about those, where is, I think, what is, less than, very well, were not.

BUILDING TRANSCRIPTION SKILLS

478 BUSINESS VOCABULARY BUILDER

adjourn To end a meeting. (Do not confuse with "adjoin," which means "to be close to.")
deprived Made to do without.
rectify To correct.

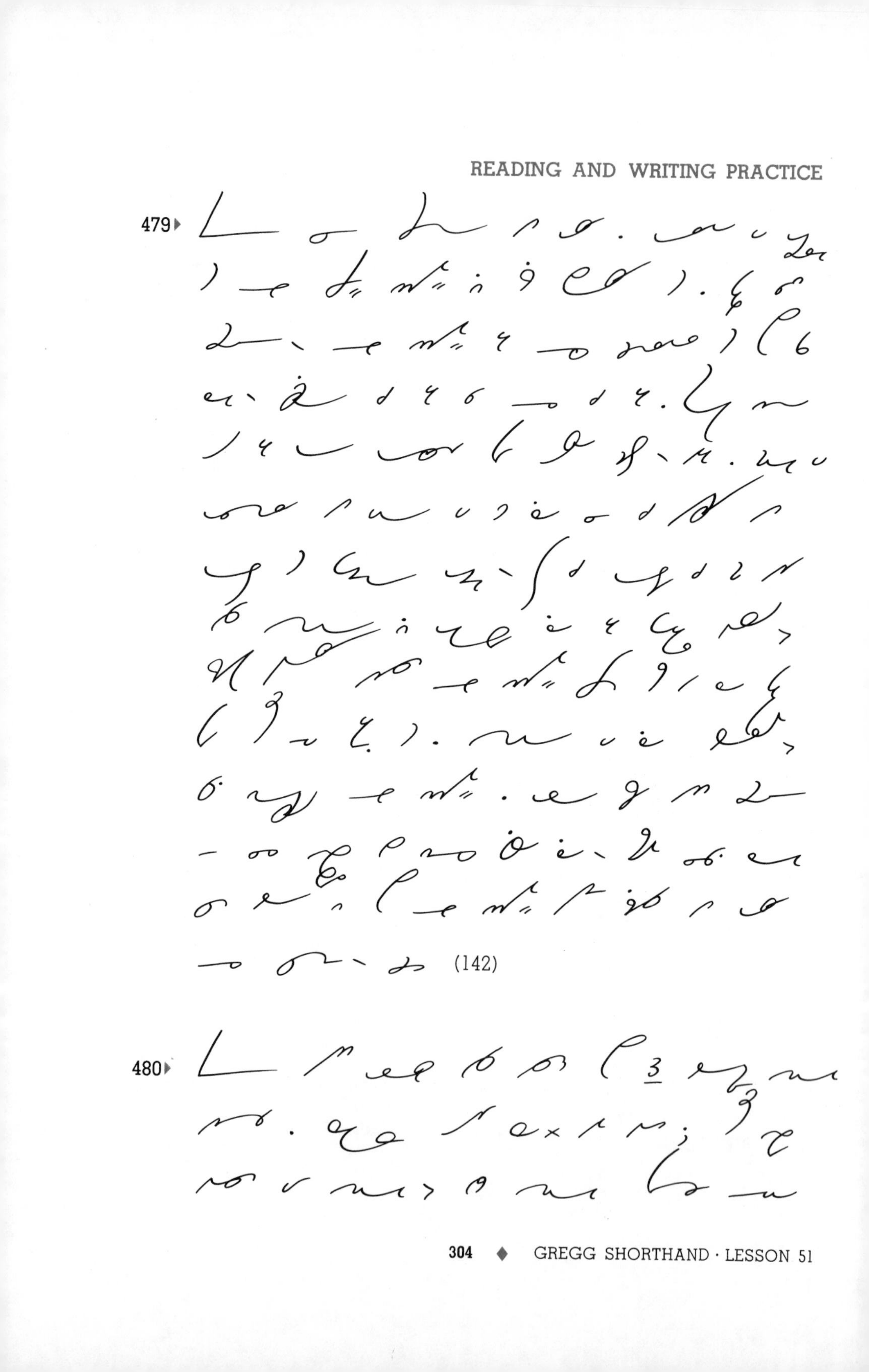

READING AND WRITING PRACTICE

479 (142)

480

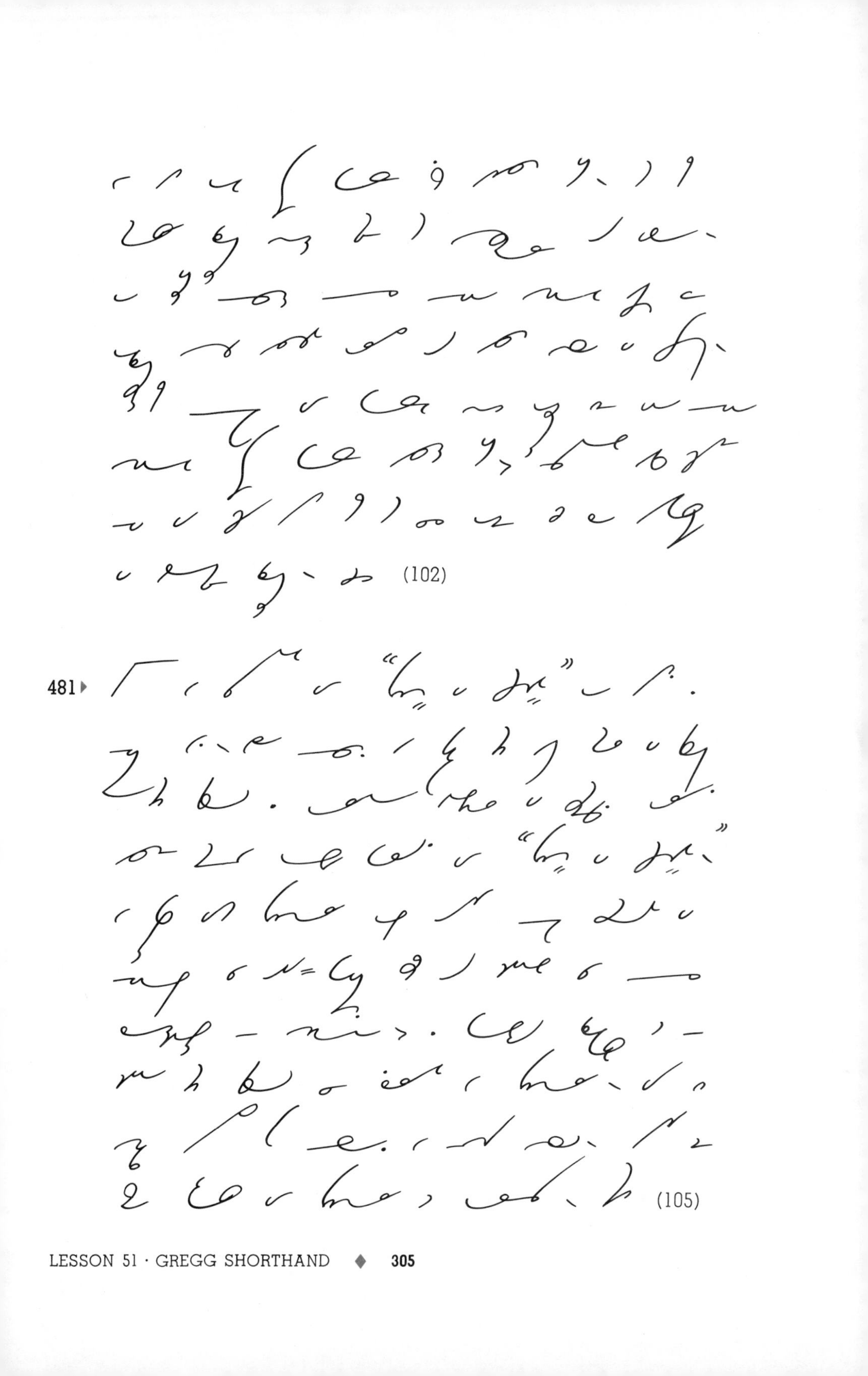

(102)

481

(105)

482

(105)

483

(98)

484

(164)

The practice material in this lesson concentrates on the shorthand principles you studied in Chapter 4.

485▸ BRIEF FORMS, DERIVATIVES, AND PHRASES

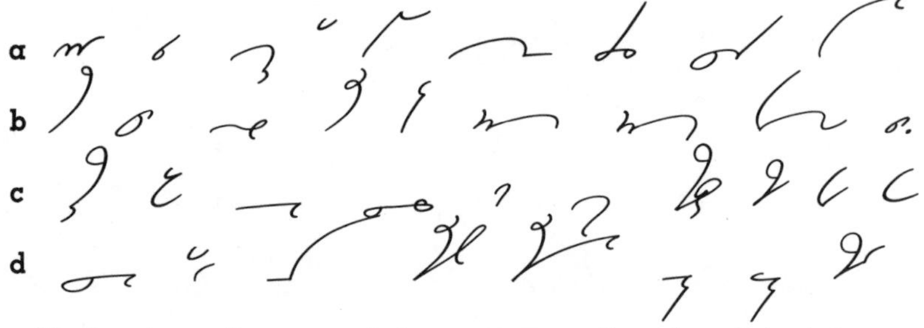

a Worth, yet, questions, over, during, gone, generally, acknowledged, times.

b Ever-every, how-out, correspond-correspondence, several, such, suggest, suggestion, bigger, using.

c Advantages, opportunity, must, immediately, wish, company, advertises, after, part, present.

d I must, over the, in time, several days, several times, in such, on such, after the.

BUILDING TRANSCRIPTION SKILLS

486▸ SPELLING FAMILIES

An effective device to improve your ability to spell is to study words in related groups, or spelling families, in which all the words contain the same spelling problem; for example, words in which e is retained before *ment* and words in which e is dropped before *ment.*

To get the most benefit from these spelling families, practice them in this way:

1 Spell each word aloud, pausing slightly after each word division.
2 Write the word once in longhand, spelling it aloud as you write it.

You will find several of the words in each spelling family used in the Reading and Writing Practice.

Words Ending in -ment

Most words ending in e retain the e before the ending *-ment.*

an·nounce·ment	**amuse·ment**	**en·cour·age·ment**	**man·age·ment**
ad·ver·tise·ment	**ar·range·ment**	**en·gage·ment**	**state·ment**

BUT

ac·knowl·edg·ment	**judg·ment**	**ar·gu·ment**

487 **BUSINESS VOCABULARY BUILDER**

induced Influenced.
daily A newspaper that is issued every day.
traveler A salesman; a representative.

READING AND WRITING PRACTICE

488

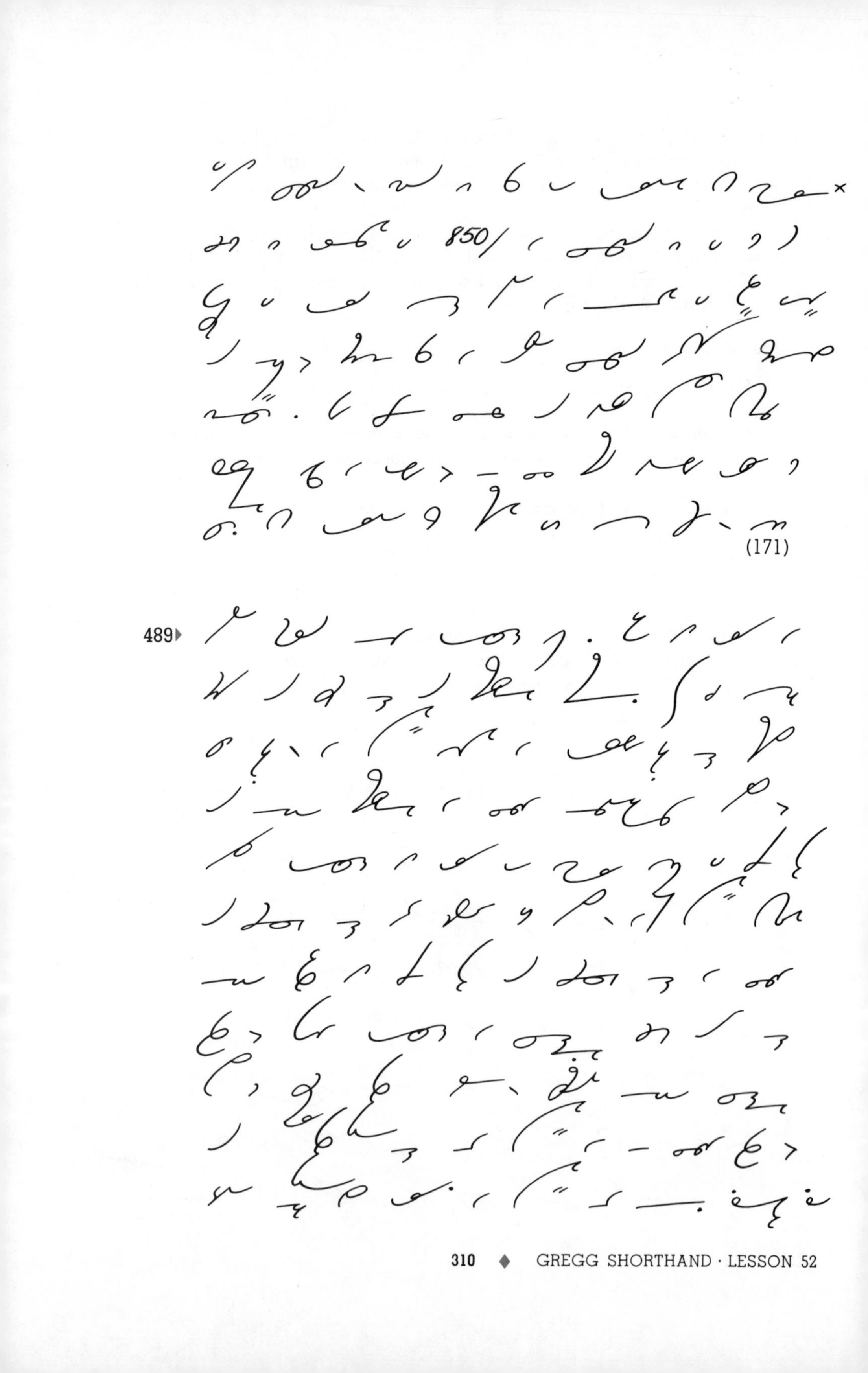

850

(171)

489

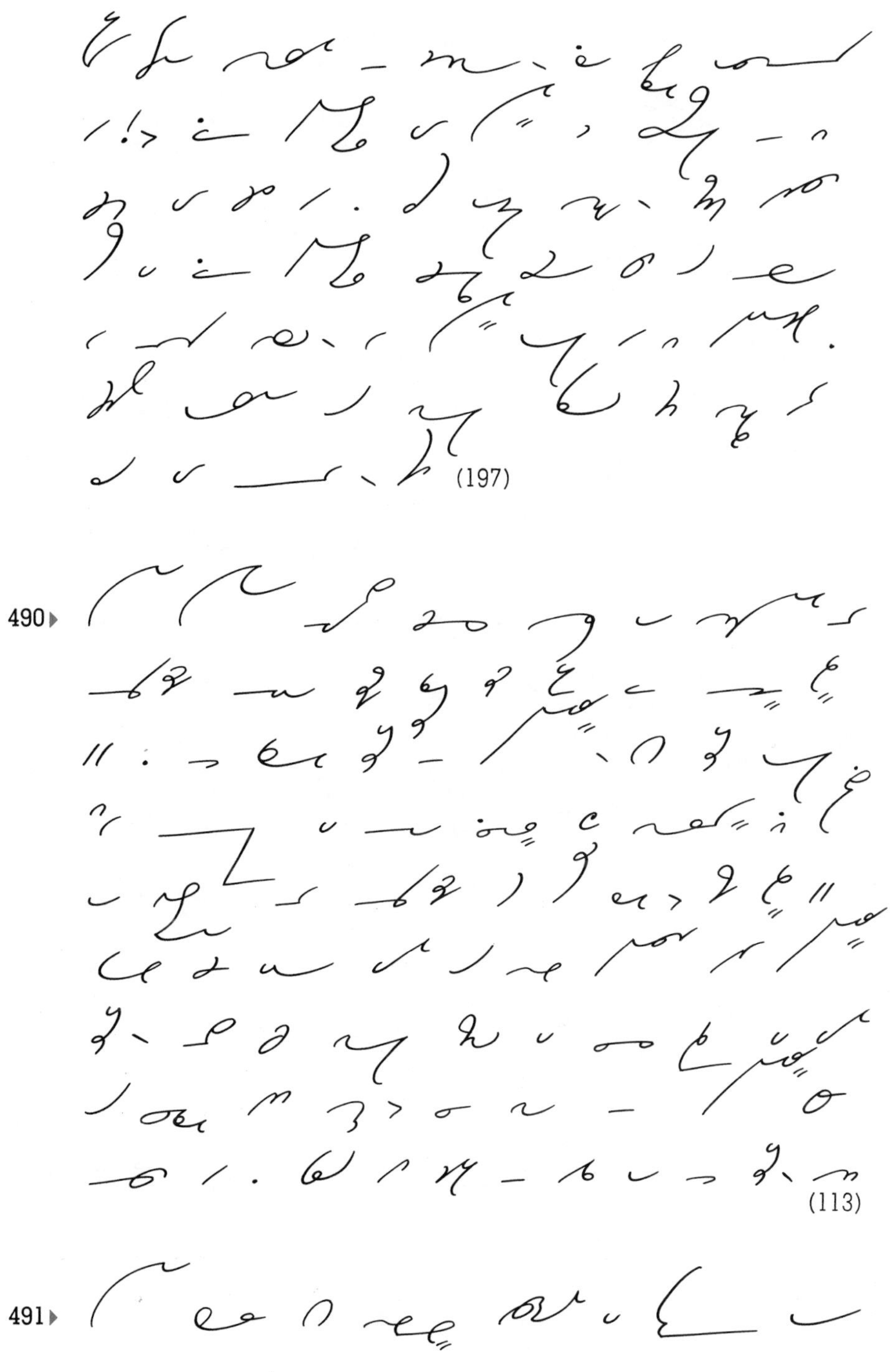
(197)
490
(113)
491

(105)

492

(99)

In this lesson you will obtain a thorough review of the shorthand principles you studied in Chapter 5.

493 ▸ **BRIEF FORMS, DERIVATIVES, AND PHRASES**

a Ordinary, publish-publication, public, organization, responsible, circular, opinions, regarding, purpose.

b Newspaper, streets, upon, subjects, ideas, speaking, regularly, probably, particularly.

c Requests, under, states, next, success, satisfy-satisfactory, progress, envelope, difficulty.

d Upon the, upon that, upon them, next time, to speak, to publish, under the, under that, under those.

BUILDING TRANSCRIPTION SKILLS

494 ▸ **BUSINESS VOCABULARY BUILDER**

associates Fellow workers.

novel New, different.

atlas A book of maps.

READING AND WRITING PRACTICE

495

41

80

(168)

496

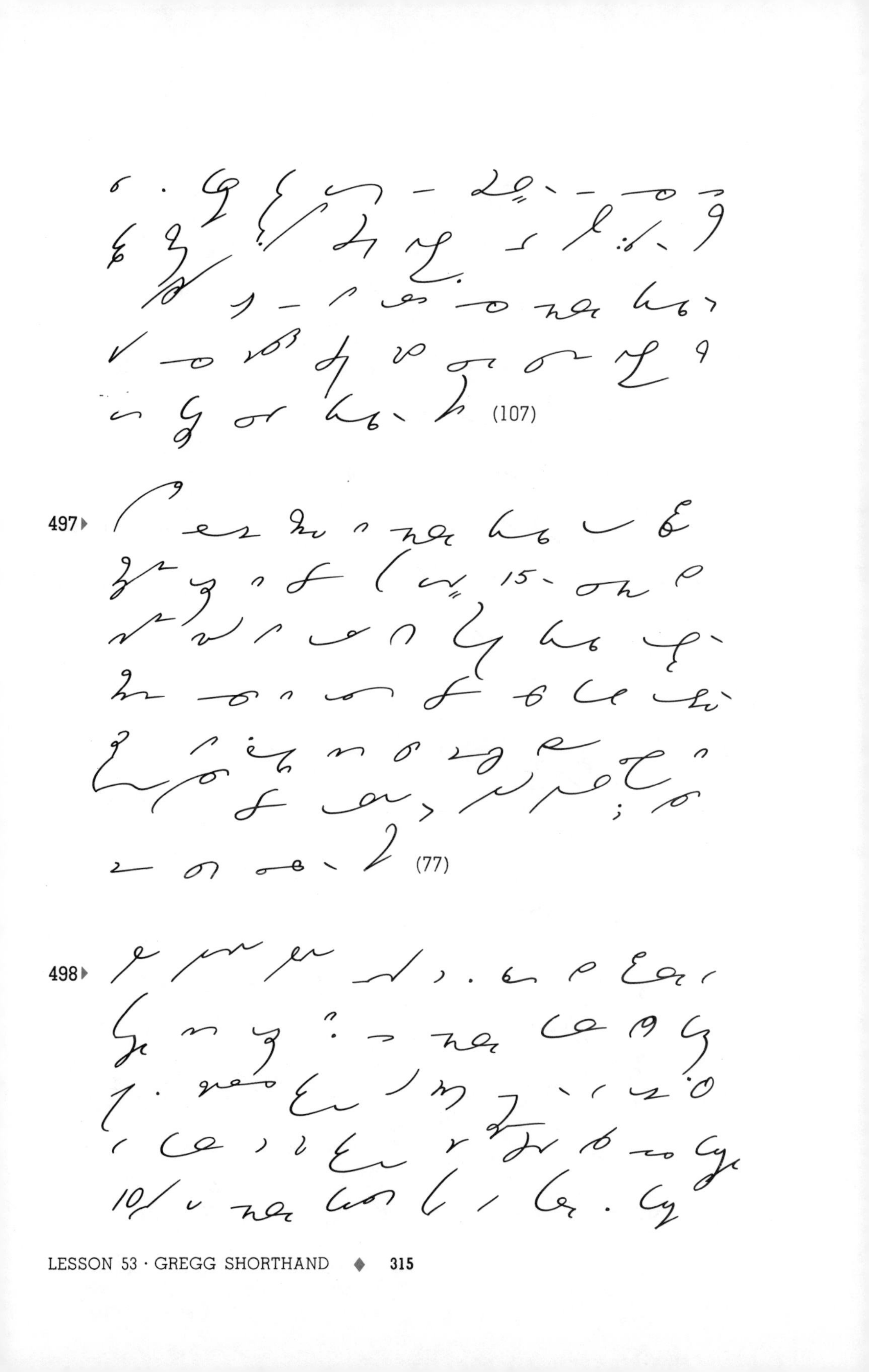

(107)

497

(77)

498

(173)

499

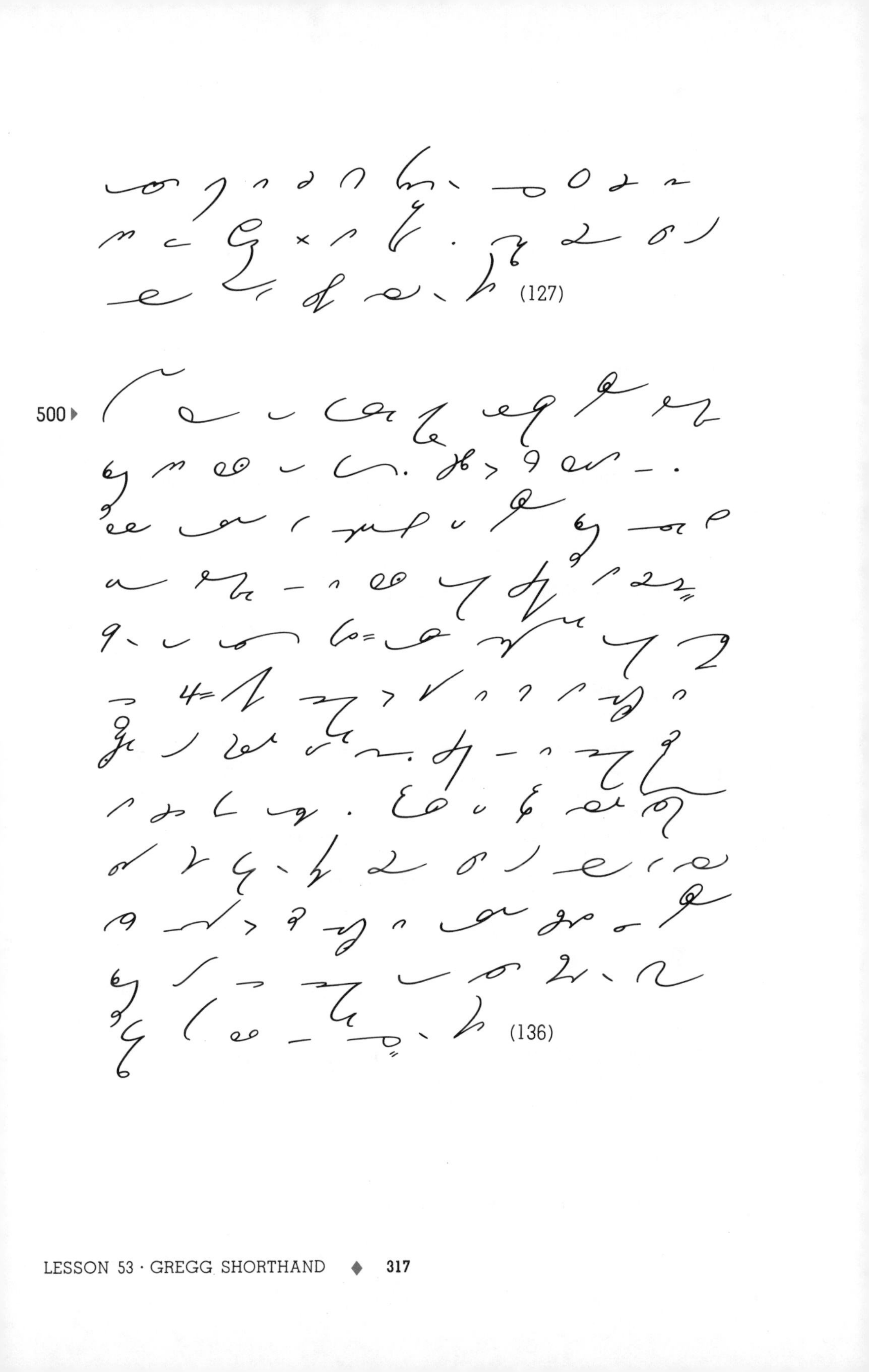

(127)

500

(136)

The practice material in Lesson 54 concentrates on the shorthand principles you studied in Chapter 6.

501 ▸ BRIEF FORMS AND DERIVATIVES

a Government, governs, characters, objected, objective, throughout, world, railroad.

b Situation, situations, quantities, short, shortly, shorter, between, experience, experiences.

c Never, recognize, recognizes, recognition, merchandise, merchant, merchants.

BUILDING TRANSCRIPTION SKILLS

502 ▸ SIMILAR-WORDS DRILL their, there, they're

their Possessive form of *they*.

Some women make their own dresses.

there In or at that place.

He went there at my request.

they're Contraction for *they are.*

They're always ready to help you.

503 ▸ **BUSINESS VOCABULARY BUILDER**

terminal Station; depot.
preliminary Coming before.
surplus That which is left over.

READING AND WRITING PRACTICE

504 ▸

Bu·reau
en·trance

thor·ough·ly
fa·mil·iar
they're

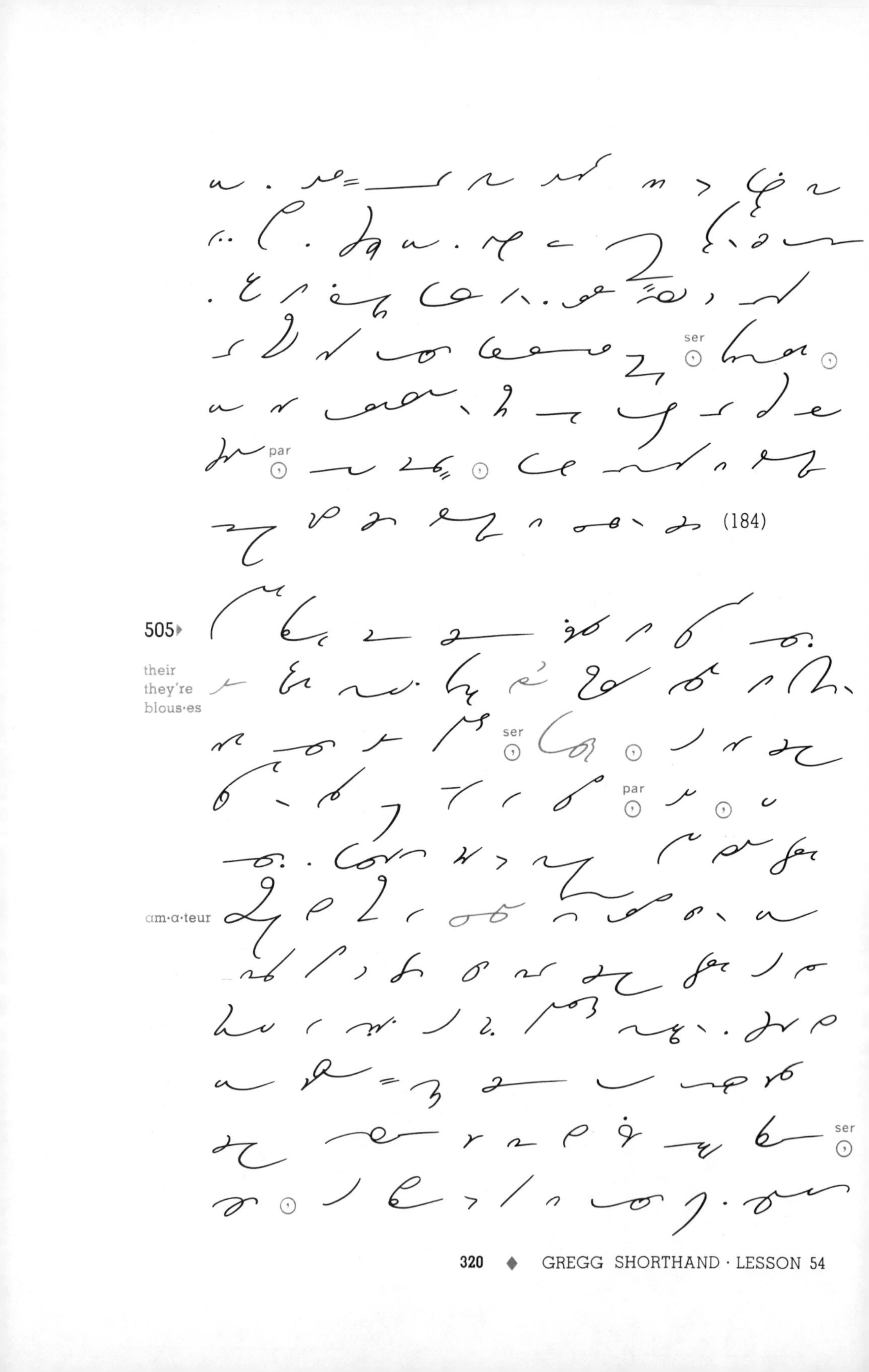

ser

par

(184)

505

their
they're
blous·es

ser

par

am·a·teur

ser

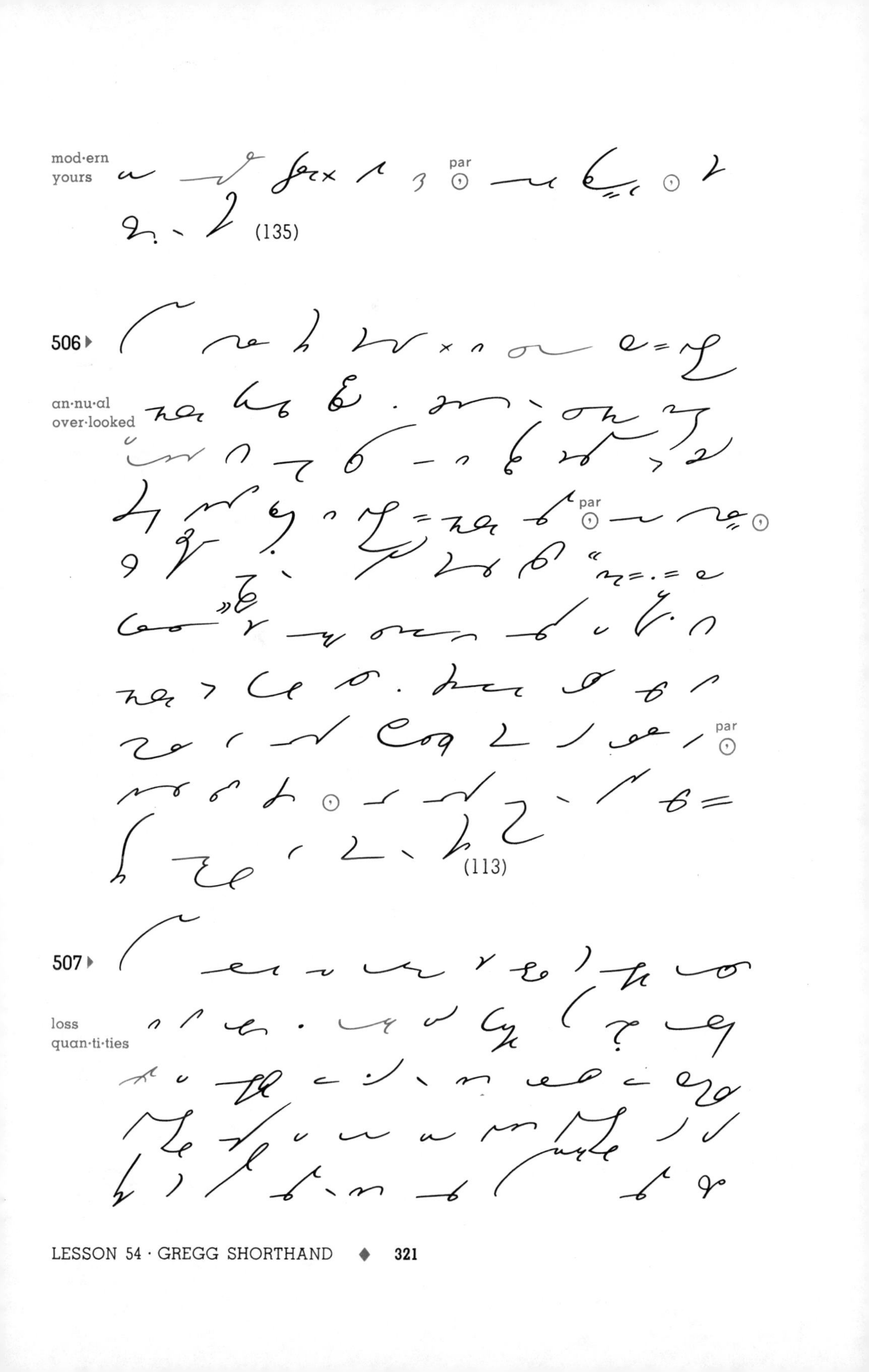

mod·ern
yours

par

(135)

506

an·nu·al
over·looked

par

par

(113)

507

loss
quan·ti·ties

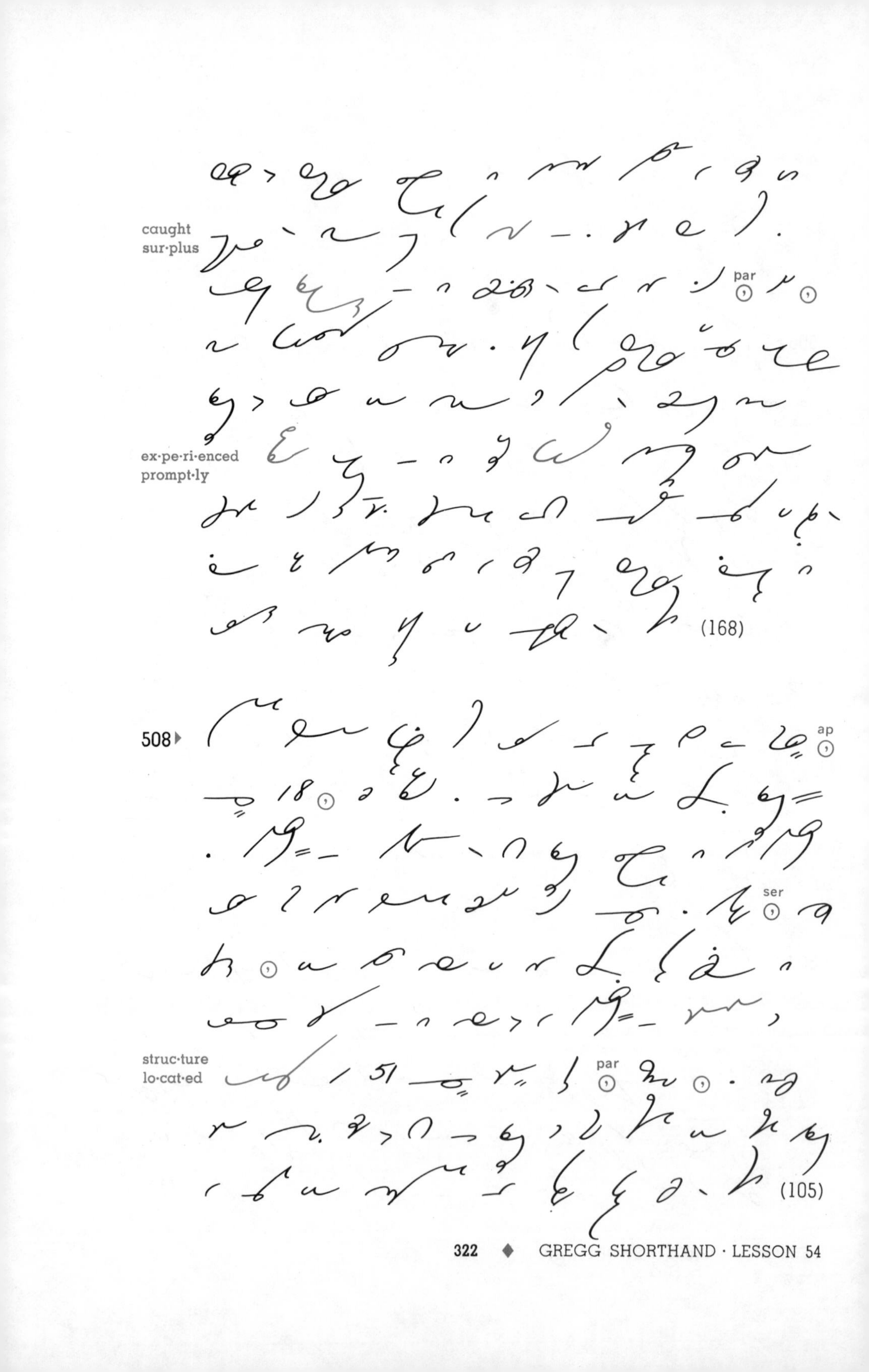

caught
sur·plus

par

ex·pe·ri·enced
prompt·ly

(168)

508

ap

18

ser

struc·ture
lo·cat·ed

51

par

(105)

In Lesson 55 you will review intensively the shorthand principles you studied in Chapter 7.

509 ▸ BRIEF FORMS, DERIVATIVES, AND PHRASES

a Particularly, timely, partly, presently, gladly, probably, immediately, generally.

b Greater, sooner, bigger, shorter, worker, manufacturer.

c To progress, to part, to present, to speak, to publish, to put, to be, to have, to which.

BUILDING TRANSCRIPTION SKILLS

510 ▸ GRAMMAR CHECKUP the infinitive (The form of the verb usually introduced by *to—to see, to be, to have, to do.*)

Careful writers try to avoid "splitting" an infinitive; that is, inserting a word or phrase beween *to* and the following word.

NO To properly do the job, you need better tools.
YES To do the job properly, you need better tools.
NO He was told to carefully prepare the report.
YES He was told to prepare the report carefully.

511 BUSINESS VOCABULARY BUILDER

equivalent Equal in force, amount, or value.
impressive Inspiring admiration.
patronage Business.

READING AND WRITING PRACTICE

512

intro ser

its
equiv·a·lent
pre·vi·ous

as

if

(125)

513

cour·te·ous
ex·ceed·ing·ly

intro

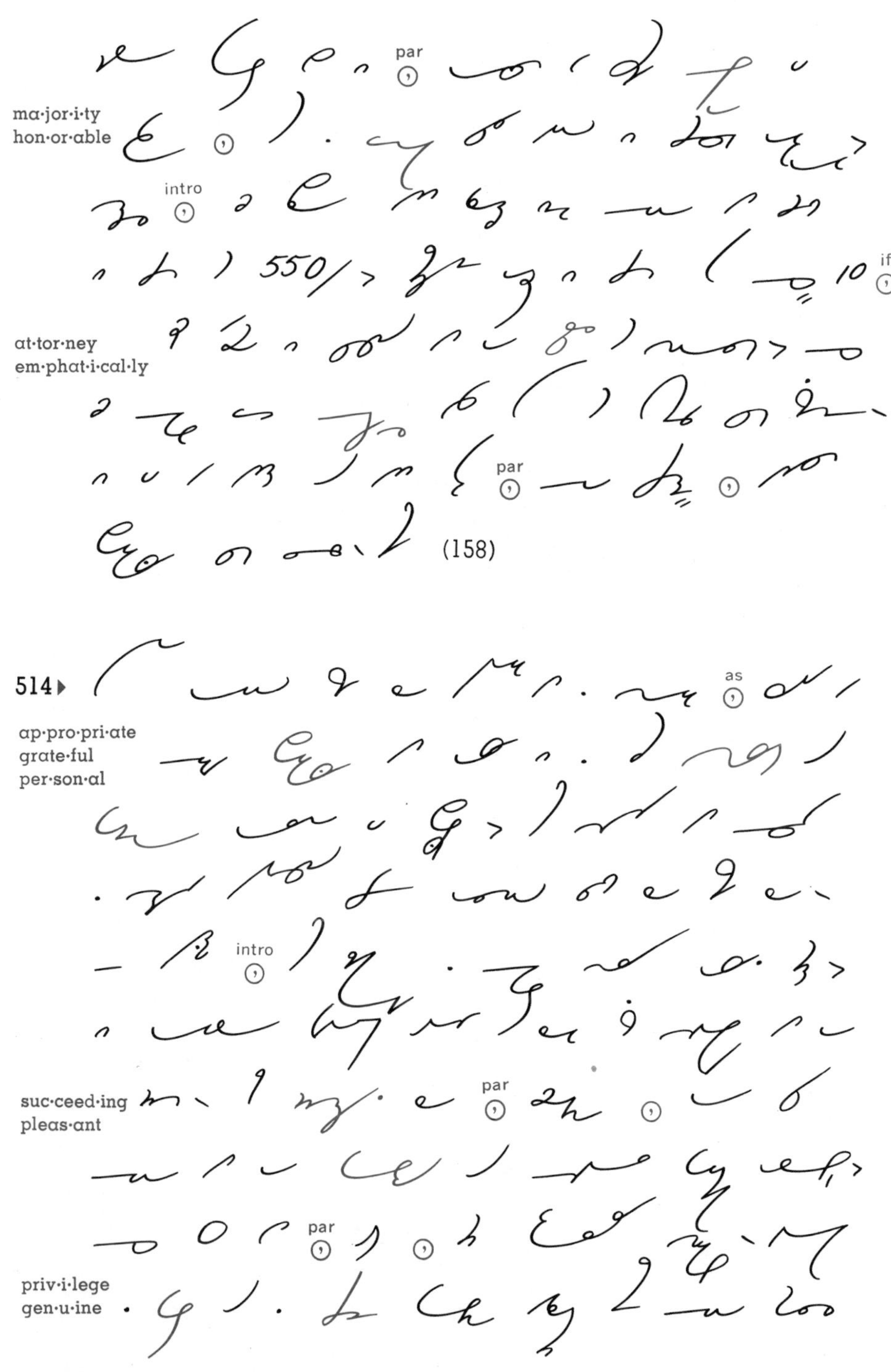
par
ma·jor·i·ty
hon·or·able
intro
550
10
if
at·tor·ney
em·phat·i·cal·ly
par
(158)
514
as
ap·pro·pri·ate
grate·ful
per·son·al
intro
suc·ceed·ing
pleas·ant
par
par
priv·i·lege
gen·u·ine

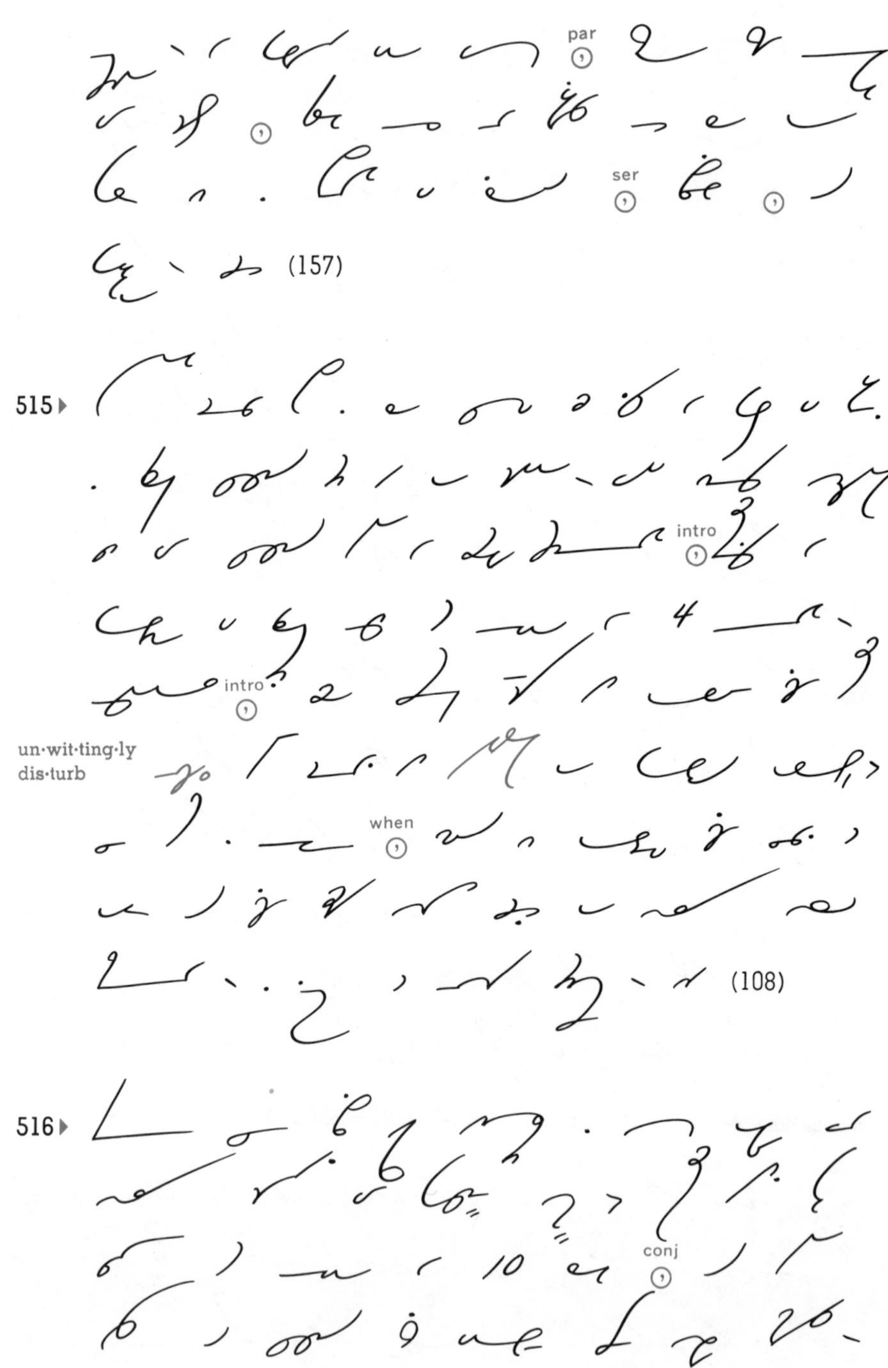

par
ser
(157)
515
intro
intro
un·wit·ting·ly
dis·turb
when
(108)
516
conj

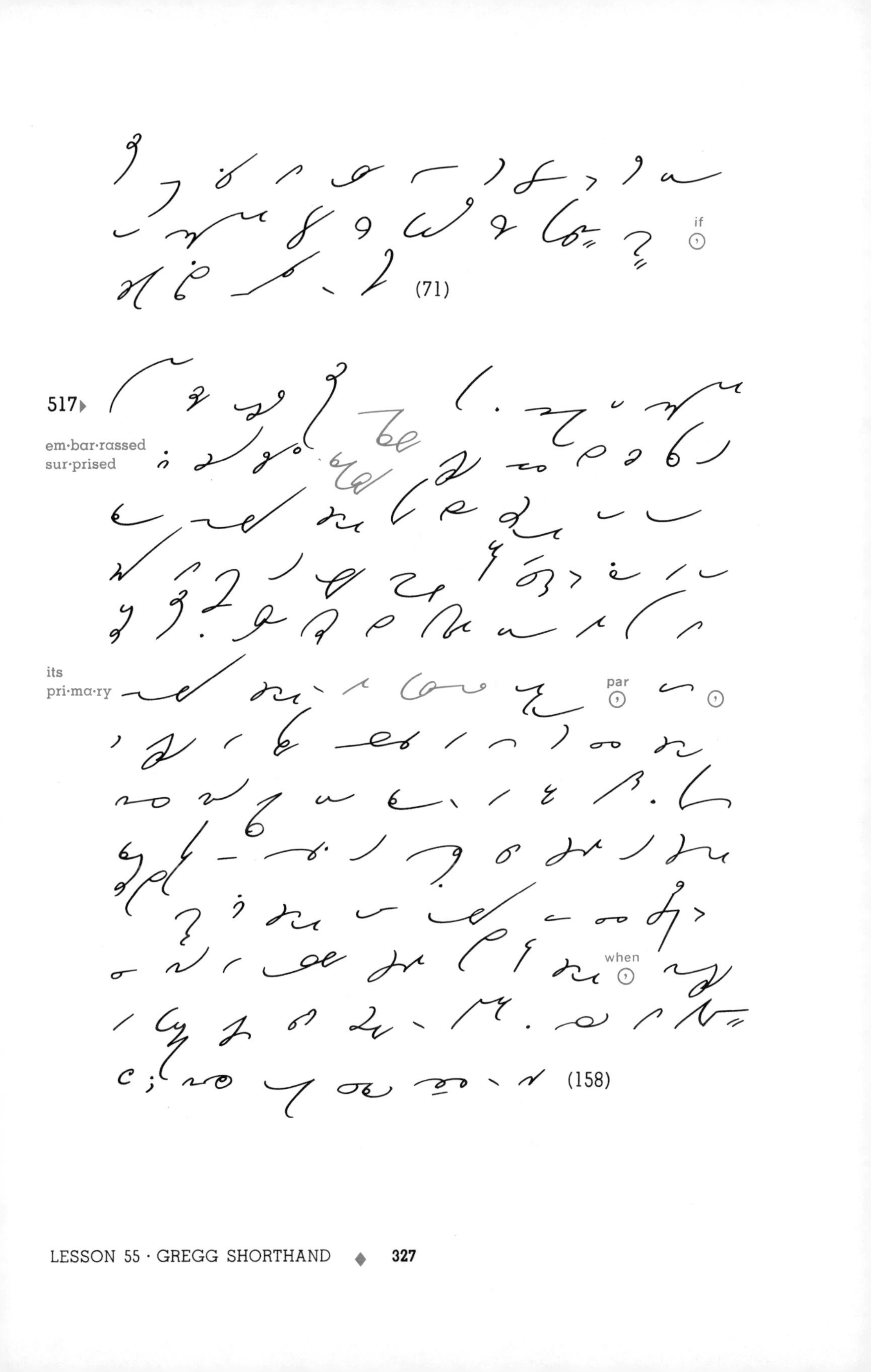

if

(71)

517

em·bar·rassed
sur·prised

its
pri·ma·ry

par

when

(158)

The practice material in this lesson concentrates on the shorthand principles you studied in Chapter 8.

518 BRIEF FORMS, DERIVATIVES, AND PHRASES

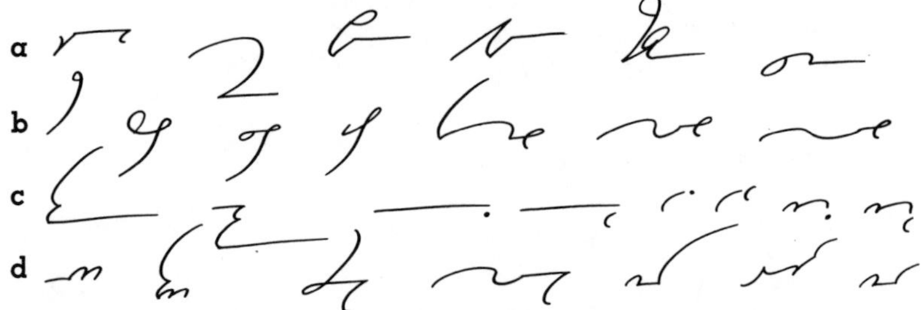

a Statements, government, apartment, department, advertisement, acknowledgment.

b Ever, wherever, whenever, whatever, bigness, greatness, gladness.

c Businessmen, newspapermen, morning, mornings, thank, thanks, working, workings.

d In the world, business world, very important, great importance, one time, throughout the, one of the.

BUILDING TRANSCRIPTION SKILLS

519 COMMON WORD ROOTS

Many English words are derived from the Greek and Latin languages. Consequently, an understanding of the meanings of Greek and Latin prefixes and suffixes will often give you a clue to the meaning of words with which you are unfamiliar.

Perhaps you never heard the word *posterity*. However, if you know that *post* means *after*, you will probably be able to figure out that *posterity* refers to those who come after, or descendants.

In each Common Word Roots exercise you will be given a common prefix or suffix, together with its meaning, and a list of words in which the prefix or suffix is used.

Read each definition carefully, and then study the illustrations that follow. A number of the illustrations are used in the Reading and Writing Practice.

Super-: over; more than

supervise To oversee.
supervisor One who oversees.
superior Over in rank; higher.
superfluous More than enough.

520 **BUSINESS VOCABULARY BUILDER**

unrewarding Not satisfying.
highlight An event of major significance.
deferment Official postponement of military service.

READING AND WRITING PRACTICE

521

if

re·liev·ing
un·re·ward·ing

and o

par

and o

intro

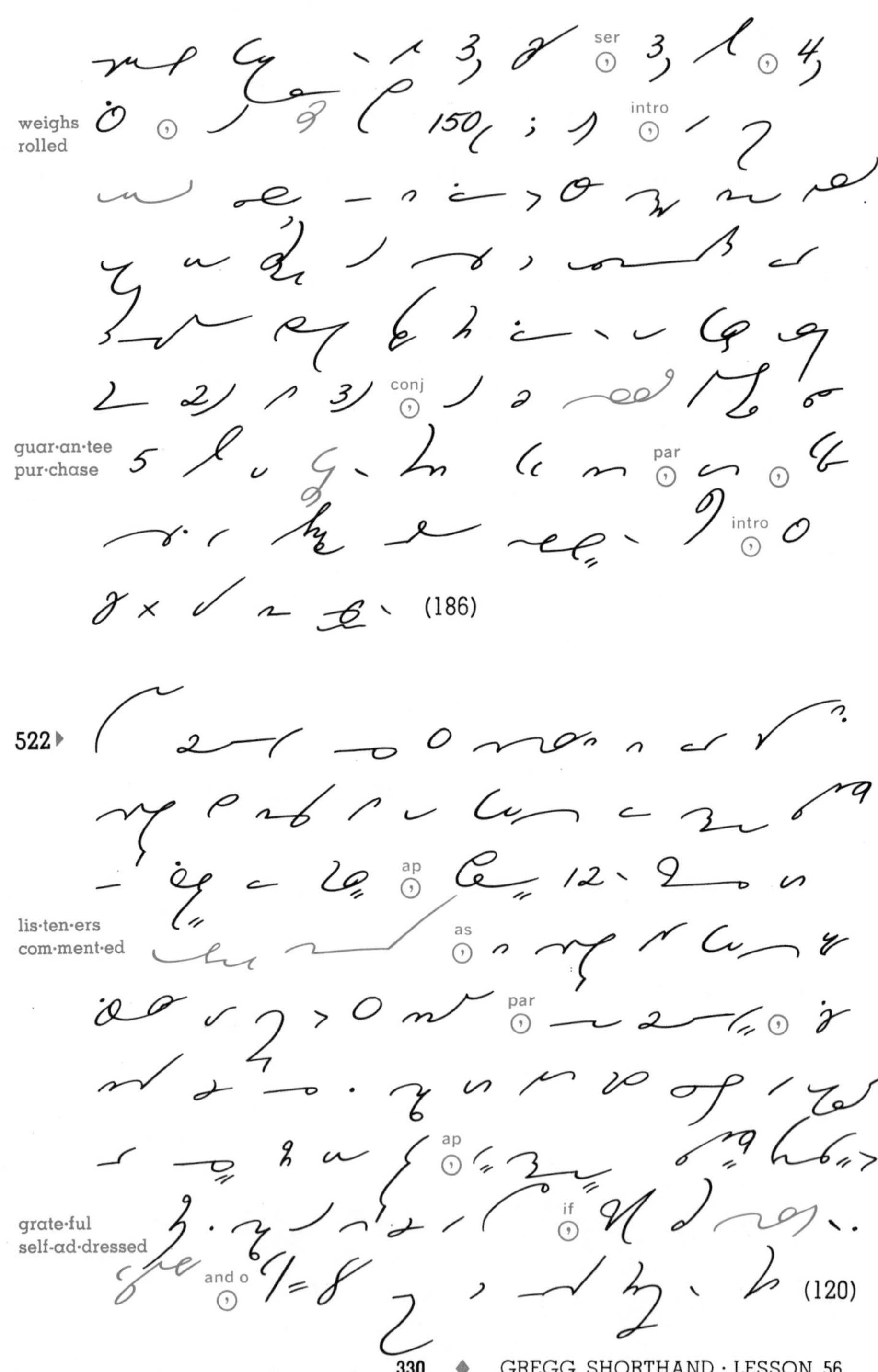
ser
weighs
rolled
150
intro
conj
guar·an·tee
pur·chase
par
intro
(186)
522
ap
12
lis·ten·ers
com·ment·ed
as
par
ap
grate·ful
self-ad·dressed
if
and o
(120)

523

su·per·sedes
pre·vi·ous

intro

par

intro

past
crit·i·cal

intro

per·son·nel
vir·tue

par

nonr

(214)

524

re·cent
sur·vey

intro

fal·la·cy
sig·nif·i·cant

par

ap

in·ves·tors
se·cu·ri·ties

(161)

525

(58)

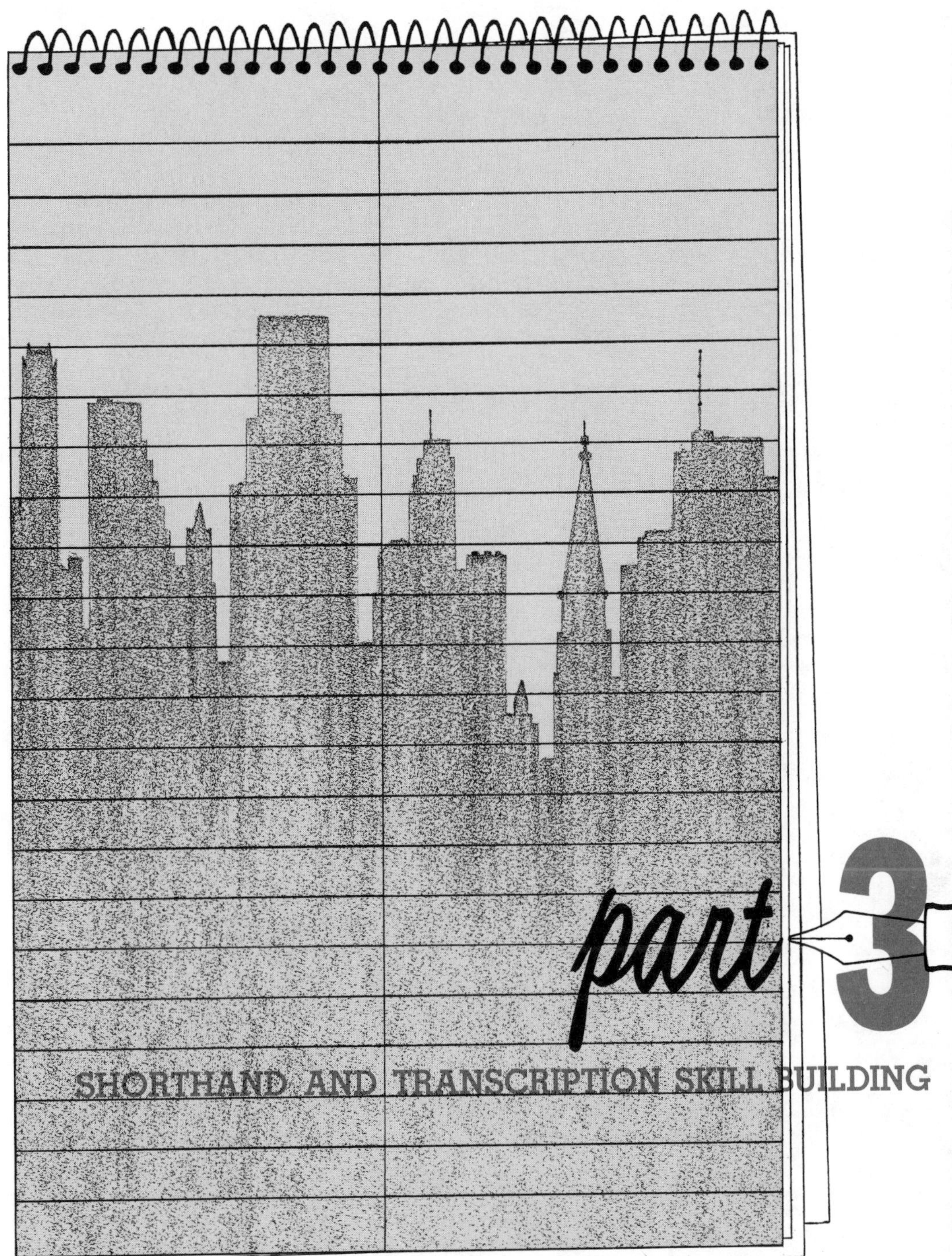

part 3

SHORTHAND AND TRANSCRIPTION SKILL BUILDING

It is easy to list the qualities the business employee should possess. He should be honest, dependable, intelligent, hard working, friendly, cooperative, ambitious. . . . But let's stop right there: *any* favorable human attribute fits. Employers can reel off at least a couple of dozen traits they'd like to observe in everyone they hire, but not a single boss really expects perfection. There are, however, four qualities the typical executive *insists* on for his secretary: excellent stenographic skill, good communication skill, poise, and good grooming.

EXCELLENT STENOGRAPHIC SKILL

"There is absolutely no substitute for good skills," the typical executive will tell you. By "skills" he means mainly shorthand, typewriting, and transcription skills. The secretary must be able to take his dictation at the rate the executive wants to give it without the plea, "You're going too fast for me." He expects her to transcribe those shorthand notes quickly and accurately on the typewriter. This calls for a typing speed of at least 60 words a minute and a good knowledge of letter and report setup.

GOOD COMMUNICATION SKILL

It could be said that communication is the secretary's main job, for her duties involve conveying meaning through the written and spoken word, through her poise, manners, tact, and facial expressions. All are methods of communicating. As to the written word, most executives expect the secretary to be their editor. When they have dictated a letter, they may say, "You 'fix' it up." This means they want her to put in the correct punctuation, paragraph the letter properly, correct errors in names, dates, figures, and word usage.

Many secretaries are expected to write letters, memorandums, and routine reports for their bosses. Letters include those that make travel or hotel reservations, acknowledge receipt of something, ask for something, follow up on an appointment or schedule, and thank someone for a favor. Memorandums and reports are written by the secretary to schedule and follow up on meetings, to report on progress, to review activities, and so on.

The secretary's voice is one of her most important assets. She greets callers, gives instructions to her employer's subordinates, communicates with other executives, and talks on the telephone to perhaps hundreds of people daily, both inside and outside the company. Occasionally she is asked to talk before an audience.

POISE

To most people "poise" simply means always looking cool, calm, and collected. Certainly these are essential ingredients in the meaning of the word. However, poise means much more than that. It includes knowing what to say to an irate customer who insists on tongue-lashing the boss (who doesn't want to be disturbed); how to explain tactfully why the executive is an hour late for an appointment with an out-of-town visitor; how to accept criticism from the boss even when she doesn't feel it is deserved; how to withhold confidential information from those who are not authorized to obtain it, no matter how persistent they are. Poise is the reflection of a mature personality, of complete confidence in one's self. It is a quality that every top executive ranks high on his list of "musts."

GOOD GROOMING

Every executive has a right to expect that his secretary will always look her best on the job. Her appearance can reflect favorably or unfavorably on him. Of course, she must be immaculately clean from head to toe. The smart secretary takes pride in herself, her job, and her boss; she never "lets herself go." This means daily attention to hair, nails, and complexion. It means getting a sufficient amount of rest so that she looks sharp and alert. And, of course, it means selecting clothing with great care and keeping it spotless and in good repair. Contrary to what some people believe, the secretary doesn't have to wear somber clothing. In fact, bright, tasteful colors are perfectly in place. The thing she must avoid is the *extreme* – the extreme in hair style and makeup, in clothing, and in accessories. The secretary who wants to look like the "belle of the ball" in the office is due for a rude awakening!

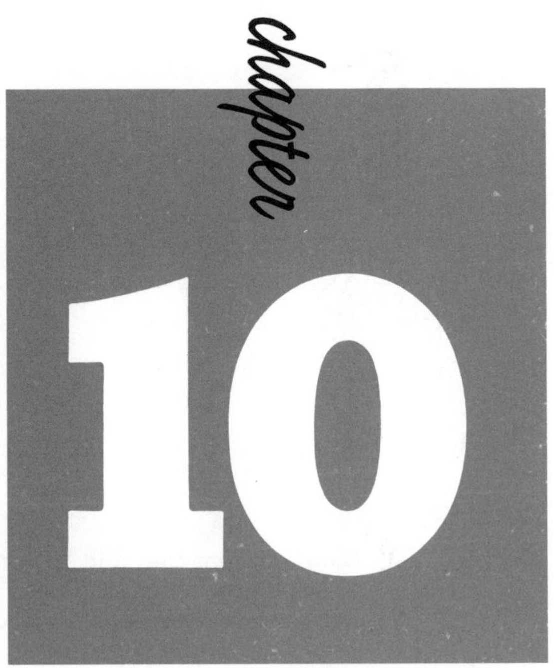

THE "IDEAL" SECRETARY

The practice material in Lesson 57 contains at least one illustration of every brief form of Gregg Shorthand. Counting repetitions, it contains 458 brief forms and derivatives. Because you have seen these brief forms many, many times, you should be able to read through the letters in this lesson with record speed!

BUILDING TRANSCRIPTION SKILLS

526 **SPELLING FAMILIES** -tion, -sion

Words Ending in -tion

ac·tion	com·ple·tion	lo·ca·tion	pro·tec·tion
ap·pli·ca·tion	il·lus·tra·tion	or·ga·ni·za·tion	pub·li·ca·tion
col·lec·tion	in·for·ma·tion	prop·o·si·tion	re·la·tion

Words Ending in -sion

ap·pre·hen·sion	de·ci·sion	per·mis·sion	pro·vi·sion
col·li·sion	di·vi·sion	per·sua·sion	ses·sion
con·clu·sion	oc·ca·sion	pro·fes·sion	tele·vi·sion

527 **BUSINESS VOCABULARY BUILDER**

apprehension Concern; fear.
merchandising Retail selling.
perplexing Disturbing.

528

ap

discuss
convene

conj

satisfactorily
overcome

intro

par

intro

(147)

529

apprehension
absence

ser

if

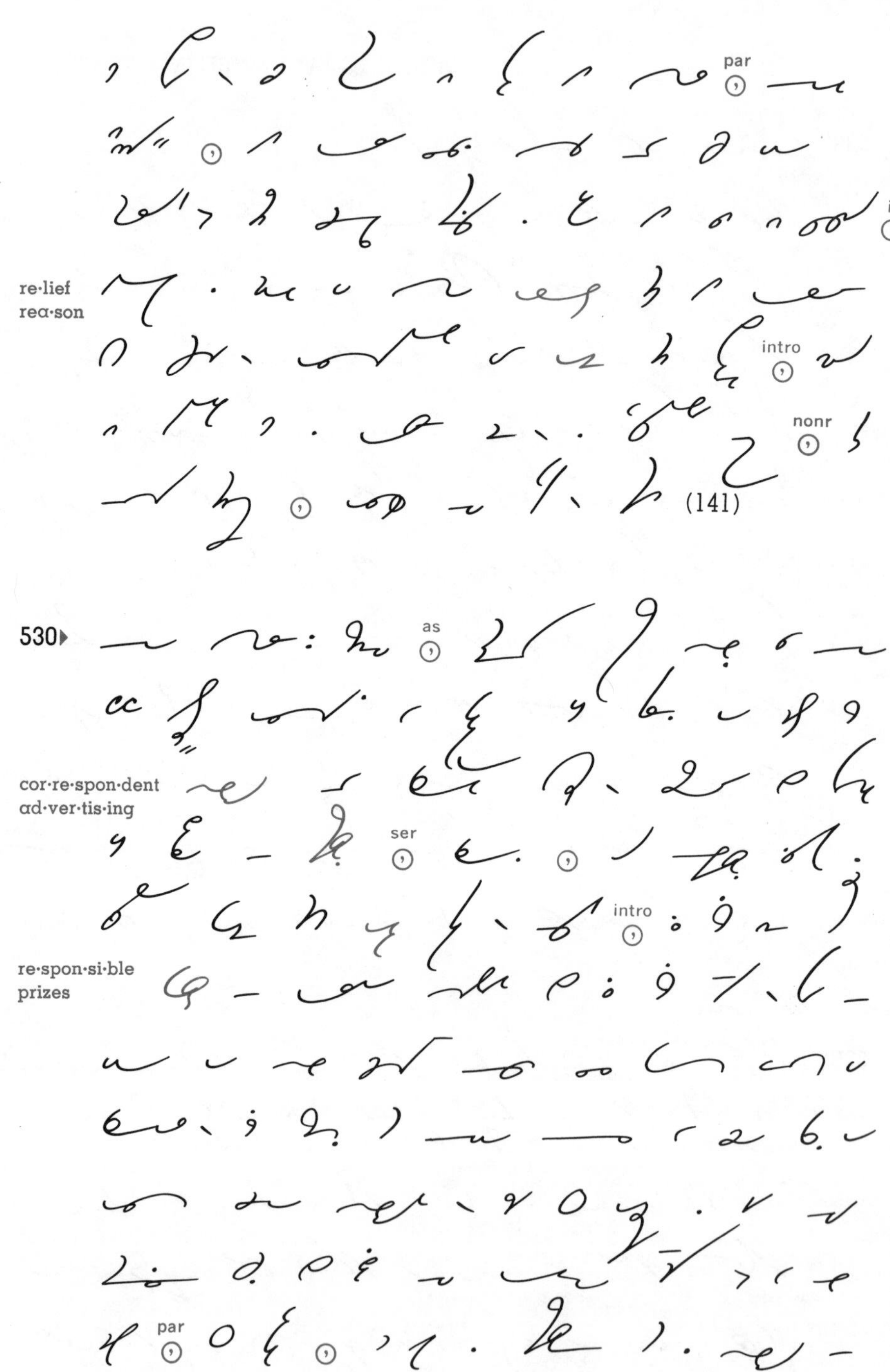
par
if
re·lief
rea·son
intro
nonr
(141)
530
as
cor·re·spon·dent
ad·ver·tis·ing
ser
intro
re·spon·si·ble
prizes
par

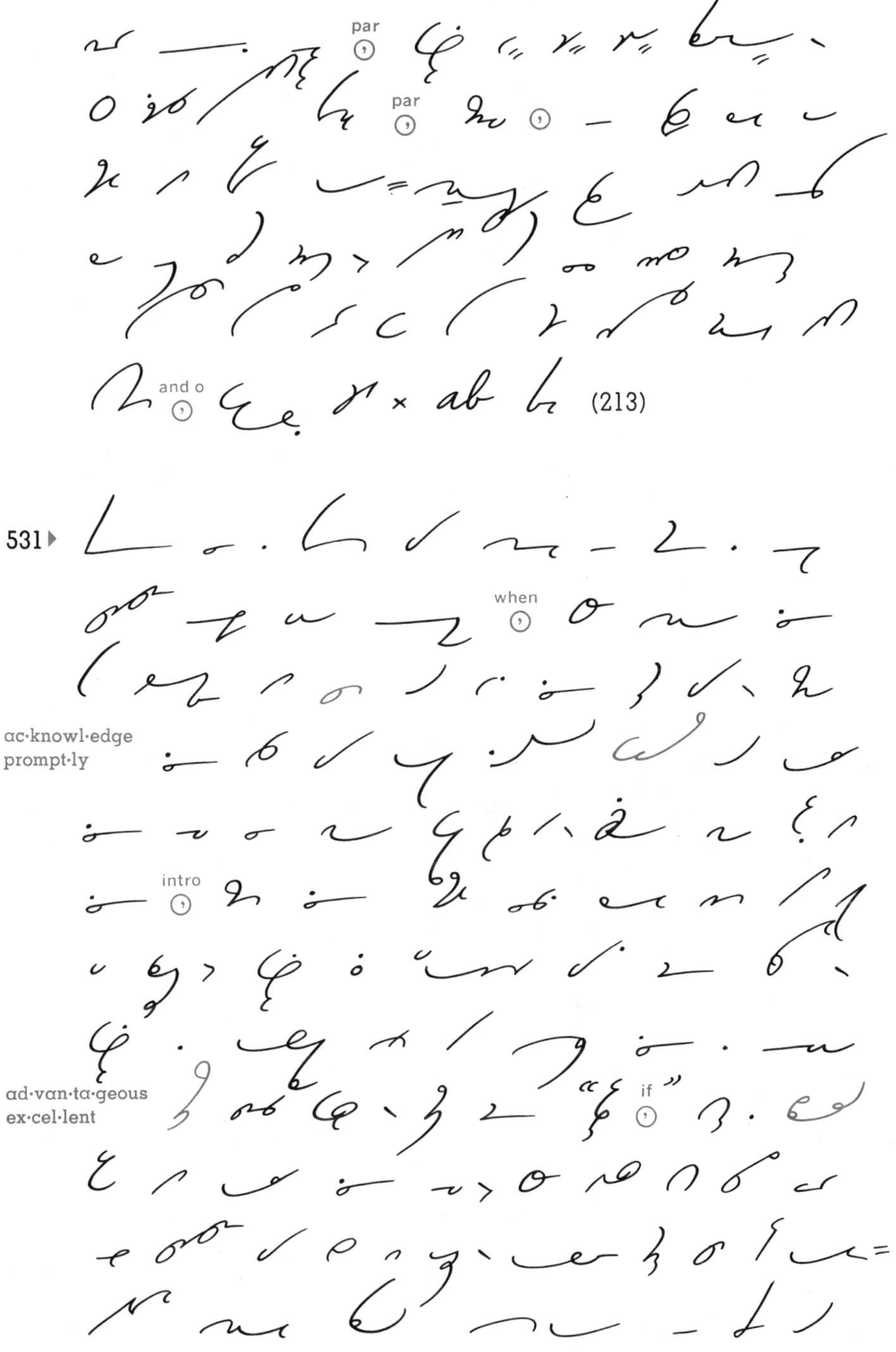
par
par
and o
(213)
531
when
ac·knowl·edge
prompt·ly
intro
ad·van·ta·geous
ex·cel·lent
if

533 TRANSCRIPTION QUIZ

In Lessons 31-56 of *Gregg Shorthand for Colleges, Diamond Jubilee Series*, you have been learning to apply ten rules for the correct use of the comma. In Lessons 57-69, you will have an opportunity to test your mastery of these rules through a Transcription Quiz – a letter in which no commas are indicated in the shorthand. It will be your job, as you copy the letter in shorthand in your notebook, to insert the commas in the proper places and to give the reasons why the commas are used. The shorthand in your notebook should resemble the following example:

At the head of each Transcription Quiz you will find the number and types of commas you should supply.

The correct punctuation of the following letter calls for 7 commas – 1 comma *as* clause, 4 commas apposition, 2 commas parenthetical.

(153)

DICTATION CHECK LIST

When you take dictation, do you—

1 Make every effort to keep up with the dictator?

2 Refer to your textbook whenever you are in doubt about the outline for a word or phrase?

3 Insert periods and question marks in your shorthand notes?

4 Make a real effort to observe good proportion as you write—making large circles large, small circles small, etc.?

5 Do you write down the first column of your notebook and then down the second column?

Lesson 58 provides you with an opportunity to increase further your ability to use the frequent phrases in Gregg Shorthand. Counting repetitions, the letters in this lesson contain 122 phrases. Several illustrations of all the phrasing principles of the system appear in the letters.

BUILDING TRANSCRIPTION SKILLS

534 GRAMMAR CHECKUP **sentence structure**

Parallel ideas should be expressed in parallel form.

NO I hope our relationship will be long, pleasant, and "of profit" to both of us.

YES I hope our relationship will be long, pleasant, and "profitable" to both of us.

NO As soon as we receive the necessary information, your account will be opened and "we will ship your order."

YES As soon as we receive the necessary information, your account will be opened and "your order will be shipped."

It is especially important to keep parallel all ideas in a tabulation.

NO Her main duties were:
1. Taking dictation and transcribing
2. Answering the telephone
3. "To take care" of the files

YES Her main duties were:
1. Taking dictation and transcribing
2. Answering the telephone
3. "Taking care" of the files

535 **BUSINESS VOCABULARY BUILDER**

parcel post A mail service handling packages.
gratifying Pleasing.
accommodations Rooms.

READING AND WRITING PRACTICE

536

conj ,

ap ,

nonr ,

sub·scrip·tion
oc·ca·sion

when ,

(153)

537

intro

par

par

al·ways
sta·tio·nery

(138)

538

if

conj

pe·ri·od
fur·ther·more

intro

if

re·take
of·fered

conj

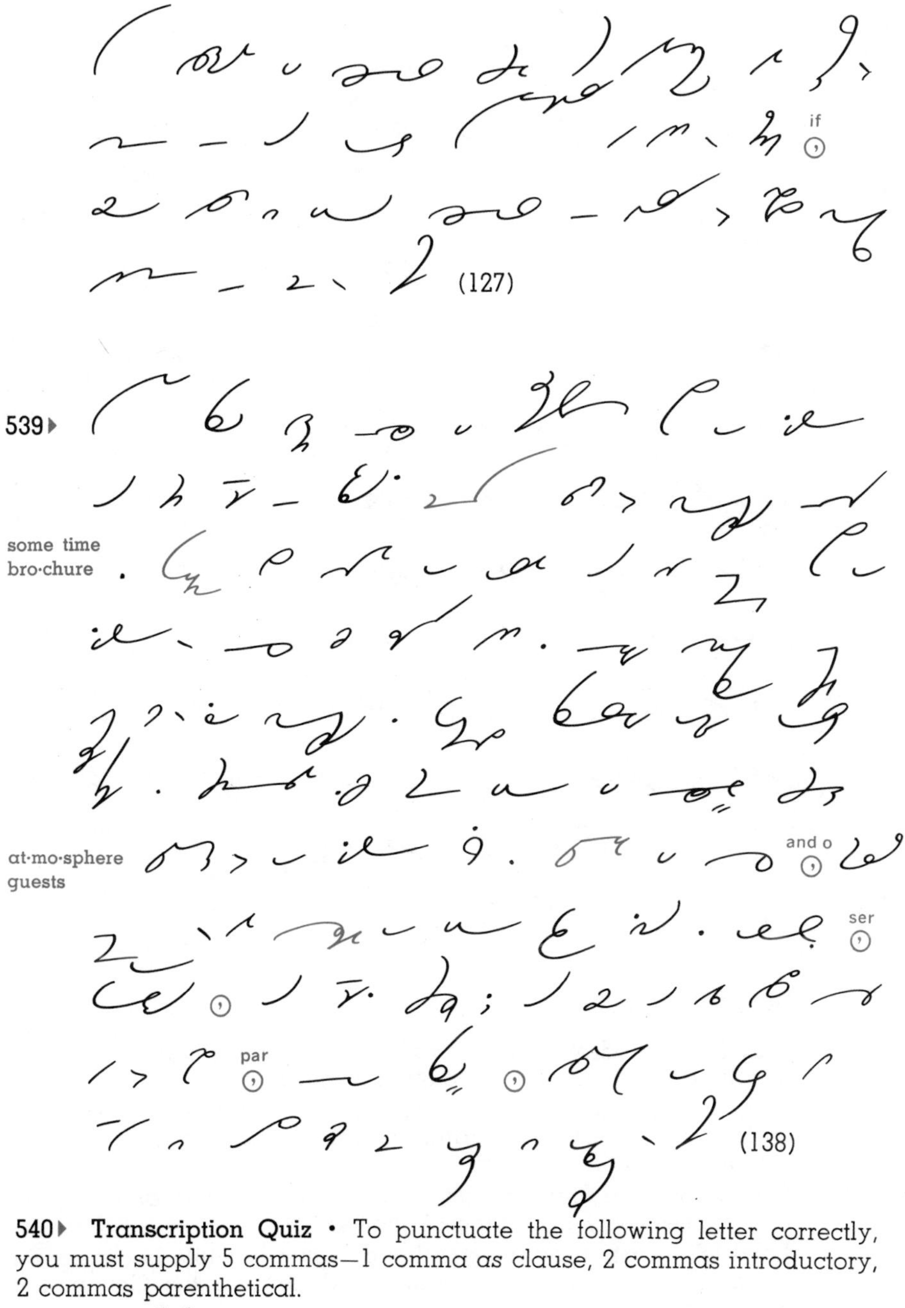

540 **Transcription Quiz** • To punctuate the following letter correctly, you must supply 5 commas—1 comma *as* clause, 2 commas introductory, 2 commas parenthetical.

(141)

DID YOU KNOW THAT —

President Woodrow Wilson was an expert shorthand writer and that he drafted all his state papers in shorthand?

Samuel Pepys wrote his famous diary in shorthand? He wrote so legibly that students of literature had no difficulty making an accurate transcript of his notes.

George Bernard Shaw did all his composing in shorthand and then had his secretary transcribe his notes?

James F. Byrnes used his shorthand regularly while he was a Supreme Court justice, a Secretary of State, and the Governor of South Carolina?

If any of the joined word beginnings are still a little hazy in your mind, here's a chance to fix them firmly in your mind. The practice material in Lesson 59 contains 98 illustrations of the joined word beginnings of Gregg Shorthand.

BUILDING TRANSCRIPTION SKILLS

541 ▸ SPELLING FAMILIES -ible, -able

A troublesome pair of endings for many stenographers and secretaries is *-ible, -able*. Unfortunately, there is no rule that tells us when to use *-ible* and when to use *-able*. In most words in the English language, the ending is spelled *-able;* but it is spelled *-ible* in a sufficient number of words that you should think twice before you type an *i* or an *a* before *-ble*.

Words Ending in -able

avail·able	**com·fort·able**	**mem·o·ra·ble**	**re·li·able**
bear·able	**con·sid·er·able**	**ob·tain·able**	**suit·able**
ca·pa·ble	**de·sir·able**	**por·ta·ble**	**un·for·get·ta·ble**

Words Ending in -ible

ad·mis·si·ble	**flex·i·ble**	**leg·i·ble**	**re·spon·si·ble**
de·duct·ible	**im·pos·si·ble**	**plau·si·ble**	**sen·si·ble**
de·fen·si·ble	**in·cred·i·ble**	**pos·si·ble**	**ter·ri·ble**

542 BUSINESS VOCABULARY BUILDER

incredible Difficult to believe.

workmen's compensation The money, fixed by law, that workmen may recover from an employer in case of accident arising out of their employment.

estate A large home with a great deal of land.

READING AND WRITING PRACTICE

543

un·for·get·ta·ble
in·ex·pen·sive

ser

par

in·cred·i·ble

ser

conj

(167)

544

em·ploy·ees
com·plete·ly

re·solved
unique

un·em·ploy·ment
work·men's

(190)

545

fea·ture
suits

par

dis·tin·guished
ad·ver·tis·ing

en·joy·able
un·in·ter·rupt·ed

and o

(120)

546 ▸

ac·cept
apol·o·gies
pre·vi·ous

intro

23^{15}

55

6^{29}

lat·ter
pri·or
re·ceipt

if

(134)

547▸ Transcription Quiz • The correct punctuation of the following letter calls for 5 commas—2 commas nonrestrictive, 2 commas apposition, 1 comma *as* clause.

21

5

4

(142)

Lesson 60 gives special attention to the joined word endings of Gregg Shorthand. There are 119 illustrations of joined word endings in the practice material of this lesson.

BUILDING TRANSCRIPTION SKILLS

548▸ COMMON WORD ROOTS **pre-:** before; beforehand; in advance

preview An advance showing or viewing.

prediction The act of telling beforehand; a forecast.

precaution A measure taken beforehand to prevent harm or to assure good.

premature Happening before the proper time.

549▸ BUSINESS VOCABULARY BUILDER

transferable Capable of being used by another.

unbiased Not prejudiced.

current Most recent; present.

READING AND WRITING PRACTICE

550▸

an·nounce·ment
an·nu·al

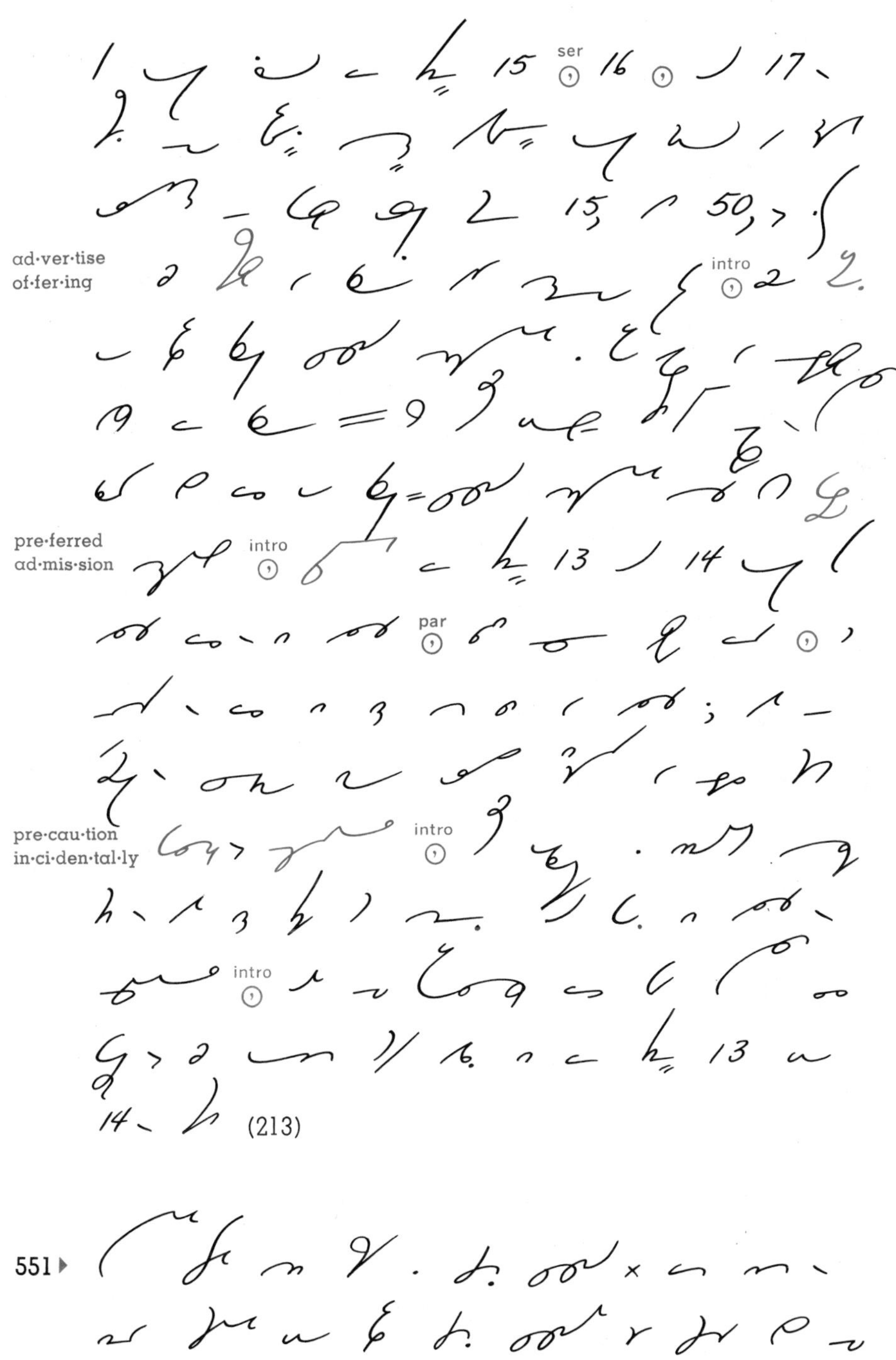

ad·ver·tise
of·fer·ing

pre·ferred
ad·mis·sion

pre·cau·tion
in·ci·den·tal·ly

551

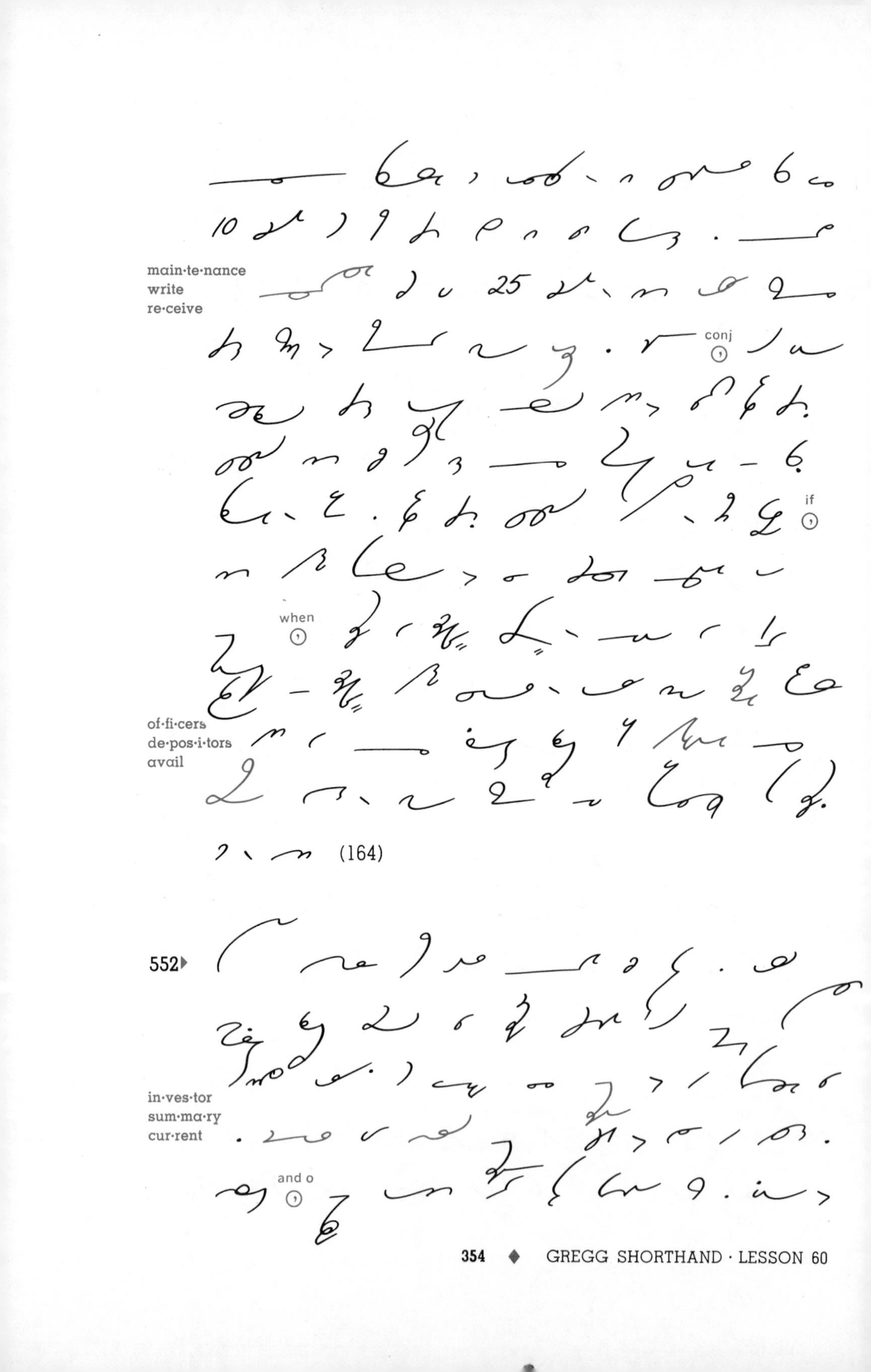

main·te·nance
write
re·ceive

conj

if

when

of·fi·cers
de·pos·i·tors
avail

(164)

552

in·ves·tor
sum·ma·ry
cur·rent

and o

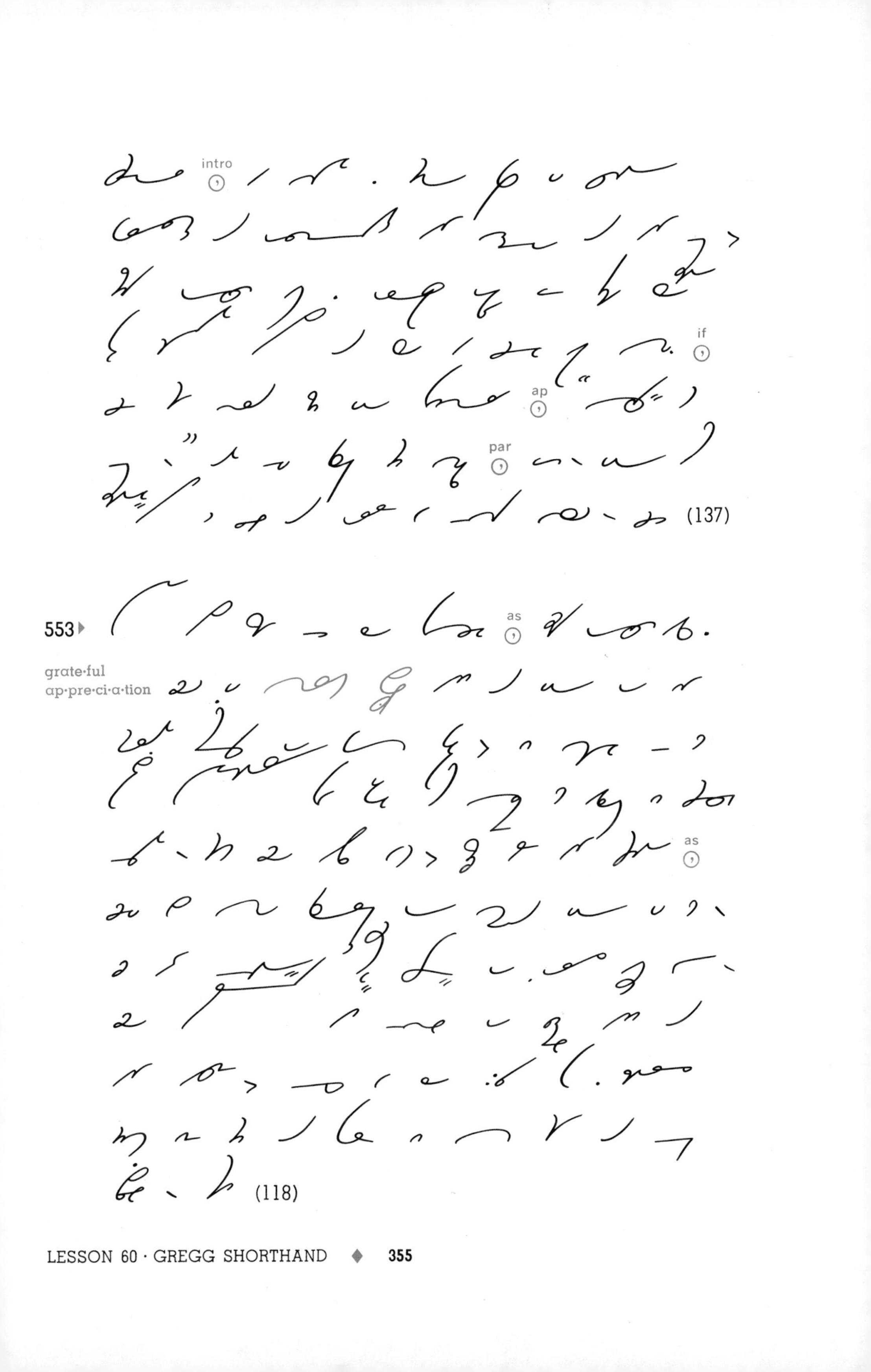

intro

if

ap

par

(137)

553 as

grateful appreciation

as

(118)

554▸ Transcription Quiz • The correct punctuation of the following letter calls for 5 commas—1 comma *as* clause, 2 commas introductory, 2 commas parenthetical.

As you copy the Transcription Quiz in your notebook, be sure to insert the necessary commas at the proper points and to indicate the reason for the punctuation.

13

65/

(143)

SPELLING AND PUNCTUATION CHECK LIST

Are you careful to punctuate and spell correctly when—

1 You write your compositions in English?

2 Prepare papers for other classes?

3 Correspond with friends to whom you must write in longhand?

In short, are you making correct spelling and punctuation a habit in all the longhand writing or typing that you do?

Disjoined word beginnings are given intensive treatment in this lesson. The letters that follow contain 39 illustrations of disjoined word beginnings.

BUILDING TRANSCRIPTION SKILLS

555 GRAMMAR CHECKUP comparisons

The comparative degree of an adjective or adverb is used when reference is made to two objects; the superlative degree is used when reference is made to more than two objects.

COMPARATIVE

Of the two boys, Jim is the taller.

Which boy is more efficient, Jim or Harry?

Is Mr. Smith or Mr. Green better qualified to do the job?

SUPERLATIVE

Of the three boys, Jim is the tallest.

Which of the boys is the most efficient, Jim, Harry, or John?

Is Mr. Smith, Mr. Green, or Mr. Brown best qualified to do the job?

556 BUSINESS VOCABULARY BUILDER

interior appointments The furnishings and equipment on the inside of a car.

transatlantic Across the Atlantic Ocean.

557

nonr

ser

intro

ar·ti·cles
year's

in·tro·duc·to·ry
de·scribes

and o

ser

equipped
con·ve·nient
elec·tri·cal·ly

conj

ap

if

(201)

558▸

and o

ef·fi·cien·cy
crews

when

peace
knowl·edge

and o

(113)

559▸

intro

ser

min·i·mum
ef·fi·cient·ly

intro

(167)

560

priv·i·leg·es
rea·son

an·noy·anc·es
con·cen·trate

ser

pri·va·cy
over·all

25

ful·ly
strict·ly
led

conj

if

(235)

561▸ **Transcription Quiz** · To punctuate the following letter correctly, you must supply 4 commas—1 comma *if* clause, 2 commas parenthetical, 1 comma *and* omitted.

(81)

Do you find that you don't know the disjoined word endings as well as you would like? Then read and copy the letters in this lesson carefully. The letters contain 52 illustrations of disjoined word endings.

BUILDING TRANSCRIPTION SKILLS

562▸ SIMILAR-WORDS DRILL **loss, lose, loose**

loss *(noun)* That which one is deprived of.

He suffered a loss through theft.

lose *(verb)* To be deprived of.

I know that you do not want to lose your paintings.

loose Unattached; not fastened.

We are forwarding to you our loose-leaf booklet.

563▸ **BUSINESS VOCABULARY BUILDER**

appraising Placing a value upon.

appraisals Values set upon properties by qualified people.

heirlooms Things of special value handed down from one generation to another.

READING AND WRITING PRACTICE

564▸

ap·prais·ing
cli·ents

56

par

and o

intro

suf·fered
loss
theft

ser

intro

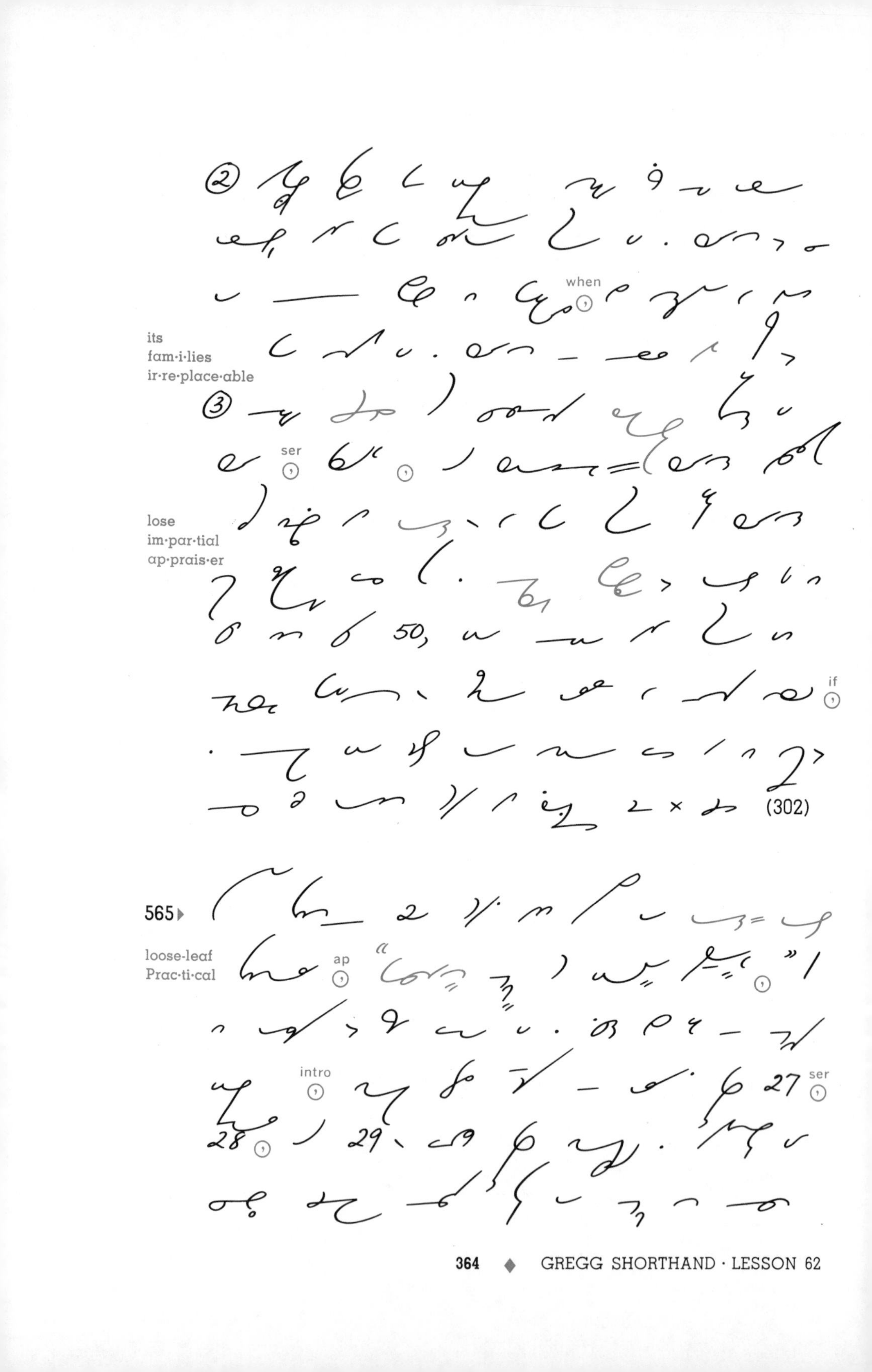

(2)

when

its
fam·i·lies
ir·re·place·able

(3)

ser

lose
im·par·tial
ap·prais·er

50,

if

(302)

565

loose-leaf
Prac·ti·cal

ap

intro

27

ser

28

29

intro

spe·cif·i·cal·ly
neigh·bor·hood

ap

en·gi·neer
fu·el

ser

and o

(218)

566

phys·i·cal
strain

ab·sorb·ing
es·pe·cial·ly

par

ser

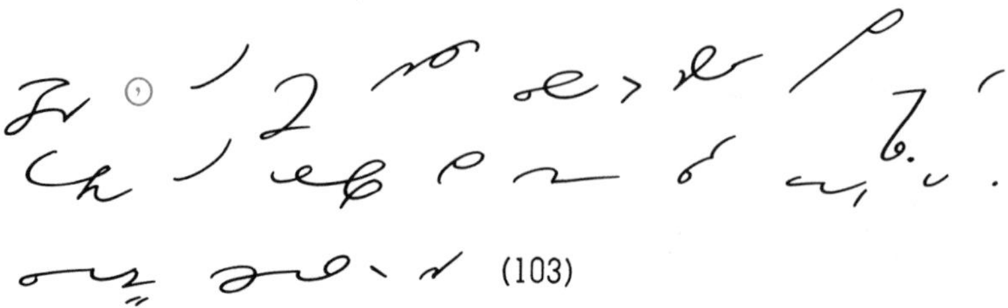

567 ▸ Transcription Quiz • The following letter requires 5 commas—3 commas parenthetical, 1 comma introductory, 1 comma *if* clause.

(134)

One of the major reasons why Gregg Shorthand can be written so rapidly and fluently is its blends—single strokes that represent two or more sounds. In this lesson you will find many words and phrases that employ these blends—118 illustrations in all.

BUILDING TRANSCRIPTION SKILLS

568 **COMMON WORD ROOTS** **co-:** with, together, jointly

cooperative Working together.

cooperation The act of working together.

coordinate To bring together.

coeducation Joint education, especially the education of boys and girls at the same school.

569 **BUSINESS VOCABULARY BUILDER**

preceding Coming before. (Do not confuse with "proceeding," which means "going ahead.")

primary First; main.

confront To face.

READING AND WRITING PRACTICE

570

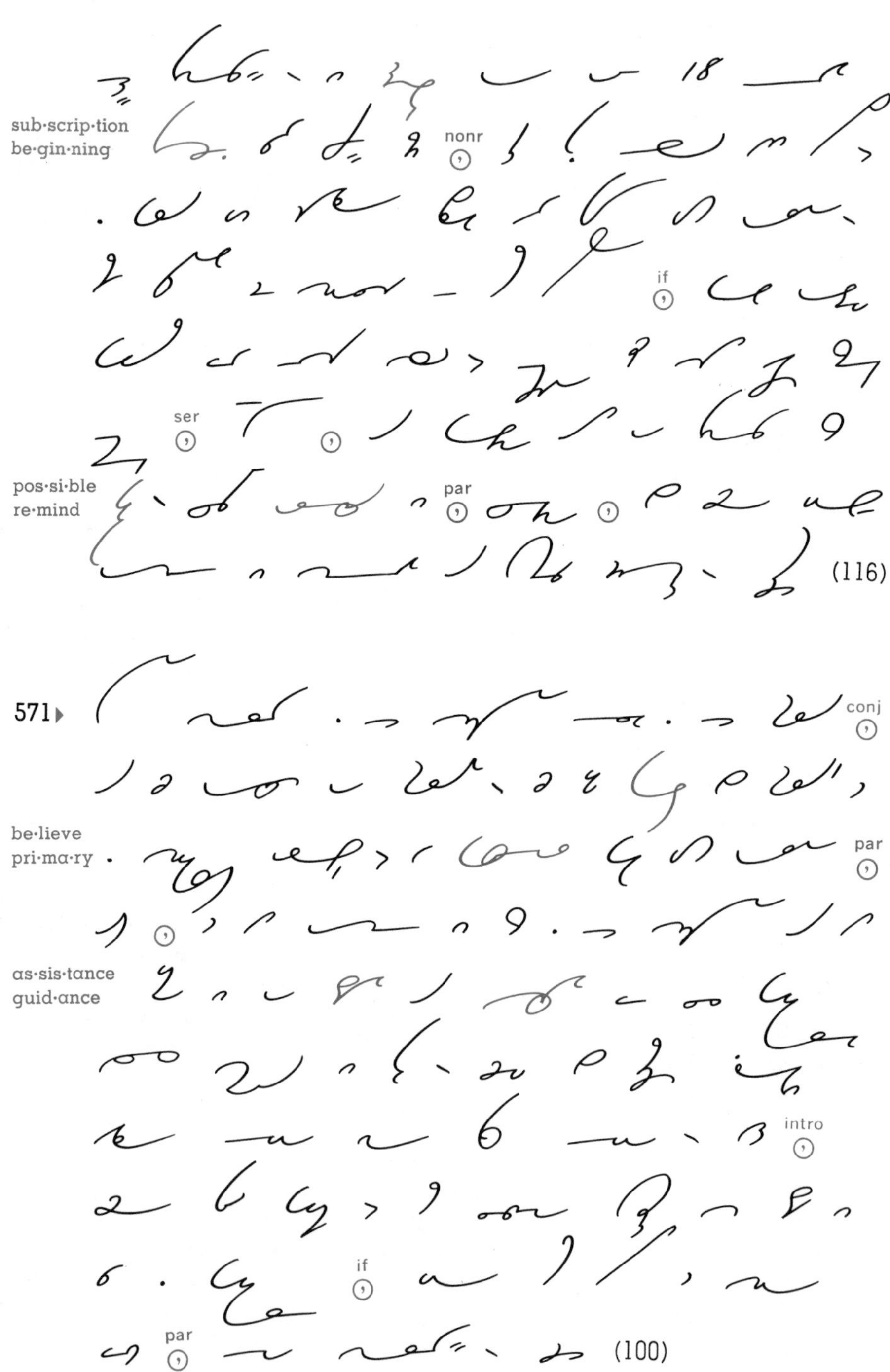
sub·scrip·tion
be·gin·ning
nonr
if
ser
pos·si·ble
re·mind
par
(116)
571
conj
be·lieve
pri·ma·ry
par
as·sis·tance
guid·ance
intro
if
par
(100)

572▸

ap

Di·rec·tors
theme

as

par

ex·pens·es
hon·o·rar·i·um

par

ac·cept
ar·riv·al

if

(150)

573▸

re·ceived
re·mit·tance

en·deav·or
pleas·ant
eco·nom·i·cal

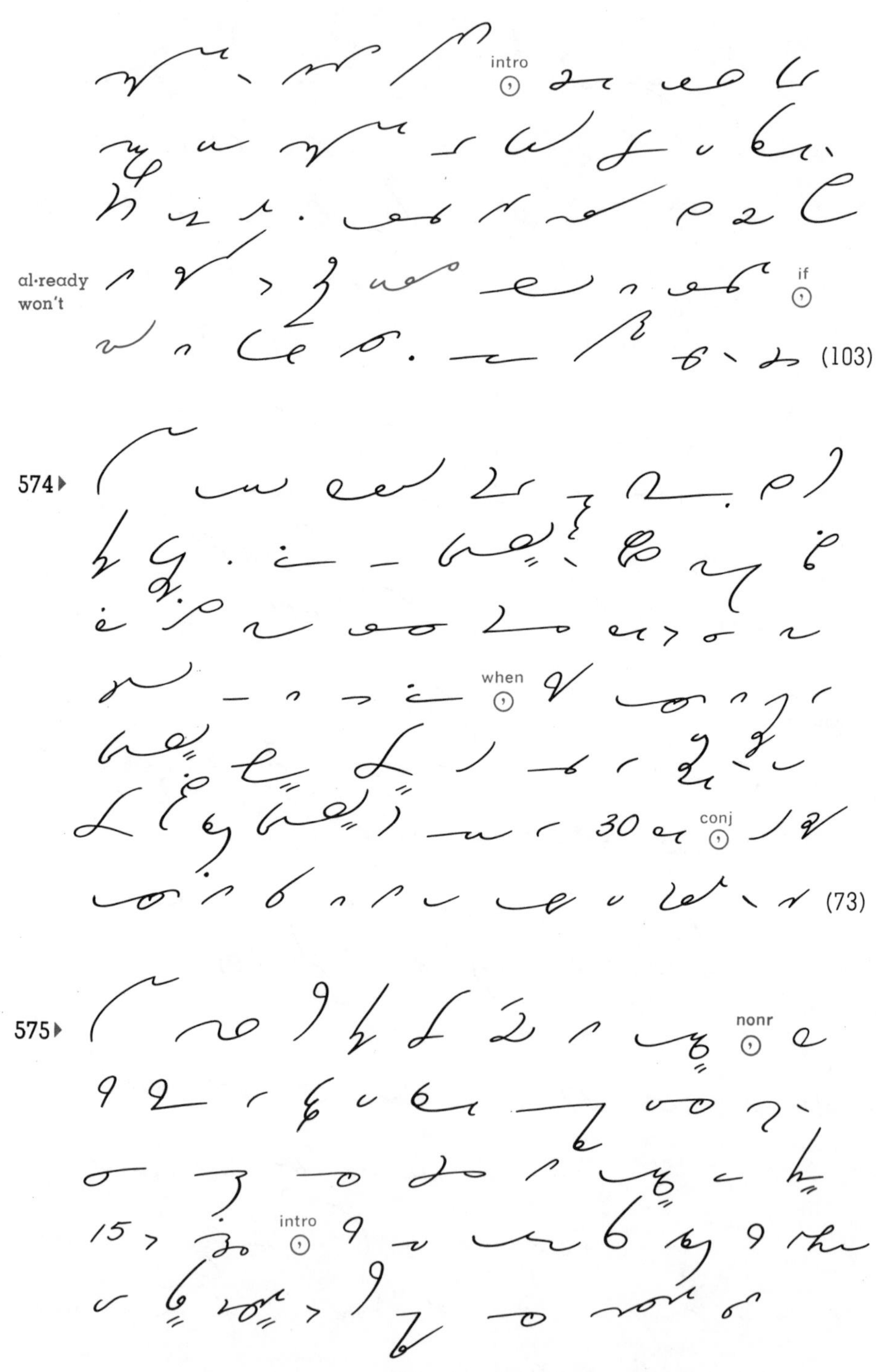
intro
al·ready
won't
if
(103)
574
when
conj
30
(73)
575
nonr
15
intro

576▸ Transcription Quiz • The following letter requires 7 commas to be punctuated correctly—2 commas *and* omitted, 1 comma introductory, 2 commas series, 2 commas parenthetical.

Remember to indicate each comma in your shorthand notes and to give the reason for its use.

(140)

As you learned during the early stages of your study of Gregg Shorthand, vowels are omitted in some words to help us gain fluency of writing. In this lesson you will find many illustrations of words from which vowels are omitted.

BUILDING TRANSCRIPTION SKILLS

577 SPELLING FAMILIES -ary, -ery, -ory

Words Ending in -ary

an·ni·ver·sa·ry	dic·tio·nary	li·brary	sec·re·tary
com·pli·men·ta·ry	el·e·men·ta·ry	nec·es·sary	sum·ma·ry
con·trary	glos·sa·ry	pri·ma·ry	tem·po·rary
cus·tom·ary	itin·er·ary	sec·on·dary	vo·cab·u·lary

Words Ending in -ery

bind·ery	gro·cery	mys·tery	re·fin·ery
de·liv·ery	ma·chine·ry	que·ry	sce·nery
dis·cov·ery	mas·tery	re·cov·ery	sta·tio·nery

Words Ending in -ory

de·pos·i·to·ry	ex·plan·a·to·ry	in·tro·duc·to·ry	sat·is·fac·to·ry
di·rec·to·ry	fac·to·ry	in·ven·to·ry	ter·ri·to·ry
ex·ec·u·to·ry	his·to·ry	man·da·to·ry	vic·to·ry

578 BUSINESS VOCABULARY BUILDER

middleman An agent between the producer of goods and a retailer or consumer.

overhead Such items as rent, heat, telephone service, taxes, etc., that are part of running a business.

inventories Amounts of goods that are kept on hand.

READING AND WRITING PRACTICE

579

gen·u·ine
re·cent
au·tho·rized

par

as

20

ap

if

(132)

580

when

intro

ser

vol·ume
min·i·mum

in·ven·to·ries
fac·tors

conj

32

par

(174)

581 ▸

Cloth·ing
for·ward

30

par

intro

privileges
approval

(124)

582

receive
renewal

par

escape
accidentally

intro

(124)

583▸ Transcription Quiz • In the following letter you must supply 5 commas to punctuate it correctly—3 commas introductory, 1 comma *as* clause, 1 comma *if* clause.

(140)

VOCABULARY CHECK LIST

Has your command of words improved since you began your study of Gregg Shorthand? It has if you—

1 Studied all the words in the Business Vocabulary Builders and added them to your vocabulary.

2 Paid careful attention to the Similar-Words Drills, so that you know the difference between *due, do; personal, personnel,* etc.

3 Learned the meanings of the common word roots presented in a number of the lessons of your textbook.

Very often in your dictation on the job you will have to write numbers. Because of the importance of accuracy in transcribing numbers, always take special care in writing numbers in your shorthand notes. The letters in this lesson will help you fix in your mind the devices in Gregg Shorthand for expressing numbers and quantities.

BUILDING TRANSCRIPTION SKILLS

584 ▸ SIMILAR-WORDS DRILL **county, country**

county A political division of a state.

Our plant will be in Rensselaer County, near Troy, New York.

country A nation.

Our country produces more aluminum than any other country.

585 ▸ BUSINESS VOCABULARY BUILDER

immeasurably Incapable of being measured; vast.

manifest Easily understood; evident; plain.

recourse A turning to for help.

586

dai·ly
fi·nal

as

88

grate·ful
en·thu·si·as·ti·cal·ly

ap

when

and o

4

50

im·mea·sur·able

30

par

25

3

per·ma·nent

when

nonr

5

21

ea·ger
ac·quaint·ed

intro

conj

(273)

587

teen-ag·ers

intro

ser

20's 19, 30's 24,

40's 20, 50's 17,

60's

par

ser

cre·ate
emer·gen·cies

10

5/

intro

5

if

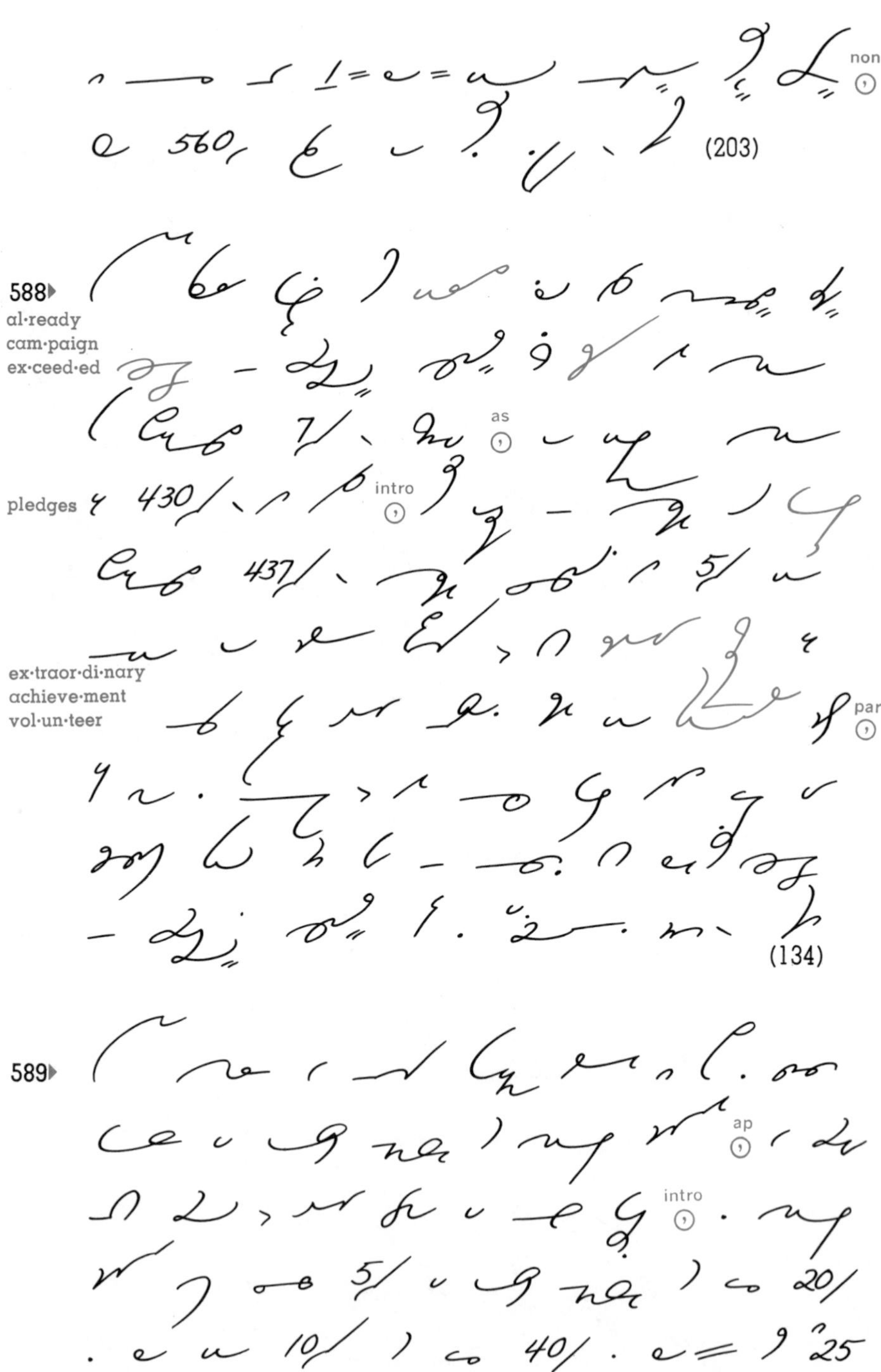
nonr
(203)
588
al·ready
cam·paign
ex·ceed·ed
as
pledges
intro
ex·traor·di·nary
achieve·ment
vol·un·teer
par
(134)
589
ap
intro

25 28 5/ 25/

10/ 50/

intro

urge
bro·chure (124)

590 ▸ **Transcription Quiz** • For you to supply: 4 commas—1 comma introductory, 1 comma nonrestrictive, 2 commas series.

24

90 24

6.65

3/

1

(151)

Lesson 66 provides you another opportunity to test your knowledge of the brief forms of Gregg Shorthand. Counting repetitions, the letters in this lesson contain 475 brief forms and derivatives.

BUILDING TRANSCRIPTION SKILLS

591 ▸ **COMMON WORD ROOTS** **un-**: not

unsolicited Not asked for; voluntary.
unusual Not usual; rare.
unhappy Not happy; sad.
uncertain Not sure.

592 ▸ **BUSINESS VOCABULARY BUILDER**

versatile Capable of doing many things.
forecast To predict.

READING AND WRITING PRACTICE

593 ▸

as

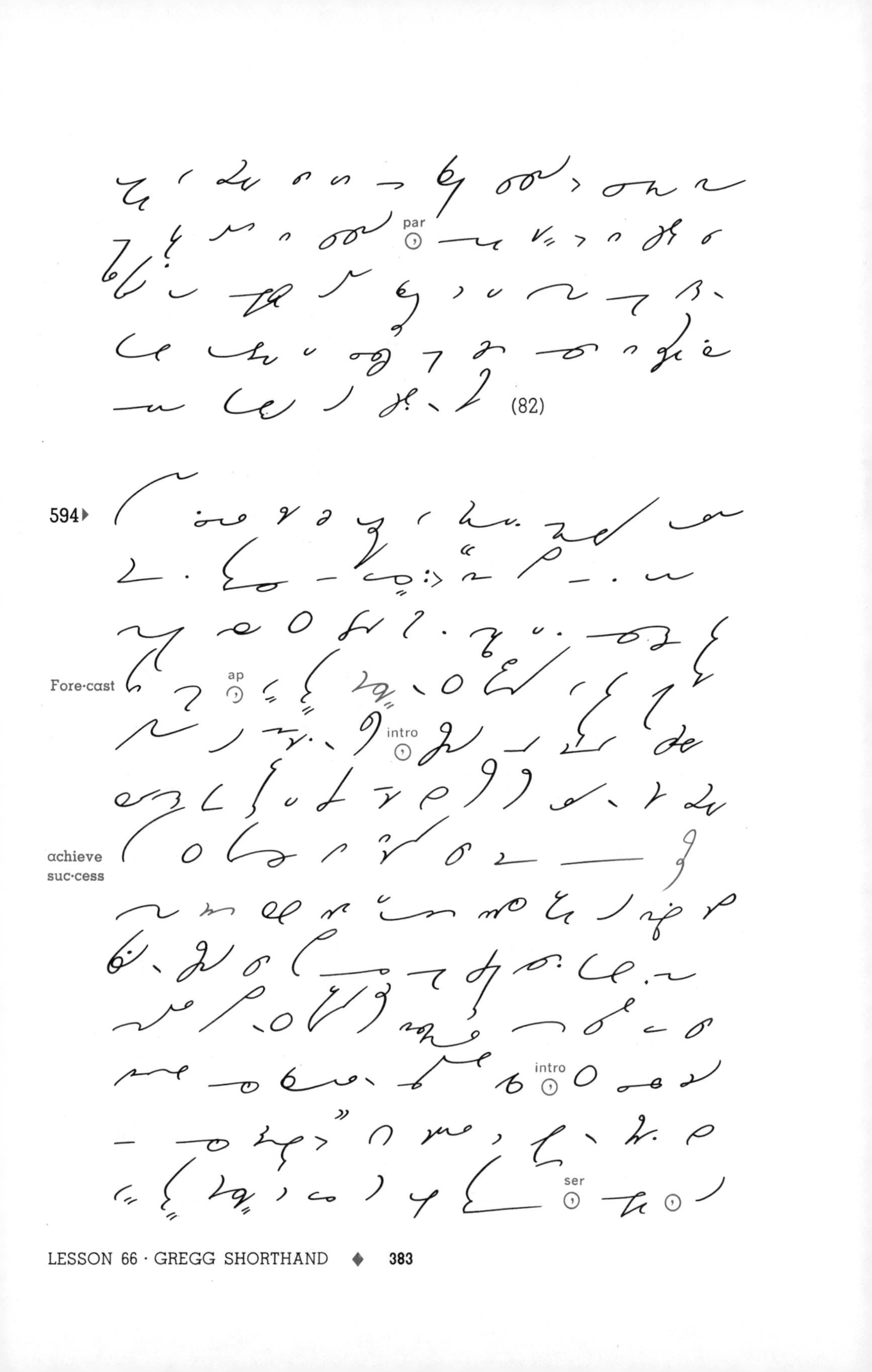

par

(82)

594

Fore·cast

ap

intro

achieve suc·cess

intro

ser

aid
sal·a·ried

if

par

par

(244)

595

re·ferred
dif·fi·cul·ties

as

par

par

par

(117)

596

ac·knowl·edge
hard·ware

nonr

15 par 18 19

par

if (125)

597 ▸

So·ci·ety
Safe·ty

conj

hearty
Coun·cil

par

as

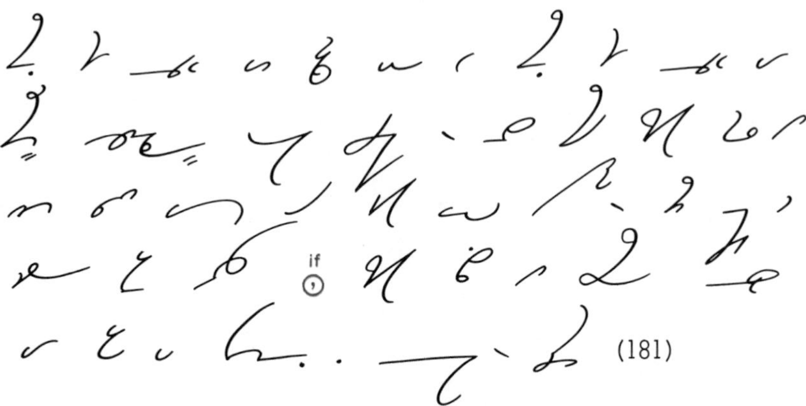

598 ▸ **Transcription Quiz** • For you to supply: 5 commas—1 comma *when* clause, 1 comma *and* omitted, 2 commas series, 1 comma conjunction.

(157)

Lesson 67 is another "phrasing" lesson. The letters contain several illustrations of all the phrasing principles of the system.

BUILDING TRANSCRIPTION SKILLS

599 GRAMMAR CHECKUP verbs—with "one of"

1 In most cases, the expression *one of* takes a singular verb, which agrees with the subject *one.*

"One" of the men on the staff "is" ill.

"One" of our typewriters "does" not work.

2 When *one of* is part of an expression such as *one of those who* or *one of the things that,* the verb following is usually plural, to agree with the plural object of the preposition *of.*

He solved one of the "problems" that "have" been annoying businessmen for years.

He is one of the "men" who "drive" to work.

600 BUSINESS VOCABULARY BUILDER

functions Activities; purposes.

complimentary Flattering. (Do not confuse with "complementary," which means "filling out or completing.")

stationery Such items as paper, envelopes, pencils, erasers, etc. (Do not confuse with "stationary," which means "remaining in one place.")

READING AND WRITING PRACTICE

601 (88)

602 (108)

al·ways
wor·ry·ing

conj intro intro intro if

as·sis·tance
ma·jor

al·ready

603

men's
shirts

and o

intro

nonr

ap

par

whole·sale

if

(158)

604

be·gin·ning
ac·cus·tomed

par

par

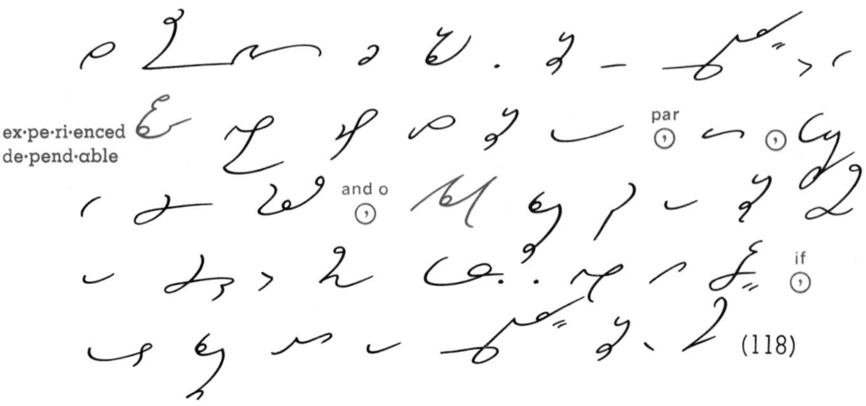

605▸ Transcription Quiz • For you to supply: 4 commas—2 commas introductory, 2 commas parenthetical.

(147)

Lesson 68 contains a general review of the major principles of Gregg Shorthand.

BUILDING TRANSCRIPTION SKILLS

606 ▸ **SIMILAR-WORDS DRILL** **due, do**

due Owing; payable.

You must pay your bills when they are due.

do To carry out; to perform.

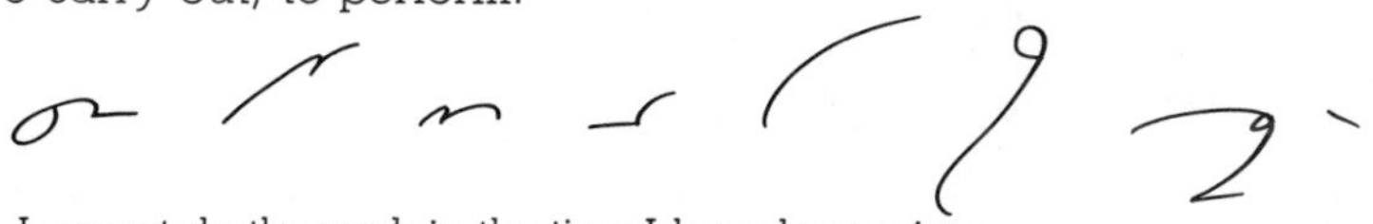

I cannot do the work in the time I have been given.

607 ▸ **BUSINESS VOCABULARY BUILDER**

decided (adjective) Clear cut; definite.

orientation Acquaintance with existing conditions or situations.

briefs (verb) Gives essential information to.

anticipate To foresee.

READING AND WRITING PRACTICE

608 ours res·tau·rant

30 60

par

prompt·ly due

as

intro

conj

150

30

if (170)

609 and o

when

guid·ance
briefs
pol·i·cies

intro

intro

ser

an·tic·i·pate
over·come

when

par

ef·fec·tive
rec·om·mend

conj

if

(186)

610 ▸

intro

par

res·o·lu·tions
won't

oc·ca·sions
for·ward

phase
as·so·ci·a·tions

(130)

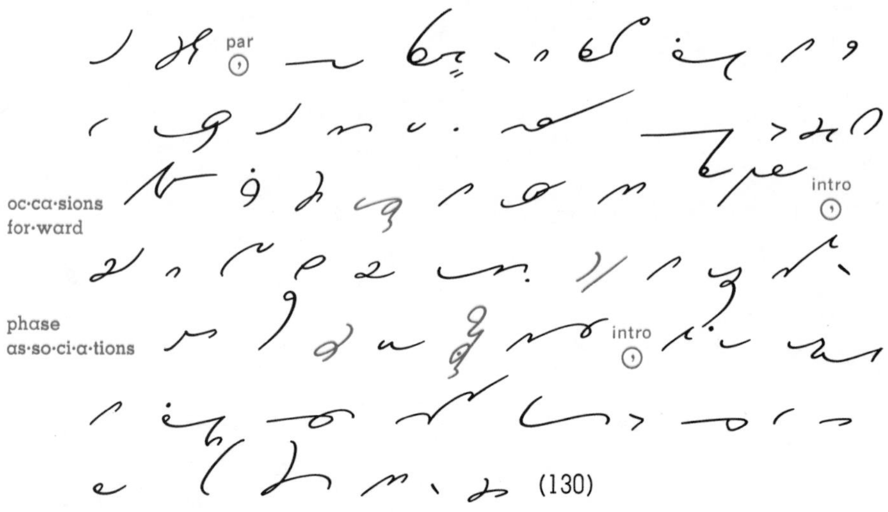

611▸ Transcription Quiz • For you to supply: 8 commas—6 commas parenthetical, 1 comma nonrestrictive, 1 comma *if* clause.

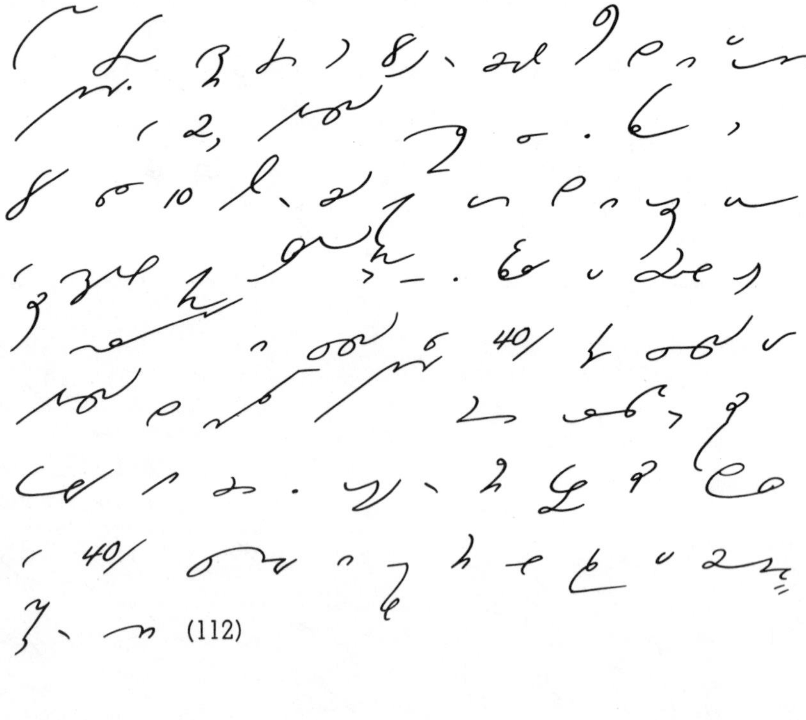

(112)

Lesson 69, like Lesson 68, contains a general review of the principles of Gregg Shorthand.

BUILDING TRANSCRIPTION SKILLS

612 ▸ **COMMON WORD ROOTS** **re-**: again

reorder To order again.
reconsider To take up again.
reconfirm To assure again.
replenish To fill or supply again.
repeat To say again.

613 ▸ **BUSINESS VOCABULARY BUILDER**

continually Endlessly; in broken occurrence but frequently. (Do not confuse with "continuously," which means "in unbroken occurrence.")
consecutively One after the other.

READING AND WRITING PRACTICE

614 ▸

fas·ci·nat·ing
ma·jor

lei·sure

con·tin·u·al·ly
sur·pris·ing

ac·cu·rate

copies
in·ter·rup·tion

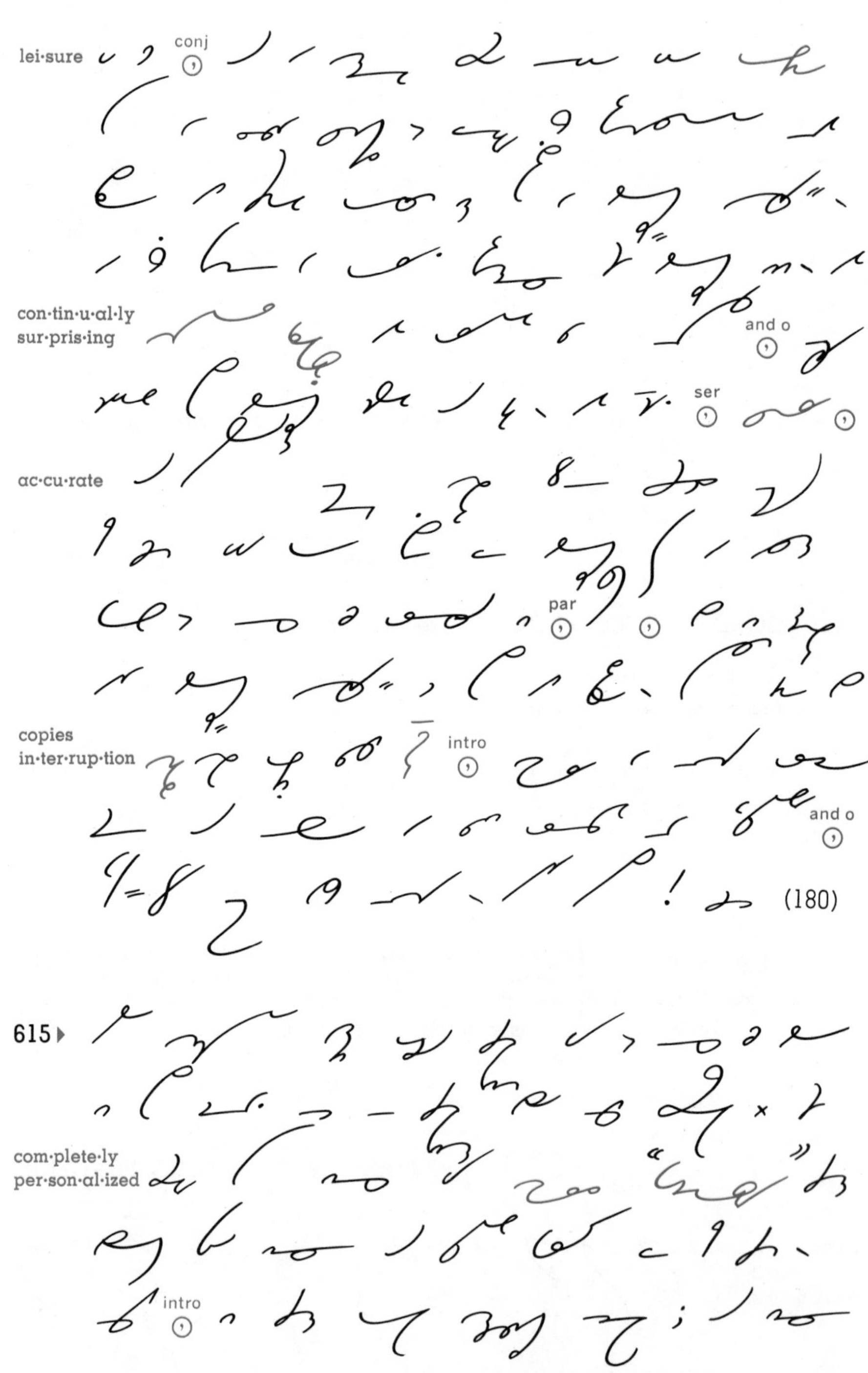

com·plete·ly
per·son·al·ized

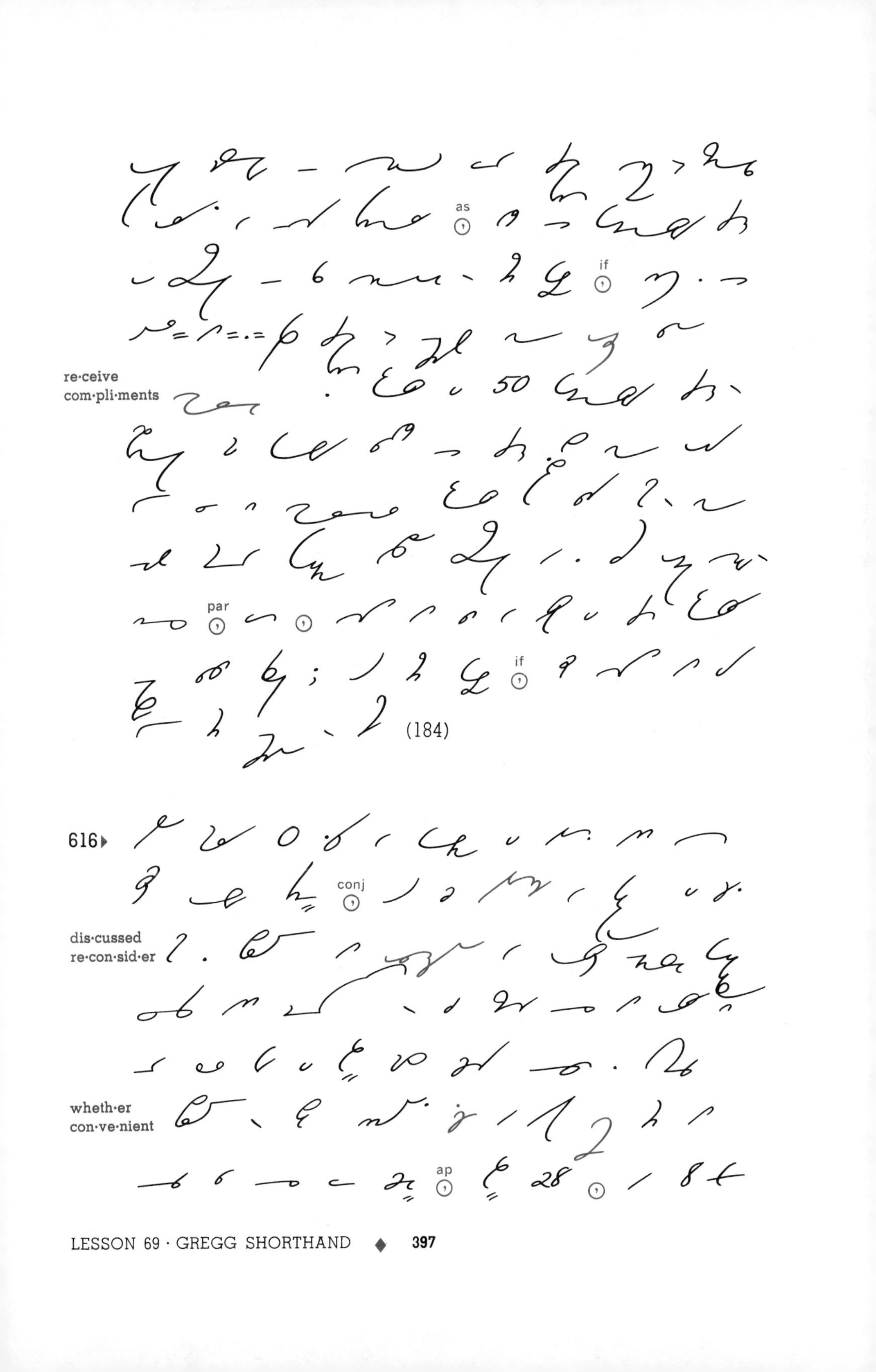

as

if

re·ceive
com·pli·ments

par

if

(184)

616

conj

dis·cussed
re·con·sid·er

wheth·er
con·ve·nient

ap

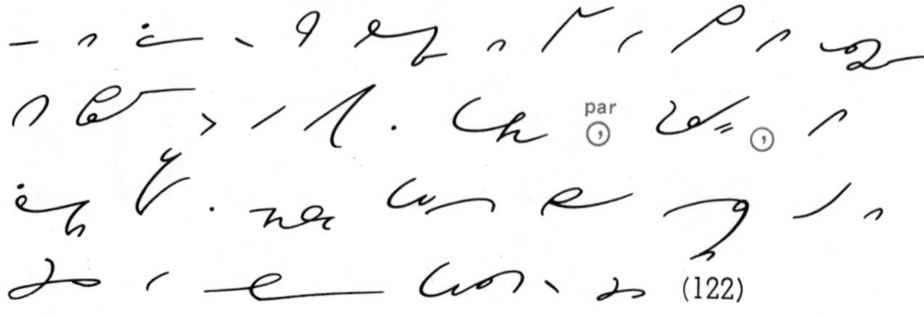

617 ▸ **Transcription Quiz** • For you to supply: 5 commas—1 comma conjunction, 1 comma *when* clause, 1 comma *and* omitted, 2 commas parenthetical.

(128)

Read carefully the article, "The Love of Work," in this lesson. It will give you an outlook on work that will help you lead a happier, more productive life.

BUILDING TRANSCRIPTION SKILLS

618 SPELLING FAMILIES -ious, -eous

Words Ending in -ious

con·scious	en·vi·ous	ob·vi·ous	spa·cious
cu·ri·ous	gra·cious	pre·cious	stu·di·ous
de·li·cious	in·ge·nious	pre·vi·ous	te·dious
de·vi·ous	ju·di·cious	se·ri·ous	var·i·ous

Words Ending in -eous

ad·van·ta·geous	er·ro·ne·ous	mis·cel·la·neous	si·mul·ta·neous
cou·ra·geous	hid·eous	out·ra·geous	spon·ta·ne·ous

619 BUSINESS VOCABULARY BUILDER

judiciously Wisely.
passive Not active.
diversion Pastime; something that amuses.
artificial Not real.

READING AND WRITING PRACTICE

READING SCOREBOARD • Now that you are on the last lesson, you are no doubt very much interested in your final shorthand reading rate. If you have followed the practice suggestions you received early in the course, your shorthand reading rate at this time should be a source of pride to you.

To get a real picture of how much your shorthand reading rate has increased with practice, compare it with your reading rate in Lesson 18, the first time you measured it.

LESSON 70 CONTAINS 507 WORDS

If you read Lesson 70 in:	10	12	14	16	18	20	minutes
Your reading rate is:	50	42	36	32	28	25	words a minute

620 ▸ **The Love of Work**

ap

er·ro·ne·ous·ly
be·lieve

intro

par

be·lief
usu·al·ly

ser

23

if

if

ar·ti·fi·cial
dis·tinc·tion

nonr

purge
self-pity
en·vi·ous

te·dious
oc·ca·sion·al

par

re·tire·ment
per·sis·tent·ly

intro

and o

when

pres·tige
spurs

(327)

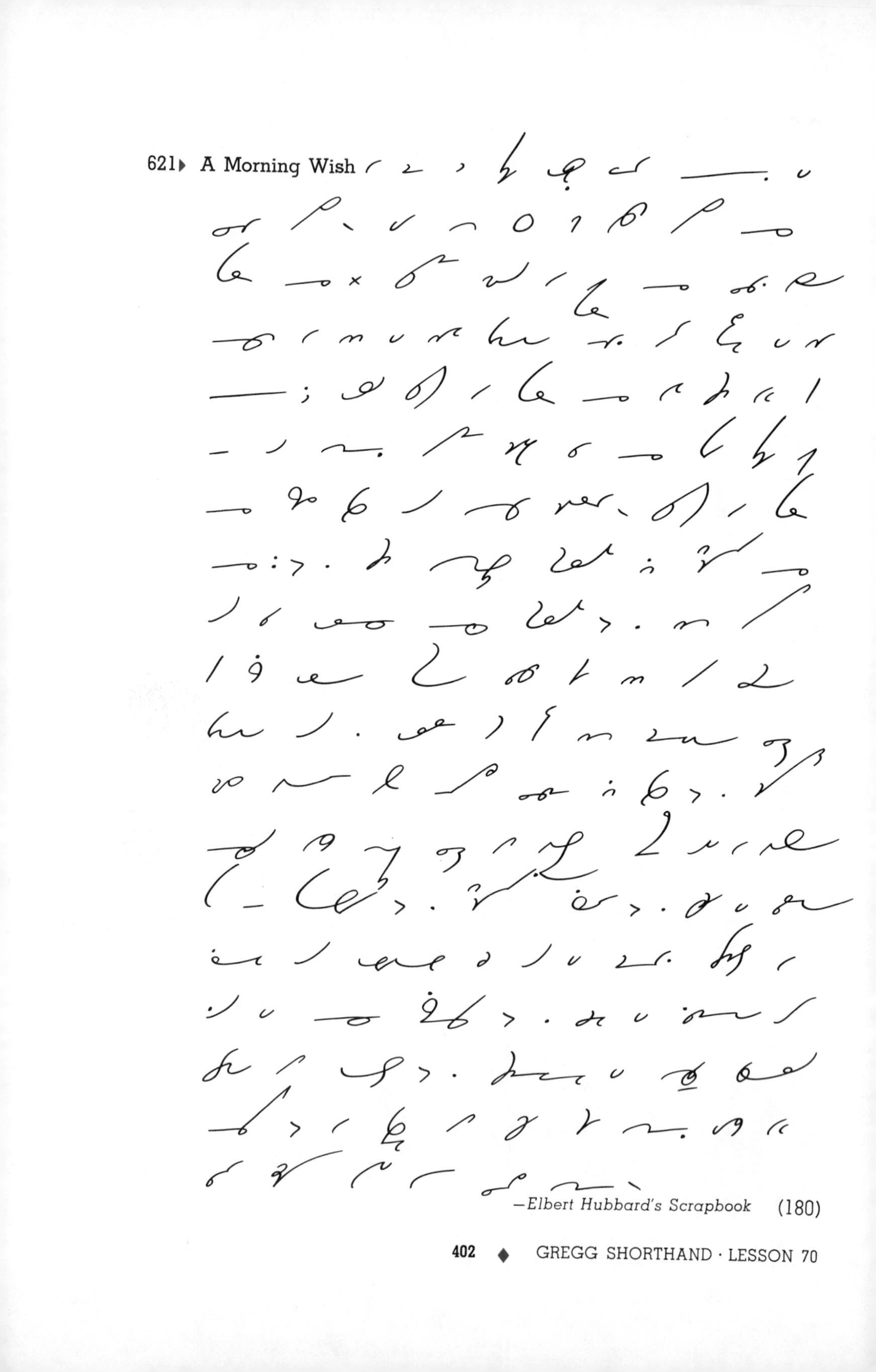

621▸ A Morning Wish

—Elbert Hubbard's Scrapbook (180)

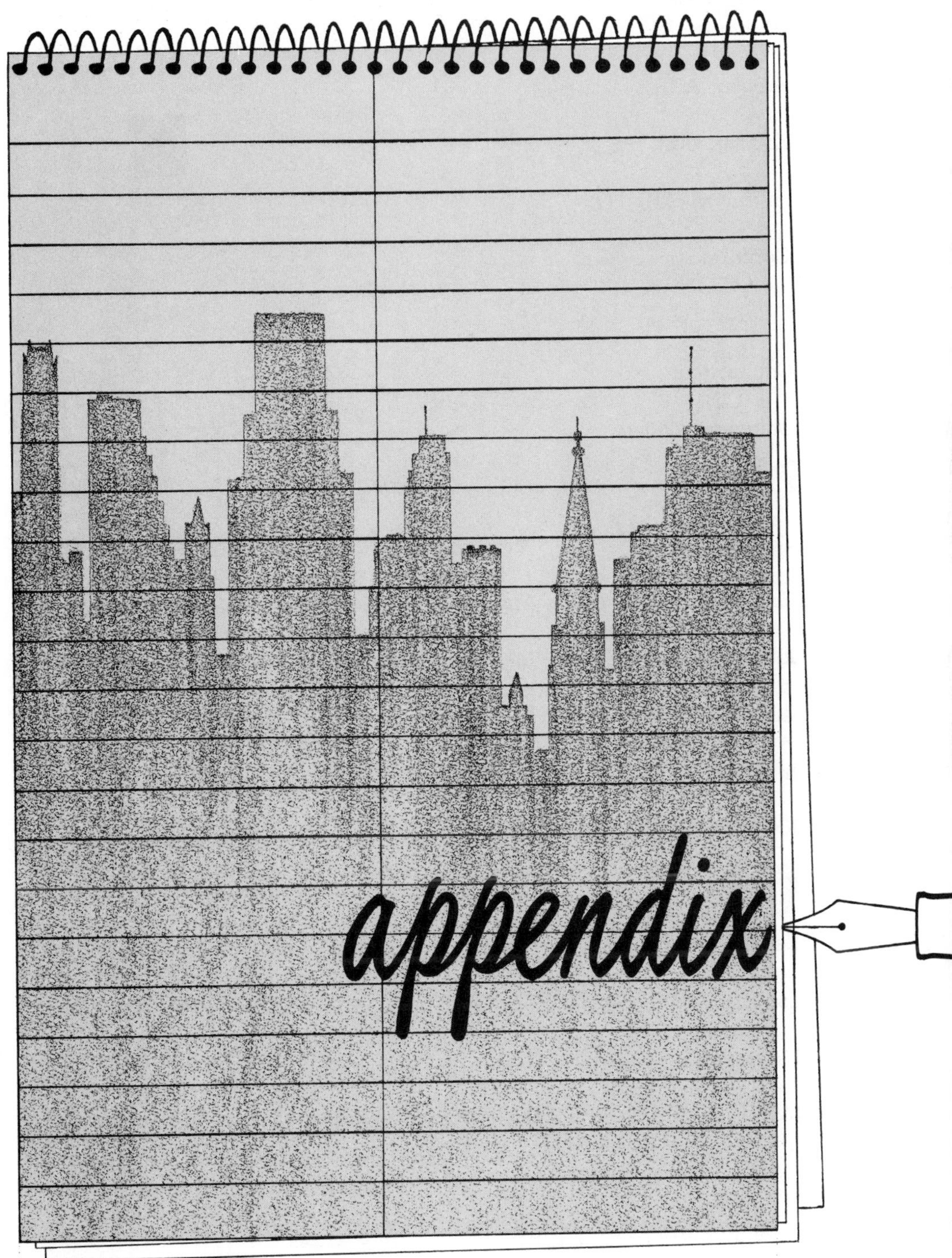
appendix

STATES

The abbreviations in parentheses are those recommended by the Post Office Department.

Alabama (AL)

Alaska (AK)

Arizona (AZ)

Arkansas (AR)

California (CA)

Colorado (CO)

Connecticut (CT)

Delaware (DE)

Florida (FL)

Georgia (GA)

Hawaii (HI)

Idaho (ID)

Illinois (IL)

Indiana (IN)

Iowa (IA)

Kansas (KS)

Kentucky (KY)

Louisiana (LA)

Maine (ME)

Maryland (MD)

Massachusetts (MA)

Michigan (MI)

Minnesota (MN)

Mississippi (MS)

Missouri (MO)

Montana (MT)

Nebraska (NB)

Nevada (NV)

New Hampshire (NH)

New Jersey (NJ)

New Mexico (NM)

New York (NY)

North Carolina (NC)

North Dakota (ND)

Ohio (OH)

Oklahoma (OK)

Oregon (OR)

Pennsylvania (PA)

Rhode Island (RI)

South Carolina (SC)

South Dakota (SD)

Tennessee (TN)

Texas (TX)

Utah (UT)

Vermont (VT)

Virginia (VA)

Washington (WA)

West Virginia (WV)

Wisconsin (WI)

Wyoming (WY)

PRINCIPAL CITIES OF THE UNITED STATES

Akron
Albany
Albuquerque
Atlanta
Austin
Baltimore
Baton Rouge
Birmingham
Boston
Bridgeport
Buffalo
Cambridge
Camden
Canton
Charlotte
Chattanooga
Chicago
Cincinnati
Cleveland
Columbus
Dallas

Dayton
Denver
Des Moines
Detroit
Duluth
Elizabeth
El Paso
Erie
Fall River
Flint
Fort Wayne
Fort Worth
Gary
Grand Rapids
Hartford
Honolulu
Houston
Indianapolis
Jacksonville
Jersey City
Kansas City

Knoxville
Long Beach
Los Angeles
Louisville
Lowell
Memphis
Miami
Milwaukee
Minneapolis
Mobile
Nashville
Newark
New Bedford
New Haven
New Orleans
New York
Norfolk
Oakland
Oklahoma City
Omaha
Paterson

Peoria	Salt Lake City	Tacoma
Phoenix	San Antonio	Tampa
Philadelphia	San Diego	Toledo
Pittsburgh	San Francisco	Trenton
Portland	San Jose	Tulsa
Providence	Savannah	Tucson
Reading	Scranton	Utica
Richmond	Seattle	Washington
Rochester	Somerville	Waterbury
Sacramento	South Bend	Wichita
St. Louis	Spokane	Wilmington
St. Paul	Springfield	Worcester
St. Petersburg	Syracuse	Yonkers

COMMON GEOGRAPHICAL ABBREVIATIONS

America	England	Canada
American	English	Canadian
United States	Great Britain	Puerto Rico

WORD BEGINNINGS, WORD ENDINGS, AND PHRASING PRINCIPLES IN ORDER OF THEIR PRESENTATION.

The number in each heading refers to the lesson in which the word beginning, word ending, or phrasing principle is first introduced.

3 Simple Phrases

7 Salutations and Closings

8 -ly

9 -tion, -cient, -ciency

9 -tial

9 T for To in Phrases

11 Been in Phrases

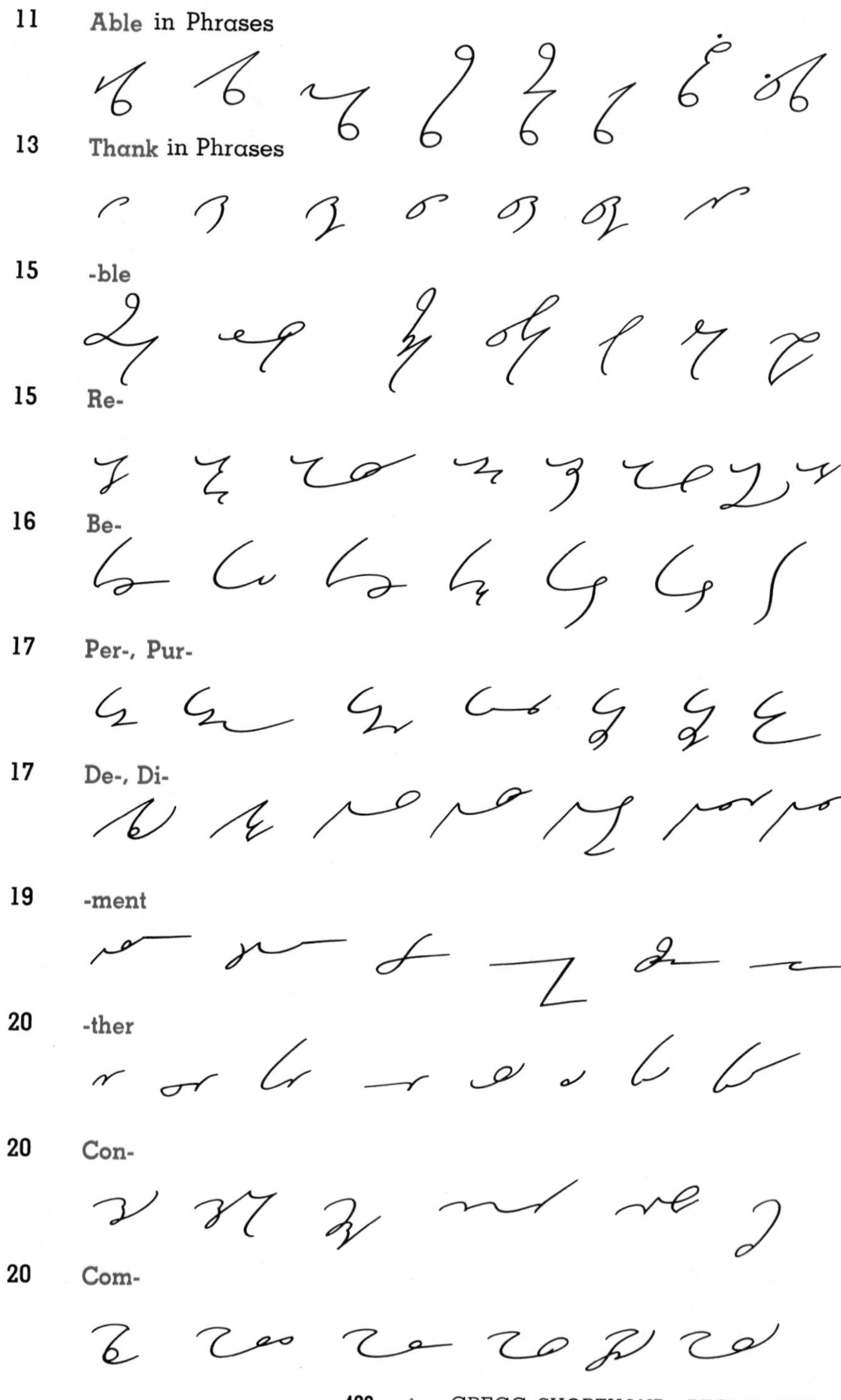
11 Able in Phrases
13 Thank in Phrases
15 -ble
15 Re-
16 Be-
17 Per-, Pur-
17 De-, Di-
19 -ment
20 -ther
20 Con-
20 Com-

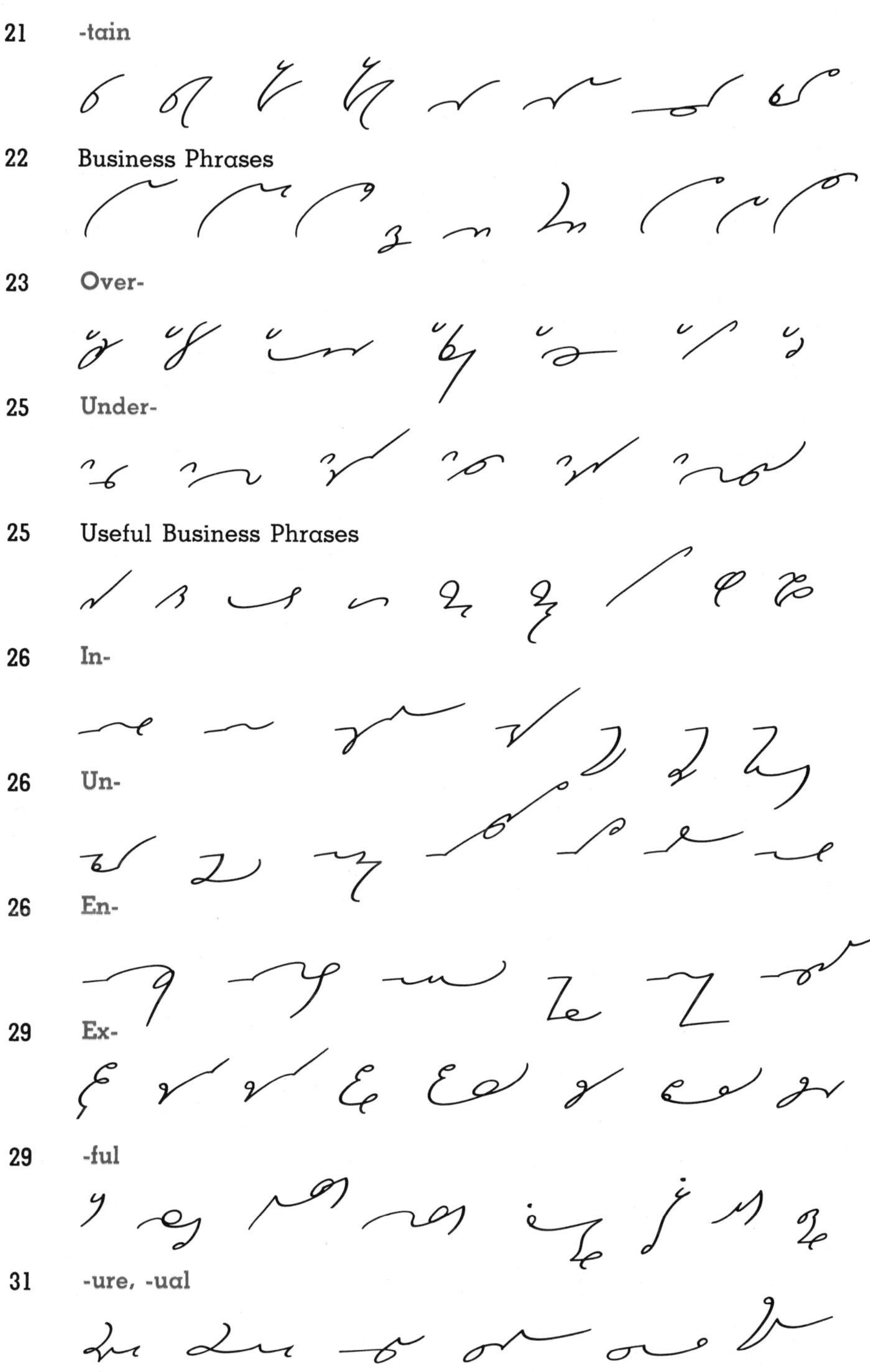
21 -tain
22 Business Phrases
23 Over-
25 Under-
25 Useful Business Phrases
26 In-
26 Un-
26 En-
29 Ex-
29 -ful
31 -ure, -ual

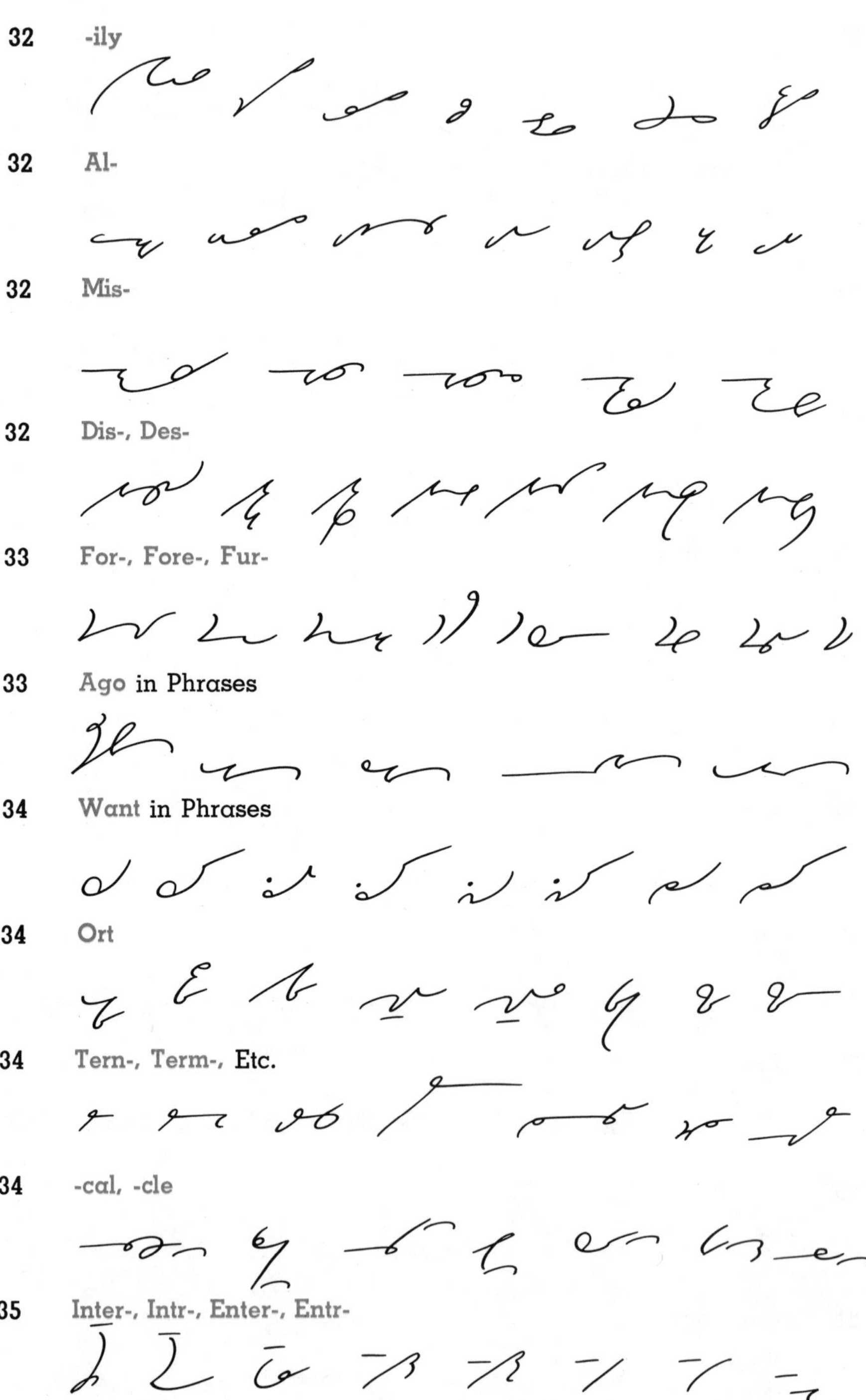
32 -ily
32 Al-
32 Mis-
32 Dis-, Des-
33 For-, Fore-, Fur-
33 Ago in Phrases
34 Want in Phrases
34 Ort
34 Tern-, Term-, Etc.
34 -cal, -cle
35 Inter-, Intr-, Enter-, Entr-

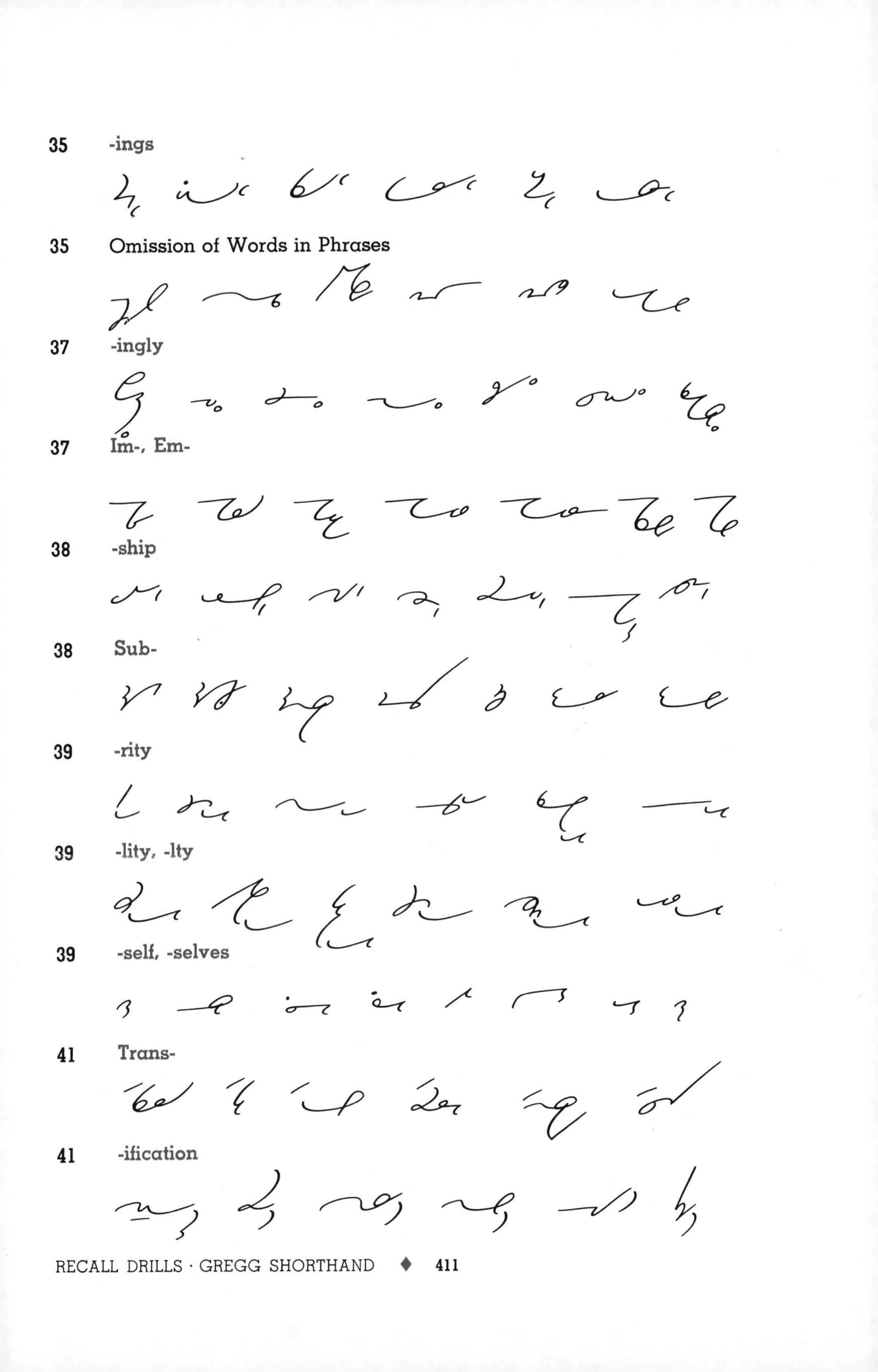

35 -ings

35 Omission of Words in Phrases

37 -ingly

37 Im-, Em-

38 -ship

38 Sub-

39 -rity

39 -lity, -lty

39 -self, -selves

41 Trans-

41 -ification

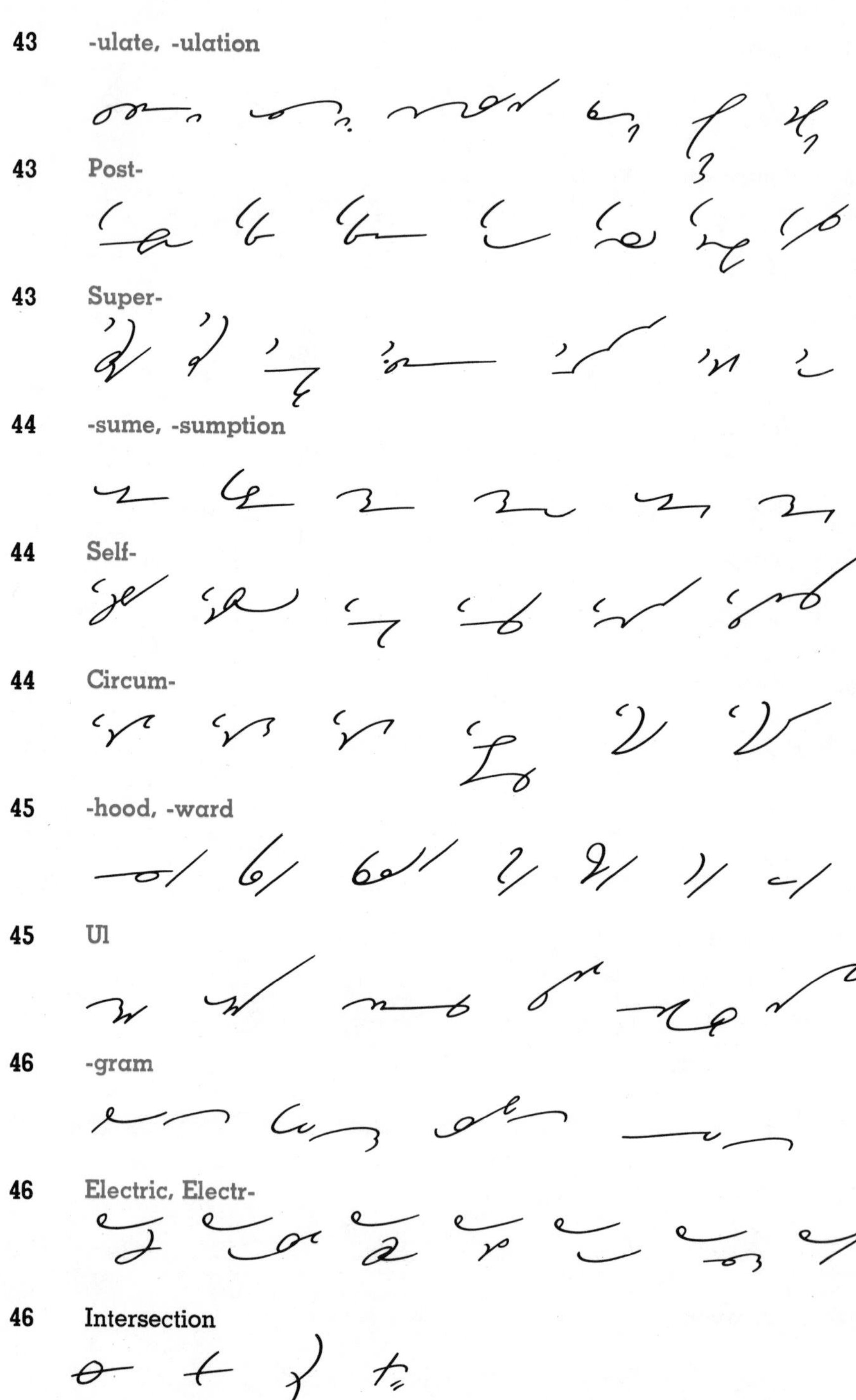
43 -ulate, -ulation
43 Post-
43 Super-
44 -sume, -sumption
44 Self-
44 Circum-
45 -hood, -ward
45 Ul
46 -gram
46 Electric, Electr-
46 Intersection

GREGG SHORTHAND

In order to facilitate finding, this Index has been divided into six main sections — Alphabetic Characters, Brief Forms, General, Phrasing, Word Beginnings, Word Endings.

The first figure refers to the lesson; the second refers to the paragraph.

PHRASING

WORD BEGINNINGS

WORD ENDINGS

BRIEF FORMS

The first figure refers to the lesson; the second to the paragraph.

BUILDING YOUR TRANSCRIPTION SKILLS

The first figure refers to the lesson; the second figure to the paragraph.

COMMON WORD ROOTS

GRAMMAR CHECKUP

PUNCTUATION PRACTICE—COMMAS

SIMILAR WORDS

SPELLING FAMILIES

FREQUENTLY USED PHRASES
OF GREGG SHORTHAND

	A	B	C	D	E	F	G
1							
2							
3							
4							
5							
6							
7							
8							
9							
10							
11							
12							
13							
14							
15							
16							
17							
18							
19							